SOLITARY

SOLITARY

**Unbroken by
four decades in solitary
confinement. My story
of transformation and hope.**

ALBERT WOODFOX

with Leslie George

Grove Press
New York

FIRST EDITION

Printed in the United States of America

First Grove Atlantic hardcover edition: March 2019

Designed by Norman E. Tuttle of Alpha Design & Composition
This book was set in 12-point Adobe Caslon Pro by
Alpha Design & Composition of Pittsfield, NH.

Library of Congress Cataloging-in-Publication data is available for this title.

ISBN 978-0-8021-2908-6
eISBN 978-0-8021-4690-8

Grove Press
an imprint of Grove Atlantic
154 West 14th Street
New York, NY 10011

Distributed by Publishers Group West

groveatlantic.com

19 20 21 22   10 9 8 7 6 5 4 3 2 1

It has been my experience that because of institutional and individual racism, African Americans are born socially dead and spend the rest of their lives fighting to live.

Echoes

Echoes of wisdom I often hear,
  a mother's strength softly in my ears.
Echoes of womanhood shining so bright,
  echoes of a mother within darkest night.
Echoes of wisdoms on my mother's lips, too young
  to understand it was in a gentle kiss.
Echoes of love and echoes of fear
  Arrogance of manhood wouldn't let me hear,
Echoes of heartache I still hold close
  As I mourn the loss of my one true hero.
Echoes from a mother's womb,
  heartbeats held so dear,
  life begins with my first tears.
Echoes of footsteps taken in the past,
  echoes of manhood standing in a looking glass.
Echoes of motherhood gentle and near,
  echoes of a lost mother I will always hear.

—Albert Woodfox, 1995

Contents

2000–2010

2011–2016

Prologue

February 19, 2016

I woke in the dark. Everything I owned fit into two plastic garbage bags in the corner of my cell. "When are these folks gonna let you out," my mom used to ask me. Today, Mama, I thought. The first thing I'd do is go to her grave. For years I'd lived with the burden of not saying good-bye to her. That was a heavy weight I'd been carrying.

I rose and made my bed, swept and mopped the floor. I took off my sweatpants and folded them, placing them in one of the bags. I put on an orange prison jumpsuit required for my court appearance that morning. A friend had given me street clothes to wear, for later. I laid them out on my bed.

Many people wrote to me in prison over the years, asking me how I survived four decades in a single cell, locked down 23 hours a day. I turned my cell into a university, I wrote to them, a hall of debate, a law school. By taking a stand and not backing down, I told them. I believed in humanity, I said. I loved myself. The hopelessness, the claustrophobia, the brutality, the fear, I didn't say. I looked out the window. A news van was parked down the road outside the jail, headlights still on, though it was getting light now. I'll be able to go anywhere. To see the night sky. I sat back on my bunk and waited.

Chapter 1

In the Beginning

I was born in the "Negro" wing of Charity Hospital in New Orleans, the day after Mardi Gras, February 19, 1947. My mom, Ruby Edwards, was 17. My father was gone. He left her, she told me, because she was from the wrong side of the tracks. We lived in New Orleans until I was five and my mom fell in love with a man named James B. Mable, a chef in the U.S. Navy. He was the first and only man I ever called Daddy. They got married and had four more children, a girl and three boys.

We moved six or seven times to different naval bases during those years. Daddy's job was to feed the crew of whatever ship he was assigned to. He used to take me onto the ships on weekends when Navy personnel were allowed to bring family. I remember walking to the edge of an aircraft carrier to see the water and he grabbed me by the back of my shirt so I wouldn't be blown away by strong winds.

I was a rebellious child. When I was seven or eight, I challenged my mom to a wrestling match. "I can beat you," I told her. "If I win you have to wear a dress all day," she said. It was the worst punishment I could think of but I agreed. She pinned me in a few seconds. I don't know where she got the dress but I wore it. At least I was keeping my word, she said. "A man ain't nothing without his word," she told me. I heard that my whole childhood.

For a while my mom was my world. Proud, determined, and beautiful, she took care of us. She couldn't read or write but she could add and subtract and was good with money; she could squeeze a penny until it screamed. Growing up in the Jim Crow South she had a lot of practice surviving on very little. When Daddy was on leave we stayed at his parents' small farm where he had grown up in La Grange, North Carolina. There, my grandparents grew watermelons, cabbage, corn, tobacco, and sweet potatoes. Behind the house was a chicken coop and farther back a forest where we picked wild strawberries. My grandmother loved to fish but was afraid of boats. I was the only one she trusted to row her out into the river, which, my mom being from Louisiana, we called a bayou.

My grandmother showed me how to clean and cook the fish we caught. She taught me how to farm. I fed the chickens and worked in the fields. I learned to drive a team of mules at a very early age. When we "cropped tobacca" I drove a slender buggy led by a mule that fit between rows of tobacco. The sides of the buggy were made of cut-up burlap sacks, nailed to posts that stuck up from each corner of the wagon. The women in the field broke off the leaves and laid them down flat in the buggy. When the buggy was full I drove it to the curing barn where women tied and hung the tobacco on sticks that were then placed inside the barn on racks. Once the barn was full the heat was turned on and the tobacco would be cured before being shipped and sold to tobacco factories. When I was nine or ten I'd hitchhike back and forth to a job at a tobacco factory in Winston-Salem, 170 miles each way. Sometimes the drivers would make conversation, other times they wouldn't. My job was to help roll the tobacco barrels to a scale. A lot of kids my age worked there.

When I was 11, everything changed. Daddy was forced by the Navy to retire after 25 years and we moved to La Grange full-time. He went from being a master chief petty officer, the highest noncommissioned rank you can achieve in the Navy, to being a black man living on a farm in North Carolina. Without the responsibility and respect he was given in the Navy, he lost his self-esteem. He started drinking and took his frustration and rage out on my mom. Daddy never hit me or my brothers or sister. He beat my mom. When he hit my mom, she screamed and tried to fight back, but she was a small woman. He overpowered her with his size and strength. We never knew when he was going to explode in anger and bitterness. Nothing warned us in advance how he would react on any given day so we lived in constant confusion and fear. One time he beat my mom so badly his sisters came around and told her they were afraid for her life. If she didn't leave, they said, he might kill her. My mom didn't want to go but some part of her knew if she stayed with Daddy she was in danger. Sooner or later the violence he used against her might be used against her children. She made a secret plan with Daddy's sisters to take us kids and run away. Because of her limited education and experience the only place she felt safe was in New Orleans, where she was born and raised. So, New Orleans was her destination.

On the day Mama planned for us to go, Daddy was getting ready to leave the house when my five-year-old sister, Violetta, said she wanted to go with him. My little brother James, who was three, said he wanted to go too. Mama spoke to Violetta: "Why don't you stay home, Vi. I think you should stay." Violetta was Daddy's favorite child and he said she could go with him. James could come too. We all watched them walk out the door. Mama turned to my aunties and said, "I ain't going. Not without my children." They told her in the strongest words possible that she had to leave because her life, and the lives of her children, depended on it. They promised they'd send Vi and James along behind us with someone. It was the hardest decision my mom ever made. She took me; my brother Haywood, who was two; and the baby, Michael, not a year yet, to the Greyhound bus station. We boarded the bus and rode all the way to New Orleans without Vi and James. Mama cried off and on the whole way. She was filled with anger, fear, and remorse because she felt as though she'd abandoned two of her children, even though she knew she'd see them in a matter of days or weeks. She never imagined that years would pass before she would see them again. Had she known, our lives would have been different, because she never would have left.

At the bus station in New Orleans, Mama called her brother on a pay phone. Uncle Joe came to get us with Aunt Gussie. They drove us to a house she was renting. I'll never forget the address, 918 North Villere Street, in the Sixth Ward. Inside, Aunt Gussie led us down a long hallway to two small rooms in the back. One of the rooms had a fireplace and became our makeshift kitchen. Mama put a bunk bed in there for me and my brothers. She took the other room as her bedroom. In order to use the toilet, we had to walk out the front door and around the house to the backyard. It was located in a little room attached behind the house. There was a bathtub in a small room that separated Aunt Gussie's kitchen from our two rooms, but my mom always made us take baths in a big metal tub in our kitchen. Mama warmed up water on the little stove and poured it in the tub for us. There was a slop jar in the corner we used as a temporary toilet at night. We put pine oil in it to keep down the odor. One of our chores each morning was to empty the slop jar.

The city of New Orleans is made up of wards, and we lived in the Sixth Ward, also called the Treme. It was a black neighborhood in those days, a mix of working-class and poor people. We lived in the poor section. Claiborne Avenue was the busiest street in the Treme because most of the businesses in the Sixth Ward were located there. It was our Canal Street, the main business area of New Orleans. Small black-owned businesses like grocery stores, hair salons, dress shops, laundromats, barbershops, bakeries, and bars lined Claiborne Ave. The middle of Claiborne was covered in grass and trees and called "neutral ground." It was a favorite gathering place for people in the neighborhood during Mardi Gras season and other major holidays. Everyone set up barbecue pits and picnics on neutral ground. After school, my friends and I played tackle football there in the shade of the trees that lined Claiborne.

When we weren't playing on neutral ground we played stickball in the street. If it wasn't too hot, children played barefoot, saving their shoes for school. Almost all the houses in the Sixth Ward were the same, we called them "shotgun houses." If you stood at the front door and fired a shotgun, the ball shot would go straight out the back door. Our house was a double shotgun. Every house on my street had a small porch or steps in the front where people gathered. Telephone poles were on either side of the street with sagging, crisscrossing wires between them. There wasn't a tall building in sight, except for a church steeple here and there and Joseph A. Craig Elementary School. Every house had a side alley lined by a fence. My friends and I jumped the

fences to take shortcuts from street to street. Later we jumped fences
running from the police.

My mom wanted the best for us, but since she was functionally illiterate
she couldn't get what would be considered a regular job. So, she took odd
jobs and did whatever was necessary to provide for us, and sometimes
that included prostituting herself. Only 28 when we moved back to
New Orleans, and in spite of having five children, my mom was still a
very beautiful woman. She worked in bars and nightclubs as a barmaid,
hustling tricks and rolling drunks. Outside there was poverty but inside
our house my mom created an oasis for us. She always made enough
money to buy us clothes, put food on the table, and pay Aunt Gussie
rent. She cared a lot about making sure we had clothes that fit. Most of
the kids I grew up with wore hand-me-down clothes that were too big
or too small. Some kids wore pants that stopped at the ankles. We called
them "ankle-whippers." Mama told us she wanted us to have better than
what she had when she was a child. She always got us something new
to wear for the first day of school. I didn't realize until I was much older
the sacrifices she made to give us these basic necessities.

She used to say, "I don't want my children to do the things I have
to do to make a living." And, "I want my children to have a better life."
But sometimes our need to survive poverty got in the way. When money
was tight and there was no food in the house I shoplifted bread and
canned goods. It never felt like a crime to me, it was survival. In every
other way, we made do. For some meals, Aunt Gussie and I would fish
for perch or mullet in Bayou St. John. If my shoes had holes on the
bottom I put a layer of newspaper inside so I could still wear them. I
was proud though. I didn't want anyone to see the holes in my shoes.
At church when it was time to kneel I would half crouch, kneeling on
one knee so I could keep the shoe with the holes flat on the floor so
nobody behind me would see the holes . One time a nun walked to
the end of my pew and loudly told me to kneel on both knees. When
I wouldn't do it, she ordered me to come out into the aisle between the
pews. I walked to where she was standing and once again she ordered
me to kneel. Now everyone was looking at me. If I knelt the whole

congregation behind me would see the holes in my shoe. I refused. She grabbed my collarbone and tried to force me to my knees. When I resisted she told me to get out. I went back to church sometimes with my mom but I never forgot the cruelty of this nun.

Aunt Gussie went to a Baptist church. Sometimes she took me to a gospel concert at her church, and I enjoyed the harmonies and voices. Aunt Gussie used to give me a dollar on Thursdays to go get her a "blessed candle" from her church. One Thursday on the way to get her a candle I noticed her pastor in the corner store when I walked by. He was holding a box full of candles, which cost 50 cents each at the store. I followed him. I wanted to watch him bless the candles, and expected to see him perform some kind of ceremony when he got to the church, but he just took the candles from the box and put them on the table for people to buy for a dollar. That was a shock because back in those days 50 cents was a lot of money.

I never believed in God, even as a child. I couldn't understand the idea of an all-powerful being. But I always considered myself to be spiritual. For me, spirituality is a feeling of connection beyond yourself. We had an old dog we called Trixie and at times I felt as though I knew what Trixie was thinking. To me that was spiritual.

During the days, my brothers and I were sometimes on our own. My mom might be sleeping off a hangover or was too exhausted to get up from hustling all night. Often, she didn't get home until six in the morning. Sometimes I snuck into her room after she went to bed and hid the money she made that night so if her boyfriend came around that day he wouldn't get it. It didn't do any good. If my mother was in love with a man she would give him anything she had, including her money.

Aunt Gussie cooked and helped out. We all did chores, cleaning the floors, ironing our clothes. I remember pressing clothes with an old-fashioned iron that was heated on the stove. We learned to take care of ourselves. We always took care of one another. When I was 12 my baby brother Donald was born. His dad was a merchant marine named Pete who had an off-and-on relationship with my mom for many years.

Everything in those days was segregated between whites and blacks. Black people weren't allowed to go to a lot of places because of Jim Crow laws. At the movies, black people could only sit in the balcony. We were barred from sitting in the seats downstairs. We weren't allowed to stand in the lobby or at the concession counter. To buy popcorn or any of the other snacks we had to wait by the lobby door until a white usher walked by so we could give him our money and order. The usher would bring back our change and candy or popcorn, or whatever was left over at the concessions.

The only time I really had contact with white people was when we went to the French Quarter or to the shopping district on Canal Street. The first time I felt that a white person could be a threat to me I was standing at a bus stop at the corner of Dumaine and Villere with my mom when two white police officers drove by in a patrol car. She put her hand on my shoulder protectively and moved me behind her. As I got older I noticed white people would address black grown-ups as "boy" or "girl" and I felt the disrespect of it.

The first time I was called a nigger by a white person I was around 12. I was waiting with dozens of other kids at the end of the Mardi Gras parade behind the Municipal Auditorium where the people on the floats, who were all white in those days, gave away whatever beads and trinkets they had left. On one of the floats the man tossing the trinkets was holding a real beautiful strand of pearl-colored beads. I thought they'd make a nice gift for my mom on her birthday. I called out to him, "Hey mister, hey mister," and reached out my hand. He pointed to me as he held the beads above his head and tossed them toward me. As the beads came close to me I reached up and a white girl standing next to me put her hand up and caught them at the same time I did. I didn't let go. I gestured to the man on the float and told her, "Hey, he was throwing the beads to me." I told her I wanted to give them to my mom. She looked at the man on the float, who was still pointing at me, then she ripped the beads apart and called me nigger. The pain I felt from that young white girl calling me nigger will be with me forever.

Most of the policemen were white in those days. They came through our neighborhood picking up black men for standing on the corner, charging them with loitering or vagrancy, looking to meet their quota of arrests. Once in custody, who knows what charges would be put on those men. My friends and I knew it would be whatever the police wanted. We always knew the police picked up the men in our neighborhood because they were black and for no other reason. We never talked about it though. We couldn't have articulated racism if we tried. We didn't understand the depths of it, the sophistication of it. We only absorbed the misery of it.

In sixth grade I attended a social studies class that taught me my place in the world. We had an African American teacher for a classroom of black children who lived in the same all-black neighborhood, using a textbook that only depicted what was happening in white America. The pictures and stories in the textbook had nothing to do with our reality. It wasn't the first time I became aware that that white people had it better. But it was the first time it began to dawn on me that everybody knew white people had it better. It was the first time I understood that something was terribly wrong in the world, and nobody was talking about it.

In that same social studies class I was taught that women like my mom, who worked in bars, were considered a disgrace to society. I had always detested the men my mom brought home but until I took this class I never judged her, it was just a way of life. I began to look down on her. I didn't realize at that time that my mom didn't have choices, that she worked in bars to take care of me and my brothers, and I was unforgiving. Deep down I never stopped loving my mom. But I hated her too. One of the greatest regrets of my life is that I allowed myself to believe that the strongest, most beautiful, and most powerful woman in my life didn't matter.

Around this age I also started to hear stories about men in the Ku Klux Klan lynching black people. Like all blacks, I was scared to death of the Klan. I didn't venture much into the white community.

For the most part, my friends and I stayed in the black neighborhoods of New Orleans. It was where we felt safe. Eventually it was where we committed our crimes. For a while I went on to excel at school, in the classroom, and in sports. I was small for my age but I was on the football team and the volleyball team. We didn't have a basketball team at my school but we often played basketball in the park. Playing sports was the only time in my life I knew what to do at any given moment. But the lessons of that sixth-grade class had weakened me in a way I can't describe. I stayed in school for three more years, but somewhere inside me I was done with school. I turned my attention to the street. There, I quickly learned everyone had one choice: to be a rabbit or a wolf. I chose to be a wolf.

1960s

Where justice is denied, where poverty is enforced, where ignorance prevails, and where any one class is made to feel that society is an organized conspiracy to oppress, rob, and degrade them, neither persons nor property will be safe.

—Frederick Douglass

Chapter 2

The High Steppers

I started to hang with other boys in the Treme when I was around 12. I had a little job in the grocery store making snowballs, cups of shaved ice covered with flavored sugarcane syrup. When the owner wasn't looking I handed out snowballs to my friends through the back window. At night, we stood under a streetlight on the corner of Dumaine and Robertson and talked shit for hours, boasting about things we never did, describing girls we never knew. Everyone called me Fox.

After school, we'd meet up and figure out ways to get things we didn't have. We shoplifted bread from the boxes outside stores, snuck into the theater to watch movies. For money, we sang and danced in the French Quarter or stole flowers from the graveyard and sold them to tourists on Bourbon Street. To eat we met at the bakery on Orleans Avenue before dawn and stole rolls and pastries from delivery trucks parked behind a tall barbed wire fence. It was nothing for us to climb over that fence if we had a pillowcase or cloth to protect our hands. We'd take a tray of baked goods from the back of one of those trucks, dump them into a bag, then run across the tracks to Brown's Velvet Dairy to steal milk or ice cream from their trucks. We carried everything to the park and ate until we couldn't eat anymore.

When we heard about a concert playing at the Municipal Auditorium we climbed up the back wall to an open second-floor window, ran down the back stairs, and charged kids admission at the back door. When the Ringling Bros. Circus came to town we signed up for day jobs to feed and water the animals. We piled hay in front of the elephants and horses and shoveled shit from behind them and hauled water to the tigers in cages. When nobody was looking we'd leave our rakes and shovels in the straw, sneak off, and find an unguarded back door where we charged for entrance, letting our friends in for free.

We never thought we were committing crimes. We thought we were outsmarting the world. But we watched out for police. Sometimes they'd come after us if they saw a group of black kids, no matter what we were doing. We had to especially be on the lookout in the French Quarter, where we "beat the box" on Bourbon Street, drumming on cardboard boxes. If the police grabbed us in those years they'd take our money and beat us until we ran away as fast as we could.

My mom saw into the future and tried to protect me from going to jail. "If I catch you stealing or doing anything wrong I'm going to whip your ass," she'd say. "I don't want you out there stealing and being a petty-ass criminal." If she saw me on the street with a kid she thought was trouble she would come up to us and tell me to go home. At home she'd yell at me and I'd yell back. I didn't think she had any right to tell me what to do. I didn't want her controlling me. We still had affectionate times some days, when I would sit close to her and we'd talk with her arm around me. She loved my hair. By age 13, though, I wasn't obedient to my mom anymore. She would tell me to be home at a certain time and I wouldn't be home at that time. My friends and I were hustling to survive, and we loved being good at it. I call this period of my life the guilt of innocence. We didn't know any better.

Around this time, we started to think of ourselves as a gang and started calling ourselves the 6th Ward High Steppers, a name we thought made us sound like winners. Being in a gang, defending your turf becomes necessary. I had to learn to fight. I wasn't a natural-born fighter so I held back at first. Fighting actually made me physically ill. When I saw boys my age fighting older, bigger kids, I thought they had something I didn't have. I wondered if I was a coward.

My friend Frank had been pushing me to fight this dude my age named Lawrence, who was constantly humiliating me. If I was eating a sandwich, when he saw me he'd take it and eat it. Once he took my belt. Mostly he demanded I give him any money I had on me. I was terrified of Lawrence, who was bigger than me.

"You can't let him do that to you, Fox," Frank said. "When are you going to stand up for yourself?"

The next time I saw Lawrence it was on Orleans Avenue neutral ground. I was scared but this time when Lawrence pushed me I swung my arm and hit him in the head. That's when I learned that courage doesn't mean you aren't afraid. Courage means you master that fear and act in spite of being afraid. Lawrence and I fought and didn't stop until I got up and he didn't. For a while Lawrence and I fought every time we saw each other. Then he gave up. I never let fear stop me from doing anything again.

We never wanted to get caught on anybody else's turf but if there was a house party outside the Sixth Ward, we risked it. If confronted by another gang we stayed and fought or hauled ass. When gang members from other wards came on our turf we beat them up or chased them out. No one had guns at that time. We only fought with fists. Gang members never attacked the family members of other gang members. If there was a feud between gangs it stayed within the gangs. It was understood that family was off-limits. Everybody honored that. After every fight, I still felt ill and went off to be by myself but I didn't tell anyone. By the time I was in my midteens I had a reputation for being very tough. Only I knew differently.

On hot summer nights when the mosquitos were tearing our asses up we broke into the pool next to the park and filled it with water. We turned on the lights by bending back the cover of the switchbox to reach the switch. Then we started the water pump and let the water run until the pool was full. People came from the nearby projects to swim. Sometimes park officials would come around and turn everything off and tell everyone to go home. If the cops came everybody broke out running. A child who got caught would be sent to juvenile hall. A grown-up would be charged with trespassing. Most of the time the police didn't come. When we finished swimming, we drained the pool and turned the lights off.

For the most part, we knew how to avoid cops. Police cruisers circled the neighborhood at the same time every day like clockwork and we wouldn't be out at those times. If police showed up unexpectedly we'd go inside or slip down an alley to avoid them. Or we'd scatter and run. We ran, and were chased, even when we weren't doing anything wrong. I got really good at jumping fences while being chased by police. If they caught us for any real or imagined crime they beat us with their fists and nightsticks or blackjacks, which we called flapjacks because they made a flapping sound when they hit us. They searched us looking for any money we had, pocketing what they found. For a while they let us go; when we got older they dragged us to juvenile hall. It never occurred to us to tell anyone they beat or robbed us. It was accepted. That was just the way life was at that time.

When I was 14 my mom asked me if I wanted to meet my real father, Leroy Woodfox. I was surprised because I didn't know they were in touch. My first thought was, no. All I knew about by biological dad was that he abandoned my mom when she was pregnant with me.

"Why?" I asked.

"He said he'd like to meet you," she said. She gave me the address of his dry cleaning business, which was nearby. I wasn't really curious about him, but I thought he might give me some money so I went. When I walked in I saw him right away. I looked just like him. I can't remember what we talked about, but we didn't say too much. He offered to clean some clothes for me. A few days later I took him some trousers and he tossed them onto a pile of clothes in the corner, telling me to come back in a couple of days. When I went back to pick up the pants I saw right away they were still on the pile in the corner. I turned and walked out the door, leaving the pants behind. I never saw him again.

One of my hustles was working the shrimp boats in St. Bernard Parish, carrying huge bags of shrimp and oysters to a warehouse. Inside the warehouse, women stood around a table shucking oysters into gallon-size cans, juice and all, one after another. They could get through a bag of oysters faster than anything I'd ever seen. Some of my pay was in oysters and shrimp, which I'd take home. I think that warehouse is where

I heard that Hurricane Carla was coming and that when it touched down it would be the "storm of the century." I always liked to stand in our backyard during a storm and listen to the rain and wondered what a hurricane would feel like. The hurricane slammed into Texas on September 11, 1961, and spawned tornadoes that reached Louisiana. The morning of the storm I made my way to Lake Pontchartrain, to the seawall steps where I'd played when I was younger. I didn't tell anyone where I was going. My mom would have kicked my ass if she knew. At low tide, nine or ten stone steps were visible coming up from the water's edge to the shore; when the tide was in, the steps were covered with water. By the time I got there it was raining hard and the tide had come in. I looked for a place to stand. I figured the water wouldn't get over the wall, but to be sure I crossed the lake road and stood against a sturdy tree, tying a rope around my waist to the tree so I wouldn't be blown away.

I was already completely soaked from the rain. The wind hit me now, mostly from the side. Usually Lake Pontchartrain is as flat as glass. I watched giant waves develop out on the lake for a long time. By the time I noticed the water had come up over the wall it was already past the grass and almost to the road that runs along the side of the lake. I was surprised watching it creep across the road toward me. When the water covered my feet. I put my hands on the rope, ready to untie it. When it got to my knees I untied myself and waded against the wind to higher ground, then made my way home.

Not long after that, my stepdad showed up at the house and dropped off my sister Violetta and my brother James. We hadn't seen them in three years. After he dropped them off we never saw Daddy again. My mom gave Vi the top bunk and the boys shared the bottom bunk, until she got a foldout couch for Vi to sleep on. It was crowded but I wasn't home much at night to sleep anyway. My brother Michael remembers me being around the house in those days, making sure that everybody got home after school and that everyone had dinner at night. My little brother Haywood says I was like a daddy to him. I hardly recall those times. I was consumed with what was going on outside. Soon, a new father figure came along for my brothers and sister. His name was Jethro

Hamlin. Everybody called him Pop Skeeter. He loved my mother. The saying was if Ruby said, "Jump," Pop Skeeter asked, "How high?" A master carpenter, he built cupboards and shelves in our two back rooms to make them more livable. Pop Skeeter brought stability to my family. Years later, my mom and Pop Skeeter married. He stayed with her the rest of her life, through thick and thin.

The most money our gang ever made in those years was from illegally parking cars, an old hustle that was passed down from one generation to another. On weekend nights, my friends and I went to the French Quarter or around the Municipal Auditorium and waved down drivers looking for parking spots. In exchange for a dollar we'd show the drivers where to park, directing them to illegal spots in alleys, behind buildings, up hills, or even on neutral ground. We were always amazed that people parked their cars wherever we told them to. We always said, "Be sure to lock your car," to gain their trust. We could make $50 parking cars on a good night. When the police were bored they'd come around with police dogs for something to do. They knew we'd be there and tried to sneak up on us. When somebody saw them, he'd yell, "Police!" and everybody would take off. Once when I was running away, a K-9 dog caught me. One of the "rewards" for a K-9 dog in those days was what was referred to as "Give 'em the bite," when the officer stood by and let the dog bite the person he caught, usually while that person was lying on the ground. This policeman let his dog chew my thigh. Sometimes they let us go, other times they took us to juvenile hall. Once in a while the officers from juvenile hall raided our operation too. Some of the officers at juvenile hall were black. One of them was Mr. Green, a substitute gym teacher at my school. He knew all of us. "I see you, Woodfox," he'd yell after me.

There was no way he could catch me.

"I'll get your ass at school tomorrow," he'd yell. "I'll call your mama!"

This was all part of the game. He and I both knew he wasn't going to call my mom. He wasn't going to get my ass at school the next day, or any day. It was like we were acting out roles, set in motion before time, without knowing why. He was probably parking cars at my age. Threads like this ran throughout my childhood. History was always repeating itself. These threads held us together, and kept us apart.

My first arrest was for parking cars. Juvenile hall was a house on St. Philip Street. Desks and chairs where the officers sat were set up in what would have been the living room. The bedrooms were converted into holding cells. The windows on the first floor had bars, but they didn't think anyone would be crazy enough to jump from the second floor, so they didn't put bars in the upstairs windows. Officially, you couldn't get out of juvenile hall until a grown-up came and signed you out. Sometimes when one parent came they would sign out their child and all of his friends. I usually didn't sit around and wait to see who would come because I didn't want my mom to know I got arrested. I'd squeeze out a partially opened window from a second-floor holding room, hang from the window ledge, and drop to the ground. If my mom found out she would be angry. She'd fuss at me but there was nothing she could do. When I was younger there might be an ass-whipping with a switch or an ironing cord but after a certain age I wouldn't accept that kind of punishment anymore.

In 10th grade, I was suspended from school for hitting a girl. It happened at a school assembly. I was head of my 10th-grade homeroom so I was on the stage with the girl who was class president. She told me in front of all the students that she had a problem with my shirt because it was untucked, which was the style then. I told her to mind her own business and she slapped me in the face. I took my seat on the stage. The humiliation of being slapped in front of everyone played over and over in my mind during the assembly. When the meeting ended I picked up a folding chair from a stack and hit the girl who slapped me from behind, knocking her out. Thankfully, the girl was OK. The principal suspended me, though, and told me to show up at school the next day with my mother. When I got home I didn't tell my mom what happened. I pretended to go to school every day for a year before she found out.

After I was put out of school I had more time on my hands and started taking more risks. With my girlfriends, I snuck into strangers' houses when they were out so we could be alone. I broke into stores at night and stole money directly from cash registers. Nothing in my days, or nights, was planned. I never considered the consequences of my actions.

I had a lot of girlfriends but I wasn't faithful or loyal to any of them. When I was 16 I went out with a very beautiful, naive, and impressionable girl I had gone to junior high school with named Barbara. I got her pregnant. We weren't together when our daughter was born in January 1964, but when I heard she had the baby I went to the hospital to see them. The sight of a newborn baby, my child, was strange to me. Barbara named her Brenda. I didn't think I was capable of any emotions at that time but something made me want to keep Brenda in my life. I agreed to marry Barbara. A preacher married us in her mother's living room and we moved into a small apartment downstairs. That arrangement lasted about three months until the street pulled me back. I abandoned them.

My only feeling of relief and release in those years came from racing horses with my friends. There was a stable on St. Ann Street that housed horses used to pull the buggies for tourists in the French Quarter. At night, my friends and I snuck into the stable, took the horses, and walked them to the park. We didn't have saddles so we raced bareback. We ran those horses until their mouths foamed. When I was riding horses, it was the only time in my life that I wasn't afraid of going to jail. My only fear was not being able to ride horses anymore.

Chapter 3

Car Chase

In the early spring of 1965 I was in love with a girl called Peewee. We heard about a party at a big community center in Houma, Louisiana, a small parish about 60 miles from New Orleans, and wanted to go. I drove Peewee, her little brother Harold, and some friends up there in a car they told me belonged to their uncle. I'd just turned 18. While we were inside the community center Peewee's brother snuck out and took the car for a joyride. He hit another car while he was out. Nobody was injured but someone got the license plate number of the car he was speeding away in and reported it to the police. He came back to the party and didn't say a word.

Afterward I was driving us back to New Orleans when a state trooper started blasting a siren and flashing lights behind us. As I was getting ready to pull over, Peewee's brother started yelling, "Don't pull over, don't pull over" from the backseat of the car. In the rearview mirror I saw him waving his arms. "I stole this car," he yelled. Without a second's hesitation, I swerved back onto the highway and pressed my foot down on the gas pedal. Fueled by the fear of being arrested for driving a stolen car, I inadvertently led a sheriff's squad car on a 17-mile high-speed chase down the highway, plowing through barricades erected by the sheriff's deputies or state troopers ahead of us. I was weaving in and out of traffic through Raceland when Peewee, who had been screaming this whole time, grabbed the steering wheel suddenly and jerked it to the right. The car made a sharp turn into the embankment of a canal and flew over the water, landing on the front two tires, breaking the axle between them in half, and somehow ending upright. For a moment, nobody moved. We were on the other side of the canal from the sheriff's deputies and state troopers. When I looked over they were already out of their cars yelling at us to get out, waving their guns.

We opened the car doors and ran as fast as we could in different directions. I came to a garage behind a house and found a large dollhouse inside where I hid, pulling dolls on top of me. Sheriff's deputies came in and looked around and left. Sometime later I climbed out of the dollhouse and walked out of the garage. As I looked around the corner I saw Peewee, Harold, and the others standing with state troopers. Peewee was crying. I didn't want any of them to go to jail. I walked over to the troopers and surrendered myself.

After we were arrested they brought us to the Thibodaux jail. The next day I told them I stole the car and that we were joyriding and nobody knew anything about it. Peewee, her brother, and their friends were released. They charged me with auto theft, resisting arrest, hit-and-run, and speeding; the police said I was going 108 miles per hour. I took a plea bargain and was sentenced to two years at the Thibodaux jail. They made me a trustee, which meant I had more freedom of movement than other prisoners. I was put on a work crew cutting grass and picking up trash along the highway. After a couple of weeks, I ran away.

As usual, I wasn't thinking ahead. I didn't have a plan. I just wanted to go home. I'd noticed that the back door of the Thibodaux jail was kept open until midnight. There was an old unlocked bicycle in the backyard. The guards watched TV with the inmates every night. I left one night while the prisoners and sheriff's deputies watched a program on TV. I got on the bike and headed for the highway. After pedaling a couple of hours, I was tired and looking for a place to pull over when I saw there were some trucks and equipment in a gravel pit off the side of the road. I thought I could take a nap in the cab of the cement mixer so I pedaled over, climbed in, and lay down on the seat. That's when I saw the keys in the ignition.

I taught myself how to shift gears in the cement mixer by trial and error while driving to New Orleans. I could only go about 10 miles per hour but it was better than riding a bike. When I was almost home

I pulled up to a light on St. Bernard and Claiborne and a police car pulled up next to me. From the corner of my eye I saw the cops do a double take when they saw me, a skinny black kid, driving a cement mixer in the middle of the city. They waved me over. I made a left on St. Bernard and pulled over, then jumped out running. They got out of their car with guns drawn and started firing at me. I ran up neutral ground on Claiborne and then got myself to an alley beside a house where I could jump fences and lose them. When I stopped to catch my breath, I realized I left my wallet on the dashboard of the cement mixer. I didn't hide. That's how stupid I was. I was sitting on the front steps of a friend's house in the Sixth Ward with her kid on my lap the next day when an unmarked police car filled with detectives from Thibodaux and New Orleans turned the corner. We saw each other at the same time. I couldn't run with her little kid on my lap so stayed where I was. They got out of their car with guns in their hands and walked over.

"Well, well, well," one of them said, holding my wallet. "Mr. Woodfox."

They handcuffed me, put me in their car, and beat the shit out of me on the way to central lockup because I had led the police on a chase. I was sent back to Thibodaux and charged with escape, theft, driving without a license, resisting an officer, and speeding. The judge told me I had a choice: I could do four years at the Houma city jail or two years at the Louisiana State Penitentiary at Angola, with an option to transfer out to the minimum-security DeQuincy jail in 90 days if I was well behaved. I'd seen guys in my neighborhood come back from Angola throughout my childhood. They were given the highest respect. I thought it would be an honor to go there. I chose Angola.

Chapter 4

Angola, 1960s

I learned from being in a gang that I could master my fear and still act. That lesson served me well at Angola. The horrors of the prison in 1965 cannot be exaggerated. Angola looked like a slave plantation, which it once was. The prisoner population was segregated; most prisoners were black. African American prisoners did 99 percent of the fieldwork by hand, usually without gloves or proper footwear. White guards on horseback rode up and down the lines of working prisoners, holding shotguns across their laps and constantly yelling at the men who were working, saying, "Work faster, old thing" or, "Nigger."

Originally one of six slave-breeding plantations owned by the American slave trader Isaac Franklin, Angola was spread out over 18,000 acres of farmland when I got to it. There was a main prison called the "big yard" that housed most prisoners and there were several "camps"—outlying compounds that contained dorms, cellblocks, a dining hall, and offices—all miles apart, separated by fields of crops and swampland. The prison was surrounded by the Mississippi River on three sides and the Tunica Hills to the east. In 1869 the slave trader's widow leased the land from four of his plantations to a former Confederate major who wanted to farm it. As part of a legal "convict-leasing" program established throughout the South after the Civil War, he "leased" prisoners from New Orleans and other city jails to work his farm. The convicts, many charged with minor crimes, were housed in former slave quarters and worked seven days a week. They were starved and beaten. Hundreds are said to have died every year, but that didn't affect the business of the former Confederate major.

There were always new convicts to lease. In 1901, the state of Louisiana took over and purchased the land, which became the state penitentiary, but it was always called Angola, after the African country where the plantation's original slaves were born. It was fitting as far as I was concerned: the legacy of slavery was everywhere. It was in the ground under our feet and in the air we breathed, and wherever we looked.

When I arrived in June 1965 I think they were picking peas. All prisoners first did 30 days at the Reception Center (RC), which was located just inside Angola's front gate. This is where we learned prison rules and met with a doctor, social worker, and classification officer. The classification officer determined our jobs and where we would live in the prison. I was scared shitless but kept it hidden. Being cool can be the difference between life and death in prison. Each dorm at RC had about 50 to 60 beds and a stream of prisoners coming and going. I didn't know anyone when I arrived, but I got close to one prisoner named T. Ratty, who was also from New Orleans.

The security guards and all of the ranking officers at Angola were white, and we called them "freemen." Freemen came from generations of white families born and raised in Angola prison. Segments of the ranking officers lived on the B-Line, a small community of houses and trailers at that time. Prisoners washed the freemen's cars, mowed their lawns, and painted their houses. The freemen ran the prison.

Since only 300 freemen oversaw more than 5,000 prisoners, they created another level of security, handing out shotguns to hundreds of white and black prisoners. Inmate guards, for the most part, oversaw prisoners of their own their race. However, in some cases white inmate guards worked over black prisoners—in the fields, the guard towers, and the dining hall, for example. There was no psychiatric evaluation of these prisoners before they were made guards. A lot of them had life sentences for murder and rape. Nobody was trained. Inmate guards learned from other inmate guards. Freemen, who often started working at the prison after high school, learned from their uncles, fathers, and grandfathers who were already working at Angola.

As soon as I arrived at RC I heard prisoners talk about "fresh fish day," the day first-time prisoners were taken from RC into the prison population. It was also the day sexual predators lined up and looked for their next victims. Sexual slavery was the culture at Angola. The administration condoned it. I saw men being raped at RC. Freemen didn't do anything to stop it. They wanted prisoners who had no spirit. They wanted prisoners to fear one another and abuse one another; it made them easier to control. If you were raped at Angola, or what was called "turned out," your life in prison was virtually over. You became a "gal-boy," a possession of your rapist. You'd be sold, pimped, used, and abused by your rapist and even some guards. Your only way out was to kill yourself or kill your rapist. If you killed your rapist you'd be free of human bondage within the confines of the prison forever, but in exchange, you'd most likely be convicted of murder, so you'd have to spend the rest of your life at Angola.

Freemen and inmate guards took advantage of these "master/slave" relationships. They were able to control some of the most violent and powerful prisoners by threatening to move their gal-boys away from them. If a prisoner was "good," he could keep his gal-boy, and a prison pimp would do almost anything to keep his gal-boy. Freemen also used violent rapists to intentionally hurt other prisoners, placing them in cells with a prisoner they wanted to punish or putting them in situations when they wanted to start lethal fights. Those prisoners were called "rape artists."

Some orderlies, inmate guards, and freeman who worked at RC sold the names of young and weak new arrivals to sexual predators in the prison population. I had to seem much more confident than I felt to keep guys from trying stupid shit with me. I couldn't look weak. I couldn't show any fear. So I faked it. Luckily, I had a reputation as a fighter who never gave up. There were prisoners at Angola I had known on the street and they knew me or knew of me. Word spreads quickly in prison. Dudes gossiped and talked. Word was if you whip my ass today you have to whip it again tomorrow. You have to beat me every day for the rest of your life if necessary. That helped me a lot.

The main prison was divided into two sides, a trustee side and what we called the Big Stripe side, named back when maximum-security prisoners wore prison-issue jumpsuits with black and white stripes on them. By sheer luck the classification officer made me a trustee. On the Big Stripe side prisoners had to walk within certain lines or they could be shot by a guard sitting in a tower. The classification officer assigned me my job: field hand. I was put on a line they called the Bully 100 because the field foreman had a reputation of working prisoners hard. That didn't bother me. I wasn't afraid of hard work. I already knew how to do farmwork from living with my grandparents.

When it was time for my group to go into the prison population, we were boarded onto an old school bus that took us to the main prison. One guard drove the bus, another one sat next to him, both inside a cage door that separated them from the prisoners. A lot of shit went down on the bus; I heard about fights breaking out, guys getting turned out right there on the bus. The freemen in the front ignored everything. Neither of them wanted to open the cage door and walk back into the bus where we were.

As soon as the bus passed through the sally port—the security gate—to the main prison we could hear the voices of the sexual predators calling out. They stood in a line, fingers poking through the chain-link fence. The freemen allowed them to yell at the incoming prisoners. The bus stopped behind the laundry room. We were told to get off and line up. Trustees would go left to their dorms; medium-security prisoners would go to the right.

I went left toward the walk. T. Ratty followed me. The walk was long. It runs the entire length of the main prison, between all the dorms. I looked straight ahead. Voices called out, "I got you, boy." "You're for me." "Look at that ass." Some of the rapists were looking for the men they had been expecting, who were turned out at RC and whose names they had paid for. Others were trying to pick out weak prisoners to intimidate. Closer to the prison dorms there were more prisoners on the other side of the fence, not the sexual predators but men searching our faces for people they knew. I saw someone I recognized from New Orleans. I didn't know his name but he waved me over, and I brought T. Ratty. The prisoner led us to our unit, called Cypress. There were four dorms in each unit. I was in Cypress 1. Each dorm was built to house 60 prisoners but the dorms were always overcrowded. You entered through what they called the day room, where there were benches and lockers. The main part of the building was the sleeping area, with rows of beds. Each prisoner had a bunk with a locker box attached to the head of the bunk. The TV room was located in the back of the dormitory. There were 26 of us who went down the walk that day. T. Ratty and I were the only two who didn't get turned out.

As soon as I got to the dorm I was challenged again. Each new prisoner had to go to the clothing room to get a towel and bedding and, while he was gone, it was open season on the possessions he'd left on his bed. Everything was stolen unless you knew somebody in the dorm who would watch your shit. I didn't have any friends there, but a few of the guys from New Orleans knew who I was, so I asked one of them to watch my few possessions and he did.

At the clothing room, there was another hustle. We got our sheets and a blanket and were supposed to get clothes suitable for our assigned jobs—gloves for field hands, aprons for kitchen workers. More often than not, instead of handing over the clothing, the inmate clerk in the clothing room made a business out of selling the clothes to prisoners. He paid the freemen to look the other way. If you didn't have any way to barter for or buy the clothes you were out of luck. They were always short on jackets, boots, and gloves. Field hands were supposed to get them but rarely did. Freemen used the clothing room as their own personal closet, stealing the clothes meant for prisoners for themselves or to sell outside the prison.

It wasn't just clothing that prison officials stole. High-ranking officials would steal food and toothpaste, soap and toilet paper, anything they wanted that was meant for prisoners. If they didn't use the merchandise, they sold it on the side. We always knew when all the meat had been taken. We'd get baloney for dinner seven days a week for months. Fried baloney, boiled baloney, spaghetti and baloney, baloney sandwiches.

I only had one incident of a prisoner trying to rape me. His name was Gilbert. I fought him off. Fighting never came easy to me, even in prison. It was always a conscious act that I willed myself to do. Sometimes I got into bullshit fights over something stupid, but most of the time I only fought when I had to: when I was protecting myself or when my reputation was at stake. To protect your reputation, you had to carry yourself a certain way. If someone challenges you and you don't fight you've lost your reputation; it's gone. What's good one day is not worth shit tomorrow. There were all kinds of dos and don'ts, a field of land mines. You don't talk to a guy a certain way, you don't look at him a certain way. Remarks like, "Fuck you talking to?" or "Were you talking to me?" could lead to a fight. I always fought to the end, until I beat the other guy or he quit or someone broke it up. Most of the time I tried to stay in the background but I fought if necessary. If you weren't willing to fight at Angola you'd get eaten alive.

I never turned anybody out. I've never raped anyone in my life. I didn't steal people's shit in prison, but one time I did break into a prisoner's box. He had been trying to boss me around; we called it "roboting." I couldn't let him robot me. If I did other prisoners would lose respect for me or try to robot me themselves. To retaliate a few of us shimmed the lock on his box and took all his property. When he came back, I felt bad. I felt bad every time I did something against my nature. I never ever let my guard down though. If it wasn't the other prisoners to worry about it was the security staff.

Freemen and inmate guards had the power of life and death in their hands and they had no respect for life. They had ultimate power over every prisoner's life. At that time, the midsixties, there were no checks and balances; there was no oversight. It was as if the cruelty of Angola's history, coming out of slavery and convict leasing, leaked into our present world. Angola was run like an antebellum slave plantation. A freeman would slap, humiliate, hit, and yell at a prisoner. If the prisoner talked back he would go to the dungeon. If he physically fought back he'd be badly beaten on his way to the dungeon. Freemen ganged up on prisoners in groups, and they beat prisoners who were handcuffed and in leg restraints. They hollowed out baseball bats and filled them with lead to use for beatings.

Being sent to the dungeon—being "locked up"—was a constant threat. I heard stories about the dungeon, a cellblock not far from the main prison. Prisoners were kept 24 hours a day in a cell shared by other prisoners. Total isolation. Bread for breakfast, lunch, and dinner. We called it "the hole." The lowest-ranking freeman could put you in the dungeon because of the way you looked at him, or if he didn't like your face; if you didn't walk fast enough, or if you walked too fast. Over and over we heard, "Nigger, do this or I'll lock your ass up, nigger." Or they called black prisoners "thing." "What are you looking at, old thing?" "Get moving, old thing, or you're going to the hole!" Prisoners could be kept in the dungeon for weeks. No paperwork was required.

It's painful to remember how violent Angola was in those days. I don't like to go into it. Freemen and inmate guards could physically assault prisoners in any way they wanted. I saw security guards beat down prisoners with baseball bats. I saw prisoners stab other prisoners outside in broad daylight on the walk. There were stabbings at Angola over nothing; prisoners would fight over a football game they were watching on TV. Everyone who wanted to be armed could be. A shank was the easiest thing in the world to get. Men wrapped magazines and phone books around their chests and backs for protection. They wore sunglasses while lying on their bunks so they could look awake while they were sleeping and fake sleep while they were awake.

Chapter 5

Prison Days

Most prisoners had nothing, so everybody was always on the hustle to survive. I prided myself on my hustle out on the street but something about the prisoners' constant manipulation and hustle got on my nerves. There was no sincere camaraderie between any of them. The biggest myth in the world is that there is honor among thieves. Guys ratted on each other left and right. They wouldn't do it in front of anyone, but if a prisoner was isolated by himself, nine times out of ten he would make a deal to get out of trouble. Some guys stood strong and didn't violate the code, and I learned from them. The code was: you didn't rat, you took your beef, and if you did something that somebody else got busted for—and it didn't look like he'd get out of it—you came forward. I prided myself on following the code. Even back then I had enough sense to have some honor.

Every prison has a black market, and the black market at Angola was epic. Not everybody goes into prison planning to get into the black market, but sooner or later you want something and somebody comes along who can give it to you and you negotiate. Everything is bought or bartered in prison: soap, socks, sewing needles, sugar. Years later, when I was in solitary confinement, I could get something as impossible as an onion in my cell through Angola's black market.

Almost anything could be bought, and nearly everyone could be paid off. For a carton of cigarettes, you could bribe an inmate clerk to change a disciplinary report from something serious, like fighting, to something minor, like arguing with a freeman. Paying off security happened all the way to the highest levels of the ranking officers. That's how prisoner drug dealers operated openly on the main prison yard. Some freemen were rumored to run drugs and other contraband into the prison.

The prisoners—mostly white clerks—who were the dealmakers for the freemen and their superiors had a lot of power. You could pay them $50 for a new job assignment, $20 for a new dorm assignment. The officer would get the cash, and in exchange the prisoner dealmaker would get free rein to gamble and pimp other prisoners without interruption. Security officers paid prisoners off too—with better jobs, safer housing, and more privileges—in exchange for information. A prison snitch was weak. He was broken. He would tell security officers whatever they wanted to hear.

Your success on the black market usually depended on what job you had. Kitchen workers had it best because they could get food and utensils, which were always in high demand. Working in the fields I had nothing to barter with. I got by because my mom always left me some money in my account when she visited. It was always a tussle for my mom to find enough extra money to visit but she came almost every month. A man in New Orleans had a bus he drove to Angola once a week for families of prisoners who had no other way to get there. It cost $12 round-trip; $6 for children. We visited in a large room lined with tables. My mom never asked about what I did on the street so we didn't talk about my case. I never told her one of the reasons I escaped from Thibodaux jail was that nobody visited me there and I wanted to see her; I wanted to be home. I didn't tell her I took the rap for Peewee's brother. We didn't talk about things like that. I asked her about Aunt Gussie, about my siblings and friends and people in the neighborhood, and she told me everything going on. I was always happy to see her. She was always happy to see me. At the end of her first visit we hugged and she promised to bring my brother Michael, who was 8; and Violetta, who was 13, next time.

Prisoners weren't allowed to carry cash but each prisoner had an account. His wages—two cents an hour—were deposited in that account along with any cash money he got from friends and family. We were allowed to buy up to $10 or $15 worth of canteen stamps per month, which could be used at the prison store in place of money. Canteen stamps were the currency of the prison. Next to stamps were cigarettes. Freemen preferred to be paid off in canteen stamps. What they weren't given, they took. The stamps came in a booklet and were torn off as they were used in the store. Prisoners weren't supposed to carry loose stamps. Some freemen would shake a prisoner down on the walk and confiscate any loose stamps found on the prisoner and keep these for themselves. When a guard shook down dorms or cells he pocketed any loose canteen stamps. Prison regulations forbade guards from having canteen stamps but a freeman could pull a roll of 50 from his pocket to pay for items at the prison store and nobody would blink.

One of the greatest hardships for me in the first few months I was at Angola was getting used to the sameness of every day. Our routine started when the whistle blew around five a.m. We got dressed, washed up, and stood in line to go to breakfast. Each unit was called to the dining hall separately. Oak Unit, where whites were housed, was always called first. Next, the three black units were called in rotating order. There were two guards assigned to each unit. One went with the prisoners into the dining hall; the other one stayed in the guard booth or on the walk, directing traffic, telling prisoners to keep moving. At the dining hall, there was an entrance for whites and a separate entrance for blacks. Each prisoner was given a spoon or fork and then stood in one of the lines in the aisles between rows of tables to get food from prisoners scooping it onto trays from behind steam tables. Blacks and whites stood in separate lines because we were called to the dining hall separately—whites were served by white prisoners—and sat at different tables. Once seated, we had 15 minutes to eat. When the freemen pointed at your table everyone at that table got up and walked out, placing everything in a bin at the door except the utensil, which we handed to a freeman under the watch of another guard. Dozens of cats congregated outside the exit doors of the dining hall and a lot of prisoners threw them scraps from their pockets on the way out. Everybody who worked that day reported to his job detail to be counted. Before lunch, we all returned to our dorms to be counted, then we went to the dining hall for the same routine for lunch. We did it all again for dinner.

After dinner, we usually had some time on the yard if we wanted. Sometimes there was a movie night (one night for white prisoners, another night for black prisoners). We could play football. Sometimes white and black prisoners played against each other. A lot of guys went back to their dorms and played cards or watched TV. This was repeated day after day. It was hard to get used to.

White prisoners did almost all the administrative work at Angola at that time. The inmate clerk jobs were exclusively held by white prisoners. White prisoners also had most of the jobs on cleaning crews, at the mechanic shops, and at the businesses on prison grounds: the sugar mill, cannery, and tag plant. Black prisoners were mostly in the field, reporting to the sally port after breakfast to be taken out to the fields on the flatbeds of 18-wheelers or on long wagons called "hootenannies," which were pulled by tractors. Our work in the field changed with the season. We planted crops: cabbage, cotton, spinach, okra, corn, and other vegetables. We harvested the crops when they were grown. There was no farm machinery to help, and most of us didn't have gloves or proper footwear. Picking cotton was one of the worst jobs in the field. If you didn't do it right you'd tear up your hands. One time we were clearing out a pasture and I found a trembling baby rabbit in the weeds. His mother was nowhere to be seen, most likely killed by prisoners ahead of me and already over a fire out on the headland, where coffee and food were prepared for the foremen. I picked him up and put him in my pocket to give to my sister Violetta when she visited next time with my mom. Back at the dorm I kept him in a shoebox under my bed. When I gave Vi the baby rabbit she called him Stuff. He became a beloved pet and got real big living in my mom's house.

The hardest job I ever had in my life was cutting sugarcane, Angola's main crop. Cutting cane was so brutal that prisoners would pay somebody to break their hands, legs, or ankles, or they would cut themselves during cane season, to get out of doing it. There were old-timers at Angola who made good money breaking prisoners' bones so men could get out of work. Cutting cane was especially hard in the winter, when it was so cold you couldn't feel your face. At the end of the day we piled all the cane knives on top of one another. When we came back the next morning they'd be frozen together. We had to set them by a fire to separate them.

We worked side by side in groups of four called crews. The two men inside were called the down row, the two outside were called the fly row. With each step you bent over and grabbed a cane stalk at the bottom with one hand and whacked it with a cane knife held in the other. These long razor-sharp knives had short wooden handles and were difficult to hold over long periods of time. Over and over, bend, whack, stand, on each step. The down row was supposed to stay ahead of the fly row to cut a center path that the fly row could push the cut cane stalks onto. We were pushed to go as fast as we could the whole time. It was the speed they pushed on us that made it so hard. They would put the fittest, fastest workers in the group that went first. Everyone else was supposed to keep up with them. Within each group, if the fly row couldn't keep up with the down row, the field foreman or freeman would start calling the prisoners' names. Some guys just couldn't keep up no matter how hard they tried. If they weren't able to speed up, the whole crew would be written up for a work offense. In cane season, we worked seven days a week. It was Angola's most profitable crop; we planted more cane than anything else.

I never got used to the verbal disrespect out in the fields: being called a nigger and constantly told to "hurry up, boy." I couldn't stand it, but I could shut it out. I wouldn't allow a freeman or an inmate guard to put his hand on me though. One day the field foreman grabbed my arm and I resisted, cussing him out. He called the patrol and told them to take me to the hole. A freeman appeared in a police cruiser and drove me to the dungeon. I was charged with aggravated disobedience.

By that time, I didn't think I could be shocked by anything, but the brutality and pain in the dungeon were worse than anything I'd ever seen. There were four or five men in each six-by-nine-foot cell. There was no bunk, table, or chair in the cell, just a toilet and a sink. Everyone was stripped of all his clothes and underwear and given a jumpsuit to wear. Nobody had any possessions. Each prisoner got two slices of bread three times a day. At five p.m., a guard passed one mattress into the cell. At five a.m., the guard removed the mattress. Usually one or two inmates ran the cell. In some cells bullies took the mattress for themselves all night. During the hours when there was no mattress they would take the jumpsuit off the back of a cellmate and make a pallet out of it to sit on, while that man was forced to stand naked.

Some men almost starved to death because the bullyboys in charge took their bread. It's hard to say how much the freemen knew of the abuse in the cells. But when they looked through the cell door to take their count, they couldn't help but notice some of the men in the cells weren't wearing their jumpsuits. Authorities never did anything to stop it.

In my cell, the first thing I did was make it clear that nobody wanted the trouble that would come from fucking with me. My reputation as a fighter who doesn't give up helped me in the dungeon maybe more than anywhere else in prison. It's easier to fight in the dungeon than in a normal cell. There's no bunk sticking out, no table; there's more room. When the mattress was handed in I suggested we share it and nobody challenged me. We put it in the middle so everyone could put his head on it, or we took turns using it. Nobody stole anyone's bread. Even so, the experience of being in the dungeon was pure misery. There were roaches, rats. There was no room. We were completely isolated. We couldn't call home. The only way we knew what was going on in the prison was if new prisoners were brought in. It got painful sitting and lying on that concrete. Hips, knees, back—all that would be hurting at one time or another. The dungeon could destroy every fragment of a man's dignity and self-respect. The harsh conditions were so hurtful that strong men would cry. They broke.

The only way anyone got out of the dungeon was if the colonel, who was head of security at Angola, let you out when he was making his rounds. He'd come every day, carrying a stack of index cards that had the names of prisoners on them and what each one had done to be put in the dungeon. He walked down the tier slowly. It played to the colonel's ego to have that much control over our lives. Some prisoners stood in there for 30, 45, or 60 days, "under investigation." Some men would beg for release in a childlike voice when they saw him, crying, "I'll be good. Please let me out." I was hurting too, but I was too proud to show it.

When he got to the door of my cell I'd turn my back on him and walk to the back of the cell behind everyone else. I was in there for 15 days.

I hated prison, but in those first months I'd adjusted to Angola. I could have transferred out after three months and gone to DeQuincy, a jail for first-time offenders, but I never did the paperwork. I didn't want to start over. I knew the routine at Angola. I was surviving. A lot of prisoners bonded over where they were from. There was a Shreveport group, a Baton Rouge group, a Lafayette group. I was in a clique of guys from New Orleans.

We had weekends off from work except when it was cane-cutting season. On Sunday, we could get visits. After dinner, there was some free time and we were allowed to stay outside, usually until dark. We played football and lay around on the yard. When freemen started to yell, "Clear the yard, count time, clear the yard," we all filed back into our dorms. When the last count of the day was done, the whistle blew and they locked the doors. If you weren't in your dorm by then you were taken to the dungeon.

Inside the dorm, it was chaos. Fights would break out over a game of cards. I saw guys get beat up and raped in the dorm. I stayed away from the violence. Sometimes I watched TV, depending on what was on. I played dominoes. Some prisoners used religion to give themselves hope in the knowledge they would never go free. They grouped together at night beside someone's bunk or went into the day room to have religious discussions and read the Bible. We called them "Holy Rollers." Most of the time the other prisoners and I would kick it, just talk. Ninety-nine percent of what we said was a lie. We had absolutely nothing to boast about from our real lives.

The musician Charles Neville was in the New Orleans group. He used to give guys tattoos. In those days, I prided myself on having a pretty lethal right punch so I told him I wanted a skull and crossbones inside my right arm. He used the stick-and-poke method, dipping a needle wrapped in thread into the ink from a pen. When he finished I asked him to put the word "DEATH" over it in capital letters.

I was always scared though. Always. I was far from home. I was constantly seeing acts of violence, constantly seeing guys being raped, and I lived with the knowledge that that could be me at some point in time. By February 1966, a week before my birthday, I had done a third of my 24-month sentence and was eligible for parole. I don't recall being asked any questions by the parole board. A freeman drove me and a few other prisoners due for release to the front gate in an old school bus. When I went through the gate I didn't have anyone waiting for me so I started walking down the 26-mile road that led to the highway. I hitched a ride to the bus station at Baton Rouge and got on the Greyhound bus to New Orleans. I had no purpose, no direction, and no goals, but I had survived Angola. I believed it was a test of my strength. Proof of my courage. Nobody would mess with me now. I would soon be 19 and I was a badass, I told myself, because to survive in the street that was required.

Chapter 6

Parole and Back Again

Having learned absolutely nothing in prison except how to become a better predator I picked up where I left off when I got home. I went to my mom's house first. Pop Skeeter had moved my mom, my brothers, and my sister out of our two rooms in Aunt Gussie's house on North Villere to a house on Bertrand Street. It was tidy and clean, the way my mom liked it. My mom housed and fed me. I stayed for a couple of weeks but couldn't settle in. My family's routines had become alien to me. My mom didn't tolerate me coming and going at all hours. Some nights when I got home the door would be locked and I'd fall asleep on the back porch. My brothers seemed so young to me, and they were. I would watch *The Jackie Gleason Show* on TV with them sometimes. I was closest to my sister, who was 14. She was just starting to date boys and I felt very protective of her.

It wasn't long before I moved in with my old friend and running partner Frank and we ran with our old friends from the High Steppers. Eight-track tapes had become very popular while I was in prison and everyone had an eight-track tape players installed under the dashboard of their cars. Stealing eight-track tapes out of cars became very profitable. We'd take them from cars and sell them to a fence, or we'd sell them directly to guys who had players. Sometimes we'd sell a guy tapes, then break into his car later, steal them back, and sell them to someone else. When we could, we stole the tape players.

While on parole I worked at different jobs. For a while I was a porter at a hotel. They called us redcaps because we wore red hats. We took guests to their rooms with their luggage, showed them how to turn the air conditioner on and off, and checked to make sure there were enough towels. I was there for about a month when the hotel hired a new hostess, a young white woman who called us "boys" instead of redcaps. She would call one of us over and say to the guests, "This boy will show you to your room." I asked her not to refer to me as a boy and told her that we were called redcaps by the management, but she didn't stop. I went to the manager, a young white dude, and told him that the new hostess they hired kept referring to the redcaps as boys to the guests. I asked him to talk to her and tell her to stop calling us boys. He said he would.

The next day when she called me over to take a couple to their room she called me a boy again. "I told you I'm not a fucking boy," I yelled at her. "I'm a fucking man. You take them to the room your motherfucking self." And then I walked off. The manager called me in and told me I couldn't talk to her like that and I told him to suck my dick. He fired me. I didn't give a shit. I was only working there because I was stealing sheets, pillowcases, blankets, bedspreads, and pillows and selling them around the neighborhood anyhow. If I could have taken the mattresses I would have. It was one of my hustles. It was a way to survive, to help put food on the table and help my mom pay rent and buy clothes for me and my brothers and sister. The only part that bothered me about being fired was that I'd just figured out how to unbolt the TVs.

After that I took a job as a car jockey at an automobile dealership. My job was to pick up cars that had to be repaired and bring them back to the dealership and deliver the repaired cars back to their owners. The dealer had a very small car that could be attached to a regular-size car so that I could drive myself to a customer or drive back to the dealership after delivering a vehicle. One night at closing time the manager asked me to deliver one last car to a customer. Since he was closing up he told me after my delivery to drive the small car home for the night and just bring it to work the next morning.

That night my sister Violetta called me from a pay phone at a movie theater saying a dude in the theater was harassing her and her friend. I told her to stay inside and I'd be right over to get her. I drove the dealership car over to the theater. By the time I got there, her friend's father had already picked up her friend, but Vi was there and when she saw me she ran outside and got in the car. We were a couple of blocks from my mom's house when I pulled up to a stop sign next to the off-ramp for I-10. A police car with four detectives in it was parked under the overpass. They motioned me to pull over. They separated me from my sister and took us to the police precinct under the bridge, then they interrogated me, asking me where I got the car. I told them the story and they called my supervisor.

My supervisor corroborated my story but told them he didn't give me permission to drive the car that night. The cops hung up and charged me with car theft. I said, "Man, you know I didn't steal the car. I wasn't riding around. I know you talked to my sister, she can tell you, I just picked her up." There was nothing I could do. What hurt the most was that I did my manager a favor and he stabbed me in the back. Vi called my mom to pick her up. They took me from the precinct to Orleans Parish Prison. Bail was set at $100 but my parole officer put a hold on me so I couldn't be released on bail. I sat in Orleans Parish Prison for about six months before I went to court. The DA gave me a deal, breaking the car theft charge down to "unauthorized use of a vehicle" with credit for time served. I pleaded guilty. But I wasn't released. Since unauthorized use of a vehicle was a parole violation I was to be sent back to Angola to finish my original sentence.

The day before I left I got into a fight with another prisoner at the parish prison. I punched him in the mouth. When it was over I didn't notice that one of his teeth was buried in my knuckle. The next morning my hand was swollen to three times its normal size. Since the officials at the Parish Prison knew I was shipping out they didn't take me to the hospital, they put me downstairs in the waiting room. By the time I got to Angola my hand was green and I had a fever. A captain at the Reception Center took one look at me and sent me to the hospital. At that time, the only doctor in the prison hospital was a prisoner, a white doctor incarcerated for killing his wife. They called him an orderly. I probably would have lost my hand if he hadn't treated me. He drained my fist, put me on antibiotics, and kept me in the hospital for four days to make sure all the infection was gone before sending me back to the Reception Center dorm. When I was released from the hospital he bandaged my hand and gave me "no-duty" status, which meant I didn't have to work until my hand healed.

On my way to the dorm I stopped to eat at the dining hall. I was in the chow line when a white inmate guard everybody called Nigger Miles got in my face. He got that name because he called every black prisoner "nigger." He was a giant. He came up to me and asked me why I wasn't at work and I told him I had no-duty status because of my hand. He said something along the lines of, "Well, I got a one-armed nigger in the field, what makes you better?" I said, "I don't give a fuck if you have a one-eyed and one-armed man in the field, I got no-duty status. I'm not going out in the field." He said after chow I'd be going to the fields, and I told him I wasn't going to no fucking field. He was an inmate guard. I knew he didn't have the authority to overrule my no-duty status. He ordered me to stand over by the door outside the dining hall that led to a bathroom used by security people. It also housed brooms and mops used by inmate orderlies to clean up.

I walked to the door and four or five white inmate guards came up to me. They pointed to some food drippings on the floor that had spilled from trays that were being carried to prisoners on Death Row, which was next door to RC. One of the inmate guards told me to mop up the mess on the floor. Another one said to go to the bathroom to get the mop. That was an orderly's job and I wasn't an orderly. I said no. They ordered me to go into the bathroom again. I knew what was about to happen so as I moved toward the bathroom I braced myself. Instead of going inside I turned around and started throwing punches. I hollered and screamed so the prisoners in the dining hall would hear me. By the time other prisoners started to arrive a captain had appeared and broke up the fight. They sent me to the hospital because my hand was bleeding. After I was rebandaged they put me in the Red Hat, the oldest and worst cellblock at Angola. Built in the 1930s, the Red Hat got its name because in the old days, prisoners from that cellblock wore straw hats that were marked by red paint so when they worked in the fields they could be identified. By the seventies nobody in the Red Hat worked; it was a dungeon. In the early seventies it was permanently closed by federal officials for being a chamber of horrors; years later it was incorporated into a museum on prison grounds.

In the Red Hat you could stand in the middle of your cell and touch the walls on either side of you. The cells were three feet wide and six feet long. The ceiling was low. The door was solid steel halfway up, with bars from the ceiling to waist level. The bunk was concrete. There was no mattress. There was a toilet in the cell but they kept the water turned off, so it didn't work. You had to use a bucket in the corner which could only be emptied when you were let out every few days for a shower. They wanted you to smell the stench of your own body waste while eating. All the prisoners in the Red Hat were served the same food, which amounted to slop. The cell was suffocating, hot. It was dark. It was a coffin. There were vermin. I was constantly thirsty. You never knew when they would come to get you for the shower. I lay on the concrete bunk. I stood on it. I moved around a lot to stay loose. I did push-ups and jumping jacks. I did 1,000 push-ups. Then more. I stood at my cell door and called down to prisoners in the other cells; we talked. Night came then day then night. The conditions in the Red Hat were a test, I told myself. My anger, my hate, the heat, the stench, the filth, the rats, and the pressure shaped me into something new. When the freeman came to let me out I met his eyes with defiance. He took me back to the Reception Center. I'd been in there for 10 days.

Nothing was different my second time at Angola. I was assigned the same dorm on the trustee side, Cypress 1. I had the same job, working in the fields. I knew the routine. I knew the psychology. I was 100 percent confident I wouldn't have to worry about being bullied or raped or "paying draft," paying someone not to bully you or beat you up or take your personal property. Everybody knew who Fox was and everybody knew you didn't fuck with me. When I came down the walk on fresh fish day there were four or five dudes who greeted me as a friend. When I put my stuff on the bunk this time before being taken to the clothing room I didn't have to ask anyone to watch it. My shit was still there when I got back, as I knew it would be.

I saw a lot of the same prisoners, heard the same stories. I didn't talk a lot. If I did I was lying, trying to create an aura of toughness I didn't actually feel. In prison, you never talk about your charge but you talk about everything else. Multiple times. Multiple ways. Multiple versions. What you (supposedly) did, what someone did to you, what you will do when you get out.

Prisoners bragged about their hustle. If you robbed people on the street with a gun you were a stickup artist. If you robbed drug dealers you were a jack artist. We called shoplifters "boosters." There were con artists, bank robbers, carjackers, drug dealers, pimps. Stories in prison are endless daydreams, described in detail, and—in the black dorms—spoken in the flow and rhythm of Ebonics. The beauty of Ebonics is that it's so specific, and forever changing. So were our stories in prison.

In prison, you are part of a human herd. In the human herd survival of the fittest is all there is. You become instinctive, not intellectual. Therein lies the secret to the master's control. One minute you're treated like a baby, being handed a spoon to eat with or being told where to stand. The next, with utter indifference, you're being counted several times a day—you have no choice, you have no privacy. The next moment you're threatened, pushed, tested. You develop a sixth sense as a means of survival, instincts to help you size up what's going on around you at all times and help you make all the internal adjustments necessary to respond when it will save your life, but never before. Taking action at the wrong time could get you killed.

Once you have a reputation you have to do what it takes to keep it; you do things you don't want to because it's expected of you. I lay low as much as I could and tried to fit into the background and play my role. I knew my survival depended on my ability to respond violently if needed. But by some grace, maybe the love of my mother, I hadn't totally lost my humanity. I was always poised to be aggressive, but I also knew it wasn't who I was.

In those days, if you didn't have a sentence of life in prison, you only had to do half your time; it was called two-for-one, the "good time" system. Every day you were in prison and stayed out of trouble you got credited for two days. My first time at Angola I did eight months—a third of my sentence—before I was paroled. When I was sent back after violating parole my "good time" was recalculated; I had to do half of my remaining 16 months. After eight months I was discharged on August 31, 1967.

Chapter 7

Stickup Artist

They gave me a bus ticket and $10 at the front gate. Still wearing prison-issue clothes I hitched a ride on an 18-wheeler packed with Angola produce to Baton Rouge. I took a Greyhound bus to New Orleans. The first time I'd left Angola I was proud that I'd survived. This time I was numb. When I got back I didn't go home to see my mom right away. I looked for Frank. It was pretty much just the two of us left. The High Steppers were long over. We never talked about our old gang anymore. Most of the guys from the gang had moved on or were in prison. Frank was my only running partner. I didn't stay with my family but I saw my mom almost every day, dropping by the house. She was a great cook and had red beans and rice with ham hocks or other dishes on the stove for anyone who came by. She knew I was breaking the law but didn't ask questions. We purely enjoyed each other's company. I liked hearing her stories; we had good conversations. She was proud that I was intelligent. "Boy, you can sit down on Monday and see Friday," she'd say. I stayed in touch with Aunt Gussie too. She worked unloading barges on the Mississippi River for years.

The Sixth Ward was the same. Still poor but life went on. Children played ball in the street, some of them barefoot, answering voices calling them home for dinner. I could vaguely remember more innocent times: Dancing in the street behind a second line band after a funeral. Collecting bottle caps to see movies. Catching pigeons for an old man named Reb who lived in the neighborhood. He used to pay us 25 cents for every pigeon we brought him. We climbed everywhere to bag those pigeons, over rooftops and under rafters, around the skylight above a bank.

At the bank, we lay across the glass skylight and watched birds inside the bank fly beneath us. It never occurred to us that we could get in the bank the same way the pigeons did and help ourselves to cash from teller drawers. It never occurred to us that Reb could do something like eat the pigeons we brought him. But that's what he did.

Now, at night, I broke into houses and took anything I could carry that I thought I could fence. Radios, TVs, stereos, nice clothing. If I was lucky there would be jewelry or money lying around. Sometimes we stole a car to use for a night so we could get everything to our fence quickly. We'd leave the car near where we took it. Other times we stole cars and drove them to chop shops, selling them for parts.

I never smoked. When I was 14 or 15, I accidentally got very drunk at a dance; I didn't know the 7-Up I was drinking had vodka in it. I got so sick I passed out and threw up for two days afterward, including all over a new sweater my mom had just bought for me. I felt so bad about ruining that sweater. I never touched alcohol again. When I was 20, shortly after I got out of Angola the second time, I let a guy I used to run with named Leroy give me my first shot of heroin. I didn't want to do it—I had popped pills occasionally but never used habit-forming drugs and didn't want to start. I was at his house when he was shooting up and he started messing with me, telling me I couldn't handle it. I told him, "Shit, I can handle it, give me some." That high you get when you first start shooting heroin is the best feeling I ever had. But at some point, I no longer experienced that wonderful high. I started shooting to keep from getting sick.

I was a weekend junkie at first. I thought I was handling dope because I never got sick during the week. Then I got busted for something and while I was in Orleans Parish Prison my nose started running and I was cramping up. A friend of mine on the tier said, "Man, you got a habit." I denied it. He said, "I know what withdrawal looks like."

I became so sick that I was taken to Charity Hospital. I heard the guard tell the doctor I was a stinking-ass junkie. They gave me a shot for the nausea and I was supposed to be taken back for a shot every day but I was never taken back to the hospital. I kicked that habit in prison. When I beat the charge and was released, I went back to shooting dope again. That's how I knew I was addicted. I wasn't getting high. I was shooting to be normal, to function. On the streets of New Orleans we were buying $12 bags of heroin that had been cut down. Someone told me we could get uncut heroin for $2 a bag in New York City so in 1968 I started driving to New York with a friend to buy dope. We bought it in Harlem and sometimes shot up in Central Park. When we drove home we brought it back with us.

One night I broke into a car and was rifling through the glove compartment when I found a gun. I stared at it in my hand, then put it in my waistband and walked quickly away from the car. A new feeling came over me, a confidence I'd never felt before in my life. My chances of survival, I thought, had just increased by 100 percent. The irony of it, the stupidity of it, was that I had no idea what to do with it. I'd never fired a gun in my life. I didn't tell anyone for weeks. I kept it hidden under my shirt. One night I walked up behind a dude on the street and pulled the gun out of my waistband and pointed it at his head. "Give me your money, motherfucker," I yelled. I was real nervous, forcing myself not to show it. After a while it became normal, like anything else you do. When I needed money, I went out and got it from a person walking down the street. I was a stickup artist. Later, I started robbing dope dealers. I went up to them in the alley or on a street corner where they were selling and made them take me to where they hid their stash, or I'd go to their homes and threaten them. I was a jack artist.

After about a year of being addicted to heroin I didn't want to be loaded anymore. My girlfriend at the time was named Slim. I asked her to help me kick dope. We bought some groceries and went to our apartment. I warned her that I was going to get sick, throw up, and shit myself, but that no matter how sick I got, no matter what I said to her, no matter what I did, she was not to let me out of the apartment. I said, "I mean it, Slim, no matter what I say, no matter what I do, don't let me leave. Do whatever you have to do to keep me from leaving." She promised.

Within several hours I was sweating, stinking, sick. Of course, I changed my mind. I tried to leave. I told her to let me go. But Slim was true to her word. We tussled and fought for the next week, falling on the floor, the bed, all over the apartment. She held her ground. When I was too weak to fight I ran a guilt trip on her like the pitiful disgusting piece of shit I was. I told her if she loved me she wouldn't let me suffer. I said anything I could think of to make her feel sorry for me. She didn't waver. Eventually, I started to get an appetite. Slim fed me warm milk and chicken soup. I threw everything up. My stomach was too raw and tender to let me eat. My bones ached. In about two more weeks I gradually started to feel better. After that, I never touched drugs again.

Writing about this time in my life is very difficult. I robbed people, scared them, threatened them, intimidated them. I stole from people who had almost nothing. My people. Black people. I broke into their homes and took possessions they worked hard for; took their wallets out of their pockets. I beat people up. I was a chauvinist pig. I took advantage of people, manipulated people. I never thought about the pain I caused. I never felt the fear or despair people had around me. When I look back on that time I see that the only real human connection I had in those years came from my visits with my mom and those hours I spent at her house and around my family, but at the time I didn't think of it like that. Her house was nothing more than a rest stop for me. I only thought of myself. In the year and a half after being released from Angola the second time, from August 1967 to February 1969, I was in and out of jail. For city charges, like shoplifting or traffic tickets, I'd be taken to the House of Detention, which we called the House of D. For charges of robbery and assault I'd be taken to Orleans Parish Prison.

Each time I went to the parish prison was worse than the last. It was extremely overcrowded, filthy dirty, and dangerous. I wasn't a bully but I never backed down, so I was in a lot of fights. Once, to punish me and "put me in my place," prison officials put me on C-1, a tier that housed gay prisoners, snitches, and other prisoners who'd asked to be checked off their tiers out of fear. The officials were trying to tarnish my "bad boy" reputation, to give the impression that I was a rat or that somebody punked me out. The windows were sealed shut from the out-side with metal plates because the tier was on the first floor. There were four bunks in each cell, 15 cells on each side of the hall. During the day, the cell doors were open and we could go to a pen at the end of the hall called a day room or stay in the cell. At night, we were locked down in our cells. The tier was stifling hot and unsanitary, never cleaned. When someone came to clean the tier after a few weeks, he did nothing more than push the filth around with a mop and a pail of dirty water. The food was inedible. The air was so bad it could get difficult to breathe.

Even worse, I believed the longer I was on that tier, the more it could hurt my reputation. Some people might start to think I was a coward. A prisoner's reputation and his word were all he had. As a form of protest, and to escape the heat and filth, some of the prisoners started to talk about cutting themselves. I didn't want to join them, but I decided to do it. It might get me off the tier. Maybe with more than a few prisoners at the hospital at the same time someone would do something to help us. I wrote a note on a piece of paper to my mom, telling her I was in the hospital, and I put her phone number on it. I folded two nickels in the paper and stuck it in my waistband.

About a dozen of us cut ourselves. I sliced my upper right arm and my left wrist with a razor blade. In those days, there were no dispos-able razors, so razors with blades were passed out, used by prisoners, then passed back to security. The razors were always checked for blades when they were returned but one way or another razor blades could be acquired on the black market inside the prison. About eight or ten of us cut ourselves. A prisoner yelled for the tier guards and they came in, swearing, giving us towels to wrap around our wounds. Before they shackled us, I put the note in my hand, and when we got to the hospital I flipped it over to some black guys standing by the admittance desk; one of them picked up my note and called my mom.

Since she lived within walking distance of Charity Hospital she was there in about 15 minutes with my brothers and my sister. I tried to talk to her and tell her about the terrible conditions on C-1 but the prison guards who brought us told her to stand back. I told her over one guard's shoulders to call the prison the next day and report what was going on. It didn't do any good. After the hospital staff stitched our wounds and bandaged us they sent us back to the parish prison and we were put on the same tier, C-1. Cutting myself was a worthless act. Nothing changed. I was housed there another few months awaiting disposition on a burglary charge when I was released to make room for other prisoners. It was a common practice then—and is to this day—for the DA's office to keep prisoners with weak, or even nonexistent, cases in prison to "sweat" the prisoner, hoping he'd plead guilty. If they needed space during that time for new prisoners, though, they'd go back through those cases and let out everyone they didn't think they could convict. I remember being so relieved when I beat that charge and got back to the street. I thought I was free.

Chapter 8

Tony's Green Room

After robbing people on the streets and jacking dope pushers I eventually started robbing bars and grocery stores while they were open. I walked into a bar, pointed the gun at the bartender or somebody sitting at the bar, and yelled, "Nobody move, motherfucker. I'll kill you." I yelled to everyone to put wallets and watches in a paper bag or pillowcase. I ordered everybody to lie on the floor, then I ran out. It became like a job to me; it was my hustle, a way to support myself and fit in and maintain my reputation.

I gave my mom some money that I stole but spent most of it on bullshit. I was never into jewelry but I used to dress nice. One year I traded a van full of cigarettes I got in a robbery for a red-and-white 1963 Thunderbird and some cash from one of my fences who owned a used car lot. I liked my Thunderbird but I loved Corvettes. A woman who lived next to me happened to have a 1963 Corvette and she loved Thunderbirds. We sometimes traded cars.

I've never raped anyone but I was charged with rape twice. The first time was because I was messing with a married woman. Her husband found out about us and, to get back at me, he forced her to lie to the police and say that I raped her. Because there was no evidence and the woman changed her story so many times, the DA's office reduced that rape charge to aggravated battery. I pleaded guilty to aggravated battery to avoid staying in Orleans Parish Prison for two to three years waiting for trial. I was sentenced to 18 months in the parish prison, but I'd already been there for nine months so I was released under the two-for-one program.

The second time I was charged with rape it was a case of the police "cleaning the books." I was arrested for one charge—armed robbery—but when the police arrested me they charged me with every unsolved robbery, theft, and rape charge they had. We called that cleaning the books. It was a common practice by the police then and is now. Everybody knew about it. To the police it didn't matter if the DA was able to prosecute the charge or not. The police just wanted to wipe their books clean. The DA's office didn't mind; they could use the additional charges to intimidate guys and pressure them to take plea deals instead of going to trial. Innocent men took plea deals all the time and went to prison versus lying around in the parish jail for two or more years waiting for a trial.

The night they cleaned the books on me I had been picked up for an armed robbery. On February 13, 1969, Frank, a friend of ours named James, and I walked from Frank's apartment around the corner to Tony's Green Room to rob it. Someone outside saw us walk in holding guns and called the police. Midway through the robbery the police came in and started shooting. I heard Frank scream. He was shot in the face. In all the commotion, I hid my gun and pretended I was a customer. When the police told everyone to leave I walked out the door and went home.

Frank's girlfriend, not knowing I had been with Frank, called me, distraught, asking me to go to the hospital with her. She told me Frank had been shot. I ran to her house on foot because I'd left my Thunderbird in front of the apartment building that Frank lived in. On the way, I formulated a plan to go with her to the hospital, find out where Frank was, and go back later to break him out. I went inside the apartment to get her. We walked outside and to the car. When I opened the car door police rushed out from behind parked cars and out of the alleyway with their guns drawn. James had given the police my name and the description of my car. After the police arrested me, they took me and Frank's girlfriend back into her apartment. They put me in the bedroom and her in the kitchen. While some of them were beating me and kicking me in the bedroom I could hear the others in the kitchen threatening to take her children, asking her what she knew about the robbery. She was crying and telling them she didn't know anything about it.

The police took me to central lockup. Upstairs they put me in a room and questioned me about the robbery. I denied knowing anything about it and told them a story about how I was just there to help Frank's girlfriend get to the hospital. There were four or five detectives in the room. First one of them hit me in the head with a big leather book. After I'd been hit on my head several times while continuing to deny anything about armed robbery, one of the detectives came up behind me and put a plastic bag over my head, twisting it at the end so no air could get inside. When I was about to pass out they took the bag off. After doing this over and over they gathered around me and picked me up in the air and beat me around my body and in between my legs. Although I was in great pain I still denied knowing anything about the armed robbery. The next day I was transferred to the parish prison and that's when I found out I had been charged with armed robbery and other charges, including theft and several rapes.

The DA dropped all the charges against me for lack of evidence except the armed robbery at Tony's Green Room. All those other fake charges stayed on my record though. As years passed I thought about having them expunged but I kept putting it off. That decision would haunt me decades later. I was offered a plea deal for the robbery at Tony's Green Room. If I pleaded guilty I'd get 15 years but would only have to serve half that—seven and a half years. I didn't take it. I knew that if I held out for a trial I was taking a risk. Judges were known to add extra time in sentencing men who were found guilty, to discourage other men from going to trial. But I didn't want to go back to Angola for one year, much less seven and a half. If there was a chance I didn't have to go, I wanted to take it. I met the public defender who was representing me once before my trial. I was found guilty.

Afterward the DA's office charged me as a habitual felon, which meant they could enhance my sentence. The state of Louisiana passed one of the first "three strikes, you're out" laws in the country, except in the city of New Orleans it was more like "one strike, you're out" under the habitual felon law. If you had even one felony conviction in New Orleans and got a new charge, your sentence could be increased if you were found guilty, up to life in prison, even for nonviolent crimes. I knew when I was sentenced I'd be thrown away. That's what we called it.

Chapter 9

Escape

During my trial and after I was found guilty I was held at Orleans Parish Prison on a tier with an old friend who was about to get out. He helped me figure out an escape plan. The courtroom where I was due to be sentenced, called Section B, was a room they added to the top of the courthouse because of overcrowding. The elevator didn't reach it; you had to walk up a flight of stairs to get to it. My friend had been in that courtroom before. He said he could dress up like a lawyer, get inside, and leave a gun in the bathroom for me. The bathroom was located in the back room of the courtroom, where the prisoners were held.

On sentencing day, October 9, 1969, I wrapped my right wrist in a bandage to make it look like I had an injury and asked the guard not to handcuff me on that "sore" wrist. He cuffed me by my left wrist and put me at the end of the line of prisoners who were cuffed together. My right hand was free. My friend got dressed up in a suit and tie that morning and, carrying a briefcase, he had no trouble getting into the courthouse and making his way to the third floor. I was sitting with the other prisoners when I saw him come in the back room and enter the bathroom. After I saw him leave I told the sheriff I had to use the toilet, so he uncuffed me from the line of prisoners and walked me to the bathroom. I was nervous but I'd had weeks to think of this moment. I knew it was do-or-die time. Inside the bathroom I opened the paper towel dispenser. My friend had left a goddamn German Luger in there. I was expecting to see a small gun that would be easy for me to hide. I slipped the Luger inside the waistband of my pants and opened the door. I thought the gun would slip down the front of my pants the whole time I walked back to my seat and was cuffed to my position in the prisoners' line.

One by one the prisoners in my group were uncuffed to go before the judge, then brought back and cuffed together again. When it was my turn I stood before the judge with the gun hidden in my pants and listened with my hands at my side as he called me derogatory names. He said I was an animal and sentenced me to 50 years. Back at my seat I was again cuffed to the end of the line. We walked in a line down a short flight of stairs to the elevator, followed by a deputy.

When the elevator doors opened on the second floor we all stepped inside. An unarmed deputy was seated next to the control panel. As soon as the doors closed I pulled the gun from my pants with my free hand and held it to his head. I told him to keep the doors closed and take us to the basement or I would shoot him. I didn't mean it but that's what I said. I told the other deputy to unlock my handcuff and cuff himself and the elevator operator to the elevator railing. As he did that somebody in the basement was pressing the call button over and over. When we got to the basement the elevator doors opened and two armed cops were standing there. For less than a second we all froze. But their shock at seeing a prisoner in the elevator with a gun gave me a moment's advantage and I took it. I told them to get inside the elevator and told the deputy to close the doors. I held the Luger on the two cops and told them to hand me their guns, which I dropped down the elevator shaft through a gap in the floor. Then I handcuffed the two cops to the railing. I turned to the other prisoners to ask if any of them wanted to go; one guy, a white dude, said yes, so I uncuffed him.

The next time the elevator doors opened the two of us left running. We had to make it through another set of doors to get to the street. Once outside I ran as fast as I could toward Tulane and Broad, where a childhood friend of mine told me he'd be parked. I jumped into the backseat of his car and covered myself with a blanket.

My friend drove me to an apartment where I stayed the night. From there I watched the search for me unfold on the television news. The prisoner who ran out with me had already been captured. For some reason, the police thought I was holed up in a block of old empty houses and they surrounded the area. They called my mom and she went down to the houses where they thought I was hiding. I watched her on the news crying; they said she was begging me to turn myself in. Years later my brother told me Mama ran to the abandoned houses not to help the police find me but to beg the police not to kill me. The next morning my friend drove me across the state line to Mississippi. I took a bus to Atlanta. After lying low for a few days I boarded a Greyhound bus for New York City.

Other than a phone number a friend gave me of someone to call in Harlem when I got there, I didn't have a plan. I was so out of my element it wasn't funny. I went to a bar and restaurant to use the pay phone there. After I dialed the number two policemen walked in the front door. I hung up the phone and left. I never tried again. My friends had given me some money before I left New Orleans. I found a cheap room in a motel where women turned tricks.

Harlem had changed since the last time I had been there, to buy drugs. There seemed to be less prostitution and drug use visible on the street, less brutality. I watched as men and women my age wearing leather jackets and berets moved through the neighborhood, selling newspapers and talking to people. They escorted women on "check days" to get their groceries, protecting them from being robbed on the way to the store. I couldn't have described it at the time, but they were unifying Harlem, bringing people together. I found out they were members of the Black Panther Party. I'd never seen black people proud and unafraid like that before. They were so confident, even around police. I was used to seeing a certain look in black people's eyes, fear, especially when they were around police. These Panthers weren't intimidated. Instead, it was the police who seemed scared. I wanted to meet the beautiful Panther sisters who wore their hair in African styles and their skirts above their knees. I went by the Panther office in Harlem and looked around, picked up a newspaper, and left.

Within a few weeks I was running out of money when I heard about a guy running a book uptown in a grocery store. It was November, still football season; I bet on a game, putting $100 on a 10-to-1 bet. The team I picked won. The next day I went to the store to collect my winnings and the butcher who worked there said I had to go upstairs to get my money. Stupidly, I followed him. Once we got in the apartment he and the owner jumped me from behind and beat me damn near to death. Then they called the police and said I tried to rob them. When the police came my eyes were swollen shut and I was floating into and out of consciousness but I could hear the butcher telling the cops I held them up at gunpoint. I tried to speak, to say he was lying, but I couldn't move my jaw. The police weren't interested in my story anyway. They took me to the hospital. Later, when they asked me my name I gave them the name of one of my oldest childhood friends, Charles Harris.

Right after I was released from the hospital I was taken to a judge for arraignment. A bail hearing was set and a public defender was assigned. That kind of speed was unheard of in Louisiana, where you could be arrested on a charge and lie in jail for weeks before you were arraigned.

From court they took me to the Manhattan House of Detention, known as the Tombs, a high-rise building. It was a shock to see. Angola was a farm. Standing outside the Tombs you wouldn't know it was a city jail. I was taken in an elevator to a cellblock on the eighth floor. The Tombs was integrated. For me, being from the South, it was strange at first to have a white cellmate. He didn't protest having a black cellmate. I didn't protest either. Other than that it wasn't much different from Angola. Prison is prison. First you figure out the routine, which doesn't take long because every day is the same. Then you learn the culture and how to play between the lines. The faster you do that the quicker you adjust. At any prison there is always a pecking order. The strong rule over the weak, the smart over the strong. All the threats, games, manipulations, stories, and bullying were the same in the Tombs, overseen with the same kind of cruelty and indifference by the prison administration.

Conditions were horrible—filthy, overcrowded, and run-down. There weren't enough beds in the Tombs, so prisoners were forced to sleep on the floor in cells and in the day room. The toilets would back up and it could take days for maintenance crews to come around and fix the plumbing. Trustees were supposed to mop up but seldom did. The food was the worst I'd ever had; the same thing every day, boiled and with no seasoning. There were bedbug and lice epidemics. Security would come in and spray the floors, walls, sheets, and mattresses with poison. Every few months prisoners were stripped naked and sprayed for bedbugs and lice.

Soon after I arrived a prisoner on the tier tried to intimidate me. It started in the shower. He made comments about my body. I kept on showering. I dried off, put my clothes on, and went into the day room. He was sitting at a table playing cards. I grabbed a mop bucket, walked up to him, and split his head open with it. He was taken to the hospital, where he was treated, and he was returned to the same floor and cellblock where I was. Now he knew not to fuck with me and so did everyone else. I expected to be put in the dungeon for that but I never got busted for it. The prisoner told officials he was hit from behind and didn't know who did it. It was violent in the Tombs but nowhere near as violent as at Angola. At Angola men would stab each other over a game of dominoes. In the Tombs if there was a fight there was usually more of a reason.

Since I lied about my identity I couldn't write to or call my mom. She was the only one I knew who would send me money. I started a little laundry business to get by. I used to wash dudes' underwear, T-shirts, socks. They paid me with commissary items. There was a lot of cash money floating around in the Tombs too. For cash, I gave haircuts with a razor and comb. When I had enough saved up I played loan shark, loaning prisoners money. They paid me back with interest. As usual I lay low, but I didn't tolerate any threat or any bullshit. One month passed into the next, 1969 rolled into 1970. I continued to maintain that I was Charles Harris. I knew eventually they would find out my true identity, but you never know what might happen, I told myself. There is always hope.

1970s

Understand that fascism is already here, that people are already dying who could be saved, that generations more will die or live poor butchered half-lives if you fail to act. Do what must be done, discover your humanity and your love in revolution. . . . Join us, give up your life for the people.

—George Jackson

Chapter 10

Meeting the Black Panther Party

In April 1970, the *New York Times* reported on a questionnaire taken by 907 prisoners awaiting trial in the Tombs. "More than four out of ten prisoners said they had seen a guard assault an inmate," the newspaper reported. "Fewer than one out of ten said they had a mattress and blanket their first few days in the Tombs. About half said they obtained a mattress and blanket a week or more after entering, often from another prisoner who was leaving the jail. Nine out of ten prisoners who had blankets said they were filthy. About half the inmates said a total of three men were assigned to their cells designed for one; a large proportion of the respondents complained about the presence of rats, roaches and body lice and a severe shortage of soap."

That spring, three new prisoners were placed on the eighth-floor tier of the Tombs. They introduced themselves as members of the Black Panther Party for Self-Defense. Unfortunately, I only remember the name of one of the men—Alfred Kane. But I've never forgotten the men themselves. They taught me my first steps. I noticed they had the same pride and confidence that I had seen in the Panthers on the streets of Harlem. The same fearlessness, but there was also kindness. When they talked to someone, they asked him his name. "What do you need?" they asked. Within a few days they ran the tier, not by force but by sharing their food. They treated all of us as if we were equal to them, as if we were intelligent. They asked us questions. "Does everyone know how to read?" they asked. "We will teach you." They set up meetings and invited all of us to come. I was skeptical but curious, so I went. The concepts they talked about went over my head: economics, revolution, racism, and the oppression of the poor around the world. I didn't understand any of it. But I kept attending the meetings.

Over time I learned they were part of the Panther 21, arrested the year before with 18 other members of the Black Panther Party in New York City. Thirteen of them were on trial, indicted on a total of more than 100 charges, including conspiracies to kill police and bomb department stores, police stations, and the New York Botanical Garden in the Bronx. Bail for each of them was set at $100,000, astronomical in those days. They told us they were innocent. The charges and high bail were manufactured to get them off the street so they couldn't do the work of the party in their neighborhoods. That work included breakfast programs for children before they went to school, forming alliances with local business to support the breakfast program and other community projects, distributing the Black Panther Party newspaper, and having meetings in black neighborhoods to recruit more members. When I heard about the false arrest, trumped-up charges, and excessive bail I was surprised they weren't angry. They acted like they weren't even in prison. They told us about great black people from history and great achievements made by African Americans. They spoke of providing health care to black people in their communities. They said this country had been treating blacks horribly and that change was coming. I didn't understand anything about how change could happen. I didn't think one person could make a difference. Then a prisoner on the tier gave me a book called *A Different Drummer*, by William Melvin Kelley. It opened my mind.

I read the entire book in two days. Then I reread it. The story takes place in a fictional Southern state and features a main character, Tucker Caliban, who is descended from a great and powerful African. That African, brought over in the hull of a slave trader's ship, was so strong it took the ship's entire crew to contain him. After being dragged from the ship in chains he broke free; gathering his chains in his hands he ran away from the slave traders, eventually leading a band of escaped slaves who freed other slaves, until he was shot and killed. His baby son was taken into captivity. The generations between the son of the African and Tucker's grandparents had been born into slavery. As the story opens the time of chattel slavery has passed but Tucker isn't free. He works for the descendants of the family who had owned his ancestors. He lives in a small, Southern, racist town.

He tries to find peace buying former plantation land, but it gnaws on him that he is only allowed to buy what a member of the family allows him to buy. He builds a house and plants crops he owns, but it feels wrong to work the land where his ancestors were enslaved. It feels wrong that his life is still connected to the family who owned his people. He wants a life that is not dictated by white people. He wants to control his own destiny but he also knows he can't be someone different and live his old life at the same time. Tucker covers his land in salt so nothing will grow there again. He kills his livestock. He sets his house on fire and it burns to the ground. He and his wife and child move north. "Tucker was feeling his African blood," a white character says. His actions are a revelation to other black people in the town who had felt just as trapped. Word spreads and a mass migration of blacks eventually leave the state.

I knew how Tucker felt. Like him, I wanted to burn my past to the ground. At one time my greatest dream was to go to Angola prison. Maybe that's all I'd been allowed to dream. To survive Angola, I had become a man who acted against his true nature. Now I wanted to go as far as my humanity would allow me to go. After reading *A Different Drummer* I started to believe, for the first time in my life, that one man could make a difference.

The words the Panthers spoke started to make more sense to me. The Panthers explained to us that institutionalized racism was the foundation for all-white police departments, all-white juries, all-white banks, all-white universities, and other all-white institutions in America. It was purposeful and deliberate, they told us, and it wasn't just blacks who were marginalized. It was poor people all over the world. On the tier, in the dining hall, on the yard I started to see the black men around me as if for the first time. I thought of my neighborhood where three out of every four kids were petty thieves. We were all so poor. I was so used to it being that way. It was illegal for us to go to places where white people went. Racism was the law. The Voting Rights Act wasn't passed until I was 17. Although blacks were allowed to vote before that, we were usually intimidated and told by powerful white men who and what to vote for. We had no knowledge of the history of African people and their contributions to civilization. We didn't know anything about African American scientists, statesmen, historians, writers. Without knowing black history, we knew nothing about ourselves.

I thought of my mom, living under the dehumanizing Jim Crow laws in a world of white supremacy that didn't care about her. All the textbooks in a black child's classroom in the South were already used— passed down by white schools under Jim Crow laws. Out of date and worn out, many of them had cruel and racist remarks about black people handwritten in the margins. My mom used to tell us she missed a lot of school because she only went when she had shoes. I had judged her harshly for not being able to read.

I thought of the most violent and depraved prisoners I'd encountered at Angola and in New York. I couldn't bring myself to hate them. Uneducated, they were surrounded by racism and corruption in prison, threatened by, and often the victims of, violence and beatings because of their race, forced to live in filth, worked to death, and barely fed. Treated like animals they became subhuman. They became animals. All the principles I was being taught by the Black Panther Party I now started to understand. We want freedom. We want power to determine the destiny of our Black Community. We want an end to the robbery by the capitalists of our black and oppressed communities . . . decent housing, fit for shelter of human beings . . . land, bread, housing, education, clothing, justice, peace. I not only got it with my mind, I felt it with my heart, my soul, my body. It was as if a light went on in a room inside me that I hadn't known existed.

Chapter 11

What Is the Party?

[If] any white man in the world says "Give me liberty, or give me death," the entire world applauds. When a black man says exactly the same thing, word for word, he is judged a criminal and treated like one.

—James Baldwin

The Black Panther Party for Self-Defense was started in October 1966 by two college students in Oakland, California—Huey Newton and Bobby Seale—who wanted to stop police brutality in their neighborhoods. In the sixties, police were regularly raiding black neighborhoods while armed with guns, dogs, and cattle prods. Black people were harassed, intimidated, chased, beaten, shot, and killed by police in their neighborhoods on a daily basis. Newton and Seale created a program they called "copwatching" to monitor police activity in their neighborhoods. They started carrying legally acquired firearms to police incidents in black neighborhoods, for self-defense they said, to protect the people in the neighborhood if necessary. Newton carried law books in his car. "Sometimes," he wrote in his autobiography, "when a policeman was harassing a citizen, I would stand off a little and read the relevant portions of the penal code in a loud voice to all within hearing distance. In doing this, we were helping to educate those who gathered to observe these incidents. If the policeman arrested the citizen and took him to the station, we would follow and immediately post bail. Many community people could not believe at first that we had only their interest at heart," he wrote. "Nobody had ever given them any support or assistance when the police harassed them, but here we were, proud Black men, armed with guns and a knowledge of the law. Many citizens came right out of jail and into the Party, and the statistics of murder and brutality by policemen in our communities fell sharply." The Black Panther Party for Self-Defense grew from that.

It's a common myth that the Black Panther Party was a racist organization. Racial hatred was never taught in the party. In the late sixties, Illinois Black Panthers Bob Lee and Fred Hampton, chairman of the Illinois chapter of the party, formed an alliance with a group of white youth from Chicago's poverty-stricken North Side whose roots stretched back to Appalachia. The white group called themselves the Young Patriots Organization and wore Confederate flags on their jackets. Like the Black Panther Party, the Young Patriots Organization was formed to combat police brutality in impoverished neighborhoods. The Panthers reached out to the Young Patriots because they shared common goals: equal opportunities as well as the end of white supremacy, the end of racism, the end of housing discrimination, and the end of police brutality. The Young Patriots started wearing BLACK POWER buttons on their jackets. Lee and Hampton created other multiracial alliances—with the Young Lords and the Native American Housing Committee, among others. Hampton called this fledgling movement the Rainbow Coalition. Who knows what could have been? Fred Hampton, at the age of 21, was assassinated in his bed by police in a 1969 predawn raid at his Chicago home. His pregnant fiancée, who was lying next to him, was shot too. Jesse Jackson used Hampton's phrase when he created the National Rainbow Coalition for his 1984 presidential run.

The Black Panther Party wasn't a violent organization. If you check the history you will see that whatever violence Panthers were involved in was a response to being attacked first. Bobby Seale said, "Our position was: If you don't attack us, there won't be any violence; if you bring violence to us, we will defend ourselves." One of the rules laid out by party leaders was, "No party member will use, point, or fire a weapon of any kind unnecessarily or accidentally at anyone."

"The nature of a panther is that he never attacks," said Huey Newton. "But if anyone attacks him or backs him into a corner, the panther comes up to wipe that aggressor or that attacker out." Yet the mainstream media painted the Panthers as a violent militia. The sight of black men legally carrying guns was so terrifying to the establishment that even the National Rifle Association (NRA) supported a measure to repeal the California gun law that allowed the public to openly carry loaded firearms. In 1967, a Republican assemblyman from Oakland introduced the bill that became the Mulford Act. To protest the bill, which party members knew was created to stop them from being legally allowed to patrol their own neighborhoods, 30 Black Panthers in leather jackets and berets gathered on the steps of the California state capitol in Sacramento, legally carrying their guns. Some party members made their way into the assembly chamber and were arrested. Outside the capitol, Bobby Seale read a statement against repealing the gun law. In part, he said, "The Black Panther Party for Self-Defense calls upon the American people in general and the black people in particular to take careful note of the racist California Legislature which is considering legislation aimed at keeping the black people disarmed and powerless at the very same time that racist police agencies throughout the country are intensifying the terror, brutality, murder, and repression of black people." Two months later, Governor Ronald Reagan, a longtime member of the NRA and supporter of gun owner rights, signed the Mulford Act into law.

Much of the violence attributed to the Black Panther Party was caused by infiltrators on the FBI's payroll. Only one year after Bobby Seale and Huey Newton founded the party and released its 10-Point Program, in 1967, FBI director J. Edgar Hoover expanded the bureau's covert "dirty tricks" operation known as COINTELPRO—which stands for Counterintelligence Program—created in 1956 to fight communism, in order to focus on and attack the Black Panther Party. The FBI spent millions of dollars to infiltrate the Black Panther Party, create divisiveness and mistrust among its members, murder and incarcerate its leaders, hamper fund-raising for community programs and lawyers, and leak false information to the press and law enforcement authorities, all to destroy the party. (It was an FBI informant, acting as 21-year-old Fred Hampton's bodyguard, who reportedly set up Hampton's murder by Chicago police.) The FBI constantly surveilled Panthers and harassed their family members and anyone who supported the party. COINTELPRO-like tactics were used by local police and DA offices across the country to persecute party members: to charge them with crimes they didn't commit and to keep Panthers in jail, separating them from the party and disrupting chains of leadership and communication within the organization. Arresting Panthers tarnished their reputations and called into question the motives of the Black Panther Party to the public at large. The arrests distracted party members on the street by forcing them to raise funds— which would normally go to the community—to use for bail and to hire attorneys for Panthers being persecuted by police, DAs, and the judicial system. (In the end the FBI won; the party wouldn't officially end until 1982, but it was decimated from inside out by the early seventies.)

When Panthers raised a clenched fist, it was for unity. If you raise an open hand your fingers are separate, you are vulnerable. When you close those fingers and your hand comes together into a fist you have a symbol of power and unity. The mainstream media turned the Panther salute of a raised clenched fist for Black Power into a rebuke against other races, which it was never intended to be, instead of a call for unity, which is what it was. A raised fist was for unity between Panthers, unity within black communities, and unity with anyone waging the same struggles for the people, for empowerment and equality and justice.

Countless peoples' movements for human rights around the world have raised fists as a form of protest and solidarity, and outsiders seem to understand those struggles for human rights. However, when black men raised a fist, it was seen as something different, a threat. I think of Tommie Smith and John Carlos, African American athletes who won gold and bronze medals for the 200-meter dash at the 1968 Summer Olympics in Mexico City. After they raised their fists and bowed their heads on the winners' stand, they were torn apart in the American press. They were called "renegades" who were "angry, nasty, ugly"; their actions were described as an "insult" and "embarrassment" to the United States. Some people wanted to take their medals away. How many people ever knew they were speaking from a well-thought-out human rights platform created by the Olympic Project for Human Rights, an organization of nonprofessional black athletes they belonged to?

Smith and Carlos raised their fists for Muhammad Ali's right to protest the Vietnam War and refuse to be drafted, and for the return of his championship belt that was stripped from him. They raised their fists to demand the removal of Avery Brundage, the anti-Semitic, white supremacist head of the International Olympic Committee (IOC), who was responsible for resisting a U.S. boycott of the 1936 Olympics in Nazi Germany. They raised their fists to demand the IOC hire more African American coaches and to protest the inclusion at the Olympic Games of countries ruled by apartheid. They stood without their shoes on to call attention to poverty in black communities in the United States and wore beads and scarves around their necks to protest lynching. Smith, who broke the world record in that 200-meter race, and Carlos sacrificed personal fame, future endorsements, and possibly jobs to stand against apartheid, the Vietnam War, discrimination, poverty, lynching, racism, anti-Semitism, and white supremacy—but what most people saw, and many condemned, was two black men who dared to raise their fists.

The phrase "Power to the People" was a rallying cry for black people and for all disempowered people to come together and fight for what we all didn't have: equal education, equal opportunities, equal justice, equal treatment, and respect. At various times party members referred to police, politicians, DAs, and judges as "pigs." I did too. It comes from George Orwell's book *Animal Farm*, in which one of the characters, a pig, is a corrupt, power-hungry opportunist who turns against his followers and betrays the principles of democracy. On the street, the word "pig" was—and still is—used to describe any corrupt official, any-one in power who betrayed the people, any policeman who brutalized people, white or black. Black policemen who hurt people, black DAs who framed people were, and are, pigs. When you have no power you often use language as a defense mechanism. We lived in a world where a black person who stood up for other blacks could go to jail. In many cases language was all we had.

When I first became interested in the party I was acting more on emotions than intellect. I was a knucklehead with a newfound sense of awareness. My ability to form theories and understand ideas was very limited at that time. The party's 10-Point Program was my guide to doing the right thing. I was impressed by the principles, even though I didn't understand the depths of them. As I began to educate myself I began to understand more and more the social forces—mostly economic forces—that caused Bobby Seale and Huey Newton to formulate the 10-Point Program. Even though I didn't understand what was behind it when I first read it, I knew what it was saying.

10-Point Program of the Black Panther Party

1. We want freedom. We want power to determine the destiny of our Black Community.

2. We want full employment for our people.

3. We want an end to the robbery by the capitalists of our black and oppressed communities.

4. We want decent housing, fit for shelter of human beings.

5. We want education for our people that exposes the true nature of this decadent American society. We want education that teaches us our true history and our role in the present-day society.

6. We want all Black men to be exempt from military service.

7. We want an immediate end to POLICE BRUTALITY and MURDER of Black people.

8. We want freedom for all Black men held in federal, state, county, and city prisons and jails.

9. We want all Black people when brought to trial to be tried in court by a jury of their peer group or people from their Black Communities, as defined by the Constitution of the United States.

10. We want land, bread, housing, education, clothing, justice, and peace.

Chapter 12

NYC Prison Riot

The Panthers were moved off my tier after a few months. As the steaming-hot summer progressed in New York City, life in the overcrowded Tombs remained horrible. The food was unsanitary. The tiers were filthy. We couldn't get towels or other supplies; prisoners had to hire lawyers to receive medical care. Tensions were rising. There were 14,000 prisoners incarcerated in New York City in 1970. More than half had not even been found guilty of a crime—they were waiting for trials or to see a judge. The Tombs was built for 900 prisoners; at least 1,500 of us were being held there. The cells were so crowded that during mealtimes, prisoners had to take turns sitting at the table in their cell or alternate sitting on the floor or standing while eating. We were all aware that the prison was on the brink. The word through the grapevine that summer was that a protest was coming.

The protest broke in August. It started above us, on the ninth floor. We heard loud banging, then all of sudden the gigantic glass block windows from above us exploded like bombs on the ground. The men upstairs hollered down to us through the pipe chase, telling us how to push the windows out on our floor: rip off the tabletops in the day room, and use the table legs as battering rams to knock out the window blocks. Prisoners stood in the opened windows, calling down to spectators. Some made signs on sheets and hung them outside the prison. On my tier, prisoners took strips of sheets and knotted them around the bars of the locked gates at the front of the cellblock so security officers couldn't open the gates with their keys. We piled up mattresses against the gates.

It would take only seconds for those officers to break through when they wanted to, but it seemed like a good idea at the time. Desperation will make men do irrational things. Prison officials eventually agreed to meet with prisoner representatives from each floor in the library. I went with two or three other men from the eighth floor.

The prisoners from the ninth floor took the lead and read a list of grievances they'd written. "We the inmates on the ninth floor of Tombs city prison, Manhattan, New York, submit this petition of grievances and we solicit your attention in this matter," one prisoner read. He went on, noting prisoners had to wait on average eight months to a year for a trial. Bails were excessively high. Prisoners weren't given preliminary— or any—hearings. They were pressured by the Legal Aid Society, the state-funded agency representing most prisoners, to make guilty pleas. Prisoners were not given access to law books from the library. Blankets were dirty, mattresses were infested with bedbugs, cells built for one were sleeping three. The kitchen served moldy bread, rotten potatoes, and half-cooked powdered eggs. The prison was "ridden with body lice, roaches, rats, and mice." Prisoners had to wear the clothes they had on when they entered prison for months.

Our most urgent demand, the letter stated, was to end the excessive violence against prisoners, largely directed against black and Puerto Rican prisoners, by officers wielding "blackjacks, nightsticks, fist, and feet," who beat prisoners to unconsciousness, after which, prison doctors colluded with officials to write up fake accident reports.

"It is a common practice for an inmate to be singled out," the prisoner read, ". . . because he did not hear the officer call his name or because the officer did not like the way this or that inmate looked or because of the manner in which the inmate walked or because the officer brings the turmoil of his own personal problems to work with him, and together with other officers, beat the defenseless inmate into unconsciousness, often injuring him for life physically and mentally or both.

"These acts," he continued, "would not and could not happen without the knowledge and consent of the Commissioner of Correction, the Assistant Commissioner of Correction, the Warden of Tombs Prison, the Deputy Wardens of Tombs Prison, and the Captains of Tombs

Prison." He added, "We reject all official denials [to the effect] that such things do not happen here, as we have experienced these sadistic attacks." It was common knowledge by every official in that room, and every prisoner, that nothing goes on in prison without the prison staff being aware of it. As the saying goes, the prisoner read, "Not one leaf of a tree could turn yellow without the silent knowledge and consent of the tree itself."

The prisoners ended their statement asking that there would be no repercussions of any kind against the inmates who participated in the protest, and that the list of prisoner grievances would be released to the press. Not all prisoners who participated in the protest were beaten after we returned to our tiers, but the goon squad, a group of five or six corrections officers in vests and helmets brandishing sticks and bats, went to the ninth floor first. Many prisoners were sent to other prisons, including me. The document of prisoner grievances and demands that the prisoners on the ninth floor wrote and read aloud to prison authorities was not released to the press by the authorities.

I was taken to the Queens House of Detention, which we called New Queens. Since no actions were taken by officials to improve conditions for prisoners in August it wasn't a surprise to any of us when the Tombs erupted again, two months later. Facilities in Brooklyn, in the Bronx, and in Queens where I was staying joined in solidarity. This time the protests lasted for more than a week. Local papers reported that during the uprising 1,400 prisoners had control of 23 hostages. My tier didn't take hostages but we barricaded the end of our tier with mattresses and lockers. Our demands included: no more than two men to a cell, the right to exercise religious freedom and follow related dietary guidelines, more sanitary conditions, edible food, adequate medical care, and affordable bail. One of the prisoner demands was for bail hearings to be held in public, to show people that black and Puerto Rican prisoners consistently received excessively higher bail for petty crimes than did white defendants. After eight days riot police stormed the prisons across the city.

Guards and police retook the city's jail with brutal force. At New Queens, there was no way to hold them off. It wasn't even close. We had a wall of mattresses and boxes. They had gas guns, shields, bats, and axes. They sprayed canisters of CS gas onto the tier and chopped through our barricade and sprayed more tear gas on us. The CS gas, meant to be used outside to control riots, was blinding inside, burning our eyes, mouths, nostrils, and lungs and making it almost impossible to breathe. While we were choking and disoriented they forced us back into the cells on the tier, beating us with riot sticks and baseball bats.

We were ordered to strip naked in the cells. As we undressed, guards with ax handles, billy clubs, blackjacks, and bats lined up on either side of the hallway outside our cells. One by one we were called out by our cell number and ordered to the day room. As each prisoner was forced into the hall he was beaten and poked in the genitals with nightsticks; bats and clubs rained down on him. The men in the first four cells had the shortest distance to go. The farther back your cell, the more you got beaten. I was in number 15, the last cell on the tier. When they got to my cell I cupped my genitals with one hand and put my other arm over my head and came out running. A couple of prisoners ahead of me had fallen and the guards were stomping them. I could see unconscious prisoners being dragged to the day room. I ran over a floor slippery with blood from busted heads, mouths, and faces. With each running step my only thought was, "Don't fall, don't fall," over and over. I felt the blows all over.

I made it to the day room without falling but had been badly beaten. I felt excruciating pain in my left arm. Blood was pouring from a gaping wound on the top of my head. In the day room they herded us like animals and forced us to lie on top of each other while guards made cruel and racist remarks like, "Put that dick in him, nigger." Prisoners who refused to lie on the other men were beaten mercilessly. I didn't want to be on the bottom of this pile so I ran and jumped up on top of the stacked bodies. Other prisoners were moaning: "Lord help me. Don't let me die. I can't breathe." Some of them were screaming.

The cries of the other prisoners hurt me the most. I was in physical pain but the greater pain was seeing men break. I understood their agony and suffering, but in my mind no matter what happens, you don't cross a certain line. Crying, begging, calling some of the guards "boss," saying, "Please don't hit me," "Please, man, have mercy on me," or "I'm going to be good." The things they were saying were so degrading. It was humiliating to me to see men reduced to that. I was in a lot of pain, but I was determined not to beg these animals. I was not going to plead. I was not going to ask for anything. Even while being screamed at, poked with nightsticks, with blood rushing out of my head, I didn't say a thing.

While we were being forced to lie in a pile in the day room guards went into our cells and threw away our property—eyeglasses, photographs, letters. When they finished trashing our cells we were ordered back onto the cellblock, where they put five or six men in each cell. There was no room for all of us to sit and everyone was badly injured. That night was agony. The next day they took me to Lenox Hill Hospital, where a doctor put a cast on my fractured arm and stitched up my head. Back at the prison they packed five of us into single cells again. We stayed like that for about a week.

After four or five days, they came around with peanut butter and jelly sandwiches. I don't know how long it was until we had a hot meal. It took a long time to heal. To this day I have problems with my hip from being hit there with a bat. My scalp has a scar where my head was busted. But I never regretted taking part in the protest.

I was moved back to the Tombs and was sitting in the day room waiting for a court appearance when a guard told me my lawyer was there to visit me. I didn't have a lawyer. When I walked into the room the attorney said, "Charles?" The lawyer offered me a deal meant for a real Charles Harris who was locked up somewhere in New York. He told me if I pleaded guilty to a burglary charge he could get me two to three years on Rikers Island, but I had to make the plea deal that day. I'd heard prisoners talk about the work crews at Rikers, and how the crews were brought to work on the streets every day. If I could get a job in one of these work crews I thought I might be able to escape. I pleaded guilty. Later that day they took me to Rikers. After I was processed, they told me my job would be working on a street-cleaning crew in Brooklyn. I felt hopeful for the first time in months.

That night there was a blizzard. When I woke up the next morning the windows were white with snow. We weren't allowed to go outside to our work details. The next day, more snow. They kept us inside for a week. I was in the day room when I heard a corrections officer call, "Where is Charles Harris, aka Albert Woodfox?" My prints had finally come back. They moved me off the tier and put me in a one-man cell in an empty wing.

At first being segregated from everyone else didn't bother me. I was too busy worrying about the possibility of being killed by police when I got back to New Orleans. I thought they would kill me for escaping. The idea of going back to Angola also weighed on me. But by this time my level of consciousness had been raised by the Black Panther Party and I had become politicized. Things would be different. I didn't know how, but that's how I felt. Now that they knew who I was I could finally write to my mom. I told her I got caught, that I was in jail. She got somebody to write back to me once. Before they could ship me back to Angola I had to be tried on the bogus aggravated robbery charge brought by the bookie. I was sent back to the Tombs.

In mid-May 1971, I heard on the radio that all 13 of the Panthers of the Panther 21 who had been on trial, including the Panthers I had met on the eighth floor, had been exonerated on all counts. It took the jury foreman, James I. Fox, 20 minutes to read the verdict, "Not guilty," 156 times. The Panthers had told me to agitate. To educate. I started thinking about how to talk to prisoners about the conditions we were living in.

I was quickly found not guilty at my trial for aggravated robbery because while I was in jail the Harlem bookie and butcher who set me up had been arrested for strong-arming and setting up other people the way they did me, which came out during my trial. I fought extradition back to New Orleans and lost. In June 1971, I was put on a plane back to New Orleans. On the outside, nothing had changed from the day I had escaped the courthouse 20 months earlier. I was a black man with a long prison sentence ahead of me. Inside, however, everything had changed. I had morals, principles, and values I never had before. Looking out the window of the plane, I saw into the window of my soul. In the past, I had done wrong. Now I would do right. I would never be a criminal again.

Chapter 13

Hostages

My actions in the New York City jail uprisings became part of my permanent record. I was labeled a militant. When I arrived at Orleans Parish Prison they put me on C-1, which they now called the "Panther tier." The last time I was on this tier I cut myself to get off. This time it was radically different. Less than half the tier was full. It only housed members of the Black Panther Party. I was nervous at first because I was unfamiliar with everyone. But I also knew these men weren't ordinary prisoners. It was still suffocating, hot, filthy, and dark. The windows were still sealed shut, covered from the outside with steel plates. The Panthers were all from the New Orleans chapter of the party and were in prison awaiting trial for defending themselves against a police attack on their headquarters, located in the Desire housing projects, months before. As the days passed I watched the men conduct themselves the way Panthers in New York had, with poise and purpose, focused on self-education and self-discipline. Among the Panthers I met there were Ronald Ailsworth (Faruq) and Donald Guyton (Malik Rahim), both cofounders of the New Orleans chapter of the party. It didn't take long for us to accept one another. At the daily meetings Malik tore books into sections to give each of us a part to read so we could then report back to the others what we had learned. We had debates and talked about society and the world. They got their friends—local Panthers from the New Orleans chapter—to visit me. The New Orleans Panthers attended our court hearings. We had copies of the Black Panther Party newspaper smuggled onto the tier. I became more outspoken than I was in New York.

One day I suggested we clean up the tier. Orleans Parish Prison had always been a filthy, rat-infested pigsty with broken toilets, rotten food, and overcrowded cells. All of us kept our own cells spotless and we cleaned the day room, but the rest of the tier hadn't been cleaned for months. At our meetings we practiced collective criticism, so if someone had a beef or wanted to bring up something going on, it was brought in front of everybody. I brought up that our tier was a disgrace. "How can we live on a tier that's filthy and dirty like this?" I asked. "Shouldn't we have more pride?" Everybody agreed and in the following days we cleaned out the empty cells.

On any given weekday prisoners were summoned to court and transferred from their tiers to a holding pen on the second floor of the prison, where they sat until it was time to be led through a series of corridors to the courthouse. There, they were taken to smaller bullpens located in the back of each courtroom. On an average day there could be 20 to 30 prisoners sitting in the bullpen at the prison. On court days we had a chance to talk to prisoners who weren't on our tier, and we used that time to talk about the party. One time in the bullpen Faruq broke into a Black Panther Party song called "Power to the People." All the prisoners joined in.

> Power, power, all power to the people.
> We're going to pick up the gun and put the pigs on the run.
> There just ain't enough pigs to stop the Black Panther Party.

Some of the prisoners were clapping, others were keeping rhythm drumming on the metal benches we were sitting on. The guards ordered us to stop. We kept singing. They came back with tear gas, spraying all of us. My eyes were still swollen shut and tears were streaming down my burning face when it was my turn to go to court. There was so much gas on me that the deputy who put restraints on me got sick walking me through the corridor.

When deputies brought me into the courtroom I didn't walk to the table where I was supposed to sit. I walked to the middle of the courtroom, in front of the spectators—some of them Panthers—and raised my handcuffed hands as fists to my chest, as high as I could in restraints, and yelled, "Look what these racist pigs have done." Two deputies were on me in seconds, dragging me out as I heard the judge holler, "Get him out of here." The Panthers in the audience stood and were yelling after me, "Leave that man alone." In the back deputies punched and kicked me. I couldn't defend myself because my hands were cuffed to my waist, but I was cursing them, calling them names. The judge came in and told the deputies to stop beating me and get the gas off me. They brought me wet paper towels to wipe my body and hair and gave me a new jumpsuit. Before he went back into the courtroom the judge told me to stop acting up.

We believed that being in prison we were at the forefront of social struggle and it was our responsibility to respond to the issues. Our list of grievances was long and similar to what had been happening in the Tombs. Men in the parish prison were held for months without being arraigned; they weren't given bail, or their bail was set too high; they had no access to law books; they were forced to sleep on the floor, three or more to a cell. The prison was infested with roaches, lice, and rats. The food was disgusting. We talked among ourselves about how to get these stories outside prison walls. I knew from my experiences in New York that we had to do more than get the prison adminis- tration's attention: we had to speak directly to the media; otherwise they would only report on one side, the side of prison authorities. We decided to take a hostage and not release him until we could talk to the press. We would also demand to speak to the first African American woman to be elected to and serve in the Louisiana House of Representatives, Rep. Dorothy Mae Taylor, who was working for prison reform in those days.

We passed a note outlining our plans to another tier through an orderly and they wrote back saying they would take a hostage the same day. We'd put two guards under house arrest at the same time, one guard from each tier.

On Monday morning, July 26, 1971, a young black prison guard brought some Panthers going to trial out on the bridge where their personal clothing was being held, and we confronted him. We didn't hurt him. We told him, "Look, man, we need to put you under house arrest. Don't resist. We're going to put you in a cell in the back for your own safety. If you come with us, it won't get physical." He handed us his keys. We opened the lockbox that contained the controls for the cell doors and opened them. We walked the guard back to a cell. We asked him if he wanted anything. Then we closed and locked the cell door.

I pressed the intercom button and told the security people working in the processing area at the front of the prison that we'd taken a guard hostage and we wanted to see the media and Dorothy Mae Taylor to talk about prison conditions. They said, "Don't hurt him, don't hurt the guard." I said the only way we'd hurt him is if they came on the tier. News reporters and cameras were allowed on the exercise yard. Representative Taylor arrived. We knocked the metal plate off one of the windows so we could talk through the window. She asked to see the guard we were holding hostage, so we brought him to the window. She asked him if he had been harmed in any way. When he said no, she agreed to talk to us. We read out our list of grievances to her. After we released the guard, Representative Taylor read our demands aloud to the press.

Soon after this I was told by prison officials that I was being sent back to Angola. On the tier we discussed whether or not we should resist, but as a group we decided I should go and recruit Panthers for the New Orleans chapter. Later, Malik got word to me from Oakland that we should start a separate chapter of the party—a prison chapter—at Angola.

Before I left Orleans Parish Prison, I took an oath on C-1 to become a member of the Black Panther Party. On my last day there, one of the Panthers gave me a copy of the *Little Red Book*, a collection of quotations from Mao Tse-tung. The Panthers told me, "Don't forget the party. Don't forget what the party stands for. Don't forget the 10-Point Program and the principles of the party. Educate. Agitate. Be strong. Stay strong."

Chapter 14

Angola, 1971

Prison is designed to break one's spirit and destroy one's resolve. To do this, the authorities attempt to exploit every weakness, demolish every initiative, negate all signs of individuality—all with the idea of stamping out that spark that makes each of us human and each of us who we are. Our survival depended on understanding what the authorities were attempting to do to us, and sharing that understanding with each other.

—Nelson Mandela

Nothing had changed at Angola. Sexual slavery was still a part of prison culture. Violence was still a constant threat. Armed inmate guards were still in use, on cellblocks, in guard towers, on horseback in the fields. Stabbings and beatings happened every day. Angola was the same. But I was different. I came with orders to start a chapter of the Black Panther Party. I was told to resist, educate, agitate. When I joined the party, I dedicated my life to social struggle. I gave my word that I would live my life by the principles of the party. I was prepared to sacrifice my life to keep my word.

The prison was still segregated. I was put in a black dorm at the Reception Center. I'd only been there for about a week when I saw a prisoner named Joseph Richey follow a boy who was 17 into the bathroom. In prison, you learn the signs of what's going on before it happens.

I borrowed a knife from a prisoner in the dorm and put it under my shirt and went into the bathroom. Richey had the boy in the shower, threatening him, trying to make him take his clothes off. "What the fuck is going on in here?" I said.

"This ain't your business," Richey said. "You ain't got nothing to do with this."

I said, "I'm making it my business." I walked toward them. "You're not raping that kid." I looked at the boy. "Come on out," I said, "ain't nothing going to happen here." The boy didn't move at first, then slowly inched his way toward me against the wall. He walked by me and left through the door.

I pulled the knife out from under my shirt. Richey pulled his weapon out, and I said, "Let's do this." I made a lunge for him and he backed up and dropped his knife. I told him as long as I'm in the dormitory he's not raping that kid or anybody else. When I walked out of the bathroom I stood on a table in the day room and announced to the room, "All you motherfuckers in here who rape people, you are on notice. You're not raping anybody while I'm in this dorm." I can proudly say that after I stopped Joseph Richey from raping that kid not one prisoner was raped in the RC dorm I was living in.

After 30 days, I was brought before the classification board and assigned a job in the scullery, washing pots and pans used in the dining hall and kitchen. This time I wasn't on the trustee side; I would be in the main prison. The walk was long and covered to keep the rain off. Railings ran down either side. There were four units down the walk, each composed of four one-story rectangular cinder-block dormitories. Each dorm held about 60 prisoners. Two dorms in each unit faced each other across the walk. The front door of each dorm opened onto the walk. The sides had huge windows from waist level to ceiling, and there were narrow walkways on either side of the dorm that led to the back. Between two of the dorms in each unit on the left side of the walk—dorms 1 and 2—there was a guard booth. The walk and all the buildings were elevated, about three or four feet off the ground. Four or five steps went down to the yard between units. Officially, prisoners weren't allowed to congregate on the walk but sometimes they did or they stood in groups off the walk in the grass between the units. Each guard booth had room for two officers to sit. One of the guards from each unit was often on the walk, keeping it clear and sometimes shaking down prisoners searching pockets, jacket linings, and shoes for contraband as they walked by, while the other sat in the booth.

Each unit was named after a species of tree. White prisoners lived in the Oak dorms, the first unit on the walk. Next came the all-black units: Pine, Walnut, and Hickory. The whole area, including a huge treeless yard and a clothing room, just inside the security gate, was surrounded by a 12-foot chain-link fence topped by barbed wire. Freemen and inmate guards manned the towers overlooking the walk and the yard. There was a baseball field in the yard and another area up a small hill where we played football. The dining hall and control center were on the other side of the security gate, which we called the "snitcher gate," at one end of the walk.

I talked about the Black Panther Party to prisoners in my dorm and on the walk. I talked about the 10-Point Program. "We want freedom; we want the power to determine our own destiny," I told them. I carried the *Little Red Book* with me wherever I went. "Do not steal," I told the men, reading, "not even a needle or a piece of thread from the people." Some of the guys who knew me from before watched me, thinking I was still in the game, trying to figure out what my game was. Other prisoners felt threatened and avoided me. I spoke to the men about what the Panthers taught me. "In prison," I said, "first they reduce your value as a human being, then they break your will." I told them they had to reeducate themselves, that we had to come together and work together. I told them they had to stop raping and stabbing each other. "They want you to fight among yourselves so you don't resist," I said. "You deserve better than what you're getting."

It took me a while to catch my stride and learn how to talk to the prisoners. Through trial and error, I learned that the best way to reach each man on the yard was at his own level of consciousness. I started to talk a lot about the food and how bad it was. I learned that asking questions was more effective than lecturing, so I asked a lot of questions.

"How do you feel not having rain clothes when you have to work out in the field?" I asked. "How do you feel eating baloney over and over when we see trucks bringing in chicken and beef meant for us?" "How do you feel about being paid two cents an hour?"

At the same time, I was still integrating my newly learned code of conduct into my day-to-day life. I had the idealistic passion of a revolutionary but at age 24, after five years in and out of four different prisons, I had the emotional maturity of someone much younger. If a dude did something to me or threatened me I retaliated. But I was determined to keep going. I kept coming back to the principles of the party. Over time I realized that my own personal conduct—the way I behaved—was almost more important than anything I said. The Panthers taught me you don't fight fire with fire, you fight fire with water. I came to understand that meant if a prisoner challenged or threatened me, I had to find the opposite within myself to deal with that individual and use the teachings and values of the Black Panther Party rather than resort to violence.

I worked in the dining hall, a huge building that held the kitchen, pantries, and freezers where food was stored; a bakery; a butcher shop where inmates got vocational training; an empty room in the back for workers to hang out between shifts; and, at the very back, the scullery. There was always one huge tub of water boiling in the scullery. We wore rubber boots that went to our knees, rubber aprons that fell from our necks to the tops of the boots, and insulated rubber gloves to work around the scalding water. We lowered the pots and pans to soak in the boiling water first, using broken-off broomstick handles, then lifted them out the same way, tossing them into a corner where we rinsed them with a power hose. After they were hosed down we set them on drying racks. Usually there were three of us working and we took turns at the tub of boiling water; sometimes there were only two of us. We had to work fast but I was careful; I never got burned.

In most of the prison, blacks and whites did not work together. But jobs in the dining hall were mixed. The white prisoners had the "better" jobs, cooking and working as clerks in the pantry; the blacks did the cleaning and serving at the steam table. (White prisoners had their own steam table and were served by white prisoners.) Most of us worked 16-hour days, every other day, and between meals we were allowed to sign out and go back to our dorms or to the yard, or we could stay in the back room. It was different for the black dining hall workers in the front, who served the food, wiped up the floor and tables while prisoners ate, and poured Kool-Aid and other drinks. They were forced to work 16-hour days six or seven days a week, and between meals they weren't allowed to leave. After a couple of weeks working in the scullery I started to stay in the dining hall between my shifts to talk to the workers there. "What you're doing is slave labor," I told them. "There shouldn't be different rules for you than the rest of us." I suggested they put together a petition and send it to the warden.

In the back room of the kitchen I spoke to white prisoners as well. "You have a better job for being white and that benefits you individually, but as a group you still suffer," I said. "We are all victims of the same corruption, the same brutality, the same beatings, the same sexual slavery that is allowed by the administration. We all experience the same degrading inhumane conditions in the dungeon. The same lack of medical care. All of us," I told them, "white and black prisoners, suffer for the same reasons." They listened to what I had to say. I felt I was making progress.

In August, I got into a beef with a freeman. I don't remember what it was about but I was put in the Red Hat for a few days. Outside the temperature was in the 90s. Inside the three-by-six-foot cell in the Red Hat, it felt double that. I sat on the concrete bunk. I stood and sweat ran off me from thinking. Sometimes I felt cheated, knowing that being born black pretty much determined where I'd wind up. I thought it was sad that I had to come to prison to find out there were great African Americans in this country and in this world, and to find role models that I should have had available to me in school. What helped me was that I knew I wasn't a criminal anymore. I considered myself to be a political prisoner. Not in the sense that I was incarcerated for a political crime, but because of a political system that had failed me terribly as an individual and a citizen in this country. This crystallized within me in the Red Hat.

I remember the day I was released, August 21, 1971, because it was the day George Jackson, field marshal for the Black Panther Party, was shot and killed by guards at Soledad prison in California. After being locked in the stinking coffin of the Red Hat for three days I didn't think my resolve to uphold the principles of the Black Panther Party could get any stronger. When I learned of George's murder, my commitment only grew.

A few weeks later I was listening to the radio when I heard that prisoners at Attica penitentiary in upstate New York had taken 42 prison employees as hostages. Conditions at Attica had been notoriously bad for years. I heard rumors about it when I was in the Tombs. Prisoners were given a bucket of water and a filthy towel once a week instead of a shower; they didn't have soap, medical care, or adequate food; and there was severe overcrowding. I tried to find news about the riot on the radio but deep in Louisiana there wasn't any. Days later we found out that New York governor Nelson Rockefeller ordered prison guards and various police departments to take back Attica. We learned later that prisoners at Attica were lied to by prison officials, who said that a negotiation would take place to end the riot and hostage situation. As helicopters hovered over the prison yard on the morning of September 13, prisoners were expecting members of the Department of Correction and the governor's office to land in the yard to talk to them. Instead, prisoners were ordered to put their hands on their heads and lie down on the ground. Military-grade tear gas was released by the helicopters onto the yard. Without any warning, more than 500 armed uniformed state troopers, along with hundreds of national guardsmen, sheriffs, and police from several upstate New York counties, stormed the yard and fired indiscriminately, hitting unarmed prisoners and hostages alike. Prisoners who had formed a protective circle around the hostages were gunned down. Ten hostages and 29 inmates were killed.

None of the hostages were killed by prisoners, but on the day of the massacre officials reported prisoners had slit the throats of four hostages and castrated another one. One official told reporters outside the prison that he "saw" the castrated hostage "with my own eyes." The following day the local medical examiner, Dr. John Edland, came forward with the truth: The ten dead hostages were killed by police bullets. No hostages had their throats slit. No hostage was castrated. The governor ordered two other autopsies, which corroborated Edland's findings. In exchange for his integrity and bravery, Edland and his family received death threats. He was called a traitor and a "nigger lover."

We wouldn't know any of this until much later but based on my experience as a prisoner I knew that what happened at Attica did not go down the way it was being reported on the radio at the time. After the slaughter in the prison yard, the barbaric treatment of the prisoners who were left alive began. I was frustrated and angry and felt so much pain for the men slaughtered and brutalized at Attica. But even as I was horrified that these men, these human beings, were suffering such brutality at the hands of New York State authorities, I kept coming back to one thought: the prisoners at Attica had come together. The lines that usually divided prisoners—racial, religious, economic—seemed to have disappeared for 1,280 men in that prison yard. It validated what I learned from the Black Panther Party. The need to be treated with human dignity touches everyone. And the key to resistance is unity.

Chapter 15

Herman Wallace

I first heard Herman Wallace's name when I was in Orleans Parish Prison. Like me, he came from New Orleans, was incarcerated for armed robbery, and had his world changed after meeting members of the Black Panther Party in prison. While I was learning from Panthers up in New York in the Tombs, he was learning about the party from Panthers in the parish prison. "In prison I met Chairman Mao, Marx and Engels, Chou En-lai, Fidel, Che, George Jackson, Ho Chi Minh, Kwame Nkrumah, and especially Frantz Fanon," Herman once wrote. "I learned a whole new mode of thinking." He vowed to follow the Black Panther Party principles of Huey Newton and Bobby Seale, as I had. I never knew him on the street but got to know him by sight in the parish prison. We were on separate tiers but passed one another from time to time on the way to or from court or on a lawyer call-out. Everybody called him Hooks because of his bowlegged walk. I was known as Fox, but he always called me Albert. We'd raise our handcuffed fists at our waists in solidarity when we saw each other. "Power to the People," we called out.

When I got back to Angola Herman was there, but he was at Camp A, unreachable from the main prison where I was housed. One day I heard the health department had condemned Camp A and Herman was among the prisoners moved to the main prison. I went to look for him on the walk and found him in the Pine 1 dorm. When he saw me he smiled and we hugged. Herman had one of those smiles that light up a person's whole face. He was unguarded and open to me, which made me trust him. In temperament, we were opposites. Hooks was an in-your-face extrovert, aggressive and bold, and I was more reserved and diplomatic, an introvert. But we had the same goals and the same morals and principles. He told me about organizing prisoners at Camp A. I told him what I'd been doing. We both knew nobody wanted us to do what we were doing—not the freemen, not the powerful prisoner kingpins who made money off prostituting other prisoners, not the drug-dealing prisoners or anyone who made a profit off the corruption that was rampant at Angola. We both knew there would be retaliation, that we would have to make sacrifices. I could see he was willing to accept that and he saw the same in me. Together we set out to create a chapter of the Black Panther Party at Angola. To this day I don't understand how or why, but we believed we were invincible.

We held party meetings on the yard where we played football. As the men tossed the ball to one another on the football field in the evenings Herman and I talked to them. "In order to be liberated you must first liberate yourselves," Herman told the men. "You don't deserve to be treated like chattel slaves," I said. "You are not property, you are men," we said. "You have to find the dignity and pride within yourself," I told them. "I am proof that it's possible."

We explained the concept of institutionalized racism and how it contributed to them being locked up—how police departments and courthouses discriminated against blacks. "I used to think I kept getting arrested because I had bad luck," I told them. "It wasn't bad luck. I was targeted because I am black, that's why I kept getting arrested." We told them we needed to come together as a group against the administration because it was the only way to make change; we had no power when we were only looking out for ourselves. We went over and over the principles of the Black Panther Party. Number 1: "We want freedom, we want the power to determine the destiny of our black community." Number 4: "We want decent housing, fit for shelter of human beings." Number 7: "We want an immediate end to police brutality and murder of black people." Number 9, "We want all black people when brought to trial to be tried in court by a jury of their peer group or people from their black communities." Herman and I realized that a lot of these men had never before been told that they were anything good. The oppressed will always believe the worst about themselves, Frantz Fanon wrote, and we found that to be true.

We were very aware of the sex slave market that existed in Angola but at first we were so busy trying to organize prisoners we didn't focus on that. Then one day I was sitting on my bed when a kid who was raped by another prisoner sat down across from me. When I looked at his face I realized, for the first time in my life, the brutal consequences of rape. I was seeing the face of a person who had his dignity taken, his spirit broken, and his pride destroyed. It was one of the most heartbreaking moments of my newfound awareness. In his face, I saw a human being who was completely destroyed. Before, I had thought of rape as physical violence and I felt it was my duty, as a Black Panther, to try to prevent it. Now, I saw that rape went way beyond a physical act. Rape brought about the complete destruction of another human being.

I felt a new awareness in my core that harming another human being—in any way—was morally wrong and completely unacceptable, and with that came a lot of shame, because I was flooded by memories of fighting and physically hurting people. I had been violent and cruel to survive the street. With the recognition that I'd been wrong came a great deal of pain. And a new moral principle was born within me: to do no harm. This was a profound moment for me as a man, and as a human being. This was me evolving at my center.

The next day I went to find Herman. I opened the door of his dorm and hollered that I needed to talk to him. We stood on the walk by the railing and I told him what happened and how angry and sad I was; how for the first time I realized that I felt as if some of the things I'd done to other human beings in my life were an attack on all humanity. He said he felt the same way and we discussed what to do about it. Later that day we brought it up with the prisoners who came to our meeting on the football field. As Panthers, we told them, we had to take a stand against rape. Not just to say it was wrong, but we had to do something to stop it. The prisoners agreed to help us. We would start by trying to protect the new prisoners coming into Angola. Black prisoners were bused to the main prison from the Reception Center on Thursdays. On those days we would meet the new prisoners and escort them to their dorms. (The unchecked rape happened in both white and black prisoner populations on fresh fish days, but black and white prisoners were sent down the walk on separate days.)

Herman and I called it an "antirape squad." We set up guidelines for the other prisoners who wanted to stand with us: Work in pairs; never alone. Use violence only as a last resort. Every Thursday on fresh fish day we armed ourselves and went down the walk, introduced ourselves to the new prisoners, and told them they were now under the protection of the Black Panther Party. We escorted them to whatever dormitory they were assigned to and we explained the type of games that a prisoner played to sexually assault or rape another prisoner, or coerce him into becoming a sex slave. "Don't borrow anything," we told them. "Don't take anything that's offered, don't ask for favors, don't accept favors. If you do you are opening yourselves up to being in debt to sexual predators." We told them if they needed anything to come to us. We'd help them find what they needed—whether soap, toothpaste, deodorant, or "zuzus," the term we used for snacks like potato chips and candy. If we came upon anyone threatening another prisoner with rape we stopped it. Sometimes all it took was to say something—"Brother, leave that, go ahead on" or "This ain't gonna happen"—and that would be enough. Other times we had to fight. We put the word out that if you messed with someone under our protection you had to deal with the Black Panther Party. As the presence of the party grew on the walk we knew the prisoner "shot callers"—those who had profitable gambling, drug, and prostitution businesses within the prison—were watching us. I never had a direct confrontation with any of them, but we always traveled in groups of two or three. That wouldn't protect us from being attacked but it made us feel better.

Wherever we were, in the dorm, at our jobs, on the chow line, on the walk, Herman and I talked about the Black Panther Party. Some guys would make remarks to me like, "Damn, man, that's all you talk about, the Panthers." I didn't deny it. For me it was always the Panthers. Our list of enemies was long. It wasn't just the prisoner pimps and drug dealers, both white and black, who hated us. Snitches gravitated to us too, trying to get information they could sell. Security officers overheard us. We knew we were a threat to the status quo. I got scared of being killed sometimes. But I believed what I was struggling for was more important than me. It never occurred to me to stop what we were doing.

Herman and I had about six or seven months together in the main prison. During this time we formed the first official chapter of the Black Panther Party behind bars. It wasn't a normal chapter. We didn't have the reading material to pass out or share. We couldn't hold daily political classes. We couldn't watch over the men to see how they were developing in their political awareness or moral conduct. We couldn't require the men to read two hours a day, as the Panthers did on the street. A few men who came to our meetings grasped the Black Panther Party concepts right away and pledged to honor them and did. Many who initially joined didn't have the strength or will to keep going. Most men who came to our meetings didn't make any kind of commitment to the party, but I liked to think they were influenced by what we talked about.

Chapter 16

April 17, 1972

On April 17, 1972, I got dressed, brushed my teeth, and waited for the freeman to unlock the door and call, "Chow," for breakfast. There were usually two freemen assigned to every unit. During meals one guard stayed on the walk directing traffic while the other, usually more senior guard, went to the dining hall with the inmates in their unit. When they unlocked the doors for the Hickory dorms that morning all the other units had already been let out and the walk was crowded. I walked to breakfast with a prisoner named Everett Jackson. I didn't know him but he was a legal clerk and I'd asked him to help me with my case. A prisoner named Colonel Nyati Bolt was also walking with us. We could see there was congestion ahead of us; inmates were being held back at the snitcher gate. Word came down the line there was a "buck," the word we used for a workers' strike in the dining hall. I wasn't surprised. I'd been talking to the kitchen workers about their rights for weeks. The dining hall workers were refusing to work until they spoke with the warden. After about five or ten minutes the whistle blew and all of us on the walk were sent back to our dorms to wait out the buck. Prisoners who were out walking the grounds or working out at the weight pile also had to return to their dorms when the whistle blew. The dormitory doors were locked once we were inside. I lay down on my bunk. About 20 minutes later they blew the whistle for chow, the doors were unlocked, and we exited onto the walk again.

This time the line moved quickly because the strike was over. I again walked to the dining hall with Everett. In the dining hall, we sat together. Bolt sat with us. At some point I noticed that a prisoner named Chester "Noxzema" Jackson was also at our table. He wasn't a friend, or a Panther, but he wanted to be a Black Panther and hung around the fringes of wherever Herman and I were. A former "gal-boy" and known snitch, Chester Jackson tried to pass himself off as a member of the party before we got to Angola. He wore a black beret and had a panther drawn on his jacket. He asked everyone to call him "Panther," but it didn't stick. Everyone called him Noxzema. He wasn't a Panther and Herman and I didn't trust him but we had a "wait-and-see" attitude about everyone. That's what the Panthers taught. And, being in prison, we didn't really have any other choice.

I wasn't working that day so after breakfast I walked Everett to the control center where the inmate counsel office was located to get some paperwork I needed. He left me on the walk and went inside for the papers, then brought them back and gave them to me in less than 10 minutes. I went back through the snitcher gate and down the walk to my dorm and went back to sleep.

I woke to a scream of whistles blowing and a lot of yelling outside the dorm. A freeman was at the door, yelling, "All you niggers get up. Get on the walk and line up. Get outside." I walked out and got behind hundreds of other prisoners. Freemen were running through the yard carrying machine guns and rifles.

We were at the end of the line and none of us knew what was going on at first. I thought maybe it had something to do with an incident the day before, when a freeman was attacked in a guard shack on the walk. A prisoner walked up to the guard booth and threw gasoline on the 20-year-old guard in the booth, Mike Gunnells, while another one threw some burning material into the booth, setting the guard's clothes on fire. (Gunnells said he saw the prisoner Rory Mason lighting a piece of paper but didn't identify the prisoner who threw the gas. Only Mason would be tried and convicted for the crime.) But I also knew it could be anything. Angola was a breeding ground for chaos in those days. There were the daily battles on the yard over prostitution, drugs, and gambling. There were the daily conflicts between racist inmate guards and freemen against prisoners. There was an ongoing battle behind the scenes within the administration—a power play between the current warden, C. Murray Henderson; his right-hand administrator, Lloyd Hoyle; and the old families at Angola who had been running the prison for generations. The head of security, Hayden Dees, who came from a long line of Angola families, had been acting warden and expected to be named warden before Henderson was hired. When Henderson, who was from Tennessee, was hired in 1968 it was an unwelcome shock to the "old guard." Henderson was an outsider. By all accounts, Dees had been cheated.

Tensions increased between Henderson and Dees when the Justice Department started looking into the prison in response to a prisoner lawsuit in 1971. An inmate named Hayes Williams and three other prisoners sued the governor and the secretary of the Louisiana Department of Public Safety and Corrections alleging that the substandard living conditions at Angola violated their constitutional right against cruel and unusual punishment. After the Williams lawsuit was filed, lawyers from the Justice Department got involved and Warden Henderson was pressured to integrate the prison, get rid of inmate guards, and create proper disciplinary and housing records for prisoners. Henderson, in turn, was trying to force Dees to make these changes. It wasn't working. Dees was the most powerful person at Angola at that time, running the prison in every way except on paper, and he wanted to run things like a plantation, the way they'd always been run.

Word started coming down the line among the prisoners that a security guard had been killed. That surprised nobody. There were also a hundred crimes or fights a guard could stumble upon that would get him killed. And there were a thousand reasons a prisoner would be pushed to the brink and erupt in rage, revenge, and violence against a freeman at Angola. Working in the fields without gloves, being beaten in restraints, earning 32 cents a day for 16 hours of work, lack of medical care—prisoners were forced to use home remedies that they were taught by their families to treat their injuries. Men were forced to bow their heads and endure constant disrespect, name-calling, threats, and physical violence from prison officials and security guards. You can only kick a dog so many times before he turns around and bites.

Meanwhile, there was also a struggle for human and civil rights sweeping America at that time, and a growing number of prisoners and prisoner groups were doing what we were doing with the Black Panther Party, speaking out and calling for resistance. Outside the prison some black lawmakers were pushing for prison reform. In February of that year, two months before the guard's murder, U.S. Rep. John Conyers from Michigan addressed a national hearing on penal reform that was held in New Orleans, organized by Louisiana state representative Dorothy Mae Taylor and the Black State Legislators Association. Conyers's appearance made the front page of the newspaper because he called all black prisoners in America "political prisoners," because, he said, "they came out of an environment that made crime conducive for them to survive." Two black former prisoners who spoke at the hearing described atrocities at Angola. One, Andrew Joseph, said he witnessed guards firing into a gathering of prisoners who were protesting bad food, shooting prisoners "down like dogs." Another, Lazarus Smith, said he saw "as high as 60 men" die of wounds for lack of treatment at Angola. He said he once stabbed a prisoner in a fight and a guard "rode him [the wounded man] around the grounds until he died."

None of this publicity went over well with those in charge at Angola. For all their strife, Henderson and Dees seemed to agree on this: no black person had a right to speak up against the brutality and poor conditions at Angola. (Prison officials successfully blocked Representative Taylor from visiting Angola more than once.) Any prisoner who complained or resisted became a "militant" in their eyes and had to be put down, whether he had political beliefs or not.

In retrospect, when word came down the line that a prison guard had been killed that day, I should have known right away what was about to happen, but I didn't. Slowly the line moved toward the clothing room, where Hayden Dees was questioning prisoners one by one with local law enforcement.

When I got to the door of the clothing room Dees and a local deputy sheriff named Bill Daniel were standing behind the counter with three or four freemen on either side of them. Dees looked up at me when I walked in. "Woodfox, you motherfucking nigger, you killed Brent Miller," he yelled.

"No, I did not," I said.

Deputy Sheriff Daniel pulled a revolver from under the counter, pointing it at my face. "I'll blow your fucking brains out, nigger," he said. "If you think I'm scared of you because you're a Black Panther you don't know who I am, motherfucker. You Black Panthers need to bring y'all ass down to St. Francisville, we'll show you something."

I wouldn't show any fear. "Man, you better get that fucking gun out of my face," I said.

They cursed me and ordered me to strip. I took off the gray sweatshirt, blue jeans, and rubber boots I was wearing and they tossed my clothes into a pile in the corner. Someone handed me a tattered white jumpsuit to put on. They handcuffed my wrists to my waist on a leather strap and put restraints on each of my ankles, connected by a chain. I was barefoot. Two guards on either side of me, one carrying a machine gun, walked me out the door, through the snitcher gate, and up to the dining hall, where we turned right and passed through the control center to the dungeon. In the stairwell of the dungeon they beat me. Then they half pushed, half carried me up the stairs and locked me in the shower at the front of the tier. They closed the shower door and removed the restraints through the bars. They knew if they removed the restraints in the shower I would keep fighting them. All day men were brought in. The blows and the prisoners' pleas and screams in the stairwell echoed through the walls. Some prisoners would curse at the guards and try to fight back; others begged for mercy. They packed five men into cells made for one. They didn't put anyone in the shower with me.

I didn't know Brent Miller except by sight but I knew of the Miller family. Miller and his brothers were raised at Angola, and the family went back generations at the prison. His father ran the prison's hog farm. That explained the beatings. They weren't out for justice, they wanted revenge. Fuck them, I thought. Any human feeling I might have felt for Brent Miller or the Miller family had just been beaten out of me.

I wondered where Herman was. Herman and I always knew one day they would find an excuse to get us off the walk. The suddenness of being locked up reminded me that in prison, everything can change in the blink of an eye. All through the night freemen and deputies brought prisoners into the dungeon, beat them in the stairwell, and packed them into cells like sardines. I was still alone in the shower. I don't know how much time passed before Brent Miller's older brother Nix and seven or eight other freemen came onto the tier.

"There that nigger is, in the shower," he yelled, pointing at me.

"Open the shower door," he yelled to the freeman.

The freeman said, "The warden said don't let nobody in the shower." I heard him say something like, "If you want to open it I'm leaving the key in the box and you can open it yourself."

Nix and his friends were already walking toward me.

"You motherfucker, nigger, you killed my brother," he yelled.

They were standing in front of the shower now.

"Come to these bars, motherfucker, come to the fucking bars," he screamed.

I yelled back, "Are you losing your fucking mind? I'm not coming to the fucking bars. Come in and get me."

Some of the prisoners in the other cells started making noise, banging in their cells and hollering. "Leave that motherfucking man alone," they called out, shaking their bars. "Come down here and jump *me*."

I was standing now, watching the shower door, expecting it to slide open at any moment. I was too furious, too full of adrenaline to be scared. They could have pulled me out of the cell and beaten me to death. I would fight back with all I had. One of the tier guards must have called a ranking officer because somebody showed up and ordered Nix and his group off the tier.

After they left I sat back on the floor, leaning against the concrete wall, and watched the entrance to the tier. At first, I thought they had put me in the dungeon because they were making an example of me. I knew they had no evidence, no proof, nothing that would link me to Brent Miller's murder. I did not kill that man. But the longer I sat in the shower, the more I believed they might try to set me up. I was the first person they locked up. They had walked me in broad daylight across the yard to the dungeon, with armed guards on either side of me. By now everyone in the prison knew that my name was for sale. They didn't need evidence.

Later I learned Brent Miller had been stabbed to death in the Pine 1 dormitory. He was 23 years old. Former inmates told our investigators years later that prisoners who lived in Pine 1 were allowed to go back into their dorms that night; Brent Miller's blood was still on the floor.

Chapter 17

CCR

The next day freemen came to the shower and put shackles on my ankles. My wrists were handcuffed to my waist by a leather strap. These restraints would become standard for me for decades to come. They walked me to a car and I got in. A captain next to me started elbowing me in my chest, face, and ribs. They drove me to a building just inside the front gate that housed the Reception Center and Death Row. Inside was a cellblock called Closed Cell Restricted, or CCR: another name for solitary confinement. In the stairwell they beat me viciously. I couldn't fight back or defend myself because of the restraints. I tried not to fall so they couldn't kick me, but they tripped me. One of them kicked me in the eye. They grabbed me and dragged me up the stairs, still punching and kicking me. They took me to one of the tiers in CCR. I later found out this was B tier. They opened the security gate leading onto the tier and took me to cell 15. They put me inside and continued to punch and kick me. When they left, they closed the door and told me to come to the bars. I stepped to the bars and held my handcuffed hands up so they could uncuff them. They removed all the restraints through the bars.

Inside the cell there was a bare bunk attached to a wall on the left, a ceramic toilet and sink attached to the back wall, and a small metal table and bench attached to the wall on the right side of the cell. There was no mattress or blanket. I started to check myself to see what injuries I had. My body was badly bruised from being beaten but I was still able to move around the cell on my own. I walked to shake off the pain. The cell was nine feet long and six feet wide. I could take four or five steps up and back the length of the cell. When I heard the security door open at the end of the tier I stood at the bars and listened, trying to recognize voices.

I called down the tier to ask the prisoners their names when security left the tier. They called back. I didn't know them. In the late afternoon, the guards brought Herman in and put him in the cell next to me. He had been beaten badly in the dungeon and in the stairwell of CCR. I couldn't see him but we stood at our bars next to each other and talked. Herman used to live in the Pine 1 dorm and knew Brent Miller. That morning he had left Pine 3, where he lived now, went to breakfast, and was at his job in the tag plant when they were all pulled out to be questioned. He said multiple people must have seen him at breakfast and at the tag plant that morning. We talked about how we could let our families and party members know what happened to us. We both thought that the Black Panther Party would save us and there would be a movement to free us. I thought there would be mass protests in the street. "The people will rise up and not let us be railroaded," Herman said. That's how naive we were. (We didn't know it, but by that time the FBI's COINTELPRO, working with other federal agencies, local police, prosecutors, and the judicial system, had pretty much gutted the party. There was still a Black Panther newspaper and die-hard members around the country, including in New Orleans, but the infrastructure and unity of the party as we knew it were in ruins. Herman and I still didn't know that; we didn't even know what COINTELPRO was.) Freemen came onto the tier to taunt us, telling us we were going to die in the electric chair. They told us we'd be put first in line for the chair, ahead of everyone else waiting for execution.

The beatings of prisoners in retribution for Brent Miller's death did not stop with us. Prison administrators felt the need to reestablish control of the prison and the way they chose to do it was through fear and by using brutality. We heard through the grapevine that prisoners were beaten for days and that prison officials allowed local deputies and farmers from outside the prison to come in and "help." Some men were dragged from their cells in the middle of the night for "questioning." A prisoner named Shelly Batiste wrote an account of the abuse that he managed to get out of the prison. It was published in the Black Panther newspaper:

> Prisoners were beaten unmercifully . . . left to suffer from head and body injuries and acute burns with no medical attention. We were all locked in 5' by 8' cells (in groups of four, five and six, etc.). We are unable to sleep because there is only one mattress in each cell. The food is cold and has been cut. We aren't allowed to shower. . . . The guards have come to the dungeon several nights, in consecutive order, dragged Brothers out of their cells, through arbitrary selection, for looking like what they have called militant and then have beaten these Brothers unmercifully. One Brother in Angola, Wayne, was so viciously beaten he had to be taken to a hospital in Baton Rouge, and a guard checks his cell every hour to see if he is still living. The others who weren't beaten nearly to death were made to sit while 2, 3 or 4 pigs cut their hair in all directions, then made to crawl back in their cells. Their shock treatment consists of baseball bats, iron pipes, pick handles, gas and mace sprayed in Brothers' faces, so those who attempt to fight off the blows can't see. The Brothers who weren't locked down, but continued to work in the fields are being worked seven days a week; shots are being fired at them. They can't get out of line, they're beaten with bats and forced to say they are "whores"; and after these sadistic accomplishments, they are forced to finish working in a badly bruised condition.

The day Brent Miller was killed, Deputy Warden Lloyd Hoyle was interviewed by the New Orleans *Times-Picayune* and told a reporter there was no explanation for the incident. On the morning of April 18, the paper published his account. "The thing we've got to remember," Hoyle said, "is that we've got quite an adverse-type population up here. It could have been any number of things." Hoyle also said there was no information to link the incident of the guard being burned in the shack on the 16th with Miller's murder.

Sometime that day or the next morning, Warden Henderson gave reporters a different story. In the afternoon edition of the *State-Times* newspaper on April 18—the day after Deputy Warden Hoyle told reporters there "could have been a number of things" behind the guard's murder—Warden C. Murray Henderson was quoted as saying that "black militants" murdered Brent Miller and that his "investigation" into Miller's killing had already turned up "four or five prime suspects." (Going by the timing of this published report Henderson blamed "black militants" before every black prisoner on the walk had even been questioned. No white prisoners had been interviewed at this time.) Henderson also told the paper that on the previous Sunday, the day the guard was burned and the day before Miller was killed, prison officials had "intercepted" a typewritten letter that was addressed to the Baton Rouge *Sunday Advocate*, taking credit for the burning of guard Mike Gunnells that day. (A letter assistant warden Hoyle apparently had no knowledge of.) Warden Henderson said in that letter Angola officials were found "guilty" of "extreme racism" at a "people's court" allegedly held the same day the guard was burned. The letter supposedly went on to say that the public was as guilty as "the racist pigs who hold us captive," and said "more will come." It was signed, "The Vanguard Army, Long Live the Angola Prison Involvement."

I'd never heard of the Vanguard Army and don't believe the letter, if it existed, was written by a prisoner. No black prisoner could get access to a typewriter in 1972. There were no typewriters in the black dorms, none in the dining hall or kitchen where I worked, none in the tag plant where Herman worked, certainly none in the yard or in the fields. The only prisoners who may have had access to a typewriter were inmate clerks, and they were white. Prison authorities had a way to identify prisoners by their handwriting; they had samples on file for every prisoner in Angola. Similarly they had access to every typewriter at the prison and could have tested each to see where the letter was typed. If a letter giving authorities a motive for Miller's killing had been intercepted on Sunday, wouldn't the deputy warden have known about it on Monday when he spoke to reporters? The letter was never produced at any trial related to Brent Miller's murder.

In the account Warden Henderson gave the *State-Times* that was published the day after Miller's killing, on April 18, Henderson also said he believed the "sit-down strike of inmate workers" in the dining hall that took place the morning of Miller's murder was staged as a "diversionary tactic" to draw guards away from the walk. Guards were not called away from the walk that day. There were always only two guards per unit on the walk. Standard protocol was that during meals, one of those guards accompanied prisoners to the dining hall and the other was left on the walk. The morning of the strike that didn't change. One guard who was on the walk that morning would later say that he didn't even know there was a kitchen workers' strike. Contradicting himself, at the end of the *State-Times* article Henderson admitted as much, saying, "The man [Brent Miller] was supervising four dormitories by himself in an area where the original plans called for it to be manned by five. We've had a chronic problem in leaving a man by himself in an area like that. We've constantly asked for more money for more supervision but we haven't been able to get it." Henderson's claim that "militants" killed Miller, insinuating it was because he was white, would stick. The day after the *State-Times* article the Associated Press headlined an article about the killing "Militants Said Cause of Death, 'Black Power' Backers Blamed at Angola."

The freemen came onto our tier and cut everybody's Afro, saying there was a new rule that everybody's hair had to be short. Eventually they brought each of us a mattress, a blanket, and some of our possessions. I started getting notes on my food tray saying things like, "You're going to die," "Eat this food and you eat my dick," or "This food will kill you," all signed by "the KKK." I threw out the food. I received many letters threatening me. I could tell they came from inside the prison because there were no stamps on the envelopes. I searched the food on my tray for ground glass for the next year, even when there wasn't a note.

We were locked down 23 hours a day. At first, I ignored the pressure of the cell. There was so much going on. And I never for one moment thought I'd be confined to such a small area for more than a few weeks or months at the most. Once a day, usually in the morning, all 16 of our cell doors opened at the same time and we were let out onto the tier for an hour. During that time we could shower and walk up and down the hall on the tier. Sometimes I looked out the window across from my cell. There was no outside exercise yard for CCR prisoners. There were prisoners in CCR who hadn't been outside in years. We couldn't make or receive phone calls. We weren't allowed books, magazines, newspapers, or radios. There were no fans on the tier; there was no access to ice, no hot water in the sinks in our cells. There was no hot plate to heat water on the tier. Needless to say, we were not allowed educational, social, vocational, or religious programs; we weren't allowed to do hobby crafts (leatherwork, painting, woodwork). Rats came up the shower drain at the end of the hall and would run down the tier. We threw things at them to keep them from coming into our cells. Mice came out at night. When the red ants invaded they were everywhere all at once, in clothes, sheets, mail, toiletries, food.

Our meals were put on the floor outside our cell doors. We stuck our hands through the bars to pull the trays underneath the door into our cell. Anytime we were taken off the tier, even if we were moving just outside the door to the bridge, we were forced to strip, bend over, and spread our buttocks for a "visual cavity search," then after we got dressed we were put in full restraints. When we got back to the cell we were strip-searched again when the restraints came off. If we were taken outside the prison—to a hospital or to court—a black box was put over our cuffed hands. That was very painful because you couldn't move your hands at all with the black box on.

If there is one word to describe the next years of my life it would be "defiance." White inmate guards virtually ran CCR at the time, overseen by freemen who would come and go throughout the day. These inmate guards were brutal in their treatment of prisoners housed in CCR. They liked to threaten and taunt us, but they made sure to do it only if they were outside our cells or when we were in restraints. They weren't stupid enough to put their hands on us if we weren't restrained. They hated me and Herman because we didn't put up with their racist comments. If they talked trash to us we talked trash back just as bad. Nothing that came out of their mouths could hurt us. They couldn't match us with words and they couldn't stop us. We talked back to them. We talked down to them. We resisted orders. If they were jumping a prisoner we shook the bars and yelled. Any act of resistance ended the same way: four or five of them would come into the cell and jump us. It's a hell of a feeling to stand when you know you're going to be beaten; you know there will be pain but your moral principles won't let you back down. I was always scared shitless. Sometimes my knees would shake and almost buckle. I forced myself to learn how not to give in to fear. That was one of my greatest achievements in those years. I didn't let fear rule me. I'd say, "Fuck you, come in here. One of you motherfuckers ain't leaving." You don't fight to win, you fight so that when you look in the mirror the next time you don't drop your eyes in shame. They never came in alone. We were always outnumbered. I was scared, but I was mentally strong.

After a couple of weeks Warden Henderson called me out of the cell to talk to me. He didn't ask me where I was the morning Brent Miller was killed or what I was doing or who I was with. He didn't ask me about the letter that was supposedly "intercepted" the night before Miller's murder, signed by "the Vanguard Army." He asked me why I killed Brent Miller. I told him I didn't kill Brent Miller. He asked me why I hated white people. I told him I didn't hate white people. By the time I got back to my cell I knew for sure Herman and I would be framed.

On May 5, 1972, Herman and I were indicted along with Chester Jackson, age 31; and a prisoner named Gilbert Montegut, age 21. Herman was 29. I was 25. Herman and I knew why we were being charged—prison authorities wanted to wipe out the Black Panther Party at Angola. We could only guess that Chester Jackson was being charged because prison officials believed he was with the party. Neither of us knew Gilbert Montegut. It turned out he was charged because he was in the wrong place at the wrong time. Montegut had been locked up in CCR by Hayden Dees for supposedly being a "militant," along with several other prisoners, weeks before Miller was killed. Dees was forced to release him and several other prisoners from CCR a week before Miller was killed because he refused to do the proper paperwork on them. Under pressure from the federal government leaning on state officials, Henderson and Hoyle had been asking Dees for months to create paperwork behind prisoners who were locked up. Dees refused, even after Hoyle gave him an ultimatum—do the paperwork or the prisoners would be released back into the general population. Within a week of the prisoners' release Miller was killed. Dees immediately blamed Hoyle, saying one of Miller's killers must have come from the group Hoyle released from CCR. When Dees told the freemen that Miller died because Hoyle released all the "militants" from CCR, the guards were enraged, calling for Hoyle to be fired. One of the Miller brothers attacked Hoyle, pushing him through a plate glass door. Hoyle had to be hospitalized in Baton Rouge for his injuries.

Montegut was selected from that group to be charged with and indicted for the murder of Brent Miller because Hayden Dees said so. (Later we learned some inmates gave statements claiming Montegut was with the prisoners who threw gasoline and fire at the guard who was burned in his booth. He was never formerly charged or indicted for that. Rory Mason was the only prisoner convicted for that crime.) When Montegut was put back in CCR he was on my tier and I got to know him. He was no militant.

Almost 30 years later, a former prisoner named Billy Sinclair, who had been an editor of Angola's award-winning magazine *The Angolite* for years, wrote to one of my lawyers that one of the reasons he believed Herman and I were innocent was "the character" of Gilbert Montegut and Chester Jackson. He described them as "petty criminal hoodlums, incapable of forming a single, solitary political thought, much less possessing a political ideology." Sinclair continued, "To conclude that either Hooks or Woodfox would have joined in any kind of criminal conspiracy to kill a prison guard with these two individuals is mind-boggling."

It didn't take long for me and Herman to realize that most of the so-called "militants" they put on our tier in CCR—the men released from CCR with Gilbert Montegut before Miller was killed—were full of shit. They may have been running around the yard calling themselves revolutionaries, but they weren't. A lot of these guys were still in the game. They argued standing at the bars, which we called "bar fighting." They gambled. Every 23 hours when all the doors on the tier would open, fights broke out. One of the men might sneak into the cell of another prisoner who was in the shower and fish his box, stealing from him.

Herman and I talked about this hypocrisy and knew the men acting out were deeply flawed. We talked about the Panthers we had met in prison. I remembered how they were able to change everything around them by their own conduct. Herman and I started holding 15-minute meetings on the tier when we were all out on our hour. One or two prisoners came. We talked to them about how to make conditions better. We asked the men what they needed. Gradually more men came to the meetings. We asked the men what kind of tier they wanted, what kind of conduct they would like to see from one another. Based on that we created a list of rules to live by.

Hooks and I were lucky enough to have family members who visited regularly. At CCR prisoners weren't allowed to sit at a table with our visitors. We could only have noncontact visits. Each prisoner sat in a booth and there was a diamond-cut aluminum screen between him and his visitor. We were kept in full restraints throughout the visit. The first thing my mom asked me when she visited was if they hit me or if they threatened me. She was afraid they'd hurt me. I lied and said everything was all right. I didn't want her to deal with what I was going through. At the end of the visits she left what money she could in my account. Sometimes she could afford $15 or $20, sometimes more. (When my brother and sister got into their teens and started making money from jobs they would leave what they could too.) At the end of our visits my mom stood and kissed me through the screen.

A couple of other men on the tier also had regular visitors who put money into their accounts. Herman and I asked them to pool their money with ours for the benefit of the tier. They agreed. Next time we were out of our cells we announced to the tier that if everyone followed the rules we had created together, then everybody would be able to buy one item out of the store each week. The tier pool would pay for it. Every week we passed a piece of paper down the tier and every man wrote what he wanted; a candy bar, shower slippers, underwear, tobacco, chips, a mirror, whatever it was. On canteen day, we'd order everything on the list and each prisoner would get his item. If anyone violated the rules of the tier, he wouldn't be able to get an item that week. That's how we stopped guys from stealing from each other.

We practiced martial arts together on the tier. We read aloud. We held math classes, spelling classes. Every Friday we passed out a spelling or math test. We talked about what was going on in the world. We encouraged debates and conversation. We told each man he had a say. "Stand up for yourself," we told them, "for your own self-esteem, for your own dignity." Even the roughest, most hardened person usually responds when you see the dignity and humanity in him and ask him to see it for himself. "The guards will retaliate," we said, "but we will always face that together."

Chapter 18

King Arrives

A few weeks after Herman and I were put in CCR, we heard that Robert King, who joined the Black Panther Party in Orleans Parish Prison, was put in a cell on another tier. I first met King when I was 18, in a dormitory at Angola. The other prisoners told me he was a Holy Roller, a Bible thumper, and I avoided him. Physically imposing, he never used his strength to intimidate anyone. He spent a lot of time on his bunk, reading the Bible. He said he liked the flow of the language. He liked the parables and the Sermon on the Mount. He had tried to talk to me but I was caught up in the game, in surviving. I thought he was hopelessly out of touch. The day he was released on parole I told him, "I can now say I lived to see the last of the old-timers go home." He was 23. King would go on to become a semiprofessional boxer on the street—they called him Speedy King—and have several jobs until he was charged with and convicted of a robbery he didn't commit. (The perpetrator was described as being several years older with a different complexion and appearance.) He was sentenced to 35 years. After joining the party in Orleans Parish Prison he became involved in protests there. When he arrived at Angola they put him directly into the dungeon, charged with "playing lawyer." Then he was put in the Red Hat, and then on D tier in CCR.

I wrote him a note telling him Herman and I were on B tier, asking him if he needed anything. Over the next few days Herman and I paid trustees tobacco and candy to deliver our letters to King back and forth. We knew the freemen and white inmate guards would harass him for being a Panther. King expected this and wrote back that it was no big deal. Before King arrived in CCR I didn't have any trust or belief that, outside of Herman, anyone could go all the way with me. There was so much turmoil and brutality. In King's letters, I saw his strength. I saw his morality, his integrity. I believed I could trust him. Sitting in my cell I thought back to the time I first met him. I could see now that when he tried to talk to me all those years ago his interest was in getting me to go beyond myself and the influences of the street, to create a different human being. He still wanted that for the men around him. I wondered if my first meeting with King had set us on a path to be together again. Who knows what strange powers were at play, I thought. Herman, King, and I, Black Panthers at Angola, were in a terrible situation. But now there were three of us.

After about a month in CCR I was sitting on my bunk when I started sweating, and the walls of my cell started to move toward me at the same time. My clothes tightened around my body. I took off my shirt and pants but still felt like I was being squeezed, strangled. The ceiling was pressing down on me. It was hard to breathe, hard to think, hard to see. I forced myself to stand. I took a few steps, trying not to fall. At the end of my cell I turned and walked back to the cell door. I turned and continued, pacing back and forth for several minutes, maybe an hour. Eventually I was so tired I lay on the bunk and fell asleep. After the first couple of times this happened I started recognizing when it was coming on; my clothes tightened and I started to sweat. The atmosphere pressed down on me. Sometimes it lasted five or ten minutes, other times it lasted for hours. The only thing that helped was to pace back and forth. Usually it didn't end until I was so exhausted from walking back and forth that I could lie down. I continued having episodes like this one, which I later learned was claustrophobia, the whole time I was in prison. For about three years I slept sitting up, propped up against the wall, believing it helped prevent claustrophobic attacks. It seemed to lessen them but they never stopped.

Chapter 19

CCR Wars

Gassing prisoners was the number one response by security to deal with any prisoner at Angola who demanded to be treated with dignity. Gas incapacitates the prisoner so the guards can easily get into the cell and beat the hell out of him. Our tier was gassed many times, and guards ran into our cells, jumped us, kicking and punching us, forcing us to the floor or onto the bunk so they could put restraints on us. Whenever they beat us they tried to cause as much pain as possible. They were willing to break some part of our bodies if possible. It's very difficult to fight back in restraints but I did what I could. I'd spit, bite, head-butt the guards. Then they'd take us to the dungeon and write us up. On his tier King didn't take any shit from security either, so he was gassed and bounced into and out of the CCR dungeon like us. In the seventies we were gassed so often every prisoner in CCR almost became immune to the tear gas. It was always painful at first but after the initial cloud of gas dissipated we'd forget about it until a freeman came onto the tier to make a count and he'd be wearing a gas mask. That made us laugh.

Our resistance gave us an identity. Our identity gave us strength. Our strength gave us an unbreakable will. My determination not to be broken was stronger than any other part of me, stronger than anything they did to me. The prisoners around us saw how Herman, King, and I talked back to inmate guards and freemen who trash-talked us, how we refused to go into our cells if we wanted to talk to a supervisor. They saw we were fighting for them too. For better conditions, for more respect.

We talked to the men, explaining why we needed to protest, showing them that we had leverage. We could refuse to go back into our cells when our hour was up; we could refuse to hand back the trays after a meal. We could shake our cell doors, "shaking down," or bang on our tables or sinks with shoes, "knocking down," and this would be heard downstairs by the camp supervisor. We could refuse to come out of our cells on our hour, we could refuse to eat the next meal, or we could write a petition of grievance and all sign it. We didn't invent knocking down or shaking down, but we showed men there was more strength if we did it as a tier rather than as individuals. Any one of these actions, if we all did it together, was sometimes enough to get a ranking officer on the tier to talk to us. Prior to any action we took together as a tier we got a consensus, because usually security retaliated. Most of the time we were fighting to get supplies or make conditions more humane but if the tier guard was just an asshole and constantly fucking with us we'd take a vote on having him removed and we'd make an official request to whoever was running the camp: either move him or move us.

The response usually started with a lieutenant or captain coming up and threatening us, saying something like, "What the fuck you making all this noise for? We're going to gas you motherfuckers." And we'd say, "Man, we're trying to get toilet paper for the last couple of days. These people won't give us the motherfucking toilet paper." He might say OK, no problem and leave. Then after one hour passed, and then two hours, without any word from him we'd start shaking the bars again. Next thing we knew the dark yellowish smoke of tear gas would be rolling down the tier. Or sometimes after he left he gassed the tier immediately. Sometimes when ranking officers came they turned the whole tier into a dungeon. They'd take each man, one cell at a time, put him in restraints—if he resisted he was hit with pepper spray and beaten—and walk him to the bridge outside the tier. Then they'd go in his cell and throw everything he had into the hall, lock him back in his cell, and go to the next prisoner and walk him to the bridge, empty his cell, and so forth. After all the cells were emptied they pushed everybody's belongings into one pile at the end of the tier and we lived under dungeon rules. The pile would stay there until we could get out on our

hour again; during that time, we'd go through it to find all our possessions and put them back in our cells. What wasn't ours we'd hold up and
ask the men, "Whose is this?" and walk it down to them. It took days.

Other times the captain on duty might come and talk with some
sense of doing the right thing. Once we were complaining there wasn't
enough food on our trays and the captain came up and told the tier
sergeant, "Take these trays out and put food on them." Another time,
after being served expired and sour milk for days, we held our trays
after a meal, refusing to put them under our doors, and told the guard
we would hold them until we could see a dietician. The captain on duty
brought someone to talk to us.

The most effective way of protesting was the hunger strike. If we
didn't eat for three days prison officials were required by law to notify
the Louisiana Department of Public Safety and Corrections. The same
way freemen didn't want ranking officers summoned to the tier, ranking
officers didn't want state officials called to the prison. They might find
something wrong besides what the prisoners were protesting. Once
we voted to go on a hunger strike to get toilet paper that wasn't being
passed out. Just the threat of a hunger strike, that time, got the tier
guard to pass out the toilet paper.

Our victories were few, but each victory made up for the losses
before it. It was an adrenaline rush to win. We had to deal with some
prisoners who suddenly wanted to shake their bars about everything.
They'd say, "Man, his cinnamon roll is bigger than mine" or "I only got
one piece of bread and he got two." I had to talk to those prisoners and
make them understand that not every problem meant you have to go
through the most extreme form of protest to get it resolved. Sometimes
you can do other things. If a man got gassed, even if it was just pepper
spray in his cell, it affected the whole tier because the gas would spread.
There is no such thing as gassing one prisoner; whenever they gassed
anyone we all felt it.

Herman and I were only on the same tier in CCR for about a month
when a freeman showed up at my cell door and told me to pack. I
asked him why and he said, "You're moving." I said, "No, I'm not." He

walked away. I talked to Herman. "Man, I'm not going, I'm fighting these motherfuckers," I said.

We knew they'd be back with gas. Hooks yelled down the tier to warn everyone as I looked around my cell for something to use as a weapon to defend myself with when they came in my cell. I grabbed the motor out of my fan and put it in a sock and then put that in another sock. The sock was hidden in my waistband behind me when seven or eight freemen showed up holding cut-off baseball bats, billy clubs, and leather blackjacks. One of them carried restraints they wanted to put on me.

Herman and the rest of the tier started shaking their bars and yelling at them. "Leave that man alone." "Don't jump him, motherfuckers." My door was opened and they told me to come out. When I refused, a freeman holding a blackjack took steps toward my cell and I raised my arm holding the sock. A guard yelled, "Look out, he's got something in his hand," and pulled the freeman out of the cell. They shut the door again. Captain Hilton Butler appeared with a CS gas launcher and started firing it directly at me. One of the gas cartridges hit my chest. A very strong gas, the kind created to be used outside to disperse crowds, was filling my cell. I could hear the other prisoners on the tier screaming at me, "Put your head in the shitter. Put your head in the shitter." I put my head in the toilet bowl and flushed. Usually the vacuum created when the water leaves the bowl gives you a breath of air. It wasn't enough. I started kicking the bowl until it broke in pieces. I leaned down and put my face directly above the hole where the pipe was. Between breaths I picked up pieces of the toilet bowl and threw them at Butler to prevent him from aiming the gas gun directly at me. He moved to the front of the cell next to mine, Herman's cell, and pointed the gun around the corner through the bars into my cell, firing blindly. Hooks was cursing at him and screaming for him to stop and threw whatever he could toward him. I don't remember how long it lasted but eventually Butler stopped firing.

After a while Butler told me if I'd come out and let them put the restraints on me they wouldn't jump or beat me. I didn't believe him but I was close to passing out. The mucus in my throat was choking me. I couldn't open my eyes. I didn't want to die in my cell. When they opened the door, I walked into the hall and let them put the restraints on me. They didn't beat me. Walking down the tier I could see that everyone in the other cells was sick from the gas. I heard Herman's voice behind me, hoarse from screaming, still yelling. They ended up moving King and Herman too. While they were fighting to move me, they told King they were moving him to B tier. He didn't resist because he wanted to be on the tier with me and Herman. First, they put him on what we called the short tier, on the first floor, which had 13 cells, while they moved me. They put me in King's old cell on D tier. Then they moved King to B tier. Later, they moved Herman to A tier. That night they stripped everybody's cell in CCR and took our mattresses, turning CCR into a dungeon to punish everyone for my actions.

They thought they would stop our organizing by separating us but all they did was spread our influence. Wherever they put us, we started over, organizing our tiers. Pooling resources. Educating prisoners. Setting examples by our own conduct. In this way, we taught men the power of unity. Our efforts worked better on some tiers than others. It depended on the men. One time I was on a tier with a prisoner who was dangerous, a real bully, and he had a house slave mentality. He wouldn't protest with us. Whenever we were on a hunger strike for something he would take food off trays of other prisoners' who weren't eating. Prisoners started spitting on their food to prevent him from doing that.

In June 1972, we got word that the Louisiana House of Representatives had passed a series of bills by Rep. Dorothy Mae Taylor that would eliminate inmate guards at Angola, racially integrate prisons, and implement health protocols that would be overseen by the Louisiana Department of Health. State and prison officials would not implement any of these for years to come, but Representative Taylor was persistent. She had long been advocating for better conditions at Orleans Parish Prison and Angola and was used to being criticized for it by the racist white establishment. A week after Brent Miller was killed, the adjutant general of the Louisiana National Guard, Lieutenant General David Wade, who at one time in his career oversaw correctional programs in the state, even blamed Representative Taylor for Miller's death. "I feel very strongly about the damage that she has done . . . by stirring up the unrest at Angola," he told the New Orleans *Times-Picayune*. "As a result, we had a guard killed last week." In this same interview Wade called Representative Taylor a "phony" and said, "She's interested in appearing on television and stirring up a lot of trouble." When she visited the prison, he said, "they [referring to black prisoners] go wild." Representative Taylor never stopped pressing for reform. Her courage, as a black woman living and working in the racist "white man's world" of the South in the sixties and seventies, was remarkable and still inspires me.

That summer we were arraigned for the murder of Brent Miller. Two freemen came to my cell and put me in full restraints and walked me to a van parked just outside the gate. Herman, Gilbert Montegut, and Chester Jackson were already in the van. I got in and we were sitting there with the door open when Brent Miller's brother Nix drove up in a pickup truck and skidded to a stop alongside us. He jumped out swaying drunk and waving a shotgun, screaming at us, "Where are those sons of bitches? I'll kill you niggers." He took aim at our heads. I didn't move. None of us did. The freemen standing around the car were yelling at Nix. "C'mon Nix, you don't want to do this," one said. "Put the gun down." Another yelled, "They're going to die in the electric chair. If you kill them you'll go to prison." I was staring straight down the long road that leads to the front gate of Angola when I saw a car coming toward us with a light flashing on top. It was Hilton Butler, the captain who fired the gas grenades on our tier. He drove up to the front gate and jumped out of his car, cigar in his mouth, full head of red hair. "Nix, Nix, you son of a bitch," he yelled. "Didn't I tell you don't bring your fucking ass up here and get in trouble. Get yourself home." He grabbed the gun out of Nix's hands. "They killed my brother," Nix yelled. Butler held the gun with one hand straight out from his side and said, "You get your fucking ass home before you wind up in jail." Nix got in his truck and drove off, then turned the truck around and came back cursing us out his window. A few minutes later he peeled off. None of us said anything. They closed the van doors and took us to

a courthouse in St. Francisville where the charges against us were read
and we were assigned a public defender.

Herman, King, and I had so many battles with the administration
during the seventies that they run together in my mind now. Any one
of our protests could have gone on for a few hours or a whole day, and
there were some that lasted day and night. I broke at least three or four
toilets in CCR over the years before they switched to stainless steel
commodes. Somewhere around this time they were gassing us so often
a captain who had been summoned to King's tier by a prisoner protest
asked him, "What do you all want? I had so much gas on me last night
my wife wouldn't let me get in bed."

In adjusting to day-to-day life in the cell as the months and years
passed, every aspect of survival was a battle. Being able to read in that
environment, with the noise. Recognizing the signs of when a prisoner
was going to act out, when I would need to defend myself or stop
something from happening before it happened. Doing calisthenics every
day within the confines of the cell. I became living proof that we can
survive the worst to change ourselves and our world, no matter where
we are. Behind our resistance on the tiers, Herman, King, and I knew
that only education would save us. It still amazes me that the three of
us came to the same conclusion sitting in our cells on different tiers.
Education and looking outward, beyond the prison. If we were going
to avoid becoming vegetables, we had to keep learning and keep our
minds focused on the world outside Angola.

Sometimes a freeman would leave a newspaper between the bars of
the first cell on my tier and it would be passed down the tier for anyone
who wanted to look at it. Every time there was a newspaper on the tier
I read it. When we were finally allowed to have radios and newspapers,
I listened to a lot of news. I subscribed to the newspaper. All three of us
did, and we had heated debates and discussions about what was going
on in the world, played out in notes and letters we passed, or sometimes
we checked ourselves into the dungeon so we could talk. In those days,
a prisoner could tell the tier sergeant his head was hurting or he was
having problems and needed to be alone to think and he could be put

in the dungeon. They only had one dungeon in the building that housed CCR and Death Row. There were two big cells. They wouldn't put the three of us in the same cell but two of us would be in one and the third in another. We could spend time together and had many conversations and debates in the dungeon.

During this time, we started teaching ourselves the law. We knew getting the shit kicked out of us over and over wasn't changing anything. We would never be able to match them physically. There was a prisoner on D tier named Arthur Mitchell who had a lot of success filing lawsuits against the prison. For that reason, the guards didn't fuck with him. I borrowed a dictionary of law terms from Arthur and started checking law books out of the prison library.

I read case law, day and night, standing, sitting, or lying in my bunk. Some days I sat on the floor of my cell with four or five law books open around me. I heard through the prison grapevine that a white prisoner on Death Row named Big John was real good at the law and I wrote him a letter about my case. I knew I had an issue: the grand jury that indicted me in West Feliciana Parish, where Angola is located, had only been composed of white men. Women and blacks were excluded. That was a constitutional violation. Big John helped me in letters back and forth between us, carried by trustees or sometimes by an inmate counsel who visited both of our tiers. I filed a motion in the court pro se, without a lawyer, to quash the indictment because the grand jury had excluded women and blacks. Then I forgot about it. Herman, King, and I were fighting for our lives in CCR. I turned my thoughts away from my unconstitutional indictment, and even my upcoming trial. Both seemed far off. I wasn't experienced enough in the law to know better. I was focused on learning how to use the law to get relief in our day-to-day lives. Years later I would discover the court never ruled on that motion.

Before we could file a lawsuit related to prison conditions, we had to show that we attempted to resolve any issue we had by filing what was called a "petition of grievance" with the warden. If we didn't get a response in two weeks, we could file a lawsuit in the courts. In 1985, this process became much more complicated. The Louisiana

Department of Public Safety and Corrections installed a new grievance procedure, called the administrative remedy procedure (ARP), which required a prisoner who was reporting abuse or any issue to file the complaint, first with the officer over the camp or cellblock where he was living. If the issue was denied, he had to file it with the warden. If the warden denied it, he had to file with the Louisiana Department of Public Safety and Corrections. If he didn't get relief there, he had to file what was called a "petition of review" in state court. If the petition of review was denied, he could then file his lawsuit in state court. If a prisoner alleged a constitutional violation, however—for example, cruel and unusual punishment or a lack of equal treatment or of due process under the law, violating the 8th or 14th Amendment—he could skip filing the petition of review in state court and go directly to federal court. But he'd still have to go through the ARP process within the prison system. By instituting this new procedure, at the urging of the Department of Corrections and legislators, officials delayed the time it took for a prisoner to be heard in court by six months to a year. It was a technique to slow down the process and discourage prisoners from filing civil suits against abuse and poor conditions.

For more than 100 years state and federal judges refused to adjudicate prisoner abuses at all in their courts because legally, according to the 13th Amendment of the U.S. Constitution, prisoners are slaves of the state. The same amendment that abolished slavery in 1865—"Neither slavery nor involuntary servitude shall exist within the United States"— includes the clause "except as a punishment for crime whereof the party shall have been duly convicted." Judges used this clause as an excuse not to deal with violations and abuses against prisoners. They even had a name for it, calling it the "hands-off doctrine." In the 1960s the Supreme Court started making rulings that gave prisoners constitutional rights, opening the doors for prisoners to sue state officials in federal court.

It took me a while to understand the legal terms and language used in the courts and how the court system worked. If I came across a passage I didn't understand in the law books, I read it over and over again. I'd read a single passage 40 or 50 times until I was somehow able to absorb the meaning.

King filed on not being allowed to go outside for exercise—not having yard time—under the 14th Amendment, equal protection, pointing out that Death Row was allowed yard, and we were housed under the same conditions. If it wasn't a "threat to security" for Death Row prisoners to have yard, he pointed out, it shouldn't be a threat for CCR prisoners to have yard. Herman and I filed on other conditions that we felt violated our constitutional right to be free of cruel and unusual punishment. Our first lawsuits in the early seventies—and all Angola prisoner lawsuits at that time—were grouped under what everybody called the Hayes Williams suit: the lawsuit suit filed by Hayes Williams and three other prisoners in 1971, which outlined how conditions at Angola violated prisoners' 8th and 14th Amendment rights regarding cruel and unusual punishment and due process. In June 1975, after the trial for the Hayes Williams lawsuit, Judge E. Gordon West of federal district court found Angola guilty of violating prisoners' 8th and 14th Amendment rights. He wrote that conditions at Angola "would shock the conscience of any right thinking person" and placed the prison under federal control. The district court ordered Angola and the Louisiana Department of Public Safety and Corrections to improve conditions and decentralize prisons. It would take two years before an agreement, called a consent decree, would be established with new rules and guidelines under which Angola administrators would be forced to operate.

The first lawsuit I won, around 1974 or 1975, was against the Department of Corrections rule that didn't allow prisoners to wear any items of clothing with brand names or logos. At that time, you couldn't find sweatpants without logos. It put an unnecessary burden on prisoners. I filed a petition of grievance stating we should be able to wear sweatpants with logos, which the warden denied. I asked the court to review that decision and won. In the ruling, the judge told officials how stupid the rule was; not in those words. She said it didn't make any sense because it was almost impossible to buy any item of clothing that didn't have some logo or brand name on it.

Between filing grievances, going to court, and our constant protests on the tier to be treated humanely, we gradually gained privileges that had not been allowed in CCR before. Over time we were granted permission to have individual fans, radios, and books in our cells. We could subscribe to newspapers and magazines. In the midseventies, we got screens on the windows that kept the mosquitos out. Sometime in the late seventies, Herman, King, and I were actually allowed to share a record player. We could only pass it between tiers when a decent captain was on duty; he would have to give the OK for a guard to carry it between our tiers. Each of us would use it for a few days, then pass it down to prisoners on our tier who wanted to use it. To move it from cell to cell on the tier we left it outside our door at the end of our hour and a freeman or orderly would move it to the next prisoner's cell door. Eventually we were allowed to have cassette players in our cells. Any or all of these privileges could be taken away at any time, and they were. Then we'd protest again.

Chapter 20

My Trial, 1973

By the time I went to trial, in 1973, the Black Panther Party had long been struggling. COINTELPRO had done so much damage to the party across the country: incarcerating Panthers, killing Panthers, pitting Panthers against one another, planting fake evidence, demonizing the Panthers to society, and threatening Panthers' family members. The young organization never had a chance to resolve philosophical differences and internal struggles while it was under constant attack. Party leaders Huey Newton and Eldridge Cleaver split in 1972 and Cleaver left the country. Panthers all over the country started to go underground for their own survival; some had been under constant surveillance.

After our indictment in 1972, Malik Rahim gathered New Orleans Panthers and other activists at his mother's house and started a support committee for us called Free the Angola 4. Chester Jackson and Gilbert Montegut were not members of the Black Panther Party, but to the outside world they were linked to us as Panthers. In June of that year we were written up in the Black Panther newspaper. The New Orleans Panthers held events to raise funds to hire lawyers and circulated flyers about us. New Orleans Panthers Marion Brown, Althea Francois, Shirley Duncan, and others, many of them college students, visited us. As support for us grew, local activists Harry "Gi" Schafer and his wife, Jill, a white couple, joined our support committee and quickly took on leadership roles. They had been heading the Students for a Democratic Society (SDS) on LSU's New Orleans campus since 1969. One of them volunteered to be the treasurer of our committee. Black lawyers from Baton Rouge came to Angola to meet with us. A young white lawyer named Charles Garretson, recently out of law school, also visited us.

By the time my trial came up in 1973 our support committee was nonexistent. The fund-raising had stopped; the money disappeared. To us, inside, it seemed that everybody had moved on. Not until 1975, when someone sent me an article about Gi and Jill Schafer, did I learn the Schafers were FBI informants who deliberately broke up our support committee. They were paid $16,000 a year to infiltrate, disrupt, and destroy the SDS at LSU, acting as spies and agents provocateurs, making up stories to create mistrust among the students and anti-war protesters, and shaming many of them into taking more extreme actions than they wanted to, which led to their arrests. As a side project, they took on the Angola 4 support committee and played a part in its demise. In the summer of 1972, Huey Newton, while attempting to centralize activities within the party, called the members of the New Orleans Black Panther Party chapter to Oakland and sent replacement Panthers from Cincinnati to New Orleans. Nobody in the community trusted the people from Ohio, who were all strangers. With the New Orleans Panthers in Oakland, this gave the Schafers more power in our committee. From documents obtained through the Freedom of Information Act from the FBI, we learned many years later their job was to sabotage any attempt to raise funds to get lawyers for us, and that's what they did.

The black lawyers who visited from Baton Rouge disappeared when the money did. The young white attorney Charles Garretson stuck with us, agreeing to represent us even without being paid. Garretson was sincere and well-meaning—more than 30 years after he represented us he wrote to my attorneys offering to testify on my behalf at a new trial—but in 1973 he was young and inexperienced. And he was up against a good ol' boy network in which virtually everyone knew everyone else or lived in the same neighborhood, and all were determined to convict me, no matter what. He didn't have a chance.

My trial started in West Baton Rouge the day after jury selection in early March 1973. (Herman, Gilbert Montegut, and Chester Jackson would go to trial in 1974.) I was represented by Garretson, who took on my case pro bono. Otherwise, I was alone. I knew I would be. My mom couldn't afford to come to Baton Rouge and even if she could she had no place to stay there. When I arrived, the first thing I saw outside the courthouse was a group of heavily armed prison guards from Angola and deputies from Iberville Parish. Two armed deputies were standing on the roof. Inside, armed guards leaned against the walls. The all-white jury was already seated when I entered in shackles, flanked by two deputies. My restraints were removed at the defense table. The prosecutors were John Sinquefield and Leon Picou.

The expert witnesses testified first. According to the coroner, Brent Miller was stabbed 32 times around 7:45 a.m. on April 17, 1972. He died four minutes later, at 7:49 a.m. He had wounds on his back, chest, sides, and leg. His body was found in a pool of blood in the "day room," the room just inside the front door; prisoners passed through the day room of each dorm to enter the sleeping quarters, where their bunks were lined up in rows. There was a clear, identifiable bloody finger-print on the door that didn't match me, Herman, Gilbert Montegut, or Chester Jackson. The fingerprint didn't match any of the investiga-tors or the inmates who carried Miller's body out of the dorm. When the state police officer responsible for testing the print was asked if he compared the fingerprint with the fingerprints of other prisoners who lived on the walk, he said, "No, I did not." There was no blood on any of the beds or in the room where the beds were located. The other guard assigned to the Pine dormitories that day, Paul Hunter, testified that when he came back from the dining hall after breakfast he entered Pine 1 and found Miller's body lying on the day room floor. According to investigators, Miller "appeared to have fallen against a table in the day room and onto the floor."

A prisoner named Hezekiah Brown was the state's star witness against us. In his sixties and missing teeth, Brown looked like a harm-less old man on the stand but he was serving his third or fourth term at Angola for aggravated rape. He was heavily involved in the sex trade at Angola, and a snitch known for always currying favor. He shined the guards' shoes in the lieutenant's office and prison lore said Brown was a courier for the drug dealers on the walk. The drugs would supposedly be put in his shoeshine box while he was in the control center and he'd bring them back to his dorm to be picked up. He made coffee for the freemen. Everybody in prison knew you couldn't believe a word he said. (Decades later, former *Angolite* editor Billy Sinclair wrote about Brown to one of my lawyers: "I was on death row with Hezekiah Brown; in fact, on the same tier with him. He was, and remained up till the day he died, a ruthless, pathological liar. He was a petty snitch on death row who repeatedly fed free people false and fabricated information about other condemned inmates just to receive extra coffee and food. He bartered information for personal gain.")

Brown lived in the Pine 1 dormitory and testified that he saw the murder. He said he was alone in the dorm when Brent Miller entered for a cup of coffee and sat on Brown's bed, which was at the end of the row, closest to the entrance to the day room. Brown testified that he was leaning down to plug in the coffeemaker when I walked into the dorm with Herman Wallace, Gilbert Montegut, and Chester Jackson. All of us had handkerchiefs over our faces, he said. All of us were carrying weapons. He said I grabbed Miller from behind and "jugged" him in the back with a knife and the others began stabbing him, then we dragged him off the bed to the day room, where we continued to stab him. Afterward, he said, I "ran out" of the dorm followed by Herman, Jackson, and Montegut, leaving Brown alone with Brent Miller's body, and the door slammed behind us. "When I heard the door slam," he testified, "I knowed they was gone, well I—I don't know what made me move but I moved and went [to] the door." He said when he opened the door of the dorm the wind "made me come to my senses" and he realized he had his pajamas on. When asked how far he got before he realized he was wearing his pajamas and turned back, he testified, "Oh I didn't get—I didn't get out from under the—I didn't get out of the door good, you know, and then I come back in."

Brown testified that when he turned away from the door to go back inside and change out of his pajamas and passed by Miller, "he was laying there, that's when the last breath went out of his body." Brown testified he changed into pants and a shirt, walked past Miller's body again, and left the dorm. Outside he made a right, he said, to go to the blood plasma unit (located behind the clothing room just inside the snitcher gate), "straight as a bee martin to his hole." When asked who else was on the walk after Brent Miller was killed, he said he didn't see anyone on the walk. When asked the color of the handkerchief around my face, Brown testified, "It could have been red, it could have been blue." He settled on blue.

On cross-examination, Brown admitted that when he was first questioned by officials he gave them a different story. He first told investigators he was at the blood plasma unit the entire time. A "few days later," he conceded on the stand, he was awakened at midnight and brought to a room with Deputy Sheriff Bill Daniel, Warden C. Murray Henderson, and "the administration." There, authorities told Brown they "knew" he was in Pine 1 during Brent Miller's murder, he said, and "they told me everything that happened." That's when he gave a new statement to officials, telling officials that I killed Brent Miller with Chester Jackson and Herman Wallace. He did not mention Gilbert Montegut in the statement he gave that night but added Montegut to a third statement he gave authorities later. Brown testified that nobody promised him anything in exchange for his testimony.

Joseph Richey, the prisoner I had prevented from raping a young prisoner in RC, also testified against me. He said he was standing in his dorm, Pine 4, which was across from Pine 1, when he saw Brent Miller walk into Pine 1. The next thing he saw, he said, was Leonard "Specs" Turner run out of the dorm, followed by me, Herman, Chester Jackson, and Gilbert Montegut, contradicting "eyewitness" Brown who never mentioned Leonard Turner. Richey testified that our faces were not covered, contradicting Brown again. Asked if I ran left or right when I exited he said he didn't know, but that on my way out the door I ran into a wagon used to pick up trash that was sitting on the walk. Richey said that when Hezekiah Brown followed us out of Pine 1, he was wearing blue pajamas and "moving as fast as possible on his [bad] leg" down the walk toward the dining room before he stopped, turned around, and went back into the dorm, again contradicting Brown, who said he didn't leave the dorm in his pajamas but turned around in the doorway to change after opening the door, when the wind "made [him] come to [his] senses." Richey went on to testify that after Brown returned to his dorm, Richey was still watching the dorm when he saw Brown emerge after he'd changed his clothes. He said he himself then walked into Pine 1 and, when he saw the body of a fallen security officer with multiple stab wounds, he didn't turn around and run away but walked up to Brent Miller's body and stood there "for a minute and a half," then left the dorm and walked to the side of Pine 1, lit a cigarette, and "waited" for security to find Miller's body.

A prisoner named Carl Joseph "Paul" Fobb, who worked in the scullery with me and was almost completely blind in 1972, also contradicted Brown (and Richey). He testified that he was "on the side" of Pine 2 dorm when, "about 8:05 a.m.," (16 minutes after the coroner said Miller died), he saw me go into Pine 1, alone, and about "five, ten minutes" later I came out of Pine 1, alone, with a rag in my hand which I threw into the Pine 4 dorm, across the walk from Pine 1, where Joseph Richey, according to Richey's testimony, would have been standing. (Paul Fobb testified he didn't see Richey that morning. Richey testified he didn't see Paul Fobb.) No "rag" that I had supposedly thrown was ever introduced as evidence at my trial. Fobb said he didn't see Herman, Chester Jackson, or Gilbert Montegut and he didn't see Hezekiah Brown. He said that I was the only person he saw leaving the Pine 1 dorm after Miller was killed and that he was "stunned" to see me, an odd choice of words since at that time he wouldn't have known a freeman had just been killed. He testified I was wearing a blue prison shirt and a white T-shirt underneath it. He also testified there was no blood on me when I left Pine 1.

Fobb, who acknowledged he was completely blind in one eye from cataracts, conceded on the stand that he was "injured" in his other eye. On the stand, he attempted to describe two rambling statements he had given nine months after the murder on the reason I supposedly killed Miller. (He gave the statements nine months after being moved from a dorm to a harsh cellblock.) He testified he witnessed "two or three" altercations between me and Brent Miller and that he saw Miller "carry me out" of Pine 4 because I wasn't allowed to be there. He said he overheard me tell an unnamed "fall partner," that "I have fifty years," and that I was "going to fix that little bitch," referring to Miller. He testified it was my idea to create a kitchen workers' strike as a diversion for the freemen in order to pull guards away from the walk that day so that I could kill Brent Miller. "Well, this was the plot," he testified, "for to get the free mens from off of the walk, for to give him a chance to do what he have to do and bring them back to prowl." This testimony echoed the "theory" that Warden Henderson gave reporters the day after Miller's killing, nine months before Henderson got Fobb's statement.

Sitting at the defense table everybody looked like a liar to me, but Paul Fobb stood out as the most surreal liar. Everybody knew that man couldn't see. One of my witnesses would testify to that, about how Fobb was always running into things. (Years later my attorneys had an expert review Fobb's eye surgeries before 1972 as well as his medical records and she said his eyesight was so bad at the time of Miller's killing he couldn't have identified a person who was 30 or 40 feet away.) He could not have identified me running out of the Pine 1 dorm, much less tell whether or not I was wearing a white T-shirt under the button-down prison shirt he said I was wearing. By saying that I, alone, was the only one who ran out of Pine 1 that day he contradicted the state's star witness, Hezekiah Brown, and also Joseph Richey. Fobb said I didn't have blood on me after I supposedly just stabbed a man 32 times by myself. The kitchen workers' strike didn't "pull guards" from the walk. Standard prison protocol posted one guard from each unit in the dining hall during meals and one on the walk, directing traffic or sitting in the guard booth.

Paul Fobb's testimony to the contrary, I had no beef with Brent Miller. I knew who he was from walking past him and I knew of the Miller family, but I never had a conversation with him. Prisoners weren't supposed to enter each other's dorms but they sometimes went in and out for short periods of time. Some freemen weren't bothered by it; some were. I never got a write-up (disciplinary report) for going into a dorm. (If the freemen were following protocol the doors to the dorms would be locked at all times when prisoners weren't coming and going for work or meals, but they usually didn't lock the doors.) Brent Miller never talked to me. I never talked to him. He never threw me out of a dorm. He never wrote up a disciplinary report on me.

Most illogical of all, to me, was Fobb's testimony that I was somehow constantly talking about a "plot" to kill a guard loud enough for him to hear it. How was it that he happened to hear all these conversations I supposedly had with my so-called "fall partner"? If I wanted to hurt or kill a freeman I wouldn't have talked about it loud enough to be heard over the banging pots and running water in the scullery. I wouldn't have talked about it after a shift sitting among white and black prisoners I didn't know or trust. I wouldn't have talked about it anywhere near Paul Fobb.

Also, I wanted to ask the jury, even if I did have the power to orchestrate a kitchen workers' strike when I wasn't even there, how would I know in advance that the guards who would supposedly be "pulled from the walk" wouldn't include Brent Miller? Guards did not hang out in prisoner dorms. How would I have known that Brent Miller was in Pine 1? Indeed, later, prison officials and the state of Louisiana used the fact that Miller was in the dormitory that morning as a reason to deny his wife benefits and compensation for his murder.

It wasn't shocking to me that Fobb lied. What bothered me was the idea that the jury would take him seriously. I had a similar thought about Hezekiah Brown. Nobody in prison would be stupid enough to attack and kill a security guard in front of one of the biggest snitches in Angola and leave him alive.

Once I had hope. Then I saw how the contradictions of the state's witnesses didn't seem to matter to the jury. I saw how everyone who participated in the trial—prosecutors, lawyers, judge, guards—all seemed to know each other beyond a professional role. Based upon their conversations and interactions it was easy to see the personal friendships between some of them. When the jury was in the room they went through the motions of a trial. When the jury was out of the room they laughed and talked together in various parts of the courtroom. Some of them ate lunch together. I wondered if they were all working together to convict me.

None of the other guards on the walk that morning, at the snitcher gate, or directing traffic or in their booths were called to testify that they saw me, Herman, Chester Jackson, or Gilbert Montegut on the walk. None of them were called to corroborate that they saw any of the state's witnesses who claimed to be there.

On the day Brent Miller was killed I was wearing what I wore most days, blue jeans, a gray sweatshirt, and rubber boots that I needed for my work in the scullery. At my trial Bill Daniel, who was deputy sheriff in St. Francisville at the time, testified that he took a green army jacket, blue pants, and brown lace-up shoes from me, which were entered as evidence.

All the state's witnesses had me wearing something different. Hezekiah Brown, who first said he didn't really remember what I was wearing, testified I was wearing "penitentiary clothes," which meant blue shirt and blue pants. Brown was the only witness who said I had a handkerchief or scarf around my face. Joseph Richey testified I was wearing a "state-issue blue button-up shirt and state-issue dungarees" and "no jacket" and "definitely nothing" covering my face. Paul Fobb, who was legally blind, somehow "saw" that I was wearing a white T-shirt underneath a button-down state-issue blue shirt, and "state jeans." He said that I had no handkerchief covering my face entering or leaving Pine 1. He, alone, testified that I was wearing a hat over my Afro.

The spot of blood on the green jacket the deputy said I was wearing that day was so small it couldn't be typed. There was a stain of blood on the blue pants and one on the brown shoes; both stains were so small the crime lab couldn't determine if the blood came from a human or an animal.

A handmade knife with several layers of tape as a handle was entered as the murder weapon. The guard who found the knife under Pine 1 said it was covered in blood when he found it. A crime lab forensics expert testified that when the lab received the knife there were fewer than three drops of blood on it, not enough to type the blood. There was no evidence linking it to Brent Miller's murder. I find it strange that there was never enough blood on any of the items introduced into evidence to tell if it was human or animal blood, or determine if it was my blood or Brent Miller's blood or the blood of any of the other men charged.

A clear, identifiable bloody fingerprint was found on the entrance door to the Pine 1 dormitory. The state also recovered four simultaneous fingerprints from the same hand and two partial palm prints. None of those prints matched me, Herman, Chester Jackson, or Gilbert Montegut. The print also didn't match the prisoners who removed Miller's body or prints of the investigators. It was never tested against all the prisoners who lived on the walk, even though the prison had their fingerprints on file.

The three men who testified against me—Brown, Richey, and Fobb—were moved to better living quarters. Richey and Fobb were moved out of Angola to the more comfortable jail at the state police barracks. Richey was even given weekend furloughs and had so much freedom over the years that he went on to rob three banks while he was in prison, crimes for which he was convicted. Fobb was given a medical furlough, normally reserved for prisoners who have less than six months to live, and spent years outside prison. He was charged with several crimes during this time, including domestic abuse. Brown was moved to the most comfortable quarters at Angola, known as the "dog pen," where the prison's chase dogs were housed and trained. In 1986, his life sentence was commuted and he was released.

I had three witnesses testify on my behalf. It took a lot of courage for these men to come forward because they were immediately moved to harsher, more restrictive housing after they gave their statements. One of them was put in the dungeon. The first witness for my defense was Colonel Nyati Bolt, who lived in my dorm, Hickory 4, and testified that he walked with me and another inmate named Everett Jackson to the dining hall when the whistle first blew at seven a.m. He waited with us in line during the kitchen workers' strike and returned to Hickory 4 with us when we were told to go back to our dorms. We stayed in the dorm for about 20 minutes or so, he said, until around 7:35 a.m., when the whistle blew again and we walked back to the dining hall and ate together. After breakfast, he testified, he left me and Everett Jackson standing on the walk talking, sometime after eight a.m., and he went back through the snitcher gate to the boiler room, where he worked.

Under questioning from the prosecutor, Everett Jackson testified he'd only known me about three weeks. We lived in the same dorm but hadn't talked until I questioned him about my writ. "Woodfox and I talked about the possibility of my filing a writ for him this same morning, so this is the reason we were together that morning," he said.

He repeated everything Bolt said, adding that after Bolt left us on the walk after breakfast I walked with him to the control center, directly across from the dining hall, where he went inside to the legal aid office for legal papers to give me. It took "eight or ten minutes," Jackson said.

When he came down from the legal aid office he handed me the papers and he went back up to work in the inmate legal aid office.

Prosecutor John Sinquefield asked Everett Jackson about the period of time between the first and second call-out for breakfast that morning.

Sinquefield: You turned back to the dormitory; Mr. Woodfox was with you all of this time?

Jackson: Yes, he was. He was with me all this time.

Sinquefield: You all didn't stop off over at Pine one, did you?

Jackson: Negative.

Sinquefield: You didn't stop over there and hit a pig or nothing like that.

Jackson: What's a pig huh?

Sinquefield: Did you?

Jackson: What's a pig?

Sinquefield: I think it's street talk, it's generally referred to as a policeman, a security officer or something of that nature; is that correct?

Jackson: No we didn't stop anytime and didn't hit a pig.

Sinquefield: But you know what a "pig" is.

Jackson: I don't know what your definition of a pig is; I know what mine is.

Sinquefield: What's your definition of one?

Jackson: It's a little animal that has four feet.

The judge interrupted Sinquefield's line of questioning, saying not to use the term "pig" in his courtroom. When Sinquefield continued he asked Everett Jackson if I killed Brent Miller.

Jackson: No. Negative.

Sinquefield: He didn't leave your presence at any time?

Jackson: No he didn't.

Sinquefield: You didn't see him with no knives or nothing like that?

Jackson: No.

Sinquefield: You didn't see no blood on his clothes?

Jackson: Negative.

Sinquefield: He didn't say nothing about killing nobody or stabbing nobody over there in Pine one?

Jackson: No, not to me, he didn't.

Sinquefield: And you didn't see him do nothing?

Jackson: No.

Sinquefield: Didn't hear nobody hollering over there and begging for help?

Jackson: No.

Sinquefield: —or nothing like that in Pine one?

Jackson: No, no.

Sinquefield: Do you think you would have heard it if it went on?

Jackson: I most certainly would have. So would three thousand others approximately.

* * *

Sinquefield: He didn't sneak off at no time?

Jackson: He couldn't possibly have.

Sinquefield: He didn't go over there and commit no murder in Pine one there while you wasn't looking, huh?

Jackson: He didn't do it.

Everett Jackson was asked why he was no longer working on my case. "He's in one part of the prison and I'm in another," he said. "I can't see him or hear from him, so consequently I can't file it."

On cross-examination, he stated he was moved to a cellblock from the dorm after giving the statement that he was with me the morning of Brent Miller's murder.

Herbert "Fess" Williams, who lived in Pine 4, also testified for my defense. He said he was there, on the walk, between 7:45 and 8 a.m. and did not see me on the walk that morning and didn't see any of the state's so-called witnesses who said they were there. Herbert Williams's job was picking up trash in the four Pine dormitories and he patrolled up and down the walk with his trash wagon looking for garbage. On the morning of Brent Miller's murder, Williams testified, he didn't leave Pine 4 on the first call-out for breakfast. When the whistle blew for the second call-out, around 7:35 or 7:40, he testified, he left his dorm and walked toward the dining hall, looking for his trash wagon, which he said wasn't where he normally parked it, in the grass next to Pine 4. He said the wagon wasn't on the walk, in front of the Pine 1 dorm (contradicting Joseph Richey, who said I bumped into the trash wagon when I ran out of Pine 1), and it wasn't anywhere else he could see so he started walking toward the dining hall looking for it because sometimes crippled prisoners used it to get to the dining hall. On his way to the dining hall, he testified, he ran into Hezekiah Brown coming toward him, holding a plastic bag that contained sugar. He said he knew it was sugar because, "I was trying to get it from him." He said Brown was wearing "some kind of pajama top."

Williams testified that after he gave a statement to authorities that I wasn't at the scene of Miller's murder he was put in the dungeon and then "interrogated" four more times. In the dungeon, where he was in a single cell with four or five other men and no bed, he had his teeth knocked out when another prisoner "accidentally" elbowed him. Then he was put in a cellblock where he was locked down 23 hours a day. When my lawyer, Charles Garretson, asked him on the stand about his experience being "questioned" by prison officials, Williams corrected him and said that he was "interrogated" five times. He repeated several times that he didn't see me on the walk that morning, and he didn't see Herman or Chester Jackson or Gilbert Montegut. After the second time he was interrogated, "they locked me up," he said.

"Where did they lock you up?" Garretson asked.

"They locked me up in solitary confinement."

"For how long?"

"I been there ever since. I'm there now."

"You're in solitary confinement?"

"Yes, sir."

Prosecutors Picou and Sinquefield objected and tried to get Williams to say he wasn't put in solitary confinement. Williams testified that he was initially put in the dungeon for two or three weeks, then in the cellblock, which, to him, was no different from the dungeon—or "solitary confinement"—except in the cellblock he had a bed.

Picou then, out of the blue, asked Williams, "Do you know who I am?" reminding Williams that he was district attorney for West Feliciana Parish, which "covered Angola prison." He then asked Williams again if he was on the walk that morning. Yes, Williams said.

"And you were right there in the area?" Picou asked.

"I was right there in the area."

"You did not go to breakfast."

"I did not go to breakfast."

"Everybody went to breakfast except for maybe one or two or three people; is that true?"

"I don't know about the one or two; I didn't go."

"But you were there."

"I was right there in the vicinity."

"Who else—who else was there?"

"Had a white boy in that area."

"What's his name?"

"I don't even know his name. He don't even live there. He live up—he live in the quarters up above us."

The district attorney changed the subject. The white prisoner, who may or may not have been on the walk the morning Brent Miller was killed, was never mentioned again.

A prisoner named Larry Robinson testified he saw Hezekiah Brown at the blood plasma unit at 7:45 in the morning, the exact same time Brown testified that he was witnessing Brent Miller's murder. When asked how he knew it was 7:45 in the morning Robinson replied he had checked his watch because he was trying to get out of fieldwork that morning and he was supposed to be at the sally port at 7:45. Another witness for me, Clarence Sullivan, who worked in the scullery, testified that Paul Fobb couldn't see more than a few feet in front of him and was always bumping into things.

* * *

At the end of my trial the jurors were told by the judge to "hold the State to its burden of proof" and that "if the evidence did not establish beyond a reasonable doubt" that I was guilty of killing Brent Miller, the jury had to return a verdict of not guilty. As I sat there and looked at the jury, there was no doubt in my mind that they would come back with a guilty verdict. They deliberated less than an hour. The verdict was guilty. I would be sentenced to life in prison. I remember thinking they would not break me. I wouldn't let them break me, no matter what.

After my trial, I was held at the courthouse until dark. They loaded me into a prison van and two deputies sat on either side of me in the backseat with shotguns on their laps. Two armed sheriffs sat in the front. None of them said anything to me about where we were going but I could tell we were not driving toward Angola. We were headed out into the woods. I wondered if they were looking for a place to kill me. After some time, they pulled up in front of the West Feliciana Parish jail. The two in front got out and in a little while came back to the car. Nothing was said to me directly. After that they drove me to Angola. I don't know if they had an official reason to take me there or if they were just trying to scare the shit out of me.

"Baby, you all right?" my mom asked me on her first visit after I was convicted.

I was back at Angola. We were in the visiting room of CCR. I lied to her through the screen between us.

"Yeah, Mama, it's OK. I'm going to be all right," I told her.

I didn't let any worries show on my face or in my actions.

"I'm going to get a new trial," I said.

I didn't believe I would get a new trial but I didn't want to visit my pain and suffering upon my mom or my family. When my family visited I always went to great lengths to put my best face forward.

Back in my cell, I did the same. I'd been framed for murder, persecuted at my trial, and wrongfully convicted. But I didn't feel like a sacrificial lamb. I felt like a member of the Black Panther Party. If anything, I had become more of a revolutionary than I was before. In September of that year, 1973, I wrote to a friend:

I view Amerikkka . . . and her lies, capitalism, imperialism, racism, exploitation, oppression, and murder of the poor and oppressed people as being highly extreme. It is my opinion that anyone who views these situations as anything other than extreme is a petty bourgeois or a capitalistic fool!! History has taught us that revolution is a violent thing, but a highly necessary occurrence of life. Revolution is bloodshed, deaths, sacrifices, hardships, nothing can and will change that. The passing out of pamphlets is only a method of avoiding the unavoidable. It is the job of the revolutionary forces in this country to manufacture revolution instead of trying to avoid it.

Chapter 21

Herman's Trial, 1974

After my conviction in 1973, Herman wrote to the NAACP Legal Defense and Educational Fund (NAACP LDF) about the fact that we were indicted by a grand jury that excluded women and blacks. A lawyer from the NAACP LDF named Norbert Simmons came to see him and agreed he had a claim. He agreed to represent Herman on this issue and filed a motion to quash his indictment. Judge Edward Engolio, of the 18th Judicial District Court, granted the motion, which meant that everyone indicted by that particular grand jury—26 people in all—were no longer indicted. At first, lawyers for the state appealed the ruling. Then the state withdrew its appeal and reindicted everyone who had been indicted by that particular grand jury (except for me; since I had already been convicted I wasn't on their radar). There was another problem with the way the new grand jurors who reindicted Herman, Chester Jackson, and Gilbert Montegut were selected, but that wouldn't come to light until years later. Meanwhile, the motion I had filed the year before on the same issue had still not been disposed of; but I was still too new to the law to understand that all motions were legally required to be ruled on before trial.

Herman, Jackson, and Montegut were tried together in East Baton Rouge. Charles Garretson, who represented me, was their attorney. On the second day of their trial Garretson, Herman, and Montegut were seated at the defense table after a lunch break when Chester Jackson entered behind the prosecutor and sat at the prosecutor's table. He had turned state's evidence, which, we found out later, was his plan all along. According to state officials, he had given authorities a statement implicating me and Herman in Miller's murder two days after Miller was killed. We had no idea. Garretson also had no idea, and he had less than half an hour to compose himself before he had to question the man he had previously been defending. The knowledge that they had broken Jackson and got him to agree to testify against Herman and Montegut shook Garretson to his core. (Later, he would say, "[I] was in a complete state of shock. . . . It took everything I could glean together to maintain professionalism and sanity and intelligence to go forward after this lunch break.")

Jackson testified that he and I had walked toward the dining hall for breakfast alone that morning and we had stopped before we got there "to wait" for Herman. "After [we had spent] about 10 minutes" standing on the walk, he said, Herman arrived and asked me if I had "the weapons." Prosecutor Ralph Roy, who was questioning Jackson, asked him, Didn't he mean "the weapon," singular? Jackson changed his answer, saying Herman asked about "the weapon." He went on to say the three of us turned around and went back down the walk, stepping off the walk between two Oak dorms while Herman "scouted for a free-man to kill." When Herman returned, Jackson said, he told us there was "a man" sitting on a bed in Pine 1. He said when we entered the dorm we all placed handkerchiefs over our faces and that Brent Miller was on the bed, facing the "front of the building" (the opposite from what Hezekiah Brown had said), talking to Hezekiah Brown.

Jackson said he didn't enter the dorm right away but stayed back in the day room, which he called "the lobby," as Herman and I entered. Jackson said he was "hiding" from Hezekiah Brown because, he said, Brown was his "friend." Jackson described the wall he stood behind as "solid concrete," which, he testified, he "can't see through," and yet from that vantage point proceeded to say that he watched me pass by Miller after entering the dorm to get behind Miller and grab him in a "mug-ger's hold" and stab him in the front of his body. (Brown said I stabbed Miller in the back.) Jackson testified that after Miller was stabbed, he stood and tried to walk out the door but Herman pushed him back into the sleeping quarters. At that point, Jackson said, "everybody" started stabbing Miller, which was when Jackson said he entered from the day room. Jackson said when he came up to us stabbing Miller I handed him a knife and, on my orders, he stabbed Miller. Jackson testified that while we were stabbing the guard, Leonard "Specs" Turner, who had been in the back of the dorm, walked by us, exiting the building. Next, Jackson said, Hezekiah Brown walked out the front door of the building while Jackson was stabbing the guard, all of this contradicting Brown and Richey and Fobb. Jackson estimated the struggle with Miller lasted "10 or 11 minutes."

He testified that when he left the building, "that's when all the people from the other dormitories came in Pine 1 and I just went and changed clothes." Jackson stated that when he, Herman, and I left Pine 1, I ran "down the side" of Pine 1, and he and Herman walked over to Pine 3, diagonal to Pine 1, where he took off his bloody clothes and put them in a trash can in the corner of the dormitory. (Bloody clothes were never found in any trash cans in any dorm after Miller's killing, or if they were, they were never presented as evidence.) Jackson said Herman found some fresh clothes "behind a bed" and changed out of his bloody clothes. When asked what Herman did with his bloody clothes Jackson replied, "He left them there," then, "I can't say exactly what he did with them." When the prosecutor prompted him with, "He left with them?" Jackson changed his answer, "He left with them," he said, "out the door, you know, towards the door. . . . He had them in a bundle."

Not only did Jackson's testimony contradict Hezekiah Brown's testimony in every way, but he contradicted the statement he gave authorities two days after Miller was killed. In that statement (which we didn't obtain until years later), Jackson said he was going down the walk when he saw me and Herman standing in the yard near the Pine dorms. He said I was wearing a brown hat, "like a hunting cap," over my Afro. He said he walked up to me and Herman and after Herman walked away I told Jackson I was going to "kill a pig." Then Herman returned and said there was a "chump" sitting in Pine 1. Jackson said he walked away toward the dining hall. A few minutes later, he said, he heard screaming and circled back down to the walk to Pine 1. In the 1972 statement, Jackson went on to say he looked through a window and saw me and Herman stabbing Brent Miller. And then he said he *entered* the dormitory where Miller was being attacked and Herman pushed him to the side as he and I left the building. Jackson said he then followed us out the door. In this version, he didn't stab Miller. He didn't mention Gilbert Montegut in either account.

Under cross-examination, Jackson testified that he was interrogated four times between Miller's killing on April 17 and the evening of April 19, when he finally gave the statement in which he said he watched through the window as Herman and I stabbed Brent Miller. During his first interrogation, he told authorities he didn't know anything. The next day, he said, he was "picked up" and "put in the hole." He testified he was questioned by Warden Henderson, Captain Hilton Butler, and Deputy Sheriff Daniel. When asked if he'd been beaten he replied, "I got hit. . . . They had a tough meeting when they first locked me up." Inadvertently he indicated that he may have been so badly "hit" that he'd needed a doctor. He testified that on April 19 he told his lawyer to "go to the hospital, try to get me a doctor. . . . I told you how the people harassing me." When asked, on cross-examination, if authorities held a weapon to his head during his interrogation, which is what Jackson told Herman and Gilbert Montegut in the months leading up to the trial, Jackson testified that he "never seriously" told them that.

Jackson didn't mention Montegut once and the state prosecutors didn't ask about him, even though their star witness, Hezekiah Brown, placed Montegut at the scene, stabbing Miller. When Garretson questioned Jackson, he asked if Montegut had stabbed Brent Miller. Jackson replied, "Well, I can't say definite. I can't give you no definite answer on that." Jackson testified that Montegut was not present with us on the walk and "not during the struggle." He denied the DA agreed to reduce his charges to manslaughter in exchange for testimony, and, he testified, when prosecutors placed him and Hezekiah Brown in a room together the day before Herman's trial (which Garretson discovered the first day of their trial), they "never discussed nothing" about their testimony or what had happened the day of Miller's killing.

When Hezekiah Brown took the stand, he repeated the well-rehearsed testimony that he gave at my trial—I came up behind Miller and pulled him against me, stabbing him in the back; I ran out of the dorm with Herman, Jackson, *and Gilbert Montegut*, and Leonard Turner wasn't there—all contradicting what Jackson said. Anything that diverged from his tale, he didn't seem to "remember." When Garretson asked if my body or Herman's or Montegut's touched Miller's body while we were stabbing him, Brown said he didn't know. When asked if there was a lot of blood he said he didn't know because he "wasn't paying attention to no blood." (There was no blood on Brown's bed, where Brown said Miller was seated while he was being stabbed, and the blanket and sheet weren't ruffled.) In trying to determine the time of death, Garretson asked Brown if the sun was up when he walked out of the dorm. Brown replied he didn't know.

Brown unwittingly gave a small detail supporting our contention that we were framed that hadn't come up at my trial. He had testified at my trial that when he was questioned by authorities during his second interrogation "they told me what happened." At Herman's trial Brown let slip that the night he was pulled from his bed at midnight and brought to a room to be interrogated a second time, "select" prisoner "files"—presumably mine, Herman's, and Jackson's—were already on the table when he walked in and they were given to him. At Herman's trial Brown also implied that he added Gilbert Montegut to his statement later under duress. "I knowd if I said no, I didn't know nothing about it then ... I'm going to get punished behind it," he testified. "I'm going to get throwed in one of them cells, and I ... stayed in one of them cells on Death Row ... I couldn't stand that no more."

Another witness for the state, a prisoner named Howard Baker, contradicted Chester Jackson *and* Hezekiah Brown. Baker testified he was walking by Pine 1 when he saw Herman come out the door of Pine 1 "with blood on his sweatshirt and down the front of his pants" and "enough to become, you know, readily visible if you would look at it," and that upon exiting Pine 1 he saw Herman turn *right* toward the dining hall. Baker also testified he did not see me, Chester Jackson, or Gilbert Montegut, but he did see an inmate named Pedro follow Herman out of the dorm, "two or three seconds" after Herman, "around 7:55 or 8 a.m." Baker also testified he didn't see Hezekiah Brown, Leonard

Turner, Paul Fobb, or Joseph Richey that morning. He only saw Herman and Pedro. Nobody had ever mentioned Pedro in any statement or testimony before this.

Baker went on to state that after Herman—still covered in blood—turned right exiting from Pine 1, he walked past the clothing room and through the snitcher gate, which was manned by a security officer, and then past the dining hall to another security gate, which was manned by a different security officer, to get to the tag plant, where he worked, with no questions asked. At the entrance to the tag plant he checked in with a guard, giving his ID number and housing assignment—a requirement for all prisoners. About "six minutes later," Baker testified, he entered the tag plant and Herman, still wearing his bloody clothes, asked him for a key to a box containing work clothes. Baker said he gave him the key and Herman changed into clean clothes and placed his bloody clothes "on top of the box." Then, Baker said, Pedro entered the tag plant in his bloody clothes and talked to Herman. He said Herman then picked up his bloody clothes and carried them to a furnace in the front of the plant and burned them.

Baker didn't come forward with this story until after he'd been living in the brutal conditions of cellblock B for several months. Prison records our attorneys obtained years later showed that after he gave his statement against Herman, Howard Baker was moved to a dorm at Camp A, where he served as "clerk of security." After that he was moved to the dog pen, the same highly prized, low-security area that housed Hezekiah Brown. On the witness stand Baker said he came forward to tell his story months after Miller was killed "because of my conscience." Years later he would recant his testimony, saying he didn't think anyone would believe his statement against Herman because there was no furnace in the tag plant; there was no place to burn clothes in the tag plant and "everybody knew it."

When Joseph Richey took the stand, he repeated that he saw Leonard Turner come out of Pine 1, followed by me, Gilbert Montegut, Chester Jackson, and Herman. Only this time instead of saying I bumped into the trash wagon (which was not on the walk, according to Herbert "Fess" Williams, who testified at my trial) Richey testified that as we left the dorm the door "hit the garbage buggy" and the door was stuck open so Richey could see into the dorm, and he saw a body lying on the floor inside Pine 1. He said after Hezekiah Brown left the dorm, Richey entered it and walked up to Brent Miller's body and then left, waiting outside for the body to be discovered.

Herman had five alibi witnesses. One of them, Gerald Bryant, worked in the kitchen and testified he not only saw Herman in the dining hall at 7:30 or 7:45 that morning but also gave Herman some books. Another inmate, Clarence Jones, who testified he served Herman a breakfast tray that morning while working in the dining hall, said he saw Bryant give books to Herman. There were witnesses who testified they walked with Herman directly to the tag plant from the dining hall. Garretson showed the judge and jury the roster from the tag plant, proving Herman had signed in for work before eight a.m. on April 17. Prisoner Henry Cage testified that when he arrived at his job in the tag plant, around eight a.m., Herman was already there, working.

As for Gilbert Montegut, several witnesses, including a captain, testified they saw him in the hospital, nowhere near Pine 1, before and after breakfast the morning Miller was murdered. Captain Wyman Beck's testimony saved Montegut. Assigned to the hospital that day, he testified he saw Montegut there around the time Miller's body was discovered. Beck also testified that prison officials had called him that morning and told him to send Montegut back down the walk. A prison worker testified that he saw Montegut in the hospital between 7:30 and 8 a.m. and corroborated the captain's testimony that a warden telephoned the hospital that morning asking for Montegut to be sent to the walk. No explanation was given as to why Montegut was summoned.

The same forensics information that came up at my trial was conveyed to the jury. In summary: no clothing, no weapon, no physical evidence whatsoever linked any of us to the murder of Brent Miller. There was a clear, identifiable bloody fingerprint that didn't match me, Herman, Montegut, or Jackson.

Back in CCR, Robert King and I were following Herman's trial in the newspapers. When I read that Chester Jackson turned state's evidence against Herman I felt disgusted by his betrayal. I thought back to the first meeting the four of us had with our lawyer, nearly two years before. I remembered thinking there was something wrong with the way Jackson acted. He wasn't animated; he sat back in his chair. At the time, I wondered if it was nerves, or if he'd been broken. Now I knew. He lied on me and Herman, knowing we were innocent, to save his own ass. He also lied to all of us and our lawyer for two years. The all-white jury didn't deliberate long. Herman was found guilty of the murder of Brent Miller. Gilbert Montegut was found not guilty. In exchange for his testimony, Chester Jackson took advantage of the plea deal offered and pleaded guilty to manslaughter.

Herman was sentenced to life in prison and sent back to CCR, but not to my tier. By now we understood they would never put us on the same tier in CCR again. That year, and for decades, they tried to come between me and Herman. They tried to break our connection. What they didn't realize was that with every action they took against us, the stronger we became; the more united it made us. After being railroaded and lied about, after our unjust trials and wrongful convictions, we knew we were in this for life. That knowledge gave us a new determination, a new strength, and a new sense of dedication to our cause. There was a very strong loyalty and devotion between us. We had an expression we got from the TV show *Star Trek* to describe our bond: "Separated but never apart, never touching but always connected." That line became ours. Thirty years later I would still sign my letters to him "Never Apart." They could put us wherever they wanted, and they did, but they could never come between us. By the end of his trial we'd grown so much together in such a short time, as Panthers, as comrades, and as men. I sent Herman a note, asking him if he needed anything. He wrote back no, he was fine.

Years later we found out that less than a month after Herman's January conviction, on February 15, 1974, Warden C. Murray Henderson started writing letters to secure an immediate release for Hezekiah Brown.

Chapter 22

King Is Set Up

Between my trial and Herman's trial Robert King was wrongly convicted for the murder of a prisoner on his tier. He was set up for the same reason Herman and I were set up: to punish him for being militant, aggressive, outspoken, and resistant—and to give authorities a reason to keep us locked up. King was a leader, a Panther, an agitator. To prison authorities that meant he was a "troublemaker." He was the prisoner on his tier who talked back to freemen when they spoke to prisoners disrespectfully. He was the one who refused to go into his cell if he was protesting conditions. He didn't stop talking when ordered to "shut up." He didn't lower his voice when he was told he was being "too loud." He fought back when he was attacked by security. He spoke to the other prisoners about fighting back against inhumane conditions. His courage, determination, and strength influenced other prisoners.

The murder took place on the tier, when they were still allowing prisoners out on our hour at the same time. Two prisoners on King's tier, August Kelly and Grady Brewer, got into a fight. Both prisoners were armed. During the fight Brewer stabbed Kelly and killed him. There was no doubt that Brewer, alone, stabbed Kelly and that he did it in self-defense. A dozen witnesses saw what happened. There was a guard at the end of the tier who immediately came and saw Brewer with the weapon. Brewer was covered in blood. Brewer told authorities he stabbed Kelly in self-defense. In spite of that they charged every prisoner on the tier with murder. They did it to coerce someone to talk, and it worked; they found a prisoner who would testify against King.

King and Brewer were charged with the murder of August Kelly and would be tried together. The prisoner who testified against King (and who would later recant, saying he was in the shower when Kelly was killed) was moved out of CCR and given trustee status.

Before King and Brewer's trial in the summer of 1973, their state-appointed lawyer met with them only once. Grady Brewer was worried one meeting wasn't sufficient for the lawyer to prepare an adequate defense for him and King. He expressed his fears to the judge, in open court, repeatedly. The judge told him to stop talking. Brewer kept talking, asking the judge for a new lawyer. The judge finally told him if he talked one more time he would be gagged. Brewer spoke out again and he was bound and gagged. So was King, who hadn't said a word. Their hands were cuffed behind their backs. Duct tape was put across their mouths. They were forced to sit like this throughout their trial. Due to the lying inmate's testimony that had been coerced by authorities, King was found guilty along with Brewer. They were sentenced to life in prison. King and Brewer were sent back to CCR and, for a while, King was put on my tier.

In 1974, under the direction of Elayn Hunt, the first female director of the Louisiana Department of Public Safety and Corrections—and based on the bill written by Rep. Dorothy Mae Taylor—Angola finally banned the use of inmate guards and integrated the prison. The inmate guards were moved to an isolated camp away from the rest of the prison for their own protection and stayed there until they were released or died. When they integrated CCR they took the white inmates from their tier and put them on different formerly all-black tiers. They selected two white men to live on D tier, where I was. One of them, a white supremacist and member of the Ku Klux Klan, refused to be put on a tier with black prisoners, saying he'd rather go to the dungeon, and that's where they put him. They replaced him with another white prisoner. One of the white prisoners, named Pelts, was put next to me.

There was no problem whatsoever integrating D tier. I talked to both of the men about how we ran the tier collectively, as a group. I told them about the rules of conduct we established. I said it doesn't matter if you're white or black, we just want everyone to follow the rules and be respectful to one another. Pelts and I became friends. He didn't have any family who visited and had no money. I always remembered him when I ordered from the commissary and if he needed something I got it for him. He loved ice cream. One day I received a new radio from my brother-in-law and I gave Pelts my old radio. He told me nobody had ever done anything so kind for him before.

The next day we were standing at the bars talking and he thanked me again. I said, "No problem, man, I'm glad you can enjoy it." We both turned back into our cells and the next thing I heard was the prisoner on the other side of Pelts, a man we called Shelby, hollering down the tier, "Get the freeman, get the freeman." I grabbed my mirror and went to the bars. I could hear a gasping, strangled breathing and angled my mirror so I could see into Pelts's cell. He was on his hands and knees between the toilet and the bunk, struggling to breathe. His face was bright red. There was a huge vein as wide as a finger popping out from his neck. He appeared to be frozen but kept trying to raise his head. He raised his eyes and met mine in the mirror. "Hold on, man," I told him. "Help is coming, Pelts, they're coming. Hold on." In his eyes, I felt he was saying, *If I can just raise my head, I'll be OK*. I never saw a human being struggle so hard to do something and not be able to do it. He collapsed onto the floor and died from a massive heart attack. It's the first time somebody I had a friendship with died. It shook me up. I put the pain of it in the back of my mind to a place where it didn't affect me. It was all I could do.

At some point between 1974 and 1975 a warden was summoned by a protest on King's tier and on his way out he looked around and said to the sergeant, "Where the hell are the televisions? Get some goddam televisions in here!" Television was the one thing we never fought for. They installed the TVs on the walls across from the cells on every tier in CCR; one for every five cells at first. (Later there was a TV for every three cells.) On weekdays, the TVs went on at six a.m. and went off at midnight; on weekends or holidays they stayed on all night.

After we got the TVs, they stopped letting us all out of our cells on the same hour. For a while they allowed three prisoners out on the same hour, but three prisoners could still be too powerful when they refused to return to their cells or resisted other orders, so they changed the rule and only one of us was allowed out at a time. From then on, we were each let out of our cells on a different hour, staggered throughout the day. The TVs caused a lot of disunity on the tier; prisoners started liking different programs and then fought over which programs to watch.

In 1974 the Louisiana Supreme Court reversed King's conviction on the grounds that his trial judge had "abused his discretion" by allowing King and Brewer to be bound and gagged during the trial. King was retried in 1975. At his second trial he wasn't gagged, but he was bound at the defense table and forced to wear a prison jumpsuit. At the trial, Grady Brewer testified that he alone killed August Kelly, in self-defense, and the state's previous "witness" against King refused to testify against him at all. In spite of that, King was convicted a second time. He was sentenced to natural life and returned to CCR.

Chapter 23

Gary Tyler

Around that time, between 1974 and 1975, after our constant protests, CCR prisoners were given yard. Some CCR prisoners hadn't been outside in decades. They built six long rectangular pens out of chainlink fence topped with barbed wire. The pens extended out from one gated entrance. From the sky it looked like a hand with six fingers. We got yard for one hour—in place of our hour on the tier—three times a week, weather permitting. It was a huge relief to be outside. Some days when I hit the yard I ran laps and didn't stop the whole hour.

The recreation department put a weight pile at one end of each yard and gave us small plastic footballs out there to play catch with. We threw the ball to one another over the fences, but when the balls got caught in the barbed wire they easily tore and became useless. Herman came up with the idea to make a ball out of old socks. He put rags in a sock and folded it a certain way and put it in another sock and that launched the sock ball phenomenon. Everybody started making sock balls; we called them "big thumpers." Soon we were all running behind them when we were out on the yard. I could throw one over three pens. We always threw them to the opposite part of the pen from where the prisoner was standing so he'd have to chase after it. If you missed a catch or dropped the ball you had to do 20 push-ups or bench presses. For the most part, the freemen didn't bother us on the yard. We were loud, trash-talking each other, playing catch. Sometimes in the summer I went out there, unbuttoned the top of my jumpsuit, rolled up my pants legs, and lay down on the grass for the whole hour.

One time in winter when I got out to the yard it was freezing cold and the grass was covered in a light layer of frost. The freeman made some comment to me like, "Too bad you're going to miss yard today." I didn't like his condescending tone so I bent down and took off my shoes and ran laps in the frost with no shoes on. Many of us did this. We did it to give the impression that we were unbreakable, that we were determined, that there was no backing down within us, that the value of our struggle was more important than our own safety, our own comfort, our own lives, and our own freedom. Eventually they laid a concrete walk on each yard so we could go out even if the yard flooded with rain. It was great to feel the space of outside and breathe the fresh air. But none of that relieved the pressure of knowing we were going back into the cell.

On October 7, 1975, Herman, King, and I heard on the radio that a 17-year-old black student named Gary Tyler had been convicted of shooting and killing a white 13-year-old boy. He was sentenced to death and would be the youngest prisoner in America on death row. They were bringing him to Angola. We heard through the prison grapevine that when Gary arrived at Angola some of the freeman were going to put him in the hole with a "rape artist"—a prisoner who "specialized" in raping young prisoners. We weren't going to let that happen.

The day they brought Gary to Angola all three of us checked into the dungeon. The CCR dungeon wasn't as crowded as the main prison dungeon, usually no more than two or three to a cell. They put Gary in the cell next to us with two other guys. I don't remember all that was said but we made it known to those men that Gary was under our protection. One of the prisoners checked out that night. We introduced ourselves to Gary and told him who we were: members of the Black Panther Party. He could contact us, and whatever he needed we were there for him. I think we spent two or three days down there with him. We told him he now lived in a world of violent struggle, one we called "armed struggle," because that's what it was. They had blackjacks, bats, and gas guns. We tried to prepare him to survive. We told him he had to arm himself with knowledge and stay focused on what's going on in society and not the bullshit that happens inside prison. He told us his story, how he was framed for killing a white boy.

Gary was one of dozens of black children put on buses and sent to white schools in Louisiana to integrate them in 1974. One day more than 100 white students and adults at Gary's school, Destrehan High School, stopped the bus carrying the black students, throwing bottles and rocks and yelling racial slurs. During the riot a white 13-year-old student in the crowd, Timothy Weber, was shot and killed. The driver said the shot had come from outside the bus. The bus and students were thoroughly searched and no gun was found. The black students were brought to the police station and interrogated. Gary was charged with disturbing the peace when he resisted being bullied at the precinct, and then he was charged with murder. He was badly beaten. Later, a gun was "found" in the seat where Gary Tyler had been sitting. Years later that gun was identified by officers of the parish sheriff's department as having come from a firing range frequented by police. Eventually, the witnesses who testified against Gary recanted, saying they gave false statements because they were threatened and intimidated by police.

With grace and strength, Gary endured the unimaginable torture of being sentenced to death and locked up on death row for a crime he didn't commit, at age 17. When his sentence was changed to "life without parole," he endured more than seven years of solitary confinement at CCR, then he spent more than 30 years in the prisoner population at Angola as a mentor, leader, and teacher. In 2012, the U.S. Supreme Court ruled that a sentence of life without parole for juvenile offenders was unconstitutional, and four years later the Court ruled that the decision could be applied retroactively. Tyler was released from prison in April 2016. I'm continually inspired by Gary Tyler. Upon release, he immediately started working to help people in his community.

Chapter 24

Food Slots

One of the most degrading practices at CCR was being served our meals on the floor. There were no slots in our cell doors that a tray would fit through, so the orderlies put our food trays on the floor outside our cells and we had to slide them under our cell doors. Sometime in the midseventies it got to us. The tier was dirtier than usual. It hadn't been cleaned in a week. King was in the cell next to me. He and I started talking back and forth. "Man, I can't believe this shit. They're sliding the food across the dirt to us like we're dogs."

"They're treating us like we're animals in the zoo."

"I'm not a goddamn animal, I'm a man."

"This is degrading and dehumanizing."

"When are we going to demand to be treated like men?"

We reached out to Herman and he said, Let's go. We filed a petition of grievance with the warden complaining about being fed off the floor like animals. We asked that food slots be cut into our cell doors so that we could be fed like human beings. We asked him to get back to us within two weeks. We spent the following days talking to the other prisoners on our tiers, building a consensus. We never heard back from the warden and decided to go on a hunger strike. We circulated a letter to all the CCR tiers asking prisoners for their support. Everyone on all the tiers signed on to participate.

They still delivered our meals. Three times a day. When they put the trays on the floor outside our cells we left them there. We only drank water from the sinks in our cells. After a week or so of not eating I didn't have a lot of energy to do anything. After two weeks, I stopped going out on the yard. We sat on the floor by the bars and talked a lot. It sounds crazy but we talked about food. We described our favorite dishes in detail to one another, meals our mothers made, our women made, our favorite foods. Someone would say, "Man, nobody can fry a pork chop like my mom, with meat falling off the bone" or "My mom made the best red beans in the world." We talked about what would be the first meal we ate when we got out of prison. Occasionally an orderly came to our cells to tell on a guy down the tier who took a bite of food off his tray. We overlooked that. We didn't want to call anyone out and then have men turn on one another. It's very difficult to resist food sitting in front of you when you're starving. Even harder because the quality of the food was mysteriously improved during those weeks. They served fried chicken, sausage, and fried fish—not the normal meals. At least once a day one of the ranking officers would come onto the tier, saying something like, "You ready to eat now? You gonna eat?" Some prisoners would just say no, some would mouth off and say, "Man, what's it look like? Why you asking me stupid shit like that? No I ain't going to eat." Then the officer would say something like, "Man, I'm just doing my job," and leave.

After a few weeks, two of the tiers on CCR started eating again. D tier, where King and I were, and A tier, where Herman was, stayed on the hunger strike. It was extremely painful, sometimes excruciating. When the body doesn't get nourishment, it starts to feed on itself, at least that's what it felt like. After about 40 days King, Herman, and I wrote back and forth asking one another how long we were going to do this. Everybody's cheekbones and collarbones were jutting out from weight loss.

Just when we were discussing other strategies to get the prison to cut food slots, the administration sent a prisoner from A tier to talk to me and King. He said security officials wanted to know what it would take to call off the hunger strike. We told him we wanted slots cut in the doors. King added that while we waited for the slots to be cut, we wanted to be able to hold our trays through the bars while eating, rather than drag our food under the filthy cell doors. The next day, camp supervisors came onto the tier and announced that they were going to cut the food slots and that we could stand and eat through the bars if we wanted to. We agreed, having no idea that we would eat standing at our bars for the next year and a half. Our hunger strike lasted 45 days. The first meal served after we went off the hunger strike was breakfast. We stood at our cell doors as they were passing out the trays and I was about to reach my hand through the bars for my tray until I saw it was oatmeal. I hated oatmeal. After waiting for so long I could go a couple of hours more for lunch.

At first, we held our trays through the bars with one hand and fed ourselves with the other hand, then King had the idea to make slings from strips of T-shirt or other fabric that we could hang from our bars and rest our trays on while we ate. Someone put cardboard in his sling to make a little shelf and then we all did that. Some guys elaborately decorated their cardboard. It took us weeks to get our strength back. Over 18 months prison officials cut slots in the bars in almost every cellblock in the prison before they got to CCR. They hoped to break us during that time so we would give in and eat food passed under the cell door off the floor again. They didn't succeed. When they started cutting slots at CCR they cut all the slots on A, B, and C tiers before they got to D tier, where King and I were housed. When they finally got to our tier they cut all the slots in the cell doors except for four. They said they ran out of materials. Those of us on D tier—even the prisoners who had slots cut—continued to eat standing. Weeks later we threatened another hunger strike if they didn't finish cutting the slots on our tier. Later that day we saw the truck bringing in welding equipment out the window. They finished the job. Prison officials had hoped to break the unity on our tier that had held us together for 18 months. They couldn't.

A year later King was sent to a punishment program called Camp J for resisting strip searches. At Camp J they were still pushing trays under the cell doors at mealtimes. King had to start all over again, educating the other prisoners about their rights. He refused to touch food from a tray that had been on the floor. Prison officials wouldn't let him hang a sling on his door and eat at his bars at Camp J. So he talked to the orderlies who brought the food individually, and most allowed him to take the tray from them with his outstretched hand through the bars, and with his other hand he removed the paper plates of food, folding them to bring them through his bars into his cell. He ate like that for two years. They cut the food slots at Camp J after King was moved back to CCR.

In 1977 prison authorities finally released the "stipulation and consent decree," signed by state and federal officials, outlining the changes that would be made to decentralize state prisons, reduce overcrowding, and improve conditions at Angola. The federal government would govern Louisiana state prisons for decades to come.

A new warden, Ross Maggio, was appointed and he was credited with breaking up much of the power held by the families who had worked at Angola for generations. Violence was still prevalent in the main prison and out-camps, but over time it became less bloody, once the prison started using metal detectors to search prisoners. Guards used these on the men before they entered the dorms, and on the grounds, turning up knives and other weapons hidden there. In the following years—for decades—Angola would continually be in court for violating the consent decree, not following through on improvements or policies the state had agreed to. Twenty years after the judge's ruling, the prison was still under federal control because the administration never completely fulfilled its obligations to meet the goals and standards in the agreement. Not until 1998, when Republicans passed a law in Congress that allowed any elected official to file in federal court to dissolve a consent decree if "most" of the conditions of the consent decree had been met, did Angola get out from under the Hayes Williams consent decree. When the consent decree was newly released we requested a copy of it. We didn't know at the time that we were deliberately given an edited version that had CCR privileges redacted.

Chapter 25

My Greatest Achievement

After years in prison and solitary confinement, I'd experienced all the emotions the Louisiana Department of Public Safety and Corrections wanted from me—anger, bitterness, the thirst to see someone suffer the way I was suffering, the revenge factor, all that. But I also became something they didn't want or expect—self-educated. I could lose myself in a book. Reading was a bright spot for me. Reading was my salvation. Libraries and universities and schools from all over Louisiana donated books to Angola and for once, the willful ignorance of the prison administration paid off for us, because there were a lot of radical books in the prison library: Books we wouldn't have been allowed to get through the mail. Books we never could have afforded to buy. Books we had never heard of. Herman, King, and I first gravitated to books and authors that dealt with politics and race—George Jackson, Frantz Fanon, Malcolm X, Marcus Garvey, Steve Biko, Eldridge Cleaver's *Soul on Ice*, J. A. Rogers's *From "Superman" to Man*. We read anything we could find on slavery, communism, socialism, Marxism, anti-imperialism, the African independence movements, and independence movements from around the world. I would check off these books on the library order form and never expect to get them until they came. Leaning against my wall in the cell, sitting on the floor, on my bed, or at my table, I read.

The inmate librarians took care of these books. Years later I dropped a lawsuit because one of the prisoners who worked in the library asked me to. I was suing the prison for censoring a book about COINTELPRO they wouldn't let me get through the mail. The prisoner librarian came to the tier to talk to me. He said he was worried that if the lawsuit went through the administration would do an inventory of the prison library and we'd lose a lot of books. He told me he'd make sure I got a copy of the book I wanted, and he did.

As I started to read more I began to learn about world and American history: the 1791 slave rebellion in Haiti led by Toussaint Louverture, the coal miners' strikes and labor and union movements across the United States, President Andrew Jackson's massacre of Native Americans while they were being removed from their ancestral lands. I did a lot of soul-searching while reading. The words of the Vietnamese revolutionary communist leader Ho Chi Minh resonated with me when I read that he told the invading French army something like, "We are willing to die ten to one, are you?" That got me at my core, that willingness to sacrifice.

When I read George Jackson's *Soledad Brother*, I saw how even though he was fucked around by the system he never used that as an excuse not to step up. I was on D tier when I read that book in my cell. "The nature of life," he wrote, "struggle, permanent revolution; that is the situation we were born into. There are other peoples on this earth. In denying their existence and turning inward in our misery and accepting any form of racism we are taking on the characteristic of our enemy. We are resigning ourselves to defeat. . . . History sweeps on, we must not let it escape our influence *this time*!!!!"

Malcolm X taught me how to think of the big picture, to connect the dots.

I requested biographies and autobiographies of women and men even if I didn't agree with their politics or principles. Studying them helped me develop my own values and my own code of conduct. King was also a big reader; we read a lot of the same books and discussed them. He also loved fiction and literature and read Shakespeare, Charles Dickens, and all J. R. R. Tolkien's books many times over. We both read everything written by Louis L'Amour. I loved philosophy, geography, economics, biology, and other sciences. I could always find something valuable in whatever I read. I even appreciated books by religious writers like Mother Teresa, though I was not religious. She wrote that to be real, a sacrifice must hurt, and empty us. I could relate to that. She wrote that more than our own weaknesses, we must believe in love.

My proudest achievement in all my years in solitary was teaching a man how to read. His name was Charles. We called him Goldy because his mouth was full of gold teeth. He was a few cells down from me on D tier. I could tell he couldn't read but was trying to hide it. I knew the signs because my mom did the same things to hide the fact she couldn't read. One day I told him about my mom, about her accomplishments. I told him she couldn't read or write and asked him if he could. "It's nothing to be embarrassed about," I said. He told me he never learned to read because he didn't go to school. "When I was coming up we didn't have nothing," he said. "We had to go and get it."

"If you want to learn," I told him, "I can teach you, but it won't work unless you really want to learn." He told me he wanted to learn. We used a dictionary. I stood in front of his cell on my hour out and he came to my cell on his hour and we would go through how to read words using the sound key at the bottom of every page. The upside-down e, I told him, sounds like "eh," and I went through all those symbols and sounds with him on each word. In between our two hours a day I told him to call me if he needed help. "Anytime you can't get a word, holler, Goldy, no matter what time. Day or night if you have a question, just ask me." In the following months he took me up on that.

"Fox!" he'd yell, at all hours of the night.

"What?" I answered.

"I can't say this one," he yelled.

"Spell it out," I called back to him.

He called out the letters.

"Look at the key at the bottom of the page," I yelled back. "What do you think it is?" And we went back and forth like that until he got it. Sometime later I'd hear, "Hey, Fox!"

"Yeah, Goldy. What?" I'd say.

"What's this one?" he'd say.

The first time I heard Goldy read a sentence out of a book I told him how proud I was of all he'd learned. He thanked me and I told him to thank himself. "Ninety-nine percent of your success was because you really wanted to read," I said. Within a year he was reading at a high school level.

The world was now open to him.

Chapter 26

Strip Search Battle

By September 1977 I'd learned enough about chattel slavery to see a connection between the unnecessary strip searches for CCR prisoners and how African American men and women were treated as slaves. Forced to strip down on the auction block before they were bought and sold, black men and women had their bodies, mouths, and genitals inspected for disease as if they were livestock. It's one of the most humiliating experiences a human being can endure. We were strip-searched every time we left the tier, before and after, even though we were in full restraints wherever we went and we were always in the presence of one or two guards who were watching our every move. The strip search always entailed a visual cavity search. After removing our clothes, we had to open our mouths, raise our scrotum, lift our feet to show the bottoms, turn around, bend over, and spread our buttocks. Prisoners in CCR are among the most isolated and restricted men at Angola. The chances of a fully clothed man being able to hide contraband in his anus while handcuffed in the front to his waist were zero. Under these circumstances strip searches were merely another unnecessary cruelty.

In addition, the strip search at Angola always happened with several security people present. Some of the freemen made derogatory, crude, and humiliating remarks during strip searches, commenting about your anus and the size and shape of your genitalia. It was a punishment I could not endure anymore. King and Herman felt the same way. We held meetings with the prisoners on our tiers. The men lined up at their bars and we asked them if they would stand with us to stop the dehumanizing strip searches that we were forced to go through on a daily basis. We wrote up a petition, asking prison officials to change the strip search policy because the current system was degrading and served no legitimate security purpose. We also asked that when strip searches did have to be conducted, they be done in a more humane way. Herman got all the prisoners on A tier to sign it. King and I got everyone on our tier to sign. Sympathetic orderlies passed the petition to other tiers. Almost everyone in CCR signed the petition. We asked the warden to get back to us in within two weeks' time.

While we waited for a response King and I did some legal research and found cases where courts had ruled strip searches were unconstitutional, although they were allowed in prisons under some circumstances: after the prisoner had a contact visit with attorneys or family members, for example, or when he returned to prison after leaving prison grounds. The warden never got back to us. We exchanged phone numbers of our families with one another so we could call them if anyone was taken off the tier. Because now it would get physical.

Date of Disciplinary Report: 9/24/77
Albert Woodfox #72148
During routine strip search procedure, inmate Albert Woodfox refused to bend over and spread his buttocks. Lieutenant Horace Isaac and myself ordered inmate Woodfox to bend over and spread his buttocks and he refused to do so. Inmate Woodfox had to be physically restrained over a desk with his buttocks spread open by Lieutenant Horace Isaac. Inmate Woodfox charged into Lieutenant Horace Isaac as if to do Lieutenant Isaac physical harm. In the CCR isolation hallway inmate Woodfox punched Officer John R. Christen in the mouth, busting his lips, and loosening Officer Christen's two front teeth. Officer Christen was relieved and treated in the Feliciana Hospital. Inmate Albert Woodfox punched Officer Harry Bereas in his left jaw. Inmate Woodfox kicked Officer Emus in his left leg. An incident report has been submitted concerning this incident.
Verdict: Guilty
Punishment: 10 days in isolation

Date of Disciplinary Report: 10/5/77
Albert Woodfox #72148
Prior to entering CCR isolation, this inmate was asked by Captain
Travis Jones if he would submit to a complete shakedown. Inmate's
exact reply was quote you're not looking up my ass, you ain't quote.
Woodfox was bent over the A.U. desk [clerk's desk] by the officers,
and his cheeks were searched for contraband. In the process of
bending this inmate over the desk, he resisted us and tried to escape
from the office. He also kicked my right shin with one of his feet
while we were searching him. The only force used was [what] was
needed to restrain inmate Woodfox.
Verdict: Guilty
Punishment: 10 days in isolation

We didn't ask anyone on the tier to physically resist the strip searches.
I told the prisoners they had to make their own decision about whether
they would allow themselves to be humiliated and degraded. Those who
resisted paid a price. All of the prisoners who resisted the strip searches
were badly beaten. Some prisoners had to be taken to the hospital.
When freemen came to take King off our tier he resisted. I was afraid for
his life and immediately protested but I felt totally helpless: all I could
do was shake the bars on my cell and scream at the security people to
stop attacking him. We were all yelling and shaking our bars, cursing
at the security guards, telling them to leave him alone. They came back
and gassed the whole tier. They entered King's cell and jumped him,
beating him severely, and put him in the dungeon. Afterward, they
took him before the disciplinary board, where he was sentenced to the
Camp J punishment program. It was the harshest, most punitive camp
in Angola, a three-level "program" that had just opened. A prisoner
had to survive three levels of harsh deprivation without a disciplinary
report for six months before being allowed back in his normal housing.

They put me and Herman in the CCR dungeon. I was sentenced to
Camp J at least five different times by the disciplinary board court, but
somebody blocked the transfer every time. We heard it was because one
of the Miller brothers worked at Camp J at that time. I actually wanted

to go to Camp J, because King was there and didn't have support. He was still resisting strip searches over there, while Herman and I were resisting in CCR.

At first, they gave me 30 days in the dungeon. Each time a prisoner is put into the dungeon he is strip-searched first. So I was beaten on the tier for refusing to be strip-searched before leaving the tier, and then I was beaten when I refused to be strip-searched before they put me in the dungeon. At that time, because of the consent decree, prison officials were required to let prisoners out of the dungeon every 10 days for a 24-hour "break." After the 24 hours the prisoners were put back into the dungeon to complete their time or do the next 10 days. A lot of prisoners waived their right to the 24-hour break because they just wanted to get through their time without delay and didn't want the hassle of being moved. When I tried to waive the 24-hour break they wouldn't let me. It gave them a chance to add to my time in the dungeon because they knew I'd resist the strip search upon reentering the dungeon. It also gave them a chance to beat me for resisting the strip searches.

The dungeon had changed from when I was there in the sixties. Inmates got three meals a day. There wasn't much food in the Styrofoam containers, and there was no dessert or salt and pepper, but it was better than two slices of bread. Now we got one mattress in the cell at all times, so it was easier to trade off using it among prisoners. They were now required by law to let us have our legal material. Because I was in CCR, and not the main prison, there were fewer prisoners in the building, so there were fewer men in each cell.

In every other way, the dungeon was the same, designed to torture prisoners, to mentally break them. They turned off the water in the sink for days at a time, so I was forced to drink water from the toilet. This was one of the most humiliating acts I ever endured while in solitary confinement. It taught me how strong my desire to survive was. I got so I could sit in one spot in the cell and feel the physical limitations of it yet know that my mind and emotions were unlimited. I knew I was unlimited.

After not hearing back about our petition to the warden to stop the unnecessary strip searches, I wrote to an organization called New Orleans Legal Assistance (NOLA) asking for help in filing a lawsuit.

Goldy agreed to be one of the plaintiffs in the suit with me, even though it meant he would face repercussions from the prison administration and security. NOLA filed the lawsuit for us in the 19th Judicial District Court.

We went to trial and in six months the ruling came down. We won. The judge didn't stop strip searches completely, but he put limits on when the guards could conduct strip searches and conditions on how visual cavity searches could be carried out. The judge also ruled that any time I had remaining in the dungeon as a result of our strip search protests, around 300 days, had to be removed from my record.

Unfortunately, the judge's ruling didn't wipe out King's time at Camp J. He was kept at Camp J from September 1977 to November 1979. In July 1979, he filed a lawsuit, handwritten in the sweltering heat of his Camp J cell, citing the cruel and unusual treatment of being locked down 23 hours a day for seven years, how the poor lighting in his Camp J cell damaged his eyesight, and how the lack of exercise contributed to high blood pressure and physical deterioration. He wrote that 23-hour lockdown "violates his civil and human rights and is in direct contradiction to the laws of the United States which safeguard all its inhabitants from Cruel and Unusual punishment."

From CCR Herman also filed a habeas corpus writ in West Feliciana that same year, challenging the legality of our long-term confinement in CCR. Big John helped him file it. Both King's and Herman's cases were dismissed. Our battles with freemen continued through the seventies. They looked for reasons to put us in the hole. I made a screwdriver by sharpening the end of a piece of my radio antenna so I could open the back of my radio when I needed to. Every prisoner did this. They wrote me up saying it was a "trigger" for a zip gun. Another time a freeman was shaking down my cell and I saw him take something out of his pocket. I asked him, "What you taking out of your pocket?" He turned around and told me, "None of your fucking business." Later, they came to my cell and told me I was going to the dungeon because they found gunpowder in my toothpaste. I got a write-up for that as well.

At CCR they put a sign outside the doors to A and D tiers that read PANTHER TIER: DANGER. In the late seventies, a young prisoner named

Kenny Whitmore was brought to D tier and when he saw that sign, he told me later, he didn't know what to expect. The first book I gave him was *Native Son*, by Richard Wright. Soon after I got on his case about something, telling him he could do anything he put his mind to, he complained, "Man, you're more like a professor than anything dangerous." Kenny was very interested in educating himself and became a good friend and comrade. He and I would end up living on the same tier for 20 years. In the eighties, we gave ourselves African names. Kenny took the name Zulu Heshima; Zulu means "heaven" in the Zulu language and Heshima means "honor" in Swahili. We called him Zulu. I took the names Shaka, after the great warrior and monarch of the Zulu Kingdom, Shaka Zulu; and Cinque, after Joseph Cinque, the slave who led the revolt against slave traders on the ship *Amistad*. For me, taking African names represented freedom, to be born again, to take back my African heritage. We called them "freedom names," representing our liberation. Since we'd only read Joseph Cinque's name and never heard it spoken aloud, we pronounced it "Cin-cue." King started calling me Q. I called King the name he selected for himself, Moja, which means "one" in Swahili. One King.

Sometimes at night I wrote in my cell. I don't consider myself a poet but when strong emotions ran through me I would sometimes put them in a poem. It was a way I could express what was inside me. In 1978, I wrote one of my first poems, called "I Wait."

> 6×8 cell, and I wait!
> I wait for revolution, and I wait
> For unity, and I wait for peace!
> I wait while people shoot up dope,
> And while people smoke down grass!
> Yes, I wait, am I a fool?
> I wait, I wait and I wait!
> People party down, and I wait!
> I wait while people do the boogy,
> Robot, bus stop, and hustle our lives away!
> I wait while people drag ass!

Education, agitation, organization,
I'm still waiting!
Justice! I'm waiting
and I wait, and wait, and wait!
Gates flying open, people running,
Jumping, screaming, laughing, and
I wait!
Can I be wrong to wait?
I even wait for answers that never
Come, foolish huh! But I wait!
I'm waiting for justice for those
Murdered, pigs killing our youth,
And I wait for it to stop!
People waiting for food stamps,
hunger stalks, waiting for medical
aid, bodies die! Decent homes cause
there's too many rats, roaches, and
snails, I'm still waiting!
I wait for truth in schools, I ask
for truth, and I'm told to *WAIT!*
I wait while youth dies from my body,
death stalks my soul, and I wait!
I wait while revolutions of liberations
sweep across the world, Amerikkka, I'm
Waiting!
I wait for black man and woman to discover
love, I wait for them to discover it, yes,
I wait! I wait for the embrace of family,
sound of father, brother, black men, and son,
and I still wait! Seconds turn to years, years
turn to centuries, and I wait!
WHY!

In 1979, Herman and I happened to be outside on the CCR yard at the same time. We were in pens next to one another, so we could stand at the chain-link fence between us and talk instead of calling out across the yard the way we normally did. We asked each other if we were doing the right thing. Was it worth it to go through all the suffering we'd experienced? Should we change anything? Did we have regrets? We both came to the conclusion that everything we'd been through was necessary. We knew that we were not locked up in a cell 23 hours a day because of what we did. We were there because of who we were. Sacrifice was required in order to achieve change. Neither of us had any regrets. We never talked about it again.

Around this time, Goldy was released from Angola. Months later we heard he died on the street using dope.

1980s

Nelson Mandela taught me that if you have a noble cause, you are able to carry the weight of the world on your shoulders. Malcolm X taught me that it doesn't matter where you start out; what matters is where you end up. George Jackson taught me that if you're not willing to die for what you believe in, you don't believe in anything.

Chapter 27

"I Got You"

Living in concrete you get used to noise. Sound bounces off the floors and walls and echoes. When someone on the tier cracked you'd hear him cry or scream. Some guys would moan for hours or days. Televisions were always on and the volume was high. You heard every voice yelling up and down the tier. Sixteen times a day someone's door would be opened, then, an hour later, closed. When guys argued you'd hear it. When someone's cell was shaken down you'd hear it. When prisoners stood in front of each other's cells and talked they had to yell to be heard; you'd hear every conversation. Every time a prisoner was taken off the tier you'd hear the restraints rattle as they were carried to the prisoner's cell by the guard. Then you'd hear the chain between the prisoner's feet as he walked out and when he returned. Prisoners on different tiers could talk to each other through the pipe chase and everybody heard those conversations all day. Security had listening devices in the pipe chase. I never held conversations in the pipe chase, for that reason; everybody could hear what you were saying.

Solitary confinement is used as a punishment for the specific purpose of breaking a prisoner. Nothing relieved the pressure of being locked in a cell 23 hours a day. In 1982, after 10 years, I still had to fight an unconscious urge to get up, open the door, and walk out. All of us in CCR were dealing with strong, powerful emotions all the time, maybe the strongest that exist: the fear of losing control over yourself, the fear of losing your mind. Every day is the same. The only thing that changes is whatever change you can construct on your own. The only way you can survive in these cells is by adapting to the painfulness. The pressure of the cell changed most men. Some got depressed and went into themselves, isolated themselves, never speaking, never leaving their cells. Others talked constantly, were confused, irrational. When I saw that a man was about to break I'd talk to him, try to help him through it. I could feel what he was going through, even though I wasn't going through it at that moment, because I'd experienced it myself. I made a strong effort to distract him. I occupied the headspace he was in so he wasn't alone. It didn't always work. I'd see men who'd lived for years with high moral principles and values suddenly become destructive, chaotic.

I had to fit everyone on the tier into my life. Dealing with 15 personalities 24 hours a day, my own and 14 others, was always draining and exhausting. Every time somebody new came on the tier I had to learn his personality, likes, dislikes, and what set him off. At first, the tier goes quiet for a while until the guys figure him out and see how he's going to act on the tier, whether he will blend in or make trouble. Some of these men were damaged people, with no sense of honor, no sense of decency, no moral values, no principles. Prison is a very violent place. There was always the threat of being attacked. There were prisoners who were paranoid, who stored urine and shit in their cells to use as weapons. There were prisoners who threw hot water or human waste on someone in another cell in anger or revenge. There were psychopaths who attacked others for no reason, they just felt the need to stir up trouble.

I knew everybody's experiences in society shaped who he was in prison. I reminded myself of that when men on my tier were hard to deal with. Being in solitary confinement constantly weighed on these men, too, and could make them worse. I tried to deal with each man as an individual, in the present moment. You learn there are layers to people. You look for the good. This can set you up for disappointment. Once I did some legal work for a prisoner that reduced his sentence to "time served." He was going to be released from prison because of the work I did for him. The day after he found out he came to the door of my cell and threw human waste at me. He was pissed off because I was watching the news and I wouldn't let him change the TV channel to a different program. You can't hold on to those experiences or you become bitter. Every day you start over. You look for the humanity in each individual.

I made my bed every morning. I cleaned the cell. I had my own cleanup rag I used to wipe down the walls. When they passed out a broom and mop I swept and mopped the floor of my cell. I worked out at least an hour every morning in my cell. On the days when I didn't have yard I ran up and down the tier almost the whole hour out of my cell. Exercise is important to keep depression away. I watched an hour or two of news through the bars of my cell and read at least two hours a day. I actively stayed away from negative conversation on the tier. Sometimes I lay across my bed and propped my feet on the wall. My head would hang over the edge; it was relaxing at the time.

The repetitiveness of every day could feel very painful. I used to call it "another day in Dodge." I tried to make the routine different. I might sit on my bunk to eat breakfast for months or maybe a year. Then I'd stand to eat breakfast for months. Then I'd sit at the table to eat breakfast. Deep down I always knew it was the same routine. I couldn't really trick myself into believing otherwise.

As much as we hated the routine, though, we needed it for mental stability. It gave us familiarity, a sense of confidence and the illusion of control over our surroundings. Eldridge Cleaver talked about "territorial imperative": when people know their surroundings, they know how to survive in their environment. To have the lights go on at the same time, to eat at the same time. It brought order to our lives. Once we were used to the structure of the day it was something we could count on. The smallest change could feel devastating.

Most changes happened when a new warden or colonel was put over the camp and he wanted to use his power, even when it wasn't necessary. The old saying that unchecked power corrupts is true. I have yet to see or experience a situation where ultimate power of one human over another is benevolent, except that of mothers and fathers over their children. But there is often cruelty there too. When there was a change imposed on us it upset everybody, guards too. Prisoners felt it most. It could be something as simple as breakfast being served late.

If breakfast is at 6:30, when you get up you expect the food cart to come onto the tier at that time. When it doesn't come, you get restless. After fifteen minutes it starts to wreak havoc on your emotions. You start pacing. You believe something is wrong in the camp or in the prison. You are reminded that you have no control over your life. You have to fight off the hopelessness. You have to fight off the anger that your tray hasn't come. A change in routine could destroy a man's logic. I've seen dudes start shaking down—shaking their bars—yelling and screaming for a breakfast tray when it didn't come on time. Nine times out of ten they were gassed and put in the dungeon. I trained myself to see change as an opportunity rather than a threat. I developed a mental toughness. I told myself that I could survive anything but death.

Some changes I didn't like but I understood them. They prohibited us from hanging pictures on our cell walls because paper was a fire haz-ard. If a prisoner squirted lighter fluid and threw a lit match against the wall the paper could go up in flames. Other rules had no safety or security reason for being, they were just a pain in the ass. One time a major over CCR implemented a new rule that we could only have one Styrofoam cup in our cell. A lot of men got written up for having more than one Styrofoam cup. Now, getting a write-up didn't mean shit for years because there was nothing they could take away from us that really mattered. When we started getting contact visits in 1987, though, freemen suddenly had the power to make men squirm. If you were found guilty of a disciplinary infraction you'd lose contact visits for six months.

Some guards looked the other way when a rule was broken as long as there were no security risks. If something was wrong in your cell they give you a chance to straighten it out. Other guards took great pleasure in threatening you with a write-up. They'd walk by your cell and point toward you and say, "I got you." Their intimidation didn't work for a lot of us. I didn't give a shit about being written up, even if it meant los-ing contact visits. If anybody came up to my cell and said, "I got you," I'd say, "Fuck you. Put that in the write-up." Down the tier, I'd hear other prisoners say things like, "Write your mama up along with me."

If we were lucky the freeman who threatened us was too lazy to do the paperwork or didn't know how to read or write that well. The next major or colonel who ran the camp would impose other rules. He might not give a shit about how many Styrofoam cups we had, but there would be something else.

Cooking in the cell was never officially allowed, but for years it was tolerated, especially if we gave some of the food we cooked to the freemen on duty. In those days, our families could send us a shipment of canned food once a year or we could buy canned food, salt, and seasoning at the canteen. We rolled toilet paper into tight rings to burn for cooking heat. For food we couldn't buy in the canteen, like meat or other necessities, we relied on the black market which, for us in CCR, was a network of prisoners who had what we called "word." If a man has word he won't steal from you. He won't lie to you. He will do what he says he's going to do.

Since Herman, King, and I had word anybody who helped us knew he'd get paid. There was a prisoner in the machine shop who made cooking pots and frying pans on the side by cutting down gallon-size butter bean cans and affixing handles to the pans with metal. He'd get the pan to a trustee or an orderly who worked at CCR and that man would bring it to the tier when he was there for his job. He'd put the pan in the shower. I'd get it from the shower when I was out on my hour and pay the trustee with some kind of barter item; it might be stamps, a pair of tennis shoes or pair of jeans, tobacco, legal work, or whatever I'd negotiated with the prisoner who made the pan. Sometimes the guy who brought the pan wanted a cut, sometimes not. A lot of prisoners helped us for nothing because they'd heard about us and respected us. We went through similar steps to get anything else we needed. We cooked meals in our cells, fried chicken or pork chops and heated up red beans, black-eyed peas, whatever they had in stock.

King was famous for the praline candy he made in his cell. He used a recipe from a prisoner cook he'd met years before named Cap Pistol. He started by using pats of butter, packages of sugar, and cartons of milk he saved from his tray. Once he caramelized it in a homemade pan over just the right fire, he poured it onto a manila envelope to cool and harden. Other prisoners started giving him their butter, milk, and sugar and, eventually, he'd get more butter and sugar on Angola's black market. King's candy heating over a flame could be smelled up and down the tier. Trustees brought him pecans grown on the grounds of Angola to put in it. King regularly made a batch of candy and had it delivered to prisoners on Death Row. Occasionally a security officer brought King a pound bag of sugar in exchange for some candy.

In the mideighties, a new warden banned cooking in the cells. We still did it; we just hid it better. I moved my lockbox to the middle of the cell to cook behind it. We had what we called "peepers" on our cell bars, pieces of a broken mirror stuck on with chewing gum so we could see at a glance who was coming down the tier. If a freeman was coming I killed the fire and pushed the food and cooking pan out of sight. King made his candy on the seat of his toilet so if the freeman came he could push the fire into the water. Eventually they banned glass mirrors from the tiers, so we had to buy metal mirrors from the prison store. They were OK for combing your hair or seeing the guy in the next cell, but when you held the metal to look down the tier you could only see a little way before the reflection was warped.

Every tier on CCR had one miniature chess set and one miniature checkers set that the prisoners shared. I got a chess set for my cell from a prisoner who left CCR. Eventually Herman, King, and I each had a set in our cells and two of us often had a game going. If King and I had a game we'd call out the moves down the tier. We could play a game with Herman by passing notes. I always thought Herman could be a chess master. He could play from memory. In the dungeon King made chess pieces out of toilet paper to play with whoever was in his cell. If Herman was missing any chess pieces in his cell he made pieces out of soap. At some point Herman came up with the ingenious idea to start chess tournaments in CCR. It gave the men something to feel positive about, something to do. We taught the men who wanted to learn chess and everybody looked forward to the tournaments.

Dominoes were popular on the tier too. When we were out on our hour we were sometimes allowed to sit on the floor in front of the cell of another prisoner and play dominoes or cards, depending on which tier sergeant was on duty. I sometimes played chess, dominoes, or checkers with the man in the next cell. The game would be laid out on the floor between us. Since there wasn't much freedom of movement, we'd use a pencil to push our piece into place as needed. We all came up with "outlaw rules" for dominoes to make games more challenging. Trash-talking was a big part of any game: trying to psych your opponent out, break his concentration. If a guy's game was garbage we told him he had to stand in the garbage can.

We weren't allowed to have calendars until the midnineties. If they found a calendar in one of our cells, even a homemade one, they tore it up and threw it away. I never knew why. I wondered if it was because they wanted us to lose track of time, another way to break us. I asked a major about it once and he said he didn't know, but maybe it was because we weren't allowed to have the pictures of the women in bathing suits attached to the calendars.

No calendars were needed to tell us when spring turned into summer. The heat of a Louisiana summer in a cell is almost unbearable. Years after leaving prison men who have endured a summer in a cellblock never forget it. There is no air circulation. No breeze ever. The small fans we were allowed to have in our cells didn't do any good. The mosquitos ate us alive. Until we got screens we burned socks to keep the mosquitos away. The smoke looked like a London fog hovering over the tier. We were all in our underwear. It was so hot it was difficult to write letters because sweat would fall from our foreheads and hands and the pen would skip on the damp paper or tear holes in it. Sometimes I slept on the floor, hoping it would be cooler than my bunk, even though mice would sometimes run across my feet or legs or insects would crawl on me. It wasn't cooler. Sometimes to try to block out the sun that was coming through the windows across from us we hung sheets on our bars, even though that was against the rules.

After several years of demands for ice, the administration finally put coolers containing ice at the front of the tier in the eighties. Orderlies filled them in the morning after breakfast and in the evening after the last meal. Everyone had some kind of cup or container to use for ice.

On my hour out of the cell, I filled containers with ice for guys if asked. I filled my own container with ice before going back to my cell and put it in my sink. When it melted I soaked a towel in the cold water and wiped myself down. Sometimes I put my entire sheet in the ice water and wrapped it around me. They put a large fan at the front of the tier and, after our continued complaints and protests, they put another fan at the back of the tier. Neither of them did anything but circulate the hot air and humidity and make a lot of noise. We were in pain and suffering from the heat and kept protesting. Eventually they placed five fans on racks attached to the wall across from the cells in the hall of each CCR tier but it never got cool in the summertime, just like it never got warm in the wintertime.

In the winter I could hear and smell the heaters come on in the morning, but it never got warm in our cells. Every prisoner was given one blanket. If you could pay an orderly to bring you a blanket you'd have two. On cold days, I put on two T-shirts, two sweatshirts, a pair of sweatpants over my jeans, two pairs of socks, and a hat and I wrapped my blanket around me like I was in a papoose. Then I crawled under my second blanket and waited for warmth. What surprises me in looking back on it is how much the human body can take.

My favorite time of day was two or three in the morning. Everybody was usually asleep. There was no one on the tier out on his hour. The TV volume was low. It was relatively peaceful and quiet. I could concentrate and focus. I liked to read during this time, or think. It was my time to deal with the pressure of being confined in a six-by-nine cell for 23 hours a day, to deal with my emotions and the thoughts deep inside me. I looked back on things that happened during the day and how I'd reacted. I might think about it and ask myself why I did this or why I did that. I almost always acted based on my gut instinct. Later, I found that usually my first instinct was right. I thought about what I saw on the news during that day. Watching the news, good or bad, helped keep me stimulated. I thought about conversations I'd had or other activities on the tier. Sometimes I reread certain passages from books I liked or

I wrote out imaginary budgets for day-to-day living. I'd give myself a job making $200 a week, for example, then create a ledger on a piece of paper, listing how much I could afford to pay for rent, gas, electricity, and food on that income. I often thought of myself in the free world: having dinner with my family, driving a car, going to the store, going on vacation. I fantasized about going to Yosemite National Park, which I'd seen in a National Geographic program on TV. It was a way to reinforce my belief that one day I would be free. I learned that dreams and fantasies are not bound by physical limitations, because there are no limitations of the mind or the imagination.

Everyone always asks me if we had windows in solitary confinement. There was always a window of some kind visible to us, usually in the wall across from our cells. In the seventies, our windows looked out over the Death Row yard. In the eighties, our windows looked out over the CCR yard. On my hour out, I used to stand at the window and yell down to Herman if he was on the yard, exercising. (Whenever Herman was on a tier that looked out over the yard he would yell down to me or King on the yard, if one of us was out there, when he was out on his hour.) Once I had a cell that looked out on a forest and I could see birds and skunks and various animals but eventually they bulldozed the trees to move the forest back for security reasons. Another time, for a brief while, I had a window in my cell. It didn't make me feel any less confined but I could open and close it myself. I kept my window open when it rained, for the freshness. Looking out of windows we could never see the sky directly above us; we could see only as far as the horizon. When we were moved to a new cell all we got was a different angle of the same view. We called it the never-ending view.

By the early eighties Herman, King, and I knew we were forgotten. The Black Panther Party no longer existed. (The organization is said to have officially ended operations in 1982.) We'd written many letters to organizations asking for help. I can't ever recall getting a letter in reply. I was disappointed. In some ways I felt betrayed. We were forgotten by the party, by political organizations, by people involved in the struggle.

I felt frustrated. We were dismissed or ignored by the numerous law-yers and legal aid organizations we wrote, asking them to look at our cases. To us it was obvious there was a grave miscarriage of justice in our situation. When we didn't get any replies to our letters, though, we knew we had no choice but to continue our struggle on our own. We became our own support committee. We became our own means of inspiration to one another.

Chapter 28

Sick Call

I never went to the hospital unless it was absolutely necessary. Medical treatment at Angola was—as it is at all prisons—deplorable. There are long delays, bad doctors, and a lot of misdiagnoses in prison hospitals. At Angola, aspirin was given for everything. To be put in restraints, then driven in a patrol car to the hospital, then have to sit for hours in a small individual pen the size of a mop closet that smelled like urine and vomit for two aspirin wasn't worth it to me. I could get aspirin out of the canteen. Also, in order to see a doctor, versus a nurse, you had to declare yourself an emergency. I never felt that any sickness or injury I had was an emergency. A lot of times for cuts and bruises I used an old remedy my grandmother taught me: my own saliva. It worked well to speed healing.

For years the only system available to us to ask for medical treatment was this: a nurse or an EMT would come to the tier between one a.m. and three a.m. and call down the tier, "Sick call," from the front gate, and anyone who wanted to see a doctor had to stand at attention at the bars of his cell door. They came in the middle of the night and not during the day because they didn't give a shit about prisoner health or medical treatment. Coming at night was a way they could cut down on prisoners asking for medical care by staff.

After announcing sick call, the nurse or EMT would then walk down the tier and ask the prisoners about their symptoms, sometimes giving out over-the-counter medications on the spot. A lot of times arguments would break out, the prisoner saying things like, "You aren't a doctor. I am in pain, I need to see a doctor." We all knew an EMT or a nurse wasn't qualified to do a proper examination through the bars of a cell.

Prisoners started filing lawsuits. The claim was "deliberate indifference" to serious medical needs, a violation of the 8th Amendment. A judge wouldn't take that claim seriously unless the prisoner could demonstrate three things: that failure to treat his condition would inflict further significant injury or unnecessary pain; that there was deliberate indifference on the part of the prison, meaning that the failure to respond to a prisoner's pain or medical need was purposeful; and that there was harm caused to the prisoner by that indifference. For prisoners at Angola that was no problem. After being flooded with lawsuits the federal courts got involved and came down on the Louisiana State Penitentiary. Angola was forced to come up with a process that would allow prisoners to see doctors.

At some point in the eighties we got a new system: sick call forms. These forms were handed out to prisoners who wanted to see a doctor. We checked off the symptoms we had from many listed on the form and there was a space where we could describe in our own words what the medical problem was. We folded the form and placed it between our bars and waited. The forms would be picked up and were, supposedly, read by a doctor who made an evaluation of which prisoners could come to the hospital and which were to be treated in their cells. If a prisoner was too sick to wait for all that, if he was throwing up, for example, or bleeding, he could declare himself an emergency and he'd be taken to the hospital, eventually.

A lot of prisoners who needed to see a doctor avoided the hospital because anyone who went—for any reason—could be written up for "malingering." A prisoner could have visible signs of illness—be bowled over in pain, flushed with fever, spitting up blood, or have a rash that didn't heal—and could still be accused of malingering. That happened to me in the summer of 1982. I got a rash around my waist that kept coming and going. I reported it on a sick call form and they brought me an ointment to put on the rash. Since it was summer, the heat, as usual, was unrelenting and the rash got worse. I used the ointment they gave me and wrapped toilet paper around me like a cummerbund. The rash flared up worse. When my skin started oozing pus I declared myself an emergency and after a couple of days I was taken to the hospital. They accused me of malingering, of doing something to cause the rash, because it kept coming and going. "How am I doing something that gives me a rash that goes completely around my waist?" I asked. I finally saw a doctor who scraped the scabs off me and gave me a prescription cream. Back in my cell I realized I might be having an allergic reaction to the elastic band inside my underwear. I put the medicated cream on the rash and wore my underwear inside out, rolling the elastic waistband down under my rash, and it finally cleared up. I got a write-up for going to the hospital.

If a prisoner had a life-or-death problem usually the whole tier had to take action. We'd shake the bars and holler until someone came. Once King was out on his hour and he noticed that our good friend and comrade Colonel Nyati Bolt, who had been ill for days, was lying under his bunk. The man had been to the hospital two or three times and been sent back to the tier with aspirin. Now he was under his bunk, he said, to "escape the pain from the light." His head hurt so badly that the light hurt him through his closed eyes. King, at the risk of being beaten, refused to go back into his cell at the end of his hour until medical personnel came to the tier and took Bolt to the hospital. We later found out that Bolt was having a stroke. King may have saved his life.

For very serious illnesses, like cancer, prisoners were treated and kept at the hospital but often preferred to come back to CCR between treatments. Solitary confinement prisoners aren't put in a regular ward in the hospital; they are locked in a room by themselves with only a bed, bench, toilet, and sink.

Years of cell confinement, lack of exercise, and low-quality food had taken their toll on my health. In my thirties, I was diagnosed with high blood pressure and put on medication. I was told to cut down on salt, a difficult task in prison when most food that can be purchased from the canteen—canned meat, chips, bottled hot peppers, instant soup—is filled with salt. I didn't worry about it. I didn't dwell on it. There was nothing I could do about it. For most health problems I self-medicated by running in the yard—sweating out colds and fevers, working out swollen knees and sore joints. I drank hot tea with a dab of Vicks VapoRub in it for sore throats.

If I had what I called a "sugar crash," during which I felt faint or overly exhausted just sitting in my cell, I'd eat some candy. In my forties, I was at the hospital having a checkup when the doctor looked up from my chart and asked me, "How long have you had diabetes?" I'd never been told I had diabetes. I was put on pills, which regulated my blood sugar. Years later my mom would be diagnosed with diabetes. In my sixties, when my lawyers got me to a non-prison-doctor for the first time in 40 years, I was diagnosed with hepatitis C. I didn't ever think about the sadness of it, or the pain of it, or the unfairness. My attitude about my health has always been: I'm alive, keep moving.

Chapter 29

The Shakedown and the Sham
of the Reclass Board

Shakedowns are always part of prison. When we first got to CCR in the seventies they shook down our cells almost every day—sometimes five or six times a day—as a form of harassment. Back then freemen knew if they disrespected our possessions we'd eventually get into physical altercations with them and it gave them an excuse to gas or physically beat us. Until we won our lawsuit against strip searches in 1978, a shakedown always started with prisoners being forced to strip out of all our clothing and go through the humiliating act of raising genitals, lifting feet, opening mouth, bending over and spreading cheeks for visual inspection; then we got dressed and were put in restraints, taken out of our cells, and forced to stand against the opposite wall. After our lawsuit they couldn't strip-search us before a shakedown, but we were always put in restraints and had to go into the hall to stand against the wall.

In the eighties, there were two types of shakedown crews. One crew worked all over the prison and did shakedowns all day, every day, looking for drugs, weapons, or other forms of serious contraband; they usually didn't bother with minor violations like having too many Styrofoam cups, magazines, or books. The in-house shakedown crews looking for minor violations worked at CCR. The policy in CCR was to shake down two cells every day on each shift—four shakedowns a day on each tier. So each of us had a cell shakedown at least once every four days, sometimes more. The sergeant could order an "extra" shakedown at any time.

The way we—and our possessions—were treated during a shake-down depended on the security guards doing it. Some came into the cell like an invasion, going through our personal belongings, reading our personal mail. They would flip the mattress, throw our possessions on the floor, and walk on our things. They were allowed to open legal mail but they weren't supposed to take it out and read it. Some made us stand facing the wall while the shakedown crew tore our cells apart behind us. That was horrible because you couldn't see what they were doing, you could only hear it.

A lot of prisoners would argue with the guards, then they'd be written up for "defiance" or "threatening an officer" and be taken to the dungeon. I had learned not to let them provoke me to that point. The only time I spoke was when they started reading my legal mail. I'd say, "You can't read my legal mail, you know that." I never showed any emotion on my face. Killing them, beating them up, spitting on them, cussing them out—all of that was going through my mind. If, in that moment, any of us could have gotten our hands on them without restraints, there is no telling what might have happened.

Then there were the guards we called "robocops," the ones who weren't cruel but who followed the rules to the letter. We were only supposed to have six pairs of underwear, six T-shirts, and six pairs of socks. Anything over that the robocop threw into the hall. Whatever he said we weren't supposed to have—extra newspapers, envelopes, post-age stamps, magazines—went into the hall. An extra sheet or blanket (we were officially allowed to have only one of each) would be thrown into the hall. All of it would be swept into a pile and swept off the tier by the orderlies who went through the piles and took whatever they could for themselves.

Other guards had a kinder attitude and let you keep an extra pair of socks; they wouldn't drop your photos on the floor or empty your lockers. Some didn't even do the shakedown but just checked off in the book that they did. They would put you in restraints in the hall and come into your cell and sit on your bunk and flip through a magazine for 10 or 15 minutes and leave. Almost every prisoner had what we called a "shot book," a spiral-bound notebook that had pictures of women cut out of magazines glued into it: movie stars wearing thong bikinis or models in underwear and nude pictures from porn magazines. These books were passed around and traded all over CCR. Some prisoners made or bought shot books just to have one on hand for when the free-man came in to shake down the cell. They left it on their bunk during a shakedown in hopes the guard would sit on the bed and look at it and forget about doing the shakedown.

Most of the time, though, during a shakedown my cell was ran-sacked. All the contents of my boxes—letters, photographs, toiletries—were scattered; all my books were spread all over the floor and my bunk. It took hours to put everything back together again. I "reshelved" all my books on the floor in a row against the wall. I folded and put my clothes away along with my photograph albums, writing materi-als, mail, and paperwork into two steel boxes under my bed. To keep the insects out I usually put things like toothpaste and food in empty bleach bottles I'd cut in half. Sometimes the shakedown crew would throw the bleach containers into the hall along with the Coke can I used to heat water for ramen noodles or hot cocoa. Sometimes they left those things.

When the federal government took over running Angola in the sev-enties as a result of the Hayes Williams lawsuit, one of the conces-sions the Louisiana Department of Public Safety and Corrections had to make in the consent decree was to create a way to review prisoner housing at Angola. For prisoners housed in segregation, the lockdown review board—which we called the "reclassification," or "reclass," board—was supposed to review each prisoner's housing assignment every 90 days to determine if he still needed to be locked down, or if he could be released into the general population. The rea-son given on paper for locking down me and Herman in CCR was, "Original reason for lockdown." Prisoners always had the option to attend these hearings, and for years I went to them, even though it was immediately clear to me there was no way a prisoner could "work" his way out of CCR. There were no guidelines established that if fol-lowed by prisoners, would require the reclass board to move them to less-restricted housing. Prisoners were simply moved around at the whim of the officials in charge. If officials needed a cell in CCR, they moved a CCR prisoner into a dorm in the main prison, and someone new moved into his cell. We saw men who were behavioral problems, men who had recent write-ups for violence against prisoners, and men who had just been in the dungeon get out of CCR in this way. We saw a prisoner who pulled a knife on the warden get released from CCR. Herman, King, and I—with no behavioral problems and few write-ups—would never be released.

In the early years, they kept us there out of hatred and for revenge. They had talked themselves into believing that Herman and I killed Brent Miller and that King was involved. (From the day King arrived at Angola, in May 1972, his file said he was in CCR because he was being "investigated" for the murder of Brent Miller, even though Miller was killed a month before King arrived at the prison.) Then, they kept us locked down because of our political beliefs. They knew through our actions over many years at CCR that we weren't regular prisoners, that we were different. We constantly wanted to change our environment. We were able to unify prisoners. We believed in the principles of the Black Panther Party. Years later this was confirmed when warden Burl Cain made statements under oath that we were being held in CCR because of our "Pantherism." In a 2008 deposition he said he wouldn't let me out of CCR even if he believed I was innocent of killing Brent Miller. "I would still keep him in CCR," he said. "I still know that he is still trying to practice Black Pantherism, and I still would not want him walking around my prison because he would organize the young new inmates. I would have me all kind of problems, more than I could stand, and I would have the blacks chasing after them [Woodfox and Wallace]. He [Woodfox] has to stay in a cell while he is at Angola."

The CCR lockdown review board was usually made up of a major or captain and a reclassification officer. Normally, the prisoner would stand before the officers in front of a table while his case was being reviewed. When I went before the board they didn't even look up while they signed the paper indicating I was staying in CCR. I was never once asked a question at a reclass board. I never once had the impression that anyone ever opened my file. They'd be talking among themselves about hunting and fishing or some other subject and slide my signed paperwork keeping me in CCR to the corner of the table. Sometimes they'd be signing the paper while I was walking into the room. Once in a while the major on duty would say, "Why do you keep coming to the board, Woodfox? You know we can't let you out." Even the tier guards knew it was a waste of our time to go to the board meetings. They'd call down the tier to tell us the board was meeting and ask us if we wanted to go. If we said yes they'd say, "Why? You ain't getting out." At some point, I stopped going to the reclass board. It was a hassle to get all the restraints on just to stand before the table for a few seconds. After I quit going the tier sergeant would bring the signed paper keeping me in CCR and put it between the bars in my cell every 90 days.

We didn't have the wars on the tier in the eighties that we had in the seventies. The inmate guards were long gone; there were black correctional officers hired; and, after a decade, many of the people working the tiers hadn't known Brent Miller. A lot of guards, white and black, spent 12 hours a day on the tier and got to know prisoners and didn't hate them. They worked at Angola to feed their families and pay their bills. They could see that Herman, King, and I weren't bullies, we weren't violent, we weren't racist. We were polite. Many told us they were taught in the Department of Corrections training academy that we were examples of the "worst of the worst." They were shocked when they got to know us. Some officers told me and Herman they thought we were innocent; they didn't believe we killed Brent Miller.

There were always guards, however, who enjoyed the absolute power and control they had over another human being, guards whose whole life and identity were tied up in the way they acted out against prisoners. One of those guards once opened my cell door so another prisoner could jump me. This prisoner was a real bully and troublemaker and everybody knew he and I didn't get along. One day when he was out on his hour he came and stood in front of my cell door. I got up and started to walk to the cell door. I knew something was about to happen or he wouldn't be standing there. Then my door opened. He tried to come into my cell; we fought and I beat him up. I was written up for fighting and sent to the dungeon, even though I was obviously defending myself. I wrote to the warden, asking him to investigate the guard who had opened my cell door. I never received a response. Years later the state tried to say this write-up showed how violent I was, to use it as an excuse for keeping me in CCR.

Chapter 30

Comrades

None of us thought we would live long in CCR. From the beginning, we thought they moved us there to kill us. We had come to terms with that. But we survived. A large part of my ability to stay true to revolutionary struggle was the example that Herman and King set. I never had to question their loyalty. Their actions spoke louder than words. One of my favorite sayings is "The mouth can say anything but the ass is proof." When you put your ass behind what comes out of your mouth, that's what counts. Herman and King were never hypocritical, never saying one thing and doing something else. They lived their lives putting their asses where their mouths were. Because of that I trusted them. It took me years to really know them as individuals, and in those years, gradually, grew very strong friendships and love.

Herman Wallace was raised in the 13th Ward of New Orleans, not far from where I grew up. Since he was six years older than me I never knew him on the street. Like all black men of my age in the South he became aware of racism early. "Everything was segregated, from outhouse toilets to indoor churches," he once wrote. "You couldn't look white men in the eye, you had to have your head down when you walked around, all socially designed to keep African Americans as an inferior people." When he was eight years old he started shoplifting food to help feed his eight siblings. He pulled a wagon to the scrapyard in New Orleans when it was closed on Sundays to pick up all the loose pieces of copper and aluminum he could find from the yard. The following

Saturday he pulled his wagon back to the scrapyard to sell those pieces, using the money to help his siblings. He would later write that he did his "ultimate best" to be there for his family. "I chopped the wood to keep the house warm and for cooking," he wrote. "I washed clothes on a scrubbing board long before we got a washing machine. I ironed the family's clothes, plaited my sisters' hair before we went to school." On the street, he protected his sisters.

For a while he and his older siblings lived with his grandmother. She taught him how to cook. There weren't enough beds in her two rooms, so he and his brother slept on the floor. Eventually, he wrote, "I could not understand how my parents worked so hard and yet were so poor." As a teenager, he got into more petty crimes and spent time in the juvenile justice system. "You would sit around and wait for visits on Sunday," he said. "You feel alone, heartbroken, like it's you against the world."

In January 1967, he was arrested on a bank robbery charge. The following year he was convicted and received a 50-year sentence. In 1969, he escaped to the roof of Orleans Parish Prison, jumped to the rooftop of the building next door, and got to the street with several other inmates. He was caught in Florida and brought back to the parish prison, where he was put in the dungeon. His shoes had shrunk in the rain, so he took them off. Malik Rahim, one of the New Orleans Black Panthers I'd met when I was on C-1 at the parish prison, happened to be in the dungeon when they brought Herman in. Seeing that Herman wasn't wearing shoes Malik asked him what size he wore. Herman told him and Malik took off his own shoes. "Hey, brother, listen," he said, handing Herman his shoes, "you can have mine. My comrades won't let me go without." Malik walked away from him barefoot.

That was Herman's introduction to the Black Panther Party. From the Black Panthers, he found connection and purpose. He went on to join the party in the parish prison and participated in prisoner actions there. "We destroyed every commode, sink, and face bowl we could," he said. "Mattresses were stacked at the front of the tiers and set afire to prevent prison authorities from physically attacking us." After two days of a siege, the sheriff said he would negotiate with the prisoners without reprisal and gave the prisoners the opportunity to voice their grievances to CBS news cameramen he allowed into the prison. The sheriff told the reporters the problem was overcrowding and lack of funding, pointing out that there were four and five men in cells built for two. This sheriff kept his promise and didn't take vengeance on the prisoners who protested.

(Unbeknownst to me until later, Herman was also in the parish prison when my tier took a hostage in order to speak to Rep. Dorothy Mae Taylor; his tier also nonviolently took a hostage. Both hostages were released unharmed after prisoners talked to Representative Taylor.) Joining the Black Panther Party was the defining moment in Herman's life. Forty-one years later Herman was as devoted to the principles of the party as he was in the beginning. He proudly wore the iconic image of the black panther, created by artist and former Panther Emory Douglas, hand-drawn on his hat and clothing, even though he would often get a write-up for it.

Robert King grew up in New Orleans and Gonzales, Louisiana. His backyard in Algiers, the second-oldest neighborhood in New Orleans, and the only one on the western bank of the Mississippi River, actually bordered Malik Rahim's backyard for a while when they were children. King's grandmother raised him in a close-knit but impoverished family. She died when he was 15. Shortly afterward, King and two friends were walking down the street when they were stopped by police because they "fit the description" of men who had robbed a gas station. King was sent to the State Industrial School for Colored Youth, a state reformatory in Scotlandville, 13 miles north of Baton Rouge. After that he had several minimum-paying jobs but lost many of them due to being picked up on "vagrancy laws."

Police used vagrancy laws and "loitering" charges to meet their weekly quota of arrests, picking up black men and charging them with having "no visible means of support," whether or not those men had jobs or even owned their own businesses. A lot of black men in the sixties had small jobs that supported them but weren't official "businesses."; they'd walk the neighborhoods, sharpening knives or selling vegetables, for example. Ragmen came through with old shirts or pants. On the corner they'd yell, "Raaag maan," and people would come out and pay a dollar for this, two dollars for that. A lot of people made new clothes with these used clothes. The man selling the clothing and rags had no proof of employment.

Every black man and boy knew what it was like to be picked up by police for no reason. You could be hanging out on the corner with your friends when police on patrol would stop, get out of the car, and tell everybody to get up against the wall. They'd pat everybody down, ask what everyone was doing, and tell everybody to show proof of work. Then they'd get on their walkie-talkies and call the paddy wagon, charge anyone without a paycheck stub or other "proof" with loitering or vagrancy, and put them in jail. Police could legally hold the men for three days on vagrancy charges. After being in jail for three days men lost whatever jobs or means of support they had and had to start over.

Like most black men in those days King was forced to choose between providing for himself and his family or watching them starve to death. This was not a difficult choice to make. At 18 he was sent to Angola for the first time on a robbery charge and then he came back again when he was 23, which was when I first met him. Back on the street he picked up boxing and became a semiprofessional fighter; this is the time when he was known as Speedy King. At 28, King was arrested and charged with an armed robbery he did not commit. At his trial, his codefendant testified that he only picked King out of a mug shot lineup because he'd been tortured by police into making a false statement. In spite of that testimony King was convicted and sentenced to 35 years. He met members of the Black Panther Party and joined the party in Orleans Parish Prison. Later he'd say it was in prison that "things began to open themselves up to me regarding injustices. I felt it was a hard pill to swallow. I felt under slavery."

I trusted Herman and King implicitly. With other men in prison, there were only degrees of trust, depending on the person's character, or lack of character. It was something I had to evaluate as I interacted with each person. When I was with Herman or King it was different. My defenses were down. I trusted them not to do anything that would hurt me physically or emotionally. I trusted them to have my back, no matter what. I never had to worry if King was going to be there, if Hooks was going to be there. No matter what I did they would be there for me. They trusted me in the same way.

This kind of trust is very rare behind bars. In prison, you have to question everything around you. Prison teaches you that most acts of kindness have strings attached; something in return will be expected at some point and what is expected might be conduct you find appalling, a violation of your moral code and system of values. To preserve your dignity and honor, you learn to reject what people offer. Because Herman, King, and I trusted one another, there was kindness in our lives.

Nelson Mandela wrote that the challenge for every prisoner is "how to survive prison intact, how to emerge from prison undiminished, how to conserve and even replenish one's beliefs." He wrote about how being kept with his comrades on Robben Island helped him survive. "For together our determination was reinforced," he wrote. "We supported each other and gained strength from each other." So it was for me, Herman, and King. We supported each other and gained strength from one another. Whenever I thought I could not take another step for myself, I found the strength to take that step for Herman and King. We had to be strong so we could keep our minds and spirits free while being locked up 23 hours a day. We had to be strong so we could show other prisoners that in the fight against oppression, there is no letting up, no backing down. We wanted the other prisoners to see that our struggle for dignity was more important than our own safety and our own freedom and our own lives. We had to be strong so the prison administration could not break us.

I loved and cherished their friendship. I didn't know how so much loyalty and devotion could exist between three men. We had been through so much brutality, so much pain and suffering that we had every right to be hard, bitter, and hateful toward almost everyone and everything in life. But instead, we did not allow prison to shape us. We defined ourselves.

We didn't agree on everything. We could argue like cats and dogs. It was never personal though. We were three strong men who had different positions on some political issues and we'd get into it sometimes. But even in anger and frustration we held each other in the highest possible regard. I never doubted they were honest in their ideas and feelings and analysis. We listened to one another. We each saw great character in the others. Herman and King would rather lose their lives than betray me and I felt the same way about both of them. We never lost the faith.

Herman wrote a poem that, for me, expresses who we had to be to survive. We were men of steel.

Man of Steel
My keepers believe I'm the man of steel,
Ripping and running, in and out of my life,
As if this shit ain't real.
They frame me for murder—and when their conspiracy
is exposed, and they are all deposed, the judge
declares—case closed.

Equal access to Justice, equal access to rule,
Doctrines never meant for the man of Steel but to
terminate 40 years of his indomitable will.

Maybe my soul is that of concrete
Maybe it is that of the wind
Maybe it is that of fire
Maybe it is the spirit of the people—the spirit of my ancestors,
Whatever my keepers wish my soul to be,
The man of steel is always free.

Chapter 31

Contact Visit

In 1986, 14 years after I was locked down in CCR, prison authorities moved everyone from CCR and Death Row to Camp J cellblocks so they could make repairs and renovations to the old building. We were all put in Gar Unit at Camp J, the punishment camp, where King had been sent for two years in the late seventies for protesting strip searches. Camp J prisoners had fewer privileges than we had at CCR—no store, for example, less food at mealtimes, no salt or pepper, fewer books. While being housed at Camp J, CCR prisoners were supposed to be able to live by the same rules and regulations that we had at CCR—and not the Camp J rules—but there was always a tug-of-war. The Camp J major wanted things his way. We went on hunger strikes or would refuse to go into our cells when they tried to impose Camp J rules on us and gradually we won back privileges. Some things we couldn't change: The cells were much smaller. When we went to the shower we were locked in. We had a lot of arguments with security around that. Most of us only needed 10 or 15 minutes in the shower. Once we were locked in we had to wait until the guard came to unlock the door before we could get out, so we might have to spend 30 or 45 minutes or more in the shower. That would cut into our hour outside the cell.

Our "yard" time took place in small pens. There was no way to run, we could only jog or walk in circles. The windows were frosted so we couldn't see out of them. I filed an ARP about the frosted windows when I got there. I researched the statutes that described how much sunlight prisoners were supposed to get. (Even at Camp J prisoners were allowed to take law books out of the library because it was required by law.) I won that because there was established law supporting me. They had to swap the frosted glass for glass we could see through.

They did install black-and-white TVs for us at Camp J and, for the first time ever, we got to see cable TV stations while we were there. We had petitioned for cable long before we were sent to Camp J. The main prison had already had access to cable TV for years. We found out it came through for us when an inmate counsel visited after talking to the warden. "Say, man," he said, "they granted you cable here now. Y'all just got to go to channel 5 for Cinemax." I'll never forget, the World Series was on TV, we changed the channel to 5, and the first thing we saw was a naked woman walking on the beach from some foreign movie. That was the end of the baseball. A couple of the guys were really into sports and complained. There was some back-and-forth on the subject but since we lived by a majority-rule policy that was a short vote. I think it was something like 12 to 3 for the foreign movie.

At Camp J visiting was worse than it was at CCR. We had to wear restraints during the noncontact visit. The screens were so dark that in order for visitors and prisoners to see one another's form we had to stand back from the screen. At CCR Herman, King, and I could be in the visiting room at the same time if our families came together, and we encouraged them to do that. We wouldn't be able to see one another—we'd be brought to the visiting booths one at a time—but we could talk to one another, even though there were dividers between us. Our families laughed about how we'd be able to conduct full conversations with each other looking straight ahead. On the other side of the screen our families pushed their chairs back against the wall, which allowed us to see all of them and talk together. This was a ray of humanity for us. At Camp J, however, we were locked in individual visiting sheds, alone with whoever was visiting us, so we couldn't talk to one another on visits, and our families couldn't visit us together.

While we were housed at Camp J the prison started a bullshit work line for CCR prisoners that lasted a few months. We'd be allowed out of our cells for a few hours a day—either morning or afternoon—to work in the fields. There were two shifts for each time period—they kept me, Herman, and King on separate shifts. We were fed all our meals locked in our cells.

One day I became ill out in the field. I tried to keep working but when I felt the energy drain out of me I sat down on the ground. I had no strength whatsoever. Sergeant David Ross rode over on his horse and told me to get up and start working. I told him I couldn't work anymore, I needed to go to the hospital. He told me he wasn't calling the EMTs, and to get back to work. He rode away. When he came back I told him I needed to see a doctor because I was very sick. He said he wasn't calling an ambulance and told me to get up. Then everything went white. I must have lain down. Sergeant Ross finally called the EMT. When he arrived he couldn't get a blood pressure reading so they transported me to the hospital. They treated me at the hospital but later the medical staff denied it, covering for the guard. The doctor said nothing was wrong with me and filed a disciplinary report against me, saying that I was malingering.

I filed a civil suit against Sergeant Ross, the doctor, and the EMT, alleging they'd violated my 8th Amendment right under the Constitution to be free of cruel and unusual punishment, as well as my 14th Amendment rights, because Ross denied me equal treatment and protection under the law by ignoring statutory law, rules, and regulations governing the treatment of prisoners.

During the discovery phase I obtained medical records from the hospital that showed I'd been treated for heatstroke even though the doctor said there was nothing wrong with me. The medical records showed that when they brought me in the doctor examined me, then placed me in an air-conditioned room and gave me water to drink. At trial, I referred to those medical records when the doctor, attempting to cover up for Sergeant Ross, testified that he didn't treat me. The EMT said the reason he couldn't get a blood pressure reading from me that morning was that his gauge malfunctioned. On cross-examination, I asked him if he wrote an incident report on the broken blood pressure gauge and he said no, so I asked him if he was working every day with a broken blood pressure gauge and he said no, he turned it in to the hospital. I asked him how he could turn in a broken blood pressure gauge without filing an incident report on it, therefore jeopardizing the lives of prisoners by leaving in service a blood pressure gauge that either malfunctioned or was broken.

In the end, the judge gutted the suit, dismissing the part of the case that had all my evidence against the doctor and the EMT. He said I hadn't shown "deliberate indifference" on the part of the medical staff, so the jury could not take under consideration all of the medical proof that showed a cover-up. The only part of the suit the jury could consider was whether or not Sergeant Ross deliberately violated my 8th Amendment and 14th Amendment rights. The day of my trial, one of the two prisoner witnesses who worked in the field line with me and saw and heard everything that happened refused to testify. The other had amnesia on the witness stand and therefore gave misleading testimony. Given the fact the judge dismissed the part of the case that contained most of the evidence, all that was left for the jury to consider was my testimony and the testimony of Sergeant Ross. Based upon my experience in dealing with the court system and the fact that during my testimony the state brought up my previous arrests and convictions—the most recent being my conviction for the murder of prison guard Brent Miller—I felt there was no way that the jury would rule in my favor. I was right.

In 1987, I was working on a different case in my cell and asked the library to send me a copy of the Hayes Williams consent decree from 1975 for background research. When I started reading it I realized I'd never seen the full document before. The consent decree we were given in the seventies had been edited; I now saw that agreements in the consent decree that would have benefited CCR prisoners—like having contact visits—had been redacted by officials who didn't want us to have any knowledge of our rights under the consent decree. I immediately wrote notes to King and Herman and filed an ARP on it. Hilton Butler, the former captain who had gassed us repeatedly in the seventies, was the warden of Angola at that time. He was now forced to grant us contact visits. CCR had never had them before; now CCR prisoners were allowed to have one contact visit a month.

The contact visit was completely different from sitting behind a steel mesh screen. We were taken to an open room with tables and chairs. They removed our handcuffs and leg irons. My first contact visit in 15 years was around Christmas that year. My mom came with my brother Michael, my sister Violetta, and her oldest daughter, Nelyauna. There was no natural flow at first. I didn't feel comfortable. I had forgotten what it felt like to be physically close to people. I was used to talking with the partition between us. There was no hugging with the screen between you and a visitor. You couldn't even really see the eyes of the person across from you clearly.

It was a strain for me to stay within the flow of my first contact visit. When my mom put her hand on my leg it brought back a flood of memories. I became a kid again. I had to fight off crying. When they were getting ready to leave I had an intense wave of longing that went through me, a desire to leave with them. Everyone started to hug me and I didn't know what to do. I'd always been able to kiss my mom through the screen, touch fingers with Michael and everybody, but hugging, for the first time in 15 years, was totally foreign to me. (Later, King would say he felt the same. "It felt totally, absolutely strange," he said. "I didn't know how to hug. It was sadder than sad. I realized how much I'd missed.") It took me months to really enjoy contact visits.

We were at Camp J for more than two years, long after the renovations in the old building were complete. During my civil trial against David Ross, testimony came out that CCR and Death Row inmates had been moved to Camp J in violation of the consent decree. After state officials got involved we were moved back to CCR in 1989.

Chapter 32

Maturity

I feel safe even in the midst of my enemies, for the truth is all powerful and will prevail.

—Sojourner Truth

I believe life is in constant motion. Even in the prison cell, with the numbing repetition of the same day over and over. Even trapped on a tier with 14 other personalities I couldn't get away from—the one who is constantly complaining; the one who smells bad. Even with the constant noise and when the pain of not being able to leave my cell was too much to bear. (I cried. I cried a lot of times after the tier was locked down so no one could see.) Even with the fear that one day I would go insane like so many others I'd witnessed. I saw life as constantly changing and I allowed myself to change.

By the time I was 40 I saw how I had transformed my cell, which was supposed to be a confined space of destruction and punishment, into something positive. I used that space to educate myself, I used that space to build strong moral character, I used that space to develop principles and a code of conduct, I used that space for everything other than what my captors intended it to be.

In my forties, I saw how I'd developed a moral compass that was unbreakable, a strong sense of what was right or wrong, even when other people didn't feel it. I saw it. I felt it. I tasted it. If something didn't feel right, then no threat, no amount of pressure could make me do it.

I knew that my life was the result of a conscious choice I made every minute of the day. A choice to make myself better. A choice to make things better for others. I made a choice not to break. I made a choice to change my environment. I knew I had not only survived 15 years of solitary confinement, I'd honored my commitment to the Black Panther Party. I helped other prisoners understand they had value as human beings, that they were worth something. I could still remember the way it felt to be accepted by the Panthers in the Tombs, to see in their eyes that they valued me, that I was somebody to them, even though I was a prisoner with a 50-year sentence and I didn't value myself. As a member of the Black Panther Party, I gave my word I would make it my duty to protect other prisoners, to teach them how to stay focused on life outside prison, to show them that they belonged in this world. I kept my word.

In my forties, I chose to take my pain and turn it into compassion, and not hate. Whenever I experienced pain of any origin I always made a promise to myself never to do anything that would cause someone else to suffer the pain I was feeling in that moment. I still had moments of bitterness and anger. But by then I had the wisdom to know that bitterness and anger are destructive. I was dedicated to building things, not tearing them down.

In my forties, I fully understood all that my mom had sacrificed to take care of her children. I felt all the love she had for us, and the love I had for her. Everything my mother ever said to me came back to me over the years. Lessons she taught me that I had lost in the arrogance of childhood became the foundation of my own wisdom. "Life's got to be like throwing water on a duck," she used to say. "It don't stick." I hadn't known what it meant when I was a child but looking back I saw that she was telling me not to let the poverty and difficulties of my childhood define me. She was telling me to let the pain and circumstances of my life roll off my back. Her words came to me when I needed them, pushing me to understand their deeper meaning and find a way to keep going. "I used to complain about having no shoes," she would say, "until I saw a man with no feet." Her words encouraged me to focus on my strength instead of the agony of being separated from the world and feeling the heaviness of that. "When someone gives you lemons," she always said, "make lemonade."

In the novel *Native Son*, Richard Wright wrote, "Men can starve from a lack of self-realization, as much as they can from a lack of bread!" I never forgot those words. By the time I was 40 I'd read and educated myself enough to develop my own values and code of conduct. It started with the 10-Point Program of the Black Panther Party. In the years after the party broke up I expanded upon those values, I broadened my views on the struggle, and I found solace in the words of other great men and women who seemed to understand me and validate my life.

"If there is no struggle there is no progress," Frederick Douglass wrote. "Those who profess to favor freedom and yet depreciate agitation, are men who want crops without plowing up the ground, they want rain without thunder and lightning. They want the ocean without the awful roar of its many waters. This struggle may be a moral one, or it may be a physical one, and it may be both moral and physical; but it must be a struggle. Power cedes nothing without a demand. It never did and it never will."

Malcolm X wrote, "Every defeat, every heartbreak, every loss, contains its own seed, its own lesson on how to improve your performance the next time." Malcolm gave me direction. He gave me vision. The civil rights leader Whitney Young said of being black: "Look at me, I'm here. I have dignity. I have pride. I have roots. I insist, I demand that I participate in those decisions that affect my life and the lives of my children. It means that I am somebody." There wasn't one saying that carried me for all my years in solitary confinement, there were one thousand, ten thousand. I pored over the books that spoke to me. They comforted me.

In my forties, I was able to show my mom the man I'd become. I was able to thank her for her wisdom and the lessons of life she taught me and let her know she was my role model and my hero. I thanked her for the sacrifices she made for me and my sister and brothers. I apologized for putting her through so much pain in my youth and told her I appreciated everything she did for me. I always wanted to be a man my mother could be proud of. I was in prison, but I was able to show her that I had become that man.

By age 40 I had learned that to be human is to grow, to create, to contribute, and that fear stops growth. Fear retards the process of growing. Fear causes confusion and uncertainty. Fear kills one's sense of self-worth. By eradicating fear on the tier, I learned that men can deal with each other better. They can get along. I wondered if in society, we could build a world in which we do not fear one another.

1990s

In the world through which I travel, I am endlessly creating myself.

—Frantz Fanon

Chapter 33

Justice Delayed Is Justice Denied

I pace the cell to think. I pace to relieve tension. I lightly box the wall. My knuckles have calluses on them from boxing the wall. I do push-ups on my fists. I don't have deep thoughts. I'm practical. My needs are few so they cannot torment me by withholding anything. I don't need anything. I get through the days the way I have done a thousand times before. Will this be the day I break? I push that thought away. Mind over matter. I keep moving so later I can sleep. Sometimes I can't sleep. I work at it, try to understand why it's happening. I listen to music. Music is a refuge for me. An escape. There are days when music saves me. I play it loud to drown out the background noise. I play it softly. I don't dance to the music but sometimes I sway to it.

On February 11, 1990, the entire tier watched Nelson Mandela walk out of prison on TV after 27 years. Mandela was an inspiration to me. Arrested for his political beliefs he spent 18 years on Robben Island, where he was forced to carry limestone rock back and forth from one end of a quarry to another. He and his comrades slept on beds of straw. Guards urinated next to them while they ate. Imprisoned for opposing the white minority rule and oppression of black people in South Africa, in his first public speech upon his release he spoke of the need to end the brutality of apartheid. "Now is the time to intensify the struggle on all fronts," he stated. "We call on the international community to continue the campaign to isolate the apartheid regime. . . . Our march to freedom is irreversible. We must not allow fear to stand in our way." Mandela remained unbowed. He was an example and inspiration to me the whole time I was in solitary confinement. Sometimes it helped to think of people who had it much worse than I did and survived.

For years, Herman and I never appealed our convictions from the seventies. We didn't think about appealing. We didn't think it would do any good. King talked us into it. Since Herman's attorney didn't file an appeal in a timely matter after he was convicted in 1974, Herman had to file what was called an "out-of-time appeal." In 1990, his application was granted. In the spring of 1991, King and I started working on my application for postconviction relief. Reading my court papers, King called down to me, "What happened to that motion you filed to quash the grand jury?" I told him I had no idea; I'd forgotten about it. "I see here where it's open." he said. "It was never ruled on. If that's the case they're going to have to give you a new trial." By law judges are supposed to decide on the outcome of pretrial motions before trial. King sent law books down the tier for me to read so we could discuss my case. When one of us was out on his hour, he stood at the bars in front of the other's cell to talk about it.

We raised two issues: One was that the court never ruled on my motion. The second was "ineffective assistance of counsel," because, by failing to research my case, Charles Garretson hadn't put forth the best defense required by law. He probably didn't know about it. I'd forgotten about it. But that's not an excuse in a court of law. Effective counsel is a constitutional right guaranteed by the 6th Amendment. He was obligated to research my case before we went to trial. King wrote the postconviction application for me by hand on a legal pad. We could have manual typewriters in those days, so he typed it out on onionskin paper, with carbon paper between the pages so we could retain copies. (Carbon paper was so rare on the tier that every page was used over and over again until it was almost white.) As he typed he passed sections of it down the tier for me to read. I filed it on September 17, 1991.

Herman's appeal was denied at the appellate level in 1992 and the Louisiana Supreme Court denied review in 1993. I had better luck. On May 27, 1992, eight months after I filed, Judge Thomas Tanner of the 18th Judicial District Court in Iberville Parish reversed my conviction on the grand jury discrimination issue, agreeing that my attorney should have made an effort to have my indictment from the unconstitutional grand jury thrown out. The state appealed the judge's decision and lost. I would get a new trial. I was ecstatic, not knowing I would have to wait six years for my trial. I believed they were deliberately delaying, hoping that they would mentally break me or I'd die, and then there wouldn't have to be a trial.

Before I could be retried, I had to be reindicted. In March 1993, I was reindicted in the same place where I had been indicted 21 years before, the St. Francisville courthouse. In 1972, the grand jury had excluded women and African Americans. In 1993, the grand jury included blacks and women; one of those women was Anne Butler, the wife of former Angola warden C. Murray Henderson, the man who helped frame me. Not only was she on the grand jury, she was allowed to pass around a book that she and Henderson had written about Angola, which included a chapter about the Miller killing. It was not a journalistic account. Her "reporting" consisted of interviewing the former prison officials who made up the original story about me, Herman, Chester Jackson, and Gilbert Montegut killing Miller in 1972.

According to Butler's account I murdered Brent Miller with Herman Wallace and Chester Jackson. She admitted in her book that Gilbert Montegut had nothing to do with Miller's murder and he was framed because prison officials wanted to blame the murder on "militants" released from CCR shortly before Miller was killed. She didn't write about why her husband, the former warden, allowed Gilbert Montegut, an innocent man, to be tried for a murder he knew the man didn't commit.

She didn't write about the testimony of Chester Jackson and how radically different it was from Hezekiah Brown's "eyewitness" account, even though Jackson supposedly participated in the murder of Brent Miller. Or how every single one of the state's witnesses contradicted Brown's testimony. She didn't write about how the state's witnesses had me running in different directions after the murder, wearing different clothing, with no blood on me. She didn't write about how none of the state's witnesses saw each other, even though they were all supposedly standing in the same area at the same time. She didn't write about the bloody tennis shoes, which were found after Miller's killing and which investigators—and her husband—knew about but hid from my defense and never had tested at the crime lab. (We only found out about them years later through a public records request.)

Anne Butler called the chapter about Brent Miller's killing "Racist Pigs Who Hold Us Captive," a phrase she said came from that letter prison officials claimed they "intercepted" the day before Miller's killing. The intercepted letter, which was never brought up at my trial and which Deputy Warden Lloyd Hoyle appeared to have no knowledge of on the day Miller was killed when he spoke to the press, allegedly took credit for the attack on Mike Gunnells in the guard booth the day before Miller was killed and "promised other acts of unspecified violence," adding that a "people's court" was held and had "convicted" prison authorities of "extreme racism." It was signed, "The Vanguard Army, Long Live the Angola Prison Involvement."

She didn't write about how prison authorities never identified the author of the letter, if it existed, even though they had handwriting samples of every prisoner on file, as well as access to every typewriter on prison grounds. If the letter existed, and had been written by a prisoner, they could figure out who wrote it. If it was linked to me or Herman it would have been brought up at our trials.

In her book Butler described Brown—a ruthless rapist—as "gregarious Hezekiah Brown" who had "light duty" because of a "weak ankle" and "made coffee for the guards." She wrote he had been incarcerated for "relatively minor crimes" in Mississippi, Oklahoma, and Arkansas before coming to Angola, failing to mention his multiple aggravated rape convictions and the fact that he spent years on death row for one of his rape convictions. We heard a rumor later that initially Brown, who was free at the time of my indictment, refused to testify before the grand jury when he arrived at the courthouse, and that even though he'd been released from prison years before, a guard from Angola, his former "handler," had to be called to reassure him and literally walk him into the grand jury room, which would have been illegal since nobody is supposed to enter a grand jury room but the district attorney and grand jury members.

About Miller's killing Butler wrote:

Brent Miller's mother recalled his telling her that once during a
disturbance at Angola, other officers had given him a chain to use
in subduing unruly inmates. "He said that the inmates were begging him not to hit them, and he said to me, 'Mama, I wouldn't
hit one of them for nothing in the world, I just couldn't do that.'"
Now this fair-haired laughing baby boy who loved everybody, this
high school football hero, this new bridegroom, lay dead on the
floor, stabbed thirty-two times with at least two knives, his hands
in death rigidly clenched into fists from trying to grab and fend off
the sharpened blades.

She described Miller's wounds in detail, stating that "during the
mandatory autopsy, small medical sticks inserted into each wound
for the purpose of photographic evidence gave the body a porcupine
appearance."

This inflammatory account was what the grand jury was allowed to
read. Butler also wrote, incorrectly, that I'd been convicted of "theft" and
"aggravated rape." This was the story she was allowed to pass around to
other grand jurors. In a subsequent memoir, she wrote,

The book was in great demand as the grand jury considered this case
yet again, because with the passage of time nearly everybody had
forgotten the little details that can be so important. The attorneys
read the book; the witnesses read the book; even some of the jurors
read the book. And who should be called for grand jury duty out of
the 13,000 or so registered voters of the Parish of West Feliciana?
Me. I asked the assistant DA handling the case if he shouldn't excuse
me from duty but he insisted that it was the right as well as the
responsibility of every citizen to serve when called.

As expected, I was reindicted on March 17, 1993. When I was
arraigned two public defenders were appointed to represent me at
trial: Baton Rouge attorney Bert Garraway and Richard Howell from

St. Francisville. They immediately submitted a motion to quash my indictment since Anne Butler had passed her biased, inaccurate, inflammatory version of Brent Miller's murder around to other grand jurors. Judge Bruce Bennett refused the motion, writing, "There's nothing wrong with a grand juror having some knowledge of a case, even if they happened to have written a book about the case."

Meanwhile, Herman, representing himself, tried to ferret out suppressed evidence we figured the state had about our case by filing a pro se (without a lawyer) Public Records Act request, asking for "all documents . . . pertaining in any manner to the arrest, investigation and prosecution of Herman Joshua Wallace." On May 27, 1993, he filed another records request with the 20th Judicial District. In both cases the state refused to provide him with public records. Herman went to court and eventually both the 19th and the 20th Judicial District Courts ordered the state to provide the records he requested. The state said there were no documents pertaining to his case; a decade later we proved this was a lie. Herman then attempted to subpoena the Louisiana State Penitentiary, asking for "the entire investigative file . . . concerning the death of Brent Miller." In response, Angola claimed "there are no record [sic] at the Louisiana State Penitentiary regarding the Investigation into the [sic] Brent Miller's death."

That May, Herman challenged his 1974 conviction in an application for postconviction relief, raising, among other claims, the issue that Chester Jackson's deal with prosecutors to turn state's evidence should have been revealed to him, his attorney Charles Garretson, and the jury. To support his allegation, Herman included an affidavit he got from an inmate who swore that in 1985 he asked Jackson why he was abusing prescription drugs. Jackson told the inmate he had testified in court to things that were absolutely untrue and that Associate Warden Hayden Dees had threatened his life if he didn't sign a statement implicating himself, Herman, and me in the murder of Brent Miller. Herman asserted he was denied his constitutional right to due process of law. He didn't get a response for years.

The first time Garraway and Howell visited me at Angola they asked me if I'd be willing to take a lie detector test. I think they were surprised when I said yes. They came sometime later with a tester who brought his polygraph machine with him to Angola. I passed the lie detector test, affirming that I did not kill Brent Miller. I asked Garraway and Howell if they could get me a change of venue so my trial wouldn't be in St. Francisville, where I had been indicted twice and where a large percentage of the population either worked at Angola or were related by marriage or blood to someone who worked there.

The judge granted me a change of venue to Amite City, an hour and a half drive east of Angola and north of New Orleans. Amite was a small, white, conservative, Bible Belt community of 4,000 people located in Tangipahoa Parish, where the Ku Klux Klan had a very strong presence. I later found out that the Miller family had lived in Tangipahoa Parish, and that Brent Miller, considered a "native son," was buried outside the city of Amite. So in effect the change of venue for my trial was from the frying pan to the skillet.

Chapter 34

My Greatest Loss

Every morning in CCR I woke up with the same thought: Will this be the day? Will this be the day I lose my sanity and discipline? Will I start screaming and never stop? Will I curl up into a ball and become a baby, which was an early sign of going insane? Every day I pushed insanity away. Every day I had to find that strength. I had to find within me the will and determination not to break. I got those qualities from my mom.

The closest I ever came to breaking in prison was after my mom died, on December 27, 1994. I used to tell myself, "If you can breathe you can get through anything." When my mom died my breath was snatched from me. No matter how hard I tried, I couldn't catch my breath. I always thought if I lived long enough, I'd win. But now she was gone and I could never have her in my life again, no matter how long I lived. I wondered if, without my mom, I would ever be able to breathe again.

Ruby Edwards was born May 9, 1929. When she was a teenager the NAACP described Jim Crow to the *Louisiana Weekly* as a "modernized, streamlined slavery, that replaces shackles with 'For White Only' signs; that replaces slave quarters with the slum ghetto; that replaces three meals a day with the starvation wage of maids and porters; that replaces the master's bullwhip with the torch of the mob and the policeman's club." This was her world, but my mom didn't dwell on hardship. I can remember going to a department store on Canal Street with her when I was little. Black people weren't allowed to walk in the front door of a department store in those days and they couldn't browse in the aisles. We were allowed to spend our money at the store but not allowed the dignity of being seen in the store. We entered through the back door behind the store. She brought a picture of a dress she found in the newspaper and gave it to a white salesclerk. These young white store clerks were always rude, impatient, and disrespectful. The clerk eventually brought a dress back to my mom to look at that looked like the picture. My mom always believed life would get better though. When I was born, she was determined to make a good life for us.

The parents of my biological father, small-business owners in New Orleans, had other ideas. My father's mother took my mom to court to get custody of me, telling the judge my mom was unfit to raise me. My mother, only 18 years old and unable to read the court documents against her, had the strength and determination to prevail. She brought neighbors and family members to court to back up her claim that she was a good mother. The judge ruled in her favor, giving her sole custody of me. He ordered the hospital to put my father's name on my birth certificate and I became a Woodfox in name only.

The last time I saw my mom was about a month before she died. Weeks earlier, she had been in the hospital for a heart operation. Michael was visiting her when she told him she had severe pain in her left side. The pain got so bad she couldn't stand it so he summoned the nurse; the nurse got the doctor, who, upon examining her, rushed her into surgery. Her kidney had burst and they removed it. About two or three weeks later they did the heart operation, unclogging an artery. Then her toe was turning purple because there was no circulation in her foot from the diabetes and she allowed them to cut the toe off. At some point in time she told my brother, "You need to take me to Angola to see Albert."

I happened to be out of my cell on my hour and looking out the window when I saw my brother pushing a wheelchair toward the visitors' entrance. I thought he was helping somebody. After I was taken down to the visiting room they took off my restraints. When I turned and saw it was my mom in the wheelchair I almost collapsed. She had lost so much weight. It took every ounce of my strength and willpower to hide the shock and pain of seeing a woman who had always represented the strength of our family in this condition. I teased her and picked her up, which required no effort whatsoever, and set her on my lap. She was virtually skin and bones. In spite of her physical condition I could still see my mom in her eyes. I couldn't say anything. She told me she was tired. "Baby, these people want to cut my leg off now, and I ain't letting these white people cut on me no more," she said. "I'd rather die." After about half an hour she nodded off, falling asleep with her head on my chest. I made a sign to Michael that it was time for them to go. I knew my mom had come to say good-bye.

One of the cruelties of being in prison is that you are always the last to know what's going on in your own family. Herman learned of my mother's death before I did. His sister got word to him somehow. A trustee brought me a letter of condolence from Herman. When I read the letter I said, "What the fuck is this?" I later found out one of my brothers had called but prison officials had failed to notify me. While the lieutenant was making his rounds I showed him the letter from Herman and asked him why I hadn't been informed by someone that my mom had died. He said he didn't know anything about it but I could use the phone to call home. A guard came and put restraints on me and took me to the bridge right outside the tier so I could call my sister. She was crying. My brothers were there. I asked them questions about Mama's death and talked to them about what we had to do, which they had already done. The next day when I woke up the ceiling of my cell was an inch from my face. It was my worst episode of claustrophobia the entire time I was in solitary confinement. I closed my eyes and told myself to breathe. Just breathe. I did that for how long I don't know. I was soaking wet with sweat when I finally opened my eyes.

When everything in my cell was normal again I got up. I washed and changed. The grief hit me hard. I was also enraged. I wanted to hurt somebody. My emotions were all over the place. I wasn't accustomed to feeling out of control, so I didn't go out of the cell on my hour that day. I didn't want to lash out at anyone. I knew it wouldn't stop the pain and emptiness. I sat down and wrote to the warden, John Whitley, asking him to make arrangements for me to attend my mom's funeral so that I could say good-bye to her. At Angola, it was a custom at that time to allow prisoners to attend funerals for close relatives. I was shocked and devastated when he wrote back and told me I would not be allowed to attend my mom's funeral. He told me prisoners in solitary confinement weren't allowed furloughs. It is a very important custom in African American families to come together to say your last good-byes. Because of the cruelty of prison officials and the state of Louisiana I was once again forced to fight for sanity over insanity. There will never be words to describe the pain of this loss.

Since then the month of December has always been difficult for me. It manifests itself in different ways. I can be moody, depressed. I can feel insecure or not whole. Once in a while I still get this tremendous ache for my mom that feels like it's never going away. Sometimes it lasts for hours, sometimes days, sometimes weeks. Eventually it goes back inside.

A year after my mom passed away I was sitting on my bunk trying to figure something out when I heard my mom's voice in my head. It was like her voice echoed through the years to speak to me. In that moment, I sat on my bed and wrote this poem as a tribute to the wisdom and strength of my mom.

Echoes

Echoes of wisdom I often hear,
a mother's strength softly in my ears.
Echoes of womanhood shining so bright,
echoes of a mother within darkest night.
Echoes of wisdoms on my mother's lips, too young
to understand it was in a gentle kiss.

Echoes of love and echoes of fear
Arrogance of manhood wouldn't let me hear,
Echoes of heartache I still hold close
As I mourn the loss of my one true hero.

Echoes from a mother's womb,
heartbeats held so dear,
life begins with my first tears.
Echoes of footsteps taken in the past.
Echoes of manhood standing in a looking glass.

Echoes of motherhood gentle and near.
Echoes of a lost mother I will always hear.

Chapter 35

Preparing for My Trial

In 1995 a new warden, Burl Cain, was hired at Angola. Outside the state he would go on to become known as a "great prison reformer," who believed in "rehabilitation through Christ." In Louisiana, he was caught up in scandal after scandal over the years, much of it having to do with "side deals" he made with contractors at Angola and the misuse of inmate labor. One of his first deals at Angola was with Louisiana Agri-Can Co., a canning company that paid prisoners four cents an hour to take the labels off rotten canned goods and relabel them so they could be sold in Latin America and other places. An Angola prisoner who worked as an inmate counsel reported it to the U.S. Department of Health and Human Services. Federal officials seized cases of evaporated milk that were unfit for human consumption stacked "wall to wall and floor to rafters" in a building on Angola grounds. After the relabeling business at Angola was shut down Cain retaliated against the inmate lawyer who reported the operation by putting him to work in the fields.

Cain made other changes at the prison. He had razor wire wrapped in coils around the barbed wire that ran across the top of all the chain-link fences. He had time clocks installed at the end of every tier in CCR to guarantee guards made a count of inmates every 30 minutes. We heard the guards stamp their cards at the end of the tier every half hour. Cain replaced the leather restraint that went around our waists with a chain.

I sent my lawyers Bert Garraway and Richard Howell detailed notes about what happened during my 1973 trial, describing the witnesses, summarizing what they had said, and pointing out the contradictions in their testimony. I gave them lists of questions for each witness. For Joseph Richey alone I sent them 30 questions. I asked them to find experts that could discredit the charges against me: a blood-spatter expert who could explain the inconsistencies of the state's theory, a fingerprint expert to identify the bloody fingerprint that was found on the door of the dorm, an eye doctor who could look at Paul Fobb's medical records. I asked them to get the interview tapes that Anne Butler and C. Murray Henderson used to write the chapter in their book about Brent Miller's murder.

During my attorneys' attempt to review court records for my case we had a big break. In a box containing all of my court records, my attorneys found documents that had been withheld from my defense attorney during my first trial and had been placed under seal by the court. These documents showed that Warden Henderson and other prison officials paid Hezekiah Brown for his testimony against me during my trial. There was proof that Henderson agreed to pay Brown a carton of cigarettes every week; this was the highest form of currency in prison, used for gambling, sex trade, and day-to-day living, and the weekly payment was maintained for years by wardens after Henderson left Angola—until Brown's release. There were copies of letters written by Henderson in 1974 to a judge and to the director of the Louisiana Department of Public Safety and Corrections, asking them to support a pardon for Hezekiah Brown, less than eight years into his sentence for aggravated rape. There was even a letter from Henderson asking the prison to pay the cost of the advertisement used for Brown's clemency request. In those days, requests for pardons by prisoners had to be advertised in local papers so the community and victims of the felon's crimes could weigh in.

In a 1975 letter to the Louisiana Board of Pardons and Parole purporting to be from Hezekiah Brown, correctional officer Bobby Oliveaux, correctional officer Bert Dixon, Associate Warden for Custody Hilton Butler, district attorney for West Feliciana Parish Leon Picou (who prosecuted me at my 1973 trial), and former warden C. Murray Henderson were listed as "persons interested in appearing on [Brown's] behalf." Brown was released from prison in June 1986. His sentence of death, which had been switched to "life in prison" for aggravated rape in 1972 (when the U.S. Supreme Court found the death penalty unconstitutional), was commuted to time served. We could use all this to impeach Brown on the stand, because he testified in 1973 that he hadn't been paid anything or promised any favors in exchange for his testimony. I sent the copies of the letters that had been hidden from us to Herman. He could use them to appeal his conviction. We never had a chance to question Hezekiah Brown about his lies. He died before my trial began.

Anne Butler refused to provide copies of the taped interviews she used to write the chapter in her book about the Brent Miller murder, forcing my attorneys to go to court to obtain copies of these tapes. At an evidentiary hearing Butler argued that the reason she didn't want to turn the tapes over was that they could be damaged or destroyed. The court ordered her to turn the tapes over to it, stating that the court would make copies of them and return the originals to her. On the tapes prison officials must have been feeling overconfident since Herman and I had already been convicted and sentenced to life in prison for Miller's murder. They spoke openly and freely, not realizing that by doing so they were exposing their plot against me and Herman. During his taped interview former captain Hilton Butler said, "Hezekiah was one you could put words in his mouth. . . . Hayden kind of put those words in his mouth," thereby revealing that Brown was not a reliable witness. They also admitted Gilbert Montegut was framed because Hayden Dees wanted him to be framed.

Since Hezekiah Brown died before my trial, we asked presiding judge Bruce Bennett to block Brown's testimony from being read to jurors because we had no way to confront him with this new information—not only that he lied when he said he wasn't paid for his testimony but that he lied when he said he saw Gilbert Montegut stab Brent Miller. The judge denied our request. Brown's testimony would be read to jurors. (Judge Bennett would also allow John Sinquefield, who prosecuted me in 1973, to testify on the sincerity, honesty, and demeanor of Hezekiah Brown when Brown testified.)

Since Judge Tanner had overturned my murder conviction in 1992, my sentence at Angola went from life in prison back to the 50-year sentence I was serving for armed robbery. On April 29, 1996, I was discharged from Angola on that original 50-year sentence, having done 25 years—half the time, which was all that was required. If I hadn't been framed for Miller's murder I would have gone home that day. Instead, I packed up my possessions. I was to be transferred to a jail in Tangipahoa Parish, where I'd be held during my second trial.

The day before I was to leave, a young white prison guard came to my cell and told me I should get in touch with my family, my lawyer, and anyone else I could because he heard through the grapevine that the Millers would be waiting for me at the front gate when I was discharged and "it was decided" that the ranking officers in the building would not be there that morning. I immediately called my brother Michael, my sister Violetta and her husband, and both my attorneys. Each of them called the prison and the sheriff's office at St. Francisville and they were all guaranteed nothing was going to happen to me, that I would be OK. I called Michael later that day and he told me Burl Cain assured him I would be safe and there would be no problems.

Head sheriff Bill Daniel from West Feliciana Parish, who as a deputy had pointed a gun at my head in the clothing room almost exactly 24 years before, would take me to the small city jail in Amite, where I would live during my trial. I was put in full restraints in my cell and walked outside to meet him. I didn't see any rank except for one lieutenant. I knew then that some shit was going down so I mentally prepared myself. No matter what, I would not break. They could kill me, injure me, jump me; I would not beg, scream, or plead for mercy. I would give them nothing. I would leave nothing behind in that prison, especially not my courage.

Members of the Miller family were waiting for me at the front gate dressed in camouflage and wearing sidearms. I was signing out of the book when one of the Miller brothers began to curse and threaten me, calling me "nigger, motherfucker," telling me, "You'll be back" and "You're going to die at Angola, nigger" and that they were going to kill me. I had the ink pen in my hand and slowly made a fist around it, hiding it; I would use it if I had to. I let my cuffed hands drop in front of me, still holding the pen. He made an attempt to come around the concrete partition that separated us and a deputy put a hand on his chest to stop him. Daniel told me to get in the van. I started walking away from him toward the van, thinking any minute I'd hear gunfire ring out and I would die.

I got in the backseat and turned my head to look through the rear window. Bill Daniel and the Miller brothers were in a heated discussion. Daniel walked to the van and drove me to St. Francisville, where I was booked.

Chapter 36

Amite City

At the Amite City jail I was processed and put in a new cell for 23 hours a day. First, one with a concrete bunk and a hole in the floor as a toilet. After complaining to the deputies, I was told a cell was being prepared for me and I'd be moved soon. I waited for hours. Eventually I was moved to a cell called E-1, used for psychiatric patients, which had a big picture window built for observation. I had no privacy. One day I was sitting on the toilet with my sweatpants and underwear down to my ankles when a group of schoolchildren were brought in front of my cell on a tour. When they passed the plate glass window, the children paused and stared through the glass. It was one of the most humiliating moments of my life. I stared ahead, trying to project as much dignity as possible in that situation. After this incident, I banged on the door of the cell until one of the guards came and I demanded to see someone with authority. I talked to a lieutenant; it was decided they would give me a garbage bag that I could place over the window when I used the toilet.

I wrote to the warden telling him I had an exemplary record of conduct at Angola and asked him why I was in solitary confinement and asked to be placed in the general population. He came to my cell and told me that based on the information placed in my prison file by Angola officials I was a "high-priority" prisoner, "dangerous to self or others." The stupidity and hypocrisy of it was that while they kept me locked up by myself for 23 hours a day because I was supposedly a threat to others, they let me on the yard three times a week with other prisoners. That was a surprise. When it was time to go to yard they electronically opened my door from the control center and I walked out by myself down the hall. They told me which door to walk to and when I reached it they opened it and I got to the yard. On my first time out in the yard I started running laps when suddenly the door opened again and all the prisoners in the general population came out. It was nerve-racking because I'd just been told that because of my "high-priority" status I couldn't be around other prisoners. I thought prison officials were creating a situation in which I'd have to fight for my life. I slowed down my running and started looking at the men to see which one of them might attack me. To my surprise, nothing happened. There was no setup. Because of the prisoner grapevine, and the fact that many of these prisoners had been to Angola, a lot of these men knew who I was, what I believed in, and what I fought for. They left me alone.

After I'd been at Amite for six months a group of Cubans—some of whom had been in jail since they came to the States on the Mariel boatlift in 1980—attempted to escape from a nearby parish jail not far from where I was. One of them thought he'd be able to jump from the rooftop over a fence that surrounded the jail but he fell and shattered his leg. After he was treated at a hospital he was transferred to the Amite jail. A captain came to my cell and asked me if it would be OK to put him in the cell with me. "It's OK," I told him, "but I thought I was too dangerous to be housed with other prisoners. Tell the warden that if he's OK with putting a man in my cell why can't I be released into the main prison population?" The guard came back within the hour. "Pack up your shit," he told me. "We're putting you on the west wing." I put my possessions in a bag and picked up my mattress. At the Amite jail we had to carry our mattresses wherever we were moved. They took me to what everybody called the immigrant dorm, where they had prisoners from other countries, mostly Cubans. It was a small cellblock (called a "pod") with a day room and shower. There were eight cells total in the pod, four on an upper tier and four on the bottom tier. The cells were made for one prisoner but each held bunk beds for two. Our cell doors were opened at six a.m. and stayed open throughout the day. At count time the sergeant would tell us over the loudspeaker to "freeze" and he'd come to the door to count us. Some sergeants wanted guys in the cells for the count so we'd pile into the first-floor cells, five or six at a time, to be counted. Theoretically we were all locked down in our cells at night but sometimes they had 30 prisoners in a pod made for eight. Prisoners slept on the floor of the day room, under the stairway, or on tables. There was a food slot under the window of the pod that could only be unlocked from outside. At mealtime we stood in line and our trays were passed through the food slot.

I didn't speak a word of Spanish but through sign language and broken English the other prisoners and I were able to communicate. Since none of them could read or write in English they hadn't been able to do the proper paperwork for sick call. Unless they filled out the sick call forms authorities wouldn't let them see a doctor. I started filling out sick call forms for them and that led to some asking me to write letters to their families. Some hadn't been able to tell their loved ones where they were for months. The next thing I knew I was writing to the Immigration and Naturalization Service on behalf of many of them. Over time I started to comprehend some Spanish: "sí" for yes; "alto" for stop; "no tengo nada" means "I have nothing."

Eventually some prisoners came in who were bilingual and translated for us so I could help inmates prepare for the immigration board that met at the prison once a month. I had no idea that word spread among the Cuban prisoners in the jail. One day on the exercise yard about five or six young Cuban prisoners I didn't know started to walk toward me. I mentally prepared for a physical confrontation. When they got close they stood around me and greeted me like a friend, thanking me for helping the Cuban immigrants in my pod. It reconfirmed my faith in humanity.

Being out of the cell after 24 years was strange. When I was in CCR at Angola, everyone I talked to was always in front of me, standing at the bars outside my cell. In the pod it was unnerving at first to have people moving all around me, talking to me from all sides, coming up behind me. Being able to move around without restraints also took some adjustment. I wasn't accustomed to walking around the jail without an escort. They used cameras and electronic doors to lead prisoners from one area to another. The first time I had to go to central control for a call-out to see my lawyer, I stood at the door and heard the lock pop but didn't open it. I was waiting for a guard to come and get me. The prisoners behind me told me to open the door. I pushed the door then walked down a long hallway by myself. The whole time I thought about how for almost half my life I'd been wearing shackles and wrist restraints, with two escorts alongside me wherever I went.

In the day room, I couldn't remember the last time I'd held a phone receiver with my hand, instead of between my ear and shoulder, or watched television out in the open, instead of viewing it between the bars of a cell door. I was very conscious that I didn't know what to do with my hands. Do I put my hands in my pockets? I asked myself. Should I put them on the table? Gradually I became more comfortable and more self-assured. I ate meals with other prisoners and we played cards and dominoes at the metal tables. But the unknown factor was always there. There was the potential for danger every day, 24 hours a day. Everybody makes associations or friendships for his own protection. I did that too, but I didn't trust anyone. I was always aware that at any moment I could be attacked. It was a state of existence that I lived with.

The turnover in the pod was constant. After several months, we weren't an "immigrant dorm" anymore; there were more Americans than any other nationality. Prisoners were moved to other jails, other parishes, other pods in the Amite jail; some left to go to trial, others were released on bail, others took plea deals and got out.

I could have three to four cell partners in one day. From my bed I'd hear the cell door pop at one a.m., someone would be brought in, he'd put his mattress on the bunk to sleep, by seven that morning he'd be gone. Sometimes the guy they brought in would be so drunk he'd pissed himself. He'd throw his mattress on the floor and pass out, then they'd take him out the next day. Every time I had to be wary. I had to read the signs, the body language, how a dude talked when he came into the cell; is he normal, is he a bullyboy, is he crazy, is he timid? I had to make an instant analysis based on his body language and how he conducted himself to categorize him so I knew how to deal with him. As soon as I got used to one guy he was gone and somebody brand-new was brought in. I tried to get a cell partner who had a more serious charge, like murder, so I wouldn't have the constant turnover. I wanted somebody in my cell who would be there for a while. Even with that, there were no guarantees. My cell partner could seem normal for weeks and then go wacko and start messing with me, looking for a fight, or start beating on the toilet one night out of the blue, screaming.

Most of the prisoners were so young it broke my heart. I listened to them, trying to understand them. I asked them why they were in prison. From what they described the techniques used on them by police and the criminal justice system were the same used in black and Latino communities in the sixties. Targeting blacks and Latinos on the street, cleaning the books on them so they'd be pressured to take plea deals, sentencing them to long jail terms for minor offenses. One kid told me his parole officer had him picked up for "consorting with a known convicted felon" who turned out to be his grandmother. She had done two years in jail 30 years earlier on a drug charge. I talked to them about how important it was for them to stay focused on life outside the jail. They called me OG, for old gangster. They meant it as a term of respect.

From the beginning, I was concerned about the jury pool in Tangipahoa Parish. I knew some of the guards were Klansmen. I was in the heart of what was known as "David Duke territory." The town was very conservative. I wrote to my lawyers about it. Richard Howell wrote to me to say he was running for district attorney in Baton Rouge and would no longer be able to represent me and that a new attorney would take over my case. Clay Calhoun, an attorney practicing law in East Feliciana Parish, was named to replace him. The months passed. Two years passed.

On March 27, 1998, five years after Herman had filed his postconviction relief application, he got a hearing before the 19th Judicial District Court on the issue of whether he received ineffective assistance of counsel because of the conflict of interest created when his codefendant Chester Jackson turned state's evidence against him. Our former attorney Charles Garretson testified that all the information about a deal between the state and Jackson had been withheld from him.

Garretson testified he was "blindsided" when he returned from lunch and was "missing a defendant." "I felt that I was the only one in the courthouse that didn't know," Garretson said. "I felt that—I know all the deputies knew it. I felt the judge knew it, you know, and I felt I was the only one who did not know this." Garretson testified that before he cross-examined Chester Jackson at Herman's trial, Jackson's mother told Garretson that there was a "done deal" and if her son testified he would "get manslaughter" and "he would get a much lesser sentence" than what he was then serving. In addition, she told him, "he would get moved out of the Angola facility and put in a camp." When confronted with questions about a deal at trial, however, Jackson denied one existed.

In September 1998, Commissioner Allen J. Bergeron denied Herman's petition. He determined that when Chester Jackson took the stand and denied that he had been promised anything in exchange for his testimony against Herman, he "spoke the truth in the most narrow sense."

Chapter 37

The Crusaders

My trial was scheduled to take place at the end of November 1998. A couple of months before it was to start, two things happened that would alter the course of my life. First, a 25-year-old law student named Scott Fleming, who was volunteering for Critical Resistance—an Oakland-based organization seeking to abolish the prison-industrial complex—was reading a stack of letters from prisoners when he got to a letter Herman wrote to the organization, seeking support for my upcoming trial. Herman told our story, including how we'd been in solitary confinement for 26 years. He put my address at Amite in the letter as well as his own. Scott wrote back to both of us and asked us to call him. He wanted to help.

Second, Malik Rahim, the former Panther who had mentored and befriended both me and Herman at Orleans Parish Prison, was attending a Workers World Party event—also, coincidentally, in Oakland—when our former comrade from CCR, Colonel Nyati Bolt, approached him and told me my trial was coming up. Until that time Malik thought Herman and I were free. Malik tracked down my brother and called my lawyer.

Scott assumed we'd have a base of support somewhere in New Orleans, so while waiting to hear back from us, he called around looking for it. At a small anarchist bookstore called Crescent Wrench he found a group of activists who not only didn't know anything about us but didn't know anyone who knew anything about us. But they wanted to know more. Shana Griffin, Anita Yesho, Brice White, Icky, Brackin Kemp (Firecracker), and others created flyers about my upcoming trial and posted them around the city. They started to make arrangements to share transportation so they could attend my trial.

Malik flew to Louisiana with funds raised by Workers World Party activist Richard Becker and community organizer Marina Drummer to meet with my lawyer Bert Garraway. Garraway told Malik there was no reason for him, or anyone, to come to my trial—all he had to do was "get ready for a victory party." Malik left Garraway's office, flew back to Oakland, and with Becker in the Workers World office made 10,000 copies of a flyer about my case, all of which were distributed at events in the Bay Area the following week. He spread the word about my trial to activists and former Panthers throughout the country. (Through Malik's connections at Pastors for Peace our story even reached Cuba.) At a Workers World conference in New York City Malik printed hundreds of postcards featuring a statement from former attorney general and founder of International Action Center Ramsey Clark expressing concern about the fairness of my trial, stating that it would be monitored. While my jury was being selected hundreds of these cards were mailed to the offices of Judge Bruce Bennett and the district attorney.

When I got Scott's letter I called him collect that same day. He asked me about my lawyers and we talked about my upcoming trial. At the end of our conversation he asked me to call him every night during my trial to tell him what happened because he wanted to email the news to his network of friends, lawyers, and activists. I told him I would.

Malik talked about us to former Black Panther Party member Elmer Pratt (Geronimo Ji-Jaga Pratt)—a wrongfully convicted decorated Vietnam veteran who had been a victim of COINTELPRO and was recently released from prison. Ji-Jaga survived 27 years in the California prison system, several of them in solitary confinement, convicted for a murder that the FBI and other officials knew he was innocent of the entire time. (FBI surveillance records showed Ji-Jaga was in Oakland at the time of the killing, which took place in Los Angeles.) Ji-Jaga's conviction was finally vacated and he was released in 1997 on a judge's order based on evidence that the main witness against him was a police and FBI informant who had lied under oath. Upon his release from prison Ji-Jaga said, "I want to be the first one to call for a new revolution," describing himself as a "soldier . . . dedicated to the liberation of my people and all oppressed people." Originally from New Orleans, Ji-Jaga spread the word about me and Herman to his vast network of supporters, telling people who doubted us, because nobody had heard of us before, that we were Panthers and political prisoners, regardless of the original charges against us.

In November 1998, about a week before my trial was to start, I was reading in my cell in Amite when a young inmate came to my door and said, "Woodfox, some guy is getting ready to rape a white boy downstairs." He walked off. I put on my tennis shoes and went downstairs. I walked to the one cell on the tier that the guard couldn't see into with a camera, cell 15. There were three guys in there.

"What's going on here?" I said.

"What you got to do with it?" one of them asked me.

"You're trying to rape this kid, that's what," I said.

"It's not your fucking business." he said.

I told him I was making it my business. I punched the guy in his face, he pushed me, and we started exchanging blows. The other prisoner ran out. The white kid left. At some point during the fight I hit my face on the top bar of the bed, which blackened both my eyes. On my next attorney visit Garraway told me he wanted to push back the date of my trial. "I can't bring you in front of a jury looking like that," he said. He went to court and had a bench session with the judge. I don't know what he told the judge but he got us a two-week delay. My new trial date was December 7, 1998.

The night before my trial my brother and his then wife Pam had people stay at their house who came to my trial from outside Louisiana. Malik had people staying over in his mother's house and garage. New Orleans activist Opal Joyner had supporters staying in her house. Opal and Pam fed everybody. Malik was able to rent a car and a hotel room in Hammond, 19 miles outside Amite City, with funds raised from supporters including Luis Talamantez, a member of the San Quentin Six and longtime prisoner organizer and activist.

I knew the trial would be rough. "It is the position of the state," prosecutor Julie Cullen wrote in a pretrial memorandum, "that Brent Miller was the victim in this case, not because of who he was personally or because of anything he personally did, but rather because he was a white correctional officer."

In spite of that I was hopeful. We had proof that former warden C. Murray Henderson paid Hezekiah Brown for his testimony against us. We had former captain and warden Hilton Butler saying you "could put words in [Brown's] mouth." We had new supporters. The feeling of hope came with strong emotions of gratitude. Herman, King, and I had been on our own for so long.

I didn't yet know that my attorneys received money from the state to hire experts and track down all my alibi witnesses but did neither. I didn't know yet that a first-year law student would have known better what to do than they did.

Chapter 38

My Trial, 1998

I recognized Malik sitting with my brother as soon as I walked into the courtroom. We both had gray in our hair now. Everyone else, except for my family and my childhood friend Ernest, was a stranger: Geronimo Ji-Jaga's wife, Ashaki Pratt, was there, as well as Luis Talamantez, former Panther Gail Shaw from Sacramento, and several activists from New Orleans. I hated that I had to sit with my back to everybody during the trial. During recesses, I turned and spoke to people, even though I wasn't supposed to. Some guards kept trying to get between us but I felt such an overwhelming gratitude for these people that I kept turning to acknowledge them, to meet their eyes and nod my head to thank them.

From the first moments of my trial it was clear my lawyers Bert Garraway and Clay Calhoun were no match for Julie Cullen. No fewer than five lawyers from the DA's office sat on the prosecution's side every day. My attorneys were underprepared and outmaneuvered in every way. Cullen used every dirty trick she could to establish doubt of my innocence and to cover up the truth. She also made inflammatory statements about the Black Panther Party and about Brent Miller's murder. Miller had 32 stab wounds, including a 5¾-inch stab wound that punctured his trachea from the top of his left shoulder, allowing blood to get into his lungs, which is what killed him. Cullen asked the coroner if Miller felt pain before he died. "Yes," the coroner said.

The guard who found Miller's body said there was "a lot of blood" and Miller was lying in a pool of blood. In spite of that, Cullen got the coroner to say it was possible that Miller could sustain the stab wounds that killed him seated on Hezekiah Brown's bed (which is where Brown swore Miller was sitting when he was surrounded by four men and attacked) and not bleed on the bed. Miller could have "jumped up" from the bed immediately, the coroner said, resulting in "no blood" on the bed. Nobody asked how he could have been pulled off the bed to the floor behind where he was sitting, which is what "witnesses" testified, without ruffling the bedcovers.

Prosecutor Cullen told jurors I killed Brent Miller because I hated white people and that my affiliation with the Black Panther Party proved that I advocated violence against white people. The murder of Brent Miller, she said, was a "hate crime," a "racially motivated Black Panther murder."

To help her paint the picture of my supposed racism and militancy, Cullen told jurors about the letter I wrote—that authorities had apparently lost, because the letter was never produced—to former Panther Shirley Duncan from CCR in 1972, in which I wrote that white racists should be killed and I spelled America with three *k*s. Since Cullen didn't have the letter, she called the former classification officer who worked at Angola at the time to review a note he wrote to the warden *about* the letter. From reading that note he described the letter, testifying that Shirley Duncan was removed from my visitors list after I wrote the letter. The letter was supposedly bad enough to remove a visitor from my list but the classification officer never wrote up a disciplinary report on me for writing the letter. (His memo to the warden about the letter was also dated seven months after Duncan was actually removed from my list.)

After Hezekiah Brown's testimony from my 1973 trial was read to jurors in full (by a police officer sitting in the witness stand), Cullen called John Sinquefield, the DA who prosecuted me in 1973, to the stand. Sinquefield was allowed to describe Brown's "truthfulness," demeanor, and alleged sincerity when he questioned Brown back in 1973, saying that Brown "testified in a good strong voice, he was very spontaneous, he answered questions quickly and he was very fact-specific." Continuing, Sinquefield said, "I was proud of the way he testified. I thought it took a lot of courage." Garraway didn't object.

Furthering their narrative that I was a racist who hated white people Sinquefield testified he was in the courtroom in New Orleans the day I entered in 1970 after being gassed while wearing restraints and I raised my fists, saying, "Look what these racist fascist pigs have done to me."

Since we couldn't question Hezekiah Brown on the stand about the lies he told, we had to try to show through the testimony of other witnesses that Brown had lied. We put former warden C. Murray Henderson on the stand, and he testified that immediately after Brown "told us his story" about me, Herman, and Chester Jackson he was transferred to the more comfortable "dog pen" to live. Henderson acknowledged that he requested that Brown receive a carton of cigarettes each week in exchange for his "help" in the Miller murder and that he sent a letter to the governor asking the governor to pardon Brown. He sent another letter to the trial judge asking for a recommendation for Brown's pardon and offered to appear before the pardon board on Brown's behalf. Brown's clemency advertisement, he said, came from prison funds. (In those days prisoners had to place ads in local papers when asking for a pardon, to give the community a chance to react.) When Brown's sentence was commuted to "time served" in 1986 he had more than $900 in his prison account, even though, Henderson testified, Brown didn't have a job, suggesting that Hezekiah Brown was also paid in cash for testifying against us. "He didn't earn money at Angola," Henderson said. "He had no relatives or anybody that came to see him." Henderson also acknowledged that when Hayden Dees sent two prisoners—Joseph Richey and Paul Fobb—to the very comfortable police barracks in exchange for their testimony against me, it was not with his permission and, he confessed, it was "outside the scope of a normal investigation." The state police barracks was reserved for the most privileged inmates in the state prison system. Prisoners there worked as servants at the governor's mansion.

On the subject of Gilbert Montegut, who was placed at the scene of the murder by Hezekiah Brown but found not guilty at his trial with Herman in 1973, former warden Henderson admitted, "In my presence he [Brown] never, ever named Gilbert Montegut." Former captain Hilton Butler also admitted on the stand that he didn't think Montegut was present for Brent Miller's killing. This hadn't stopped either of them from allowing Montegut, a man they knew was innocent, to go to trial and possibly be convicted and sentenced to life in prison.

Former captain Wyman Beck repeated the testimony he gave at Herman's trial: that he saw Montegut at the hospital the morning of Miller's murder. A former prison hospital worker also testified he saw Montegut in the hospital's bullpen on the morning of the murder and that after he heard that Montegut was charged with murder he discussed it with Beck, who "didn't think he [Montegut] could have been involved," at which point his testimony was cut off by Cullen's objection. The hospital worker testified that he and Captain Beck agreed that "it would be pretty difficult for Montegut to be involved in [the murder] and be in the hospital at the same time." Meanwhile, Joseph Richey testified that after he "saw" me run from the dorm he "saw" Gilbert Montegut exiting Pine 1 after the guard's murder, "walking at a pace that made me think he was late for chow."

Former captain Hilton Butler took the stand and testified he recalled being interviewed by Anne Butler and C. Murray Henderson about the Miller killing for their book, but he "wasn't sure" if he said "you could put words in Hezekiah's mouth." The judge wouldn't allow us to play the taped recording of Butler saying that. My attorney read what he said to the jurors. The state knew there was no physical evidence linking me to the murder, so Julie Cullen presented a new, purposefully confusing theory—that the bloody fingerprint left at the scene of Miller's murder that didn't match me, Herman, or anyone officials accused of the murder wasn't really a fingerprint. An "expert witness" who worked in the State Troopers department testified the fingerprint was a "partial palm-print," undermining the significance of the fingerprint not matching me, even though it was deemed "strongly identifiable" in 1972 and 1973. The fact that the bloody fingerprint left at the scene of Miller's murder didn't match mine—along with the fact that deputies and prison officials never tested that print against every prisoner who was on the walk the day Miller was killed—might have exonerated me in the eyes of the jury. Prosecutor Cullen knew that. She intentionally muddied the waters. And she didn't inform my lawyers about her new "partial palm print" theory until right before the expert took the stand on the day of the expert's testimony, a violation of courtroom procedure. She told the judge she had not received a written report on the palm print theory. Later her own expert testified that she had told Cullen about the theory the previous year, in 1997.

I told Garraway to ask the judge for a mistrial on grounds of prosecutorial misconduct. The court denied the motion, ruling that we should have had our own fingerprint expert in court who could have disputed Cullen's witness. He reminded Garraway that state funds had been available to us for that.

Cullen repeatedly used underhanded tactics to confuse the jury. Through her line of questioning she revealed the substance of evidence the judge had ruled inadmissible. For example, she wanted jurors to see an unsigned, undated statement handwritten by a former Angola captain the night after Miller was killed that the judge ruled inadmissible. The statement was attributed to Leonard "Specs" Turner and was supposedly given to former Angola captain C. Ray Dixon the day before Turner was to be paroled. She put Turner on the stand and he testified he didn't make the statement. While she questioned Turner, Cullen essentially revealed the contents of the statement.

My attorneys didn't object once. This exchange has been edited to show Cullen's tactic, with other questions she asked in between removed.

Cullen: Do you remember us talking about Albert Woodfox's involvement in the murder of Brent Miller?

Turner: Again, I don't remember. I keep telling you the same thing.
* * *
Cullen: Now, do you remember telling me what you saw Albert Woodfox do on April 17, 1972?

Turner: No, ma'am, I surely don't remember that.

* * *

Cullen: Well, did you see Albert Woodfox do something on April 17, 1972?

Turner: I don't remember, I just told you.

* * *

Cullen: Now, did you see Albert Woodfox kill Brent Miller April 17, 1972?

Turner: I don't think I did, no ma'am.

* * *

Cullen: If you had seen someone stabbed 32 times, you wouldn't remember it?

Turner: I think I would.

Cullen: If you had been about five or six feet away from someone being stabbed 32 times, don't you think you would remember it?

Turner: May, and I may not, you know. I—I can't say what I would do and what I couldn't do.

Cullen: Didn't you tell me that Albert Woodfox and others killed Brent Miller?

Turner: No, ma'am, I never told you that.

* * *

Cullen: Did you tell C. Ray Dixon back in April of 1972 that Albert Woodfox and others killed Brent Miller?

Turner: I don't remember tellin' him that, if I did or not.

* * *

Cullen: Do you remember telling Murray Henderson that you weren't in a position to see anything, but that Hezekiah was there?

Turner: No, ma'am, I don't.

* * *

Cullen: Did you ever tell [Angola officer Bobby] Oliveaux what you had seen?

Turner: I don't remember ever tellin' him anything.

* * *

Cullen: All right, did you ever talk to [Angola officer Carl] Kimble about what you saw in the Pine 1 dormitory?

Turner: Not that I remember.

Cullen: Okay. You're not denying that you said—that you told him that, you just don't remember?

Turner: Told him what?

Cullen: That you saw Albert Woodfox kill Brent Miller? Let's cut to the chase Mr. Turner.

Turner: Let's see, I never—

Cullen: You know what we're talking about.

Turner: I never told him that.

* * *

Cullen: All right. Do you remember giving that statement to C. Ray Dixon?

Turner: No, I don't remember givin' that statement to anyone.

Cullen: All right. Do you deny giving that statement to C. Ray Dixon?

Turner: I really do.

C. Ray Dixon testified he didn't remember taking Turner's statement and that he didn't remember what the statement said, but when shown the statement, he recognized it was in his own handwriting. The judge allowed him to read portions of the statement aloud to the jury—sections that implicated me in Miller's murder. He instructed the jury that the statement was only admitted to attempt to "discredit the witness [Turner]," not to show that the contradictory statements were true. But how does a jury unhear something? (Even if Turner had made the statement, it should have been discredited by former warden Henderson's testimony. Henderson pointed out that Turner was due to leave on parole two days after Miller's killing and that he told him, as Henderson testified, "If you don't give me some information, I'm going to call the parole board and see that you do the rest of your eight years, flat.")

I had three witnesses in 1973 who testified they saw me in the dining hall at the time of Miller's murder, and two witnesses who were in or near Pine 1 that morning and said I wasn't there. I assumed my attorneys would either get them all to appear in court to testify or at least make sure their testimony from my first trial would be read to the jury. They only found one of my alibi witnesses to testify in person and could only prove they had searched for one more. The judge wouldn't allow us to read the testimony of anyone unless my lawyers could prove they had searched for that witness.

As the names of my missing alibi witnesses were discussed in open court, Violetta's husband, Michael Augustine, and our old childhood friend Ernest Johnson recognized the name Herbert "Fess" Williams. They heard he had died in New Orleans, and they thought they could get proof of his death so his testimony could be read. Williams was the inmate who was in front of the Pine 1 dorm at the time of Miller's killing and testified I wasn't there and Joseph Richey (who claimed he saw me run out of the dorm) wasn't there. Williams never changed his original statement, even after he was put in the dungeon and injured there, then housed in a cellblock. Michael and Ernest left the courthouse that day, drove the 74 miles back to New Orleans, and confirmed Williams had passed away by talking to his family. They contacted the coroner's office, obtained Williams's death certificate, and were back in court by noon the next day. In a small break, the court allowed the transcript of Herbert Williams's testimony to be read to the jury.

Sheriff Bill Daniel testified he never threatened me in the clothing room when I was being interrogated, saying, "At no time did I go in that penitentiary and interview inmates with a gun. I would always check my gun at the front gate." Years later, my attorneys found witnesses who gave statements that Daniel did not always "check his gun at the front gate" in those days. One of them said that when they were questioning prisoners, sheriff's deputies Bill Daniel and Thomas Guerin "were very agitated; they were armed."

My defense attorneys didn't call any expert forensics witnesses to dispute the state's case against me. My lawyers did not consult forensic experts who could have shed light on the sequence of events in Miller's murder by analyzing blood drops, spatters, and trails; they didn't talk to fingerprint experts. They didn't force the judge to require that the bloody fingerprint left at the scene of the murder be tested against other prisoner fingerprint files. They didn't have anyone review Miller's autopsy. They hadn't even ensured that all the alibi witness testimony from my first trial could be read to jurors. I was frustrated.

When I took the stand, I testified that I didn't know Miller except by sight; I had no altercations with him; and Miller had never written me up for misconduct, which was corroborated by prison records. On cross-examination Julie Cullen kept pushing me, asking if I was a racist. "In a letter to Sister Diane, why did you write AMERIKKKA?" she asked, "Are you a racist?" "Did racism give you the right to pull a gun on guards to escape from parish prison?" "Did being a victim of racism cause your armed robbery conviction?" "Were you a victim back when your raised your hands in the courtroom and shook your shackles and complained about white racist fascists?" I was getting tired of her innuendos and her deliberately twisting my words. At one point, she asked what I was wearing. Garraway asked what time she was referring to and she responded, "When you were killing Brent Miller."

I said, "Ms. Cullen, you know I didn't kill Brent Miller because you know I passed a lie detector test." It was not premeditated. I knew the results of polygraph tests were not admissible in court, because they are considered unreliable. I had no intention of saying it. I spoke out of frustration. The judge admonished the jury to disregard the statement.

Later, when a reporter interviewed jurors at my trial one of them told her I should have "known better" than to "slip" that in. "I think his slipping that information in may have turned the jury off," she said. "It did me. I believe that Albert Woodfox knew that that was not admissible, that we weren't supposed to hear it." The truth of my statement was less important to this juror than me knowing my place.

The trial lasted nine days. On the last day, the courtroom was packed with white-gloved, uniformed police officers, prison guards, and sheriff's deputies. It had been difficult for me to watch my family get their hopes up, , even when I knew deep in my soul what the end was going to be. I was worried about my brother Michael. He'd been so hopeful before my trial and even throughout it, whereas a lot of people in the courtroom knew my best chance was a hung jury. The jury deliberated for about five hours. When they read the guilty verdict, I turned to my brother and sister first. Violetta's eyes were filling with tears. I looked at her and met Michael's eyes. "They will never break me," I told them. "They will never break my spirit."

After the trial Bert Garraway told a reporter, "Basically, the state put the Black Panthers on trial, and the state convicted the Black Panthers." Ramsey Clark issued a statement calling what happened at my trial an example of "egregious prosecutorial misconduct." Stan Miller, Brent Miller's brother, told the Baton Rouge *Advocate*, "This is like an early Christmas present for our family."

WBAI–Pacifica Radio in New York City interviewed me the night after I was convicted. "I don't blame the jurors," I said. "They didn't have all the information." At the end of the interview I was asked what I believed in. "If you are not willing to struggle," I said, "if you are not willing to sacrifice, then you can never change things. Struggle is the essence of change and that's how I try to live my life. I've paid a heavy toll for it but I don't have one regret. If I knew everything that was going to happen to me and I could turn back the hands of time, I would not change one thing about my life—not one moment of dedication, not one moment of struggle, not one moment of physical pain that I've suffered from beatings by prison people in New York and in Angola."

Chapter 39

Back to Angola

While I was in the Amite City jail a new colonel at Angola, nicknamed Macho Man by prisoners, was making conditions worse at CCR. He oversaw Camp J and CCR at the same time and started taking away CCR privileges, making CCR more punitive. I received letters from King and Herman describing the situation. Since all prisoner mail is opened and read by prison officials, I had to read between the lines. When King wrote, "Man, shit is going down" somewhere in the prison, I knew he was talking about CCR. When he wrote, "Man, I haven't had anything to eat all day," I knew they were planning a hunger strike.

I was sentenced on February 23, 1999, to natural life without the possibility of probation, parole, or suspension of sentence. I was ready to go back and stand with my comrades. Since my conviction, I had been mentally preparing myself to be locked down again for 23 hours a day. It was very difficult to think about being put back in solitary after almost three years in the general prison population, but I didn't have a choice. The alternative to surviving it was to be broken. When I was returned to solitary confinement in CCR I was placed on B tier. My comrade and friend Kenny "Zulu" Whitmore was on that tier. Herman was on F tier and King was on C tier. Zulu passed me a cassette tape of Malcolm X speaking that I listened to in my cell that night. I'd read Malcolm's writings in books many times before. It was something special to hear Malcolm's voice. The biggest lesson I learned from Malcolm is that change is possible, that you can transition from what society has made you, as a result of your race and your economic situation, and redefine yourself. Malcolm also taught me how to look beyond my immediate surroundings.

King and Herman had already put together a petition, gotten it signed by prisoners, and filed a grievance with the warden about the stricter conditions at CCR. The warden never responded. When I arrived, notes were being passed between tiers to plan the hunger strike, encouraging guys to participate and to stay strong. Without our knowledge one of the orderlies who had been passing the notes for Herman and King was showing them to prison officials. No names were mentioned in the notes but it was easy for security to identify handwriting. Approximately 60 prisoners went on the hunger strike. King and Herman were called out of their cells for what they were told would be a meeting with the warden. They were gassed, beaten, and put in the dungeon at Camp J. They stayed on the hunger strike in the dungeon while we stayed on it at CCR.

They couldn't put me in a punishment cell because they didn't have my name or handwriting on any of the notes about organizing the hunger strike. The day they put King and Herman in the dungeon I tried to keep the prisoners on other tiers going while I was out on the yard. "Stay strong. Don't give up. Don't let them intimidate you," I yelled. I hollered up to the prisoners on the other tiers. "We're not at Camp J, they can't treat us like we are."

The next day, after yard, instead of being taken back to my cell I was taken to Macho Man's office. He asked me why there was a hunger strike. I said, "Why are you asking me?" He said, "I heard you are a ringleader; you have a lot of influence with other prisoners. If you tell them not to eat they aren't going to eat." I said, "I ain't no ringleader. You have no proof." He told me he had proof and I said, "Then why are we having this conversation? I should be at Camp J with Hooks and King." He asked me again why we were doing it. I told him, "The reason we're on a hunger strike is that you say one thing out of one side of your mouth and another thing out the other side. People don't trust you. We want the warden to come and see for himself this mess you created." He looked at the guard who brought me into the room and said, "Lock him up."

They put me in the CCR dungeon. I had a mattress, a sheet, and one blanket. I wore a jumpsuit. No radio, no TV, no possessions. I could get legal books but no other books. We were out of our cells only 15 minutes a day for a shower. Most of the men in the dungeon were mentally ill; some had already been gassed and beaten before being moved to the dungeon. They screamed or banged on their walls for hours, trying to handle the pressure however they could. I had to turn off my emotions. As usual, I forced myself to have an intellectual response to everything going on around me. Sometimes it was the only way to stay sane. I stayed on the hunger strike in the dungeon. I was never written up for it though. In all the years I was at Angola, I'd been on so many hunger strikes I can't count them, yet I was never written up for one. They wrote me up for "defiance" or "disobedience" or "aggravated disobedience." They didn't want a record of our protests.

I was kept in the CCR dungeon for 30 days. Herman, King, and I stayed on the hunger strike all that time. Once a week I was brought before the disciplinary court and told that I was being investigated for planning a second hunger strike and I was told the investigation was still ongoing. At the end of 30 days the investigative report cleared me. The major on the disciplinary board asked me if we could go off the record. "I'm caught between rock and a hard place," he told me. "There is no evidence for me to find you guilty but I got word from the very top to send you to Camp J." I said, "Do your job then." He found me guilty of something and they sent me to Camp J. I didn't mind. I wanted to be with my comrades. Years later I would read the write-up he created:

[Woodfox] then became very belligerent, and said, "You just as soon put me in Camp J because that's what it's going to come to because this shit isn't over with yet." He also stated "as far as he was concerned, it wouldn't be over as long as Wallace, King, and the other inmates put at Camp J for organizing the hunger strike remained locked up." He said they only organized the peaceful demonstration, and there wasn't anything wrong with that. He said again, "Just go ahead and lock me up at Camp J now, because that's what you're going to have to do anyway."

At Camp J, they put me on Herman's tier at Gator Unit the first night and then moved me to Shark Unit. King was in Gar Unit.

Camp J was referred to as a "punishment program," but the way it was executed at Angola it was flat-out torture. King used to say the "program" was to receive prisoners and in six months return patients. There were three levels of deprivation in the program. Most prisoners entered at Level 2, at which we were in our cells 23 hours and 45 minutes a day; we got 15-minute showers once a day. We got no dessert on our trays, no salt or pepper. We couldn't buy anything at the store except for hygiene products. We couldn't have any of our own clothing, so we wore jumpsuits. We could have six books, including a Bible if we wanted one, and writing materials. We had an hour out on the yard three times a week.

Camp J officers had no training; many of them were undisciplined and unethical, which led to brutal beatings and gassing of prisoners, especially mentally ill prisoners or prisoners who broke under the pressure of being confined to a cell more than 23 hours a day. Camp J was the most dreaded assignment for corrections officers at Angola. Guards were put there to be punished by administrative and security personnel with the authority to reassign them. The guards spent their days putting restraints on prisoners and taking them off. We were restrained on the way to the shower, unrestrained in the shower, and restrained for the short walk back to our cells. Multiply that by 15 prisoners on a tier. In the yard, they removed the leg shackles but we couldn't really exercise because they kept our hands restrained to our waists, which made it difficult to run; if you fall you can't brace yourself with your hands. Some guards who were too lazy to do their jobs would bribe prisoners with cigarettes—which were banned—to skip yard.

If a prisoner survived Level 2 for three months without a write-up he was supposed to advance to Level 3, with new privileges, such as being able to have a radio, buy snacks at the canteen, have an hour a day in the hall, and wear his own clothes. After three months at Level 3 without a write-up he was supposed to be released back to his normal housing. At any time, though, and at the whim of almost any security officer and for any reason, he could get a write-up and be sent back to

Level 2, or worse, Level 1, and have to start over. Level 1 was the harshest level and lasted 30 days. Meals consisted of a "loaf" of food made from whatever was being served to other prisoners, mixed together. Prisoners on Level 1 had no yard time and fewer possessions. Men on Level 1 had to wear paper gowns so they couldn't hang themselves. The insecurity of anyone's situation at any time in Camp J amounted to severe psychological torture. There were tiers where guards enforced total silence. A prisoner could be moved back a level for talking or for sharing food. From any level, a prisoner can be put in the dungeon at Camp J for 10 to 30 days. In the dungeon the clock stops. Those days don't count toward time in the program. The worst cell at Camp J was called "the booth" and was situated inside its own individual room. It was total and complete isolation.

Anyone who "acted out" at Level 1 or in the dungeon was put in four-point restraints, handcuffed to a bed at the ankles and wrists, which forced a prisoner to lie in his own urine and feces. Anyone who struggled and banged his head had a football helmet put on him by a security officer. I was never put in four-point restraints but I saw it in the dungeon when I walked by the other cells on my way to the shower.

With "good behavior" prisoners were supposed to be able to work their way out of Camp J in about six months. But as with all prisons, what's written down on paper is not what happens. A guard could have a bad day and take it out on a prisoner, or just be cruel; some of the officers regularly messed with prisoners to get them to react so they had an excuse to move the prisoner back a level, or they'd accuse someone of doing something they knew he didn't do to fuck with his head. Prisoners were exposed to harassment, mind games, provocation, beatings, and the constant threat of being put back a level. The threat of never being allowed to leave the program, of always losing ground, amounted to severe psychological torture. The overwhelming majority of prisoners left Camp J broken men.

When I got to Camp J after spending 30 days in the dungeon I was put on Level 2. By then we heard the CCR administration had restored all the privileges that had been taken away before our hunger strike.

They waited to do it until we were off the tier so it wouldn't look as if the hunger strike was effective. I forced myself to adjust quickly to being in a smaller cell and not having my possessions. In October, the weather got colder and since we didn't have our own clothes when we went outside for yard we were handed unlaundered sweatshirts to wear. After being forced to wear a filthy sweatshirt a few times I filed an ARP on that and eventually won the case in court. The prison's defense was they didn't have enough sweatshirts to wash them between prisoner use. The judge ruled they had to get more sweatshirts so prisoners had clean ones to wear.

When I made it to Level 3 I requested my radio out of storage. A guard came back and told me I couldn't have it because it had a cassette player attached. Cassette tapes weren't allowed at Camp J. I wasn't asking for cassettes, I told him. "I don't want to use the cassette player. I just want to use my own radio so I don't have to buy one out of the canteen," I said. Logic failed to convince him. I filed an ARP and was overruled. I had to buy what they called a "Camp J radio" out of the canteen, a tiny transistor made of see-through plastic that had terrible reception. Sometimes King and I were outside in our yard pen at the same time and we could call out to each other. For me that was a good yard day.

Years later I was touched to receive a copy of a letter written by a man who had been in a cell next to me at Camp J for a while. Someone who heard about our case and lived in Baton Rouge wrote to him, asking him if he'd ever heard of me. He sent her an unsigned letter about meeting me. When I received a copy of his letter I remembered him from his time at Camp J, but not his name. He wrote that when I was put in the cell next to his he was a "very depressed and troubled" man. He wrote,

The harshness, the evil and cruelty of prison life had begun to take its toll upon me. I became to trust no one as I seen everyone as my enemy. I found myself . . . with only two friends and their names were loneliness and pain. . . . One day a new prisoner was put in the cell next to me. I suddenly heard this voice saying "My name is Woodfox." So I say to myself "Man, don't I have enough problems already. Now I have a nut in the cell next to me." Again I hear this voice saying to me, "My name is Woodfox and I am introducing myself to you." This time I see [a] hand reaching out of the bars, in an effort to shake hands. . . . I was very skeptical about sticking my hand outside of those bars because I have seen guys whose hands hang outside the bars end up being sliced from a razor blade and some become stabbed from a homemade knife but for some unknown reason I found myself standing there, shaking Mr. Woodfox hand and the following day, he again spoke to me. And he also asked me, would I like something to read. . . . After closely observing this man, I began to see a man who has been confined to a cell for over 27 years. I also seen a man who has been condemned to die here in Angola. But yet I seen no hate within him. Nor did I see fear. But he did show that he was a man who were determined to become a better person. While realizing that he was living in a world where being better sometimes meant nothing. He showed that he was a man whose wisdom may very well be unlimited and whose strive for knowledge has become his faith. Seeing all of this and more, in Mr. Woodfox, is what inspired me to become a better person within myself. Through Mr. Woodfox I was reminded that a man who chooses not to seek knowledge is the same as a boy who choose not to become a man. I now realize that knowledge can be the key for that what sometimes seem impossible in life.

Kathy Flynn Simino, an attorney who worked for a center in New Orleans that did appeals for indigent defendants, wrote the direct appeal for my conviction on the grounds that the state withheld exculpatory evidence—that Hezekiah Brown had been paid—which was called "Brady material," after the 1963 Supreme Court ruling in *Brady v. Maryland*—and on the grounds that there were issues with the way the grand jury that indicted me was impaneled. When we took Anne Butler to court to get the tapes of her interviews with prison officials about the Miller killing before my trial, her testimony revealed that there may have been improprieties in selecting the grand jurors.

Simino filed my direct appeal in 1999. I would have three chances with this appeal in state court. First it went back to my trial judge. If he denied me, it would go before the appellate court, and if that court denied me, I would go before the Louisiana Supreme Court. I knew my appeal would be denied on every level. State judges like to be seen as tough on crime. Institutional racism was rampant, and still is. After all that, I could submit what's called a postconviction relief application (PCRA) in which we could include new evidence, which would take the same trajectory, starting with my trial judge. If denied, it would go to the state appeals court; if it was denied there, it would go before the Louisiana Supreme Court. Upon denial of my PCRA at the state supreme court level I would be able to go to federal court.

2000–2010

They tried to bury us. They didn't know we were seeds.

—Mexican proverb used by the Zapatista movement

Chapter 40

We Stand Together

January 1, 2000. Another century. In order to leave Camp J a prisoner needed to go 90 consecutive days at Level 3 without a write-up. King and Herman were 30 days ahead of me in the program, but when they were eligible to leave they refused to leave me behind. The reclass board put them back in their cells at Camp J. This was not only an act of defiance on their part but also unity. King and Herman were so insistent they weren't leaving without me that when I was eligible to leave the program a month later, prison officials moved me back first. Then they moved King and Herman back a week apart. They put us all on different tiers in CCR.

Support for us from outside the prison had grown while we were at Camp J. At first, people wrote to me because of my trial. When they found out about Herman, they extended their support to him and started writing to him. They wrote to us asking to be put on our visiting lists. We were each allowed 10 people on our list. When my list was full I directed people to get on King's list. If they coordinated visits with people on Herman's and King's lists we could all visit together. When white people started visiting us many of the security officers were shocked. It didn't compute with their belief system. Our supporters were both black and white. Shana Griffin; Brice White; Anita Yesho; Opal Joyner; former Panthers Althea Francois, Marion Brown, and Malik Rahim; and others were in New Orleans. Marina Drummer, Gail Shaw, Millie Barnett, and Scott Fleming were in California; and Leslie George and Anne Pruden were in New York. While we were locked up at Camp J, with limited access to phone and mail, they formed a support committee and started calling me and Herman the Angola 2. While I was grateful, it didn't feel right to me. We were three, not two. King was a Panther who was wrongfully accused and unjustly convicted. He made all the same sacrifices that Herman and I made. He lived by the same moral principles we did. We stood together in all the same battles and were beaten, gassed, and locked up the same. He was kept in solitary confinement because of his political beliefs too, for 28 years. The three of us had been through so much together. Now was not the time to separate. I wrote to Herman and asked: Now that we have a support committee, shouldn't King benefit from it? Shouldn't we become the Angola 3? Herman agreed.

I practically had to jump King to get him to do it. We were on the yard. He said no. He thought Herman and I should take advantage of the momentum that was growing around the Angola 2; he didn't want to take any attention away from us. I looked at him. King is one of the most selfless people I know. If he had 1,000 drops of water he'd give them to 1,000 thirsty people and go without. "King," I said, "we are stronger together. We can't start letting something come between us now." "Ask the members on the committee." he finally said. "If they agree, then OK." Herman and I wrote to our core supporters asking them to request a contact visit on a certain date. Miraculously those visits were all approved. The guard on duty allowed us to put two tables together in the visiting room so we could sit together. Herman and I told everyone our decision. Nobody objected. The A3 was born. The Angola 2 Support Committee became the National Coalition to Free the Angola 3, and it grew in numbers.

In the meantime, King, Herman, and I had been working on another civil lawsuit claiming that our decades of being locked down 23 hours a day in solitary confinement violated our 8th Amendment protection against cruel and unusual punishment. The Supreme Court had ruled that the Constitution "does not mandate comfortable prisons . . . but neither does it permit inhumane ones." The suit also claimed that our right to due process was being denied because the 90-day review board at Angola was a sham, a violation of the 14th Amendment. We also stated that our 1st Amendment right to freedom of speech was being violated because the reason we were being held in CCR for decades was our political beliefs. Herman wrote to the ACLU of Louisiana in New Orleans and asked for help. One of the organization's attorneys, Al Shapiro, got back to us and the ACLU filed the suit on our behalf on March 30, 2000, in state court in Baton Rouge against Louisiana Department of Public Safety and Corrections secretary Richard Stalder and Angola warden Burl Cain, among others. (Later state Corrections defendants removed it to federal court to obtain a whiter jury pool.) Our suit requested an injunction from the court to stop the state from keeping us in CCR, to force the prison to move us back into the general prison population. We also asked for punitive damages as well as attorney fees and court costs.

Our supporters in New Orleans met weekly, sometimes at Malik's house, other times in an empty church. They held yard sales, and second line concerts to raise money for attorneys and investigators for us. They created posters to make people aware of us. Scott Fleming, who had graduated from law school in 1999; and Leslie George, a producer and reporter for Pacifica Radio in New York, met in New Orleans and worked on tracking down new leads on our case, interviewing former prisoners and looking up old court records. Marina Drummer, in Oakland, secured 501(c)(3) status for our support committee under the name Community Futures Collective, which allowed us to actively raise funds and recruit lawyers and investigators. (Marina would serve as the fiscal and administrative center for our support committee from that time forward.) Others wrote about us on blogs and reached out to mainstream newspapers and TV news programs asking for coverage of us; none responded. The only national newspaper that wrote about us in the early days was *Workers World*, the newspaper of the Workers World Party. Even without the mainstream press, though, awareness about us grew as former Panthers across the country got involved, as well as prisoners' rights groups. Anne Pruden, of Brooklyn, became a loyal and dedicated friend, attempting to help us find a lawyer in those early days, even before knowing the details that proved our innocence.

Marina wrote to Amnesty International on our behalf in May 2000, and we were placed on Amnesty's "watch list" of "individuals at risk."

As our supporters grew in number, and under the pressure of the lawsuit, the Department of Corrections and prison administration started harassing me, King, and Herman. Censorship increased; they wouldn't let us see a lot of our mail. They started taking more interest in our books and magazines. They said any article or book that mentioned the Black Panther Party was contraband because it was "gang related." A lot of our incoming mail was "returned to sender" for various made-up reasons. Shakedowns became more aggressive. Herman, King, and I all had the same reaction to the increased pressure: Bring it on. Our personal safety was never an issue in our lives. We were willing to risk anything and everything to uphold our political beliefs. We felt the same way about backing the actions of our support committee. People asked us if they should try to protect us. "No," we said. "Don't worry what will happen to us," I told them. "That is a nonissue."

For the first time in decades there were people outside prison besides our families who cared about us. People were fighting for us. They didn't believe the district attorney's office. They didn't believe the courts. They didn't believe the prison officials. They believed us and they believed in us. They trusted us and offered us their friendship. We gave these people our friendship. At first, it was hard for me to answer their letters. I wasn't used to letting people into my thoughts and life. But one characteristic Herman, King, and I all shared was the willingness—and even need—to change. True change can be very painful because you have to let go of part of yourself. We knew from experience that by changing, we gained more than we lost. We got more awareness. We got more compassion. We used to call it "raising our consciousness." We talked about how the entire human race needed to raise its consciousness, not as individual races or groups, but as humans, as a species. If we didn't, human beings would become nonexistent, because we'd destroy one another. Change meant growth.

Now I was being asked to change again, to let my guard down. It always surprised me when I was asked for advice. "Instead of showing you how to build courage," I wrote in response to someone asking me how to be brave, "I write to you to pay tribute to and salute your courage. I embrace your courage. I lie down every night loving your courage. When I am in need of purpose or focus I thank your courage. Courage is not an ongoing thing that you walk around feeling every day. Like anything in life, it comes and goes with the challenges we meet every day of our lives!"

Chapter 41

Hidden Evidence

In 2000, Scott Fleming came on board and worked for us pro bono. First, he wrote an appeal for Herman, citing the new evidence—the Brady material—that had been kept from Herman but had come up at my second trial: that Hezekiah Brown was paid for his testimony. After Scott wrote Herman's postconviction relief application (PCRA)—as my direct appeal was wending its way through the state court system—he turned his attention to my case and oversaw the effort that uncovered new evidence supporting our innocence that I could use in my postconviction application. Working with attorneys Nick Trenticosta, Mike Rocks, Susana Herrero and investigator Gary Eldredge, Scott reinvestigated Brent Miller's murder as thoroughly as possible, 30 years after the fact. One of our first breaks was a statement Howard Baker gave to Mike Rocks, recanting his testimony against Herman. Baker was the prisoner who testified that he saw Herman run from Pine 1 the morning of Miller's death with blood on his shirt and pants and that he watched Herman dispose of his bloody clothes by burning them in a furnace in the tag plant. No longer in prison, he told an investigator he lied at Herman's trial to protect himself.

In a new affidavit Baker said that in 1972,

> Angola was life and death, buying and selling people, and the officers knew it was happening. . . . Weapons were everywhere. You could shake down for weapons one night and have just as many the next. I saw as many as four stabbings a week, week after week. I was

attacked and got 22 stitches in my head and only had an inmate to sew me up. . . . When Miller was killed I wasn't called in for questioning right away. The word went around from administration that it would be in an inmate's best interest to say what he knew about Miller's killing. So I looked at the situation like this, I got 60 something years, and I got a chance to help myself—so I was going to do something to help me get out of this cesspool. So, I gave a statement on 10/16/72, to Warden Dees, which was a lie. And my testimony based on that statement was a lie. I really thought this would help me because Dees told me my statement would get my sentence commuted. . . . Dees just wanted a statement. If they could have hung and burned the guys involved they would have. But there was too much light on the situation. I had heard that Hooks and Woodfox were suspects it seemed like five minutes after Miller was killed. It was all over the penitentiary that they were the ones that administration thought was involved. So I gave a statement. I was surprised that anyone didn't pick my statement apart. It was foolish to think that anyone could get to the tag plant with blood all over them, especially that day. And there was no furnace in the tag plant to burn clothes. There was only a heater to dry paint on the tags. You could not burn clothes in it and Dees knew that. And Dees knows that you have to go through two manned security checkpoints to get to the tag plant. You could not get there with blood on you. I never saw anyone come out of Pine 1. I was not near Pine 1 at the time Miller was killed. I lied to try to help myself.

Through the Louisiana Public Records Act, Scott Fleming obtained material that was deliberately withheld from me and my defense attorneys at both of my trials, including the original notes that sheriff's deputies Bill Daniel and Thomas Guerin took interviewing prisoners after Miller's murder in 1972. He also obtained Julie Cullen's trial notes, records from the crime lab that did the forensics testing, housing records from Angola, and FBI files on the case. He interviewed several former inmates. He met with lawyers and investigators in New Orleans and Baton Rouge. He examined the process used to impanel my jury and had

Mike Rocks study voir dire (preliminary jury examination) notes. Mike researched how grand juries and grand jury forepersons were impaneled in West Feliciana Parish, which was where I was indicted, and looked at the race and gender of nearly every grand juror who served in West Feliciana Parish for 30 years—between 1964 and 1993—in order to prove that, while African Americans served as randomly selected grand jurors in rough proportion to their percentage of the general population, they served in far lower numbers as grand jury forepersons, who were selected, discriminatorily, by white judges. Scott studied forensics testing, researching methods available to test blood, clothing, and fingerprints in 1973 and 1998. He got an expert to look at Paul Fobb's medical files to assess Fobb's vision based on the multiple surgeries he had before 1972. He turned over every stone to preserve every issue of ineffective counsel and prosecutorial misconduct he could think of. It's only because he did such a thorough job that, over the next 15 years, I was able to keep my case before the court.

In the 348 inmate interviews Guerin and Daniel conducted the day after Miller's death—interviews that the state had refused to hand over before my 1973 and 1998 trials—Scott found significant evidence that the prosecutor was obliged to turn over to my attorneys but didn't, the so-called Brady material.

To try to get around it during my 1998 trial, Julie Cullen made the deputies' notes available "in camera," meaning only the judge could see the notes. Judge Bruce Bennett stated that he would "give it a shot" and read the notes but warned, "I'm not sure that I would recognize what you would perceive to be exculpatory information . . . and I hate to be placed in the position of being the—the gate keeper of exculpatory information. . . . It's a very uncomfortable position to be placed in." The judge reminded Cullen, ". . . if I miss something that is exculpatory, then you all are going to have to live with that." Cullen responded by stating, "I fully accept that responsibility, your Honor." After the in camera review, the prosecution agreed to turn over only the notes of the sheriff's interviews with me, Chester Jackson, and Gilbert Montegut. The notes took up half a page.

We learned a great deal of information from the other 345 interviews that would have been favorable to my defense, important leads that the state's investigators ignored, leads that didn't point to us. It was as if prison officials and the sheriff's deputies were so determined to pin the blame on me and Herman that they knowingly and willingly ignored evidence and other leads, which could have proved who really killed Brent Miller. Two of the inmates interviewed by the deputies actually had blood on their clothes when questioned, according to the deputies' notes, and yet clothing from these inmates was not sent to the crime lab.

Based on their notes, Deputies Daniel and Guerin never questioned Hezekiah Brown, the principal witness who claimed to have seen Brent Miller's murder. Also, the deputies only questioned 14 prisoners who lived in Pine 1, where Miller's body was found. They interrogated three times as many prisoners—47—who lived in Hickory 4, where I lived. (Out of all the white prisoners who lived in the Oak dormitories, directly next to the Pine dorms, only seven were interviewed.)

The deputies' notes also revealed one prisoner had scratches on his "left back, near his shoulder blade"—a finding that deputies and prison officials apparently never followed up. (Forensics reports showed Brent Miller had skin and blood scrapings beneath his fingernails that were never tested.) There was a notation next to one prisoner's name that said he "heard talking the day before about something. G.K. [the initials of a prisoner] was one in the group talking." Next to this deputy Guerin wrote a single word—"plott [sic]"—which was never followed up by investigators.

When the deputies interviewed Joseph Richey after Miller's killing he first told them both that he went to Hickory 4 the morning of the murder and gave an inmate named "Crutches" cigarettes. Daniel wrote: "P-4 [Pine -4] 72037 [Joseph Richey] went to chow then went to hic-4 and gave Crutches some cigs came back to dorm." Guerin wrote: "Joseph Richey—Pine 4—72037—Gave Crutches cigarettes." At my trial both Richey and Daniel testified that Richey gave only one statement. By examining prison housing records Scott learned Richey was put in a cellblock after making his initial statement about giving

Crutches cigarettes. After a month in the cellblock he gave a second statement, saying he saw me run from the Pine 1 dorm, after which he was moved out of the cellblock and back into a dormitory. From the housing records Scott also discovered that every prisoner who testified against me got better housing afterward. Every inmate who testified on my behalf was put in more restrictive housing.

In Julie Cullen's pretrial notes Scott found even more proof that Cullen knew Joseph Richey was lying when he testified he saw me run out of Pine 1 after Miller was killed: he told her he hadn't "heard" my name associated with the murder until he overheard Chester Jackson's family talking. The file contained her personal typed note summarizing a conversation she had with Richey, who also went by the name Joseph Bowden. The note read: "When CJ [Chester Jackson] getting ready to testify and JB [James Bowden aka Richey] heard CJ's family talking was first time really realized that AW [Albert Woodfox] was involved in the murder." Years later two of Jackson's sisters would say Chester told them Herman and I had nothing to do with the murder.

In another unbelievable display of deliberate incompetence, Scott found a memo from Warden C. Murray Henderson to the FBI stating investigators found "a pair of bloody tennis shoes" in the area of the dormitory where Brent Miller was killed. Prison officials never sent the shoes to the crime lab; the blood on the shoes was never tested; the shoes were never entered as evidence at my trial or Herman's. And yet, at one time, the warden must have believed the shoes were key evidence in Miller's murder because the deputies asked prisoners their shoe size.

The day of Miller's murder I was wearing a gray sweatshirt, a pair of jeans, and rubber boots. The state always maintained I was wearing a green army jacket, jeans, and a pair of brown shoes that Bill Daniel claimed he seized from me the day of Miller's murder. Scott discovered from crime lab records that the clothes Daniel claimed he took from me were not submitted to the crime lab until a week after the murder and a week after all of the other evidence in the case had already been submitted and analyzed.

None of the above evidence was turned over to my defense. We never had a chance to investigate any of it. No jury ever heard any of it.

We could never follow up the leads that might have shed light on what happened. To us this was clearly prosecutorial misconduct. But Julie Cullen got away with it the same way all prosecutors do. There is no oversight of prosecutorial conduct in this country, even though reckless and irresponsible actions by prosecutors, who are out not for justice or truth but only for their own careers and to win, have enormous lifelong consequences on people's lives that can never be undone.

In my application for postconviction relief Scott also made note of what the sheriff's deputies' file did not contain: the names of police personnel who participated in the search for evidence; the names of police personnel who discovered evidence; photographs of the undisturbed crime scene (prison personnel had Miller's body moved before the police arrived); a complete listing of evidence collected; documentation of how, when, and where evidence was collected; and photographs or notes explaining locations from which fingerprints were lifted.

In addition to listing the Brady material, Scott raised more than 22 issues of ineffective counsel, including the fact that my lawyers Bert Garraway and Clay Calhoun did not investigate and consult with expert witnesses, did not object to flawed blood analysis, did not object to the way Julie Cullen questioned Leonard Turner on the stand, acted deficiently in allowing the prosecutor from my original 1973 trial to testify about his opinion of Hezekiah Brown's credibility and demeanor, did not investigate bloodstain evidence, did not investigate the bloody print found at the scene, and did not establish that physical evidence was lost.

Scott also included an analysis of the jury selection for my trial. He raised issues uncovered by Mike Rocks about the voir dire of the jury and the fact that none of the jurors were asked questions that would determine their feelings about race and their attitudes about black people, which should have been done to guarantee me an impartial jury, especially since we knew the prosecution was going to make my race and membership in the Black Panther Party an issue. He raised issues about the constitutionality of my grand jury and grand jury foreperson as well, noting there had been a pattern in West Feliciana Parish whereby the judge selected the jury foreperson rather than allow that person to be randomly selected.

Leonard Turner also gave a sworn statement to investigator Gary Eldredge that, after all his testimony saying he didn't see anything the morning of Brent Miller's murder, he was, in fact, in Pine 1 the morning Miller was killed. He said Herman, Gilbert Montegut, and I didn't do it, but he didn't say who did. Turner swore,

> In 1972 when Mr. Miller was killed I was an inmate at Angola in the Pine 1 dormitory. That morning I was doing cleanup in the lobby like I always did. Mr. Miller was inside the dorm talking with Hezekiah. While I was cleaning, two guys from another dorm came in. I said to them, "Hey the police in there." "We know," one of them said back. They both walked into the dorm. Then a third guy came in. He walked straight up to Mr. Miller (who had his back turned to him). The third guy grabbed Mr. Miller around the neck with one arm and stabbed him with a knife he had in his other hand. Then the other two . . . rushed up with knives and started stabbing him too. I took off. I knew Hooks Wallace, Albert Woodfox, and Gilbert Montegut. None of them were in the dorm or the lobby at the time. I saw what happened and I know for an absolute fact that none of these three guys were involved in killing Mr. Miller.

Investigator Eldredge interviewed a number of witnesses and located evidence. Scott Fleming and attorneys Mike, Nick, and Susana worked long hours for weeks to look at all our research and hammer out my appeal. In it, Scott also summed up the contradictory witness testimony against me. Scott wrote,

> In this case, the State has shamelessly presented no fewer than four irreconcilable theories of who killed Brent Miller. Hezekiah Brown said the murder was committed by Albert Woodfox, Herman Wallace, Chester Jackson, and Gilbert Montegut. Chester Jackson said it was himself, Albert Woodfox, and Herman Wallace. Paul Fobb said he "saw" Albert Woodfox alone. Howard Baker claimed it was Herman Wallace and "Pedro." For the State to have presented so many contradictory theories of the case was fundamentally dishonest. Even

without the benefit of any background knowledge as to the back-alley methods the State employed to secure its testimony against Mr. Woodfox, it is obvious that the State's witnesses must have been lying, for logic alone dictates the conclusion that such irreconcilable stories could not possibly all be true. . . .

Brown and Jackson both claimed to have witnessed the stabbing of Brent Miller. Brown testified that he and Miller were alone in Pine 1 when four men, armed with four separate knives, entered the building and killed Brent Miller. Jackson, on the other hand, claimed that three men, carrying only two knives, entered Pine 1 and found Brown, Miller, Specs [Leonard Turner], and "five or six" other men. Jackson was unable to say whether the five or six men in the back of the room participated in the attack. Brown was positive that the attack began when Mr. Woodfox stabbed Miller in the back. Jackson claimed to be equally sure that Mr. Woodfox stabbed Miller in the chest. Brown said that Miller was sitting on the bed facing the rear of the building. Jackson testified that Miller was facing towards the front of the building (which begs the question: How was Mr. Woodfox able to surprise Miller from behind after entering the room wearing a handkerchief over his face and walking directly past Miller?). Brown testified that the entire attack took one or two minutes and said Miller was incapacitated and fell (or, in his other version, was thrown) to the ground almost immediately. Jackson, on the other hand, testified that the attack took more than 10 minutes and said that Miller stayed on his feet until the very end. Richey said that he saw the men run out of the dorm only "two or three minutes" after they entered. However long it took, Paul Fobb claimed to be standing outside, "shocked and stunned" and "waiting" for Mr. Woodfox to walk back out of Pine 1. Brown said that he cowered against the wall in fear until Miller was dead and the attackers had left, after which he ran out of the building. Jackson said that Specs—whom Brown never mentioned—and Brown both ran out of Pine 1 while the attack was taking place.

Joseph Richey['s] and Paul Fobb's accounts began where Brown's left off—at the point when they claimed they saw the attackers run out of Pine 1. Richey testified that he saw Mr. Wallace, along with

Woodfox, Jackson, Montegut, Brown, and Specs, run out of Pine
1. In his trial testimony, all six men ran down the walk towards the
dining hall. In his initial statement, Mr. Woodfox went the opposite
direction, towards the Hickory dormitories, while only Brown and
Jackson went towards the dining hall. In his written statement,
Richey didn't know where Mr. Wallace or Specs went (although
he was able to remember when he testified nearly two years later).
Fobb, on the other hand, said he saw only Mr. Woodfox but none
of the people the other witnesses claimed to have seen.

Perhaps most importantly, the prosecution witnesses—who placed
themselves only feet apart from one another in the moments after the
murder—failed to notice each other. Richey said that he didn't see
Fobb. Fobb didn't see Richey (even though he claimed, by necessary
implication, that Mr. Woodfox threw a rag past Richey). Brown didn't
see Baker or Richey or Fobb. Jackson didn't see Baker or Richey or
Fobb. Fobb said he didn't "see" anybody else. All of them, in fact, said
that nobody else was present. Yet the state's witnesses would have us
believe that they were all present in and around the Pine 1 dormitory
when Brent Miller was killed. . . . This case amounted to a swearing
contest between 10 prisoners who testified for the defense (Woodfox,
Wallace and Montegut) and three who testified for the state.

Years later we came across more of what appeared to us to be prosecutorial misconduct. My lawyers were never informed that Joseph Richey
was diagnosed with schizophrenia in the 1960s and was prescribed
Thorazine, which he was taking, along with other antipsychotic medications, when he testified at both of my trials, a fact he would disclose
in a sworn statement in 2008. Before my 1998 trial, Richey said, he
told prosecutor Julie Cullen he was taking antipsychotic medications.
She told him to bring the drugs with him to court but never disclosed
to my lawyers that he was on any kind of medication. By the time we
learned about this, in 2008, it was obviously too late to include the issue
in my appeal. As usual, since there is no recourse for victims of apparent
prosecutorial misconduct against prosecutors who violate the rules of
professional conduct, there was nothing we could do.

Chapter 42

King Leaves the Belly of the Beast

In December 2000, we got the incredible news that King was granted a new trial by a three-judge panel of the U.S. Court of Appeals for the Fifth Circuit ruling on a habeas corpus petition written by Mandeville attorney Chris Aberle. Chris had been with King for a while. He was appointed to represent King by the U.S. Fifth Circuit back in the early 1990s and wrote his appeal on the federal district court's denial of his habeas corpus relief. When that appeal was denied Chris volunteered to help King get back into federal court. King always described Chris's next habeas corpus petition as "a work of art." His hearing that December was attended by dozens of A3 supporters. The court granted King habeas relief, ruling that he made a showing of innocence and that a constitutional violation had been committed in his trial.

Now the state was up against a wall. Prosecutors had no way to reindict King for the murder of August Kelly. The actual murderer had testified that he alone killed Kelly. There was never any physical evidence linking King to the murder and the prosecution's witness who testified against King at his 1973 trial recanted in the late eighties, admitting he had lied on the stand because authorities had threatened him. Prosecutors offered King a plea deal. If he pleaded to "accessory after the fact" they would give him a sentence of time served and he could leave Angola. King didn't want to take a plea. It was a lie. He wanted to be exonerated at a trial. But we all had just seen what had happened at my trial. Herman and I urged him to take the plea and get out, to go home. He didn't want to leave us behind. He didn't want us to be shorthanded. I would have felt the same way but I wanted him to leave. "Man, you gotta go home," I told him. "If one of us is free, all of us are free." King thought about it. Eventually he told us he decided to take the plea.

When he got to the courtroom on the day he was to be released, February 8, 2001, he was told the state changed the plea. Now the plea being offered was "conspiracy to commit murder." I believe the prosecutors used the lesser plea to lure him to court before they gave him the plea they planned to give him all along. It was a deliberate and duplicitous ploy to get King to the courthouse, where his family and friends were outside, waiting to bring him home. He'd already gone through the soul-searching required to take the first plea. Now this was a different lie. He was innocent. In the end King chose freedom over justice. Standing at the defense table he was told to raise his right hand to be sworn in. King raised his left hand. He took the plea. After court he was taken back to Angola to get the paperwork for his release and pick up his property. Herman was living on his tier and they said their good-byes. The tier sergeant allowed King to come onto my tier to say good-bye to me. King and I had lived on the same tier for 17 years. He had always been a stabilizing force for me. Most guys only talked about what was going on in prison; they couldn't see any further. King and I had wide-ranging conversations about philosophy and life, our political beliefs, world events, books we'd read, Supreme Court rulings, presidential elections, sports. We knew each other's weaknesses and strengths, our habits and ways. When he got to my cell door we hugged through the bars.

If King had started a new life—a life he deserved—and never looked back, Herman and I would have been happy for him. But he did something else. He met with our grassroots support committee and planned actions. He traveled with former Panther Althea Francois to universities to talk about us and speak out against solitary confinement. He planned a trip to speak in Europe with former Panther Marion Brown. Within three months of being locked in a cell 23 hours a day for 29 years, King was in New York City, telling our stories at the Black Panther Film Festival. Later that month he was back at the front gates of Angola, this time shouting through a megaphone, surrounded by supporters protesting solitary confinement and the injustice that Herman and I were facing.

On June 28, 2001, Scott Fleming argued Herman's PCRA before Commissioner Rachel Morgan of the 19th Judicial District Court in East Baton Rouge. In Louisiana, appeals in state court can go before a commissioner who reviews the case and writes a preliminary opinion before a judge gets the case. King was there with two busloads of supporters. He held a press conference on the steps of the courthouse, explaining to reporters how the state suppressed evidence that could have proved Herman's innocence. The commissioner recommended Herman get an evidentiary hearing with respect to the suppressed exculpatory and impeachment material that had come to light at my trial—the fact that Hezekiah Brown was paid for his testimony, among other things. He would have to wait years for that hearing.

That summer, using the recipe he perfected in prison, King started making bulk orders of his praline candy to raise money for A3 campaigns and for his travel. He called the candy Freelines. A friend donated large cooking pots for him to use; another friend created a package label that included the message FREE THE ANGOLA 3.

King would spend the next 15 years in courtrooms, at press conferences, on the state capitol steps, at hearings, in lecture halls, at protests and marches, in bookstores, at radio stations, at universities, and in the British Parliament, telling people about me and Herman, standing against the abuses of solitary confinement, and fighting for our freedom. "I am free of Angola," he often said, "but Angola will never be free of me." Wherever King went, support for us grew; people got involved. At every event people who were desperate about their own loved ones in prison or in solitary confinement approached him. He always took the time to talk to them. He perceived each family's struggle, each prisoner's struggle, as if it were his own. King always said being in prison was like being in a tunnel and freedom was the light at the end of the tunnel. Once he got out of prison, he told me, he discovered he was in a new tunnel and there was another light in the distance. "I think the struggle is unending," he told a reporter. "Actually, it's always beginning."

Chapter 43

Torture at Camp J

In March 2002, U.S. Magistrate Judge Docia Dalby ruled that our civil suit against cruel and unusual punishment could move forward. "Given the natural limits on the length of human life, especially one in prison, it is difficult to imagine a more atypical or extraordinary confinement," she wrote. Thirty years in solitary confinement, she continued, is "far beyond the pale."

The retaliatory harassment against us started almost immediately. Prison officials targeted Herman. A shakedown crew showed up at his cell early one morning. They didn't find any contraband. A different crew came at eight p.m. the same day, searching his cell again, finding nothing. The next day, while Herman was out on the yard, his cell was shaken down again: the third time in two days. This time a guard "found" a handmade handcuff key, what we call a "shim." Herman was immediately placed in the dungeon. Four days later he was brought before the disciplinary board. He denied having a shim and asked if he could pay for a lie detector test to prove it. They refused to let him take the test and sentenced him to Camp J for the six-month program, but first he had to spend 30 days in the dungeon.

They put him in the dungeon at Camp J. Herman wrote to me saying it seemed like prison officials were intentionally moving mentally ill prisoners out of their normal housing—the Treatment Unit (TU)—to put them in the dungeon with him. These prisoners, he wrote, "would scream, holler and talk to themselves all through the day and night." When one stopped, he said, another started. "It was as if they were doing shifts to keep the noise going." Herman wrote to the Camp J warden about his concern that keeping the mentally ill men in the dungeon was aggravating their conditions. He wrote to supporters asking them to call the prison to complain. Eventually he got word to us that Angola's lead psychiatrist finally spoke up and moved the prisoners back to their regular housing at TU.

After his 30 days in the dungeon Herman was put at Level 1 in Camp J. He wasn't getting enough food and had no way to buy any because Camp J prisoners could only buy food out of the canteen when they were on Level 3. After 30 days at Level 1, when he was supposed to be moved to Level 2, Herman was held back to do another 30 days at Level 1. I hated that they were persecuting Herman and not me. We always thought they didn't fuck with both of us at the same time because they didn't want what they were doing to be obvious. In their minds they could have deniability. They also knew that I knew what was going on at Camp J and they knew it affected me.

That spring, Scott Fleming met the UK-based human rights activist and founder of The Body Shop, Anita Roddick, out in California. He told her about us. She was shocked that we'd been in solitary confinement for 30 years and immediately wrote about us on her blog. "No major media outlet has shown any interest at all," she wrote. "I hereby challenge the media: tell the story of the Angola Three. The truth might just set them free." To my surprise she wrote to me, asking to be put on my visitors list. In August 2002, she came for a contact visit.

Very few people surprise me. Anita was like nobody I'd ever met before. A highly successful, world-renowned business mogul, founder of The Body Shop, and human rights activist was visiting me in a maximum-security cellblock in Louisiana, and she couldn't have been more at ease. She was intelligent, funny, and irreverent, so I was comfortable with her. She was humble, which impressed me. Her passion and enthusiasm for people and human rights and prisoners' rights were obvious. Her knowledge of social justice issues was extensive; her sincerity was pure. We talked about everything, no holds barred. She asked me, a man who had been in solitary confinement for three decades, if I missed having sex. I told her yes. She made me laugh. When we rose to say good-bye after that first visit we hugged and she was smiling hard. "I was just thinking about the huge party we're going to have when you and Herman get out of here," she said.

In September, she wrote about our visit on Counterpunch.org:

> I know the question people will ask when they hear I've taken up the cause of the Angola Three: Why me, why now, why 12,000 [miles] around the world to a remote prison to take up this case? And I am reminded of a quote I read on the wall of an Indian bank years ago. It was Gandhi who said, "Whenever you are in doubt, or when the self becomes too much with you, apply the following test. Recall the face of the poorest and the weakest man whom you may have seen, and ask yourself if the step you contemplate is going to be of any use to him."
>
> Albert Woodfox is not weak, by any means. But he, like his compatriots Herman Wallace and Robert [King], is worth my efforts and the efforts of all who believe that you must fight injustice where you find it.

Anita's husband, Gordon, asked Herman to put him on his list and went to see him at Camp J. On her next visit to me, Anita told me we didn't have to worry about raising money for lawyers anymore. Our support committee, which had been holding bake sales to try to help us financially, could focus on publicity and political actions now. Anita came back several times, sometimes with Brooke Shelby Biggs, a journalist who worked with Anita and who got on Herman's list; when Herman was not at Camp J, we could all visit together. Anita and Gordon Roddick changed our lives, ramping up the volume on our case immediately. When constant requests to the mainstream press failed to expose our stories, Anita paid to place ads about us in national magazines. She wrote about us on her blog and spoke about us and the abuses of solitary confinement to the BBC and British newspapers, which were more receptive than the mainstream American press. She talked about us wherever she went.

On October 2, 2002, Scott filed my application for postconviction relief. So much work had gone into it. I wondered how I could ever thank Scott. He worked so hard and made so many personal sacrifices to get to this point. About a week later Herman and I were sent programs for the 35th-anniversary reunion of the Black Panther Party through the mail by a friend. I got a note from the mail room telling me I wouldn't be allowed to have it because it was "gang related." The note told me it was returned to sender. The program sent to Herman, however, was delivered to his cell at Camp J. Shortly afterward, a guard went into his cell and confiscated it. Herman immediately wrote to the warden asking about rules concerning mail being confiscated at Camp J. He never got a response. The next day several lieutenants came to his cell door telling him to pack up all his property. He had been at Camp J for six months so he thought they were taking him back to CCR. Instead he was escorted to Cuda, the Camp J building that held the dungeon, where all his possessions had been dumped and scattered across the lobby floor. They walked him through the lobby as officers were intentionally manhandling his property. He saw photographs of his family members on the floor; guards kicked his toiletries across the room; all this was "staged to provoke rage," he wrote to a friend. "I chose to bite my tongue and said nothing other than to ask the reason I was being placed in the dungeon. I was told I would find out sooner or later." On October 28, after 17 days in the dungeon, Herman was taken to disciplinary court and learned he was found guilty of having "racist and gang-related" material—the program for the 35th-anniversary Black Panther Party event. They sentenced him to three more months at Level 2, suspending the sentence for 90 days to prolong his time there, and gave him 30 days of cell confinement. "It's a torture of the mind," Herman wrote, "giving someone privileges and then finding a way to snatch them from you. It's to demean you. To control you." They put him in a cell with 24-hour cameras trained on him.

Two weeks later Herman was back in his regular Camp J cell when his door opened at 6:20 a.m. and he was told to go to the front of the tier. He was locked in the shower while his cell was shaken down again. Guards came and took him out of the shower and put him in the dungeon. After two days, the warden told him the shakedown crew found a screwdriver and a shim in his cell. He was once again sentenced to Level 1. "My prison record has been an exemplary one," Herman wrote to a supporter. "I have never been charged with having a handcuff key, shim or knife, ever . . . but now, at the age of 61, I'm being accused of possessing contraband." His cell was shaken down weekly, he pointed out. "What sense would it make for me to leave such dangerous contraband in my cell knowing the harm it could bring me?"

Herman started documenting the experiences of the other prisoners from the Camp J dungeon, telling those who were willing to share their stories publicly that he would make sure people in the outside world would know about them. One prisoner told him he'd been held in four-point restraints for 13 days. Another was charged two dollars on three occasions for Mace used against him. One was writing a letter to his mother in his cell one day when a guard told him to remove the skullcap he had on, which he wore when he recited his prayers. When he didn't remove it right away he was gassed, and during the gassing he fell onto his cell floor and went into a seizure. When he regained consciousness, he was being beaten for not getting up when ordered, while being unconscious. Another prisoner told Herman he was losing the feeling in his arms after being forced for months to have his hands cuffed behind his back whenever he left his cell. One prisoner told Herman he had reached a point where he was afraid he might hurt himself. When he asked authorities for help he was gassed. He wrote to Herman: "They are refusing me mental and medical treatment so I'm cutting myself to get help." The prisoner unscrewed a lightbulb that night, broke it, and cut himself. "I won't take it anymore—ever again," he wrote to Herman. He was taken to the hospital, his wounds were sewn up, and he was put back in his cell. The next day the prisoner was taken to a disciplinary board hearing, where he was moved back to Level 1 and given 30 days of cell confinement. He was told he had to pay for his medical treatment, for ambulance transport, and for the lightbulb he broke. After disciplinary court, he was put back in his cell and the guard mistakenly left him wearing the jumpsuit he wore to the hearing. The prisoner took off his jumpsuit and looped it around the top bar of his cell door and tried to hang himself with it. An inmate "tier walker," paid 20 cents an hour to watch for suicidal behavior, saw him hanging, grabbed his legs through the bars, and held him up while everyone on the tier screamed and called for help. When the warden and a colonel arrived, they accused the tier walker of giving the prisoner the jumpsuit he used to hang himself. "I'm smack in the middle of this madness," Herman wrote to a friend.

Herman managed to get the stories of the Camp J prisoners out to artist Rigo 23, a longtime supporter and friend, and Rigo put these stories, along with excerpts of Herman's letters and interviews with the other prisoners, into a booklet. "No one should have to put up with such cold barbarism as you would find here," Herman wrote to Anita Roddick in 2002, in a letter that she posted online. "No one should allow it to go on; unfortunately, for right now, it is still going on. Every day, more and more of our spirit reaches out and looks out from behind these walls of shame."

Angola warden Burl Cain, interviewed by the New Orleans *Times-Picayune* about our civil lawsuit against 30 years of solitary confinement, told the reporter we were "crybabies." He said Herman and I "chose a life of crime" and should "look in the mirror and quit looking out. It's about time for them to look at themselves," he said.

Anita wrote to us and asked us to contribute essays for her book *A Revolution in Kindness*. Herman, who was sneaking food to prisoners in four-point restraints at Camp J, wrote an essay for her about teaching chess to prisoners. "I received a letter from Anita Roddick thanking me for my contribution to *A Revolution in Kindness*," Herman wrote to a friend from his Camp J cell. "I'm the one who should be thanking her, a billion times, but I don't want to bore her." (After the book was published Anita tried to send it to us but it was banned from Angola for potentially "inciting violence.")

Herman and I both knew he was being targeted because of our lawsuit. Prison officials were experts at using the disciplinary court at Camp J to torture and abuse prisoners. They'd build a case against a prisoner, write him up, take him to disciplinary court, sentence him to more time—and the cycle continues. He'd never get out of the program.

This was their way to legally inflict pain and suffering. Herman never complained in our notes back and forth. I knew he was suffering though. I also knew they would never break him. He released a poem he wrote in Camp J to our supporters:

> They removed my whisper from general population
> To maximum security
> I gained a voice
> They removed my voice from maximum security
> To administrative segregation
> My voice gave hope
> They removed my voice from administrative segregation
> To solitary confinement
> My voice became vibration for unity
> They removed my voice from solitary confinement
> To the Supermax of Camp J
> And now they wish to destroy me
> The louder my voice the deeper they bury me
> I SAID, THE LOUDER MY VOICE THE DEEPER
>   THEY BURY ME!
>
> Power to the People!
> Free all political prisoners, prisoners of war, prisoners of
>   conscience!

On December 7, 2002, to mark the fourth anniversary of my retrial, King, along with several members of the Coalition to Support the A3, and other prison activists held a demonstration at Angola's front gate, this time to protest the inhumane conditions at Camp J and the false allegations that were being used to keep Herman locked up there. Dozens of Angola security officers and armed sheriff's deputies from West Feliciana Parish surrounded the protesters. Plainclothes state troopers photographed them. King told reporters who had gathered, "Camp J is a torture camp. Numerous suicides result from inmates being held there."

The protesters stayed for 90 minutes. On their way back to New Orleans they drove in a convoy, fearful of law enforcement in that area after being surrounded by armed officers during their peaceful demonstration. Our supporters wrote to Herman, worried that their protests made things worse for him. They asked him if they should stop protesting. "Never," he wrote back. "Protest more."

I was writing a letter later that month when it started to rain. The skies darkened outside and it got hard to read. I called down to the tier officer, "Yo, man, turn the light on in cell 14." He ignored me. I called out again, thinking he hadn't heard me. No light. I asked him at least five different times to turn my cell light on. He didn't. I called down to him to get the supervisor. He said, "You ain't running nothing, I'll turn the light on when I want." Usually, I never lost control of my emotions. A guard could be trashing my cell in front of me, throwing my clothes on the floor, turning my mattress upside down, reading my personal mail and I might tell him to take his hands off my legal mail if he touched it, but I wouldn't show any emotion. That day my emotions got the better of me. I started shaking the bars. I shook the bars and yelled and screamed and didn't stop until the guard appeared at my cell door. He told me to step back. I complied. He told me I was spending the night in the dungeon and handed me a jumpsuit to put on.

As the door closed on my cell in the dungeon I sat on the bare mattress. I thought of my sister. The first time Violetta had breast cancer she got better. I knew the cancer might come back but I was unprepared when she got sick again. Violetta was a child when she started visiting me in prison. On the street, I protected her. Ten, twenty, thirty years later she still looked at me as if I kept her safe. Her loving acceptance never wavered. When former Panthers and activists came to support me at my 1998 trial my sister thanked them for coming and hugged them. She wasn't intimidated or afraid of TV news crews outside the courthouse. "We want him to come home," she said simply. "It's time for him to come home."

At her five-year checkup, toward the end of 2001, Violetta found out that the cancer had returned. She told me on a visit that the cancer had spread to her lungs. On August 10, 2002, Violetta died. She was 50 years old. The only request my sister ever made of me in more than 30 years was to be at her funeral. On her last visit to the prison she begged me to be there. She was weak and pale and so thin. I knew she was in pain. I told her I would, to comfort her. After her death, I wrote to prison authorities asking if I could attend my sister's funeral. My request was denied. I received photographs of Vi's funeral service. Her husband, my childhood friend Michael Augustine, visited me afterward. My brother Michael came twice that month. I talked to Vi's daughters and son on the phone. A3 supporters who went to her funeral came to see me.

I thought of us as children, picking strawberries behind our grandparents' farm. My sister's beauty was so natural, so effortless. Her devotion to me had always grounded me. I felt the pain of losing her in my soul.

In April 2003, King welcomed activists to the Critical Resistance South Regional Conference in New Orleans by reading a statement from the Angola 3, in which we emphasized the importance of organizing against solitary confinement and a racist prison and judicial system. Later that month, on April 17, he and our supporters were back at the front gates at Angola, marking 31 years since Herman and I had first been locked down, celebrating our resistance and protesting our wrongful convictions for the murder of Brent Miller. This anniversary gathering would become an annual event.

The following month, at an approved contact visit of Anita Roddick, Robert King, and several of our supporters with me, Zulu, and an inmate friend of ours named Roy, high-ranking prison officials came into the visiting room and terminated the visit within 20 minutes of everyone's arrival. They escorted King and our other visitors from the premises, telling them they had to leave and remove their cars from the prison parking lots within minutes. Anita, in the backseat of one of the cars, was on the phone to warden Burl Cain's office before they were out of sight of the prison. Later, prison officials said the visit was interrupted because King was a "security risk." They put Roy in the dungeon, accusing him of lying on his visiting form. The prison accused King, who was known as Robert King Wilkerson in prison, of lying about his name when in reality, after King was released from Angola and for the first time in his life got his birth certificate, he learned that his name and birth date were not what he thought they were. On his birth certificate he was Robert Hilary King, which was the name that he would use thereafter on his driver's license and every other legal document. The prison sentenced Roy to Camp J and moved him there. After our attorneys got involved and proved Roy didn't violate any prison rules, he was moved back to CCR.

Later that month, a federal appeals court ruled that King, Herman, and I had the right to sue Warden Cain and Richard Stalder, secretary of the Louisiana Department of Public Safety and Corrections, alleging we suffered cruel and unusual punishment in CCR. After that news, the persecution of Herman continued. He was held at Camp J for nine more months. During that time, Marina Drummer was writing newsletters to our supporters and expanded our email list, taking actions to align with other groups to enlarge our base of support. I got to know people on our support committee who visited me in prison, and many of them became friends. They told me about their political beliefs and actions; I was always moved by these visits.

In August 2003, King and artist Rigo 23 flew to South Africa as guests of Nelson Mandela's Institute for Global Dialogue, and there they met with African National Congress leaders. King spent the following month speaking in Johannesburg, Pretoria, Durban, KwaZulu-Natal, and Cape Town, and on Robben Island. At Angola, Herman and I stayed in touch as best we could through letters passed by trustees. A new year came. When they finally brought Herman back to CCR, in February 2004, I could see the skeleton underneath his skin. He had lost more than 30 pounds at Camp J. The fighting spirit in his eyes was unchanged.

Chapter 44

Cruel and Unusual

One way Herman and I could track King's movements was through our mail. When we received sudden batches of letters and cards from one place, we knew he'd been there: Amsterdam, Belgium, Paris, London, Lisbon, Rio. He traveled extensively throughout the United States too: Washington, DC; Boston, Los Angeles, Chicago, Houston. His words moved people to action. Dozens of supporters, journalists, and new friends wanted to talk to us and took our collect calls from prison.

We were all frustrated because the civil lawsuit we filed in 2000 against our solitary confinement seemed to be stuck in court. State officials used seemingly endless delay tactics, filing numerous appeals asking that the suit be dismissed, arguing that prison and state officials should be immune from such lawsuits. All that changed in 2005, when a team of New York–based lawyers led by George Kendall took on our civil case pro bono. George, a former staff attorney for the American Civil Liberties Union Eleventh Circuit Capital Litigation Project, had worked closely with the Innocence Project and the NAACP Legal Defense and Educational Fund on policy issues and taught courses on criminal justice issues at several schools, including Yale Law School, the Florida State University College of Law, and the St. John's University School of Law. George had heard about our case from Nick Trenticosta. At first George was only involved in our civil suit claiming that our constitutional rights were being violated by our being kept in solitary confinement for decades. To get started, he sent four lawyers to Angola to go through thousands of Louisiana State Penitentiary paper records. The task took more than two weeks. He put together a team of brilliant young lawyers to work on our case, including Carine Williams, Corrine Irish, Sam Spital, and Harmony Loube. Later, Katherine Kimpel and Sheridan England, in Washington, DC, joined the legal team (focusing on solitary confinement conditions), and Billy Sothern and Robert McDuff, in New Orleans, also joined (focusing on my criminal appeal.) (Years after we met George in 2005, his team would take on my criminal appeal, and then Herman's.)

Over the next two years, George's team deposed more than 60 witnesses for our civil case. We were bound by the limits of what we could legally ask for in terms of damages or injunctive relief, but these lawyers never had an underlying attitude of "Let's just get them out of CCR." It was always "Let's get them out of prison." I think that made a huge difference in how George and his team represented us. When George and his legal team were recruited to another firm, Squire Patton Boggs, in 2009, they didn't abandon us. One of the conditions George made was that he wouldn't move unless his new firm would continue to represent us.

Meanwhile, Herman and I were dealing with numerous delays in our criminal cases. Scott Fleming filed my postconviction writ in the Louisiana Court of Appeal, First Circuit, in 2002. It took nearly three years for the state court to deny it, on August 8, 2005. It took another year for the Louisiana Supreme Court to deny our appeal of that denial, on September 29, 2006. All together it took seven years from when I filed my original direct appeal in 1999 to "exhaust all state remedies" before I would be allowed to file in federal court.

Herman's case was also being drawn out. On September 9, 2000, he filed his application for postconviction relief, which went to a state court commissioner. A year later, on September 10, 2001, the commissioner ruled he should get an evidentiary hearing. Two years and nine months later, in June 2004, the 19th Judicial District Court ruled Herman's claim with respect to Hezekiah Brown was unwarranted and dismissed all the other claims in Herman's petition. Herman and Nick Trenticosta appealed that ruling to the First Circuit Court of Appeal, in

2005. The First Circuit reversed part of the lower court's ruling, adopting the dismissal of every issue except for the allegations concerning Hezekiah Brown, ordering a new hearing on that issue.

I didn't expect anything more. I knew from experience the judicial system is not concerned with innocence or justice. (The state had already recognized I had a meritorious grand jury discrimination claim filed in 1973 but chose to ignore it.) An innocent man could be hanged and the court system would only rule on what kind of rope was used for the hanging. In legal terms this is called "due process." But the pain of each of our denials in court was magnified for me now because of the men and women who worked on our cases and all of our supporters. I didn't want them to lose heart. I felt responsible, each time a ruling didn't go our way, to stay positive, to reach out, to encourage them. I wrote messages that were distributed to our supporters through newsletters and on websites. After my 2006 denial, I wrote,

> I say onward with the fight! . . . One must never hope to escape the battle without setbacks or injury. The art of a great soldier is not in his ability to fight but in his ability to maintain his dignity, pride, and self-respect, and most of all, his humanity in his darkest hour! To the friends, family, comrades, and supporters of the National Coalition to Free the Angola 3, I salute you for a job well done. I embrace all of you in my heart, soul, and spirit and I take great comfort in knowing that in the battle ahead for myself and Herman Wallace we will not be alone! Dare to Struggle. Dare to Win!

Herman's evidentiary hearing took place on September 20, 2006. It was held at Angola. Because so many people had attended his 2004 hearing in Baton Rouge, authorities wanted to try to thin out the crowd in attendance. Still, Herman's family and many supporters made it there. Nick Trenticosta, Scott Fleming, and Susana Herrero represented Herman, once again before Commissioner Rachel Morgan of the 19th Judicial District Court. They laid out the merits of his Brady claim that he had raised in his postconviction relief application. They showed the commissioner five letters Warden C. Murray Henderson wrote between

February 1974 and November 1975 attempting to get a pardon for Hezekiah Brown. They showed her how, even after Henderson left Angola, officials kept his original deal with Brown. In 1978, the warden at that time, Frank Blackburn, wrote to the secretary of corrections, C. Paul Phelps, asking that Brown be paid one carton of cigarettes a week. "This, I feel, would partially fulfill commitments made to [Brown] in the past with respect to his testimony in the state's behalf in the Brent Miller murder case," Blackburn wrote. In a handwritten note Secretary Phelps responded, "I concur. Warden Henderson made the original agreement with Brown . . . I think we should honor the agreement."

Bobby Oliveaux, a retired Angola guard, testified at the hearing that he was told by authorities to make sure Hezekiah Brown did not run out of cigarettes while he was in custody, and that if none were available from the prison, Oliveaux should pay for them himself. Oliveaux also testified that before Brown was released from Angola, he was moved from the dorm at the dog pen into an "outbuilding" with a TV by himself. He was also paid as an orderly but, Oliveaux said, didn't do any work. Oliveaux said he knew Brown well, that the prisoners he oversaw "were like children" to him. (Oliveaux was the "handler" who was rumored to have been called to the courthouse the day of my 1993 indictment to talk Hezekiah Brown into testifying against me before the grand jury.)

The commissioner was also shown a letter dated December 10, 1984, written by Howard Marsellus, chairman of the pardon board, to Governor Edwin Edwards, recommending clemency for Hezekiah Brown. Marsellus wrote that even though Brown's request for clemency was opposed by the New Orleans Police Department and the Orleans district attorney, "We . . . recommend that Your Excellency grant applicant a commutation of sentence to time served."

Less than two months later, Commissioner Morgan ruled in Herman's favor, recommending the court reverse his conviction. In a 27-page recommendation she found Herman's conviction was fundamentally unfair because the state suppressed material impeachment evidence. She cited Warden Henderson's promise to help Hezekiah Brown obtain a pardon for his testimony, expressed by Henderson at my trial, quoting from my 1998 trial transcript, in which my attorney Bert Garraway questioned Henderson:

Garraway: Didn't you also tell him [Brown] that if he gave you the information and proceeded to testify for the State, that you would also promise to support a pardon application for him?
Henderson: Yeah . . .
Garraway: And did you do that?
Henderson: I wrote letters for him.

Had Herman's jury known about that deal, Morgan wrote, "it could have seriously affected the jury's determination of Brown's credibility." She continued, "Such a promise, it is fair to say, could have even influenced him to lie if he was so inclined. We should not overlook the fact that Mr. Brown was not just any bystander but had served and was serving time for attempted aggravated rape and aggravated rape, respectively. He was not a newcomer to the prison system or a young naïve man. Warden Henderson's promise was made to him before he testified at trial." Herman was elated. We all were. But the commissioner's report was merely a recommendation, not a final ruling. Judge Michael Erwin of the 19th Judicial District still had to rule.

Now that I had exhausted all avenues in state court I could appeal my conviction in federal court. Attorney Chris Aberle, who won a new trial for King in 2000, wrote my petition for habeas corpus and we filed it on October 11, 2006. The Latin term *habeas corpus* means "produce the body." Prior to President Bill Clinton's signing of the 1996 Anti-Terrorism and Effective Death Penalty Act, which weakened habeas corpus for everybody, it had been referred to as the "Great Writ"—the legal procedure that prevented the government from holding a person indefinitely without showing cause. In my habeas petition we claimed that (i) prosecutors knowingly presented perjured testimony and false evidence at my 1998 trial; (ii) they suppressed exculpatory evidence, including proof that witnesses were lying and evidence of my innocence; (iii) they violated the Confrontation Clause of the Constitution by using and emphasizing out-of-court statements of Chester Jackson; and (iv) racial discrimination tainted the selection of the foreperson of the grand jury that indicted me. This federal habeas petition was assigned to Judge James Brady in U.S. District Court for the Middle District of Louisiana.

The next year, the efforts of George Kendall's team in our civil case against cruel and unusual punishment began to pay off. In August 2007, U.S. Magistrate Judge Docia Dalby ruled that being locked down at the Louisiana State Penitentiary for three decades could constitute cruel and unusual punishment. In her 50-page decision Dalby wrote: "These men, now in their 60s, do not and have not for some time, presented a threat to the 'safety, security and good order of the facility.'" She noted that officials cited only the "original reason for lockdown" as the reason we were being held in CCR, even though, as she pointed out, the prison changed its policy in 1996 and eliminated that as a justification for prolonged confinement. "By 1999," Judge Dalby wrote, "these plaintiffs had been in extended lockdown more than anyone in Angola's history, and more than any other living prisoner in the entire United States." Judge Dalby stated that prison officials should have known that "being housed in isolation in a tiny cell for 23 hours a day for over three decades results in serious deprivations of basic human needs." She noted that lockdown may pass constitutional scrutiny if imposed for short periods of time, but any reasonable officer would know that solitary confinement may violate the Constitution when imposed for going on three decades. Not only had the courts "consistently noted the severity and terrible deprivation associated with such confinement," wrote Judge Dalby, "it has long been the subject of research, and even of televisions and movies. . . . It is also a matter of common sense that three decades of extreme isolation and enforced inactivity in a space smaller than a typical walk-in closet present the antithesis of what is necessary to meet basic human needs. With each passing day," she wrote, "its effects are exponentially increased, just as surely as a single drop of water repeated endlessly will eventually bore through the hardest of stones."

This decision was a huge victory. It didn't mean that we had won, but now we would be allowed to litigate the question of whether long-term solitary confinement violated the Constitution under the circumstances of our case.

Then, we got devastating news. On September 10, 2007, Anita Roddick died suddenly of a brain aneurysm. I felt hollowed out. Anita, full of life. Anita wanted to transform the world. Her death was so unexpected. I couldn't get my bearings. She was my friend. King flew to London and spoke at Anita's memorial service. Herman and I sent statements that were read aloud, expressing our sadness and love. Anita's husband, Gordon, came to visit us. He was on Herman's visitors list and coordinated to arrive with someone on my list so Herman and I would both be called out to the visiting room at the same time. He wanted to talk to both of us. He told us he would fulfill Anita's dream for our freedom and pledged his continued support to the A3. We were touched that in his grief he remembered us and took the time to see us. Gordon and Anita's daughter, Samantha, wrote to me, asking to be put on my visitors list so she could visit me in place of her mom.

Before she passed away, Anita had told me that great progress was going to be made in our case. After she died, many of her friends and associates, who became aware of Anita's work for the A3 at her memorial service, stepped forward to help make that happen. Gordon put them in touch with our existing committee through Marina Drummer and they became a de facto advisory board. Organizer Chuck Blitz, a friend of Gordon's, set up a weekly call on Fridays, bringing everyone together to talk about A3 support strategies. That call would take place every week for the next eight years. Chuck and members of the advisory board worked with Marina to find a part-time coordinator. They hired Tory Pegram, the former director of development and public education for the ACLU of Louisiana, to fill that role.

We now had an enhanced support committee. We had our core "on-the-ground" grassroots supporters, some of whom had been with us for almost 10 years—since my trial—activists who voluntarily managed communications, raised funds, spoke at conferences, staged protests, wrote articles, painted murals, did mailings about us; who visited us, wrote to us, put money in our accounts, accepted our collect calls, called prison officials to ask about our welfare, and sent us puzzles, magazines, and books. And we had this new advisory board that became part of our committee, composed of Anita's and Gordon's friends, who were prominent social justice lawyers and experts; social entrepreneurs and business leaders; architects of national political campaigns; national NGO leaders; retired judges; communications professionals; filmmakers and actors, all of whom were no less passionate but who operated in a different stratosphere, through connections in politics and media. The goals of our committee were unchanged: to use our stories to spread the word about the horrors of solitary confinement in America, to get us out of solitary confinement and into the general prison population, and to free us.

I put Tory on my visitors list and she visited twice a month for a year, updating me and Herman on A3 meetings, King's schedule of events, press reports about us, and the ins and outs of her work for what had now become the International Coalition to Support the Angola 3. It would be impossible to capture it all.

To truly represent all the hours that each person on our support committee and advisory board spent toward freeing us, all the ideas they had, actions they took, sacrifices made, the time and money spent, the frustrations endured, the details of each victory large or small, the pain of each loss—to name all that was done on our behalf would take another book.

Herman and I made a conscious decision to give our supporters a great deal of autonomy. We could not micromanage our committee, the board, or the individual activists who worked on our behalf because of the limitations of being in prison. All our mail was read, our phone calls were recorded, the visiting rooms were bugged. We couldn't have meetings. Our stance to our supporters was: if you act with integrity, we have your back.

We had a huge legal team, which was completely separate from the support committee, and sometimes at odds with the committee, because often the legal team wanted less exposure, less activism. Sometimes our supporters disagreed with legal strategies. We never asked our legal team to change strategies based on pressures from our supporters. We never asked our support committee to tone down actions that drew attention to our case. We trusted that each group, separately, knew what it was doing, and we wanted to make sure that nobody was ever prevented from contributing what he or she did best.

On October 9, 2007, almost a full year after Commissioner Rachel Morgan issued her recommendation to overturn Herman's conviction, Judge Michael Erwin of the 19th Judicial District Court denied Herman's claim that the state had withheld exculpatory evidence that Hezekiah Brown was paid for his testimony before Herman's 1974 trial. It was the first time in the history of the state, to my knowledge, that a judge did not accept a commissioner's recommendation. Judge Erwin gave his response to the commissioner's 27-page recommendation on one page, in one sentence, with no analysis: "This court does not agree with the Commissioner's recommendation that a valid Brady claim exists," he wrote. Herman appealed to the Louisiana Supreme Court.

Chapter 45

"Are You Still Sane?"

Social workers used to come around the tier and ask prisoners if we wanted to talk to them. King, Herman, and I made polite conversation with these people but never asked for help. We knew if we did that somewhere down the line it would be used against us. A guard could threaten you with being moved to the Treatment Unit (TU), the "mental ward." Once you're taken off the tier to TU you could come back a zombie. The drug of choice for prisoners in those days was Prolixin. I don't know if they overmedicated people, or if it was the nature of the drug, but Prolixin almost made men immobile. It broke my heart to see men on this drug. It would take them damn near an hour to walk from one end of the hall to another. They stopped taking showers. Their cells became filthy.

Drugs like this were referred to as "chemical restraints." They killed the spirit. Every once in a while, when there was a security guard on duty who brought his humanity to the job, I asked the guard to open my door and allow me out of my cell to help one of these patients who was out of his cell for his hour. I swept out and mopped the prisoner's cell and gave him a shower. The prisoner couldn't do anything but stand there the whole time I washed him. Mentally ill prisoners got no help at Angola. For many years, over the late 1990s and 2000s, CCR was housed within TU. We shared a dungeon and I would see guards gas the mentally ill prisoners being held there because they wouldn't stop screaming or beating on bars. These men never should have been in the dungeon to begin with. Sometimes security guards would go into the cell and beat on them. I couldn't see it but I heard the blows.

In preparation for our civil trial Herman, King, and I had to meet with psychologists. The state wanted to show we had "adjusted" to the cells and hoped to document that we were not really harmed by being locked down 23 hours a day for decades. For our side, George Kendall wanted to know the true impact of solitary confinement on us.

Talking about our mental state and emotions was not easy for any of us. In 2003, Nick Trenticosta had asked us to meet with Stuart Grassian, a board-certified psychiatrist and former faculty member at Harvard Medical School who was an expert studying the impact of solitary confinement. Through his extensive research Grassian has documented what he believes is a specific psychiatric syndrome caused by solitary confinement, characterized by panic attacks, paranoia, hallucinations, hypersensitivity, and difficulty remembering, concentrating, and thinking. According to Grassian, even after a brief stay in solitary confinement, "a person can descend into a mental torpor—a 'fog'—in which alertness, attention and concentration all become impaired." The inability "to achieve and maintain attention is experienced as a kind of dissociative stupor. . . . The inability to shift attention results in a kind of 'tunnel vision' in which the individual's attention becomes stuck. . . . [Prisoners in solitary can] find it difficult to maintain a normal pattern of daytime alertness and nighttime sleep. Some find themselves incapable of resisting their bed during the day—incapable of resisting the paralyzing effect of their stupor—and yet incapable at night of any restful sleep. Difficulties with thinking and concentration, obsessional thinking, depression, anxiety, agitation, irritability and difficulty tolerating external stimuli [are common.]"

When I met with Grassian I felt vulnerable. I wasn't used to sharing my deepest feelings with anyone. But I knew the barbaric practice of solitary confinement had to stop. "The only way to survive the cell is to adjust to the painfulness of it," I told him. I couldn't answer all his questions, but I tried my best. "When you leave, you go back to your life," I said. "I go back to my six-by-nine-foot cell and have just minutes to erect all these layers, put all these defenses back." Every time I had a visit I had to break down the layers that I used to protect my sanity and my physical safety on the tier. When I went back to the cell, I had to put all those layers back. I had to shut my emotional system down. I buried my emotions, so that things that would normally touch me or move me didn't touch me or move me. And I only had approximately five to ten minutes between the visiting room and the cell to do it. "It is the most painful, agonizing thing I could imagine," I said. "But I have to do it in order to survive."

Herman told Grassian he missed experiences like sitting under a willow tree after working in the field to catch a breeze in the shade. He struggled to describe what confinement in a six-by-nine-foot cell felt like. Tears came to his eyes. "Pain. How do you describe pain," Herman said, hands trembling, Grassian wrote in his report. "When I start to feel the pain, it comes too much—like a flood. I have to stop it. . . . You suppress so much." King, who was already out on the street, was also interviewed by Grassian. "Perhaps the most common theme expressed by the three men during the interviews," Grassian wrote, "was that of sadness and loss, and the desperate need not to feel those feelings, for fear of being overwhelmed by them."

Several years later a psychologist hired by the state was sent to interview me, Herman, and King. With this psychologist, I answered questions without digging into my personal feelings. By the end of the second interview, though, I was getting irritated at his line of questioning and his constant insinuation that because I could have books in my cell and I could exercise outside three times a week for an hour, year after year of being locked down 23 hours a day was tolerable for a human being and was somehow acceptable. At the end of my second interview with him he asked me if there was anything I wanted to ask him. "Do you think that watching TV and being able to buy candy in the canteen makes a difference to somebody held for almost 40 years in maximum-security isolation?" I asked. He didn't respond. "Do you think being able to make phone calls alleviates the pain of sitting in a cell 23 hours a day, year after year? It doesn't," I told him. "If you can't get out of the cell nothing they give you makes a difference. The pressure of being in the cell never goes away. The fight for sanity never goes away. You want me to believe that I'm OK when you know I'm not OK.

I can't give you specifics on how being in solitary has affected me but I can tell you without a doubt it has affected me."

George Kendall asked me on his next visit what I had said to the state's psychologist. He told me the state wanted to send a second psychologist to interview me. Maybe the first psychologist dropped out because he had an attack of conscience, I told him. Maybe he realized that being locked in a cell for 23 hours a day year after year was cruel and unusual punishment. We couldn't know for sure. Herman and I didn't want to meet with another psychologist from the state. The state's lawyers fought us on that but George and his team prevailed.

George did need us to talk to another psychologist for our side, however, so they could prepare for our civil trial. He set up meetings for us with Craig Haney, a professor of psychology and researcher at the University of California, Santa Cruz, who was world renowned for studying the effects of solitary confinement on prisoners. Haney's research shows that only 15 days in solitary confinement can create anxiety, withdrawal, irritability, hallucinations, aggression, paranoia, rage, loss of control, a sense of impending emotional breakdown, hypersensitivity, self-mutilation, and thoughts of suicide.

Herman and I met with Haney on separate contact visits at Angola, and he also talked to King. During one of my meetings with Haney I ordered food in the visiting room. When my meal came the guards wouldn't loosen the chain on my handcuffs so I could eat. They would only remove the chain if I went behind the screen, so Haney and I ended up meeting with the screen between us. Haney was compassionate and knowledgeable about the impact of solitary confinement, and I liked him, but once again I felt as though I could only give enough to satisfy the purpose of the sessions, which was to establish that I'd been affected by being in solitary for so long. I had to hold on to everything else to stay sane. The fear that I might start screaming and never stop was always with me. I don't say that lightly. I described my claustrophobic attacks and my problems with sleeping—the fact that I couldn't sleep more than a few hours at a time. I told Haney I talked to myself all the time, that I had debates aloud with myself because there was nobody else to talk to. When I told him about not being able to go to the funerals of my mom and my sister, I cried. To get out of depression, I told Haney, "I refind my core and what I believe in," describing how I held on to the principles, morals, dignity, and duty that I learned from the Black Panther Party. I told him I worried about becoming desensitized. "There is a part of me," I said, "that is gone, that has been taken—my soul. I had to sacrifice that part in order to survive. It was the price of being able to make it with my principles intact."

Herman expressed similar feelings about how difficult it was to deal with emotions, telling Haney, "I stay away from things, emotional things that I skillfully put aside. I feel like there is a dam of emotions, feelings, and tears that could burst forth. I must be able to hold back. It's a reflex, the way we function in here, it is a survival mechanism. You have to repress and deny your feelings. You worry about what would happen if you release your feelings and your tears. . . . You can't break down, you can't moan out loud—if I don't [keep control] I don't know what will happen to me. I've seen too many guys let their emotions come loose and they've never returned from it. I fight every day against that."

In his report Haney wrote, "All three men have relied on a belief system that has helped to keep them strong in the face of severe deprivations. They see themselves as representing something larger than themselves—as leaders who have stood up in the name of improving the prison system at Angola—and they do not want to succumb, or even give any indication that they might be weakening, out of concern for what this would mean to others who look to them for guidance, strength and example. Thus, it is especially difficult for them to admit their own vulnerability to the harsh conditions around them."

Chapter 46

2008

On January 14, 2008, James "Buddy" Caldwell, an Elvis impersonator and the former district attorney for the Sixth Judicial District in Louisiana, was sworn in as the new attorney general for the state of Louisiana. One of his first moves was to hire the prosecutor at my 1973 trial, John Sinquefield—Caldwell's childhood friend—to be "first assistant," the number two position in the office. Unsurprisingly, we were on Caldwell's radar right away. There was the Sinquefield connection, and the fact that my case was in the attorney general's office; it had been transferred there before my 1998 trial. Also, George Kendall's team was pressing ahead with our civil lawsuit, filing motions and deposing dozens of witnesses, including current and former Angola officials. Our support committee had done a tremendous job challenging what they considered to be the lies and misrepresentations of the state's case against us. The pressure was on the state to respond, and Buddy Caldwell saw an opportunity to make a name for himself. It wasn't long before he would launch a smear campaign against me.

But first, I got news that Brent Miller's widow, Leontine "Teenie" Rogers, had written a letter supporting me and Herman, asking the state to admit its mistakes in the case, reopen the case, and find the real killers of her husband. Rogers had learned our side of the story a few years before, from an investigator, Billie Mizell, who was initially asked by our attorneys to look into our case. When I first heard that Billie wanted to talk to Brent Miller's widow I wasn't optimistic. Teenie Rogers was 17 years old when her husband was killed. She grew up hearing the story that "racist" Black Panthers killed her husband because he was white. She would later say she didn't know why she let Billie into her house on that first visit. But she thought of Brent, the "love of her life," every day. Maybe his murder always felt unresolved for her. In the year after Miller's death, Rogers sought damages from the state since her husband had lost his life at his workplace. The state responded by maligning Miller, saying it was his fault he got killed because he should have been in the guard booth, not in a prisoner dorm. Rogers's case was dismissed and she received just $45 a week in workmen's compensation for a limited period of time.

Teenie Rogers told Billie Mizell on that first visit that she didn't go to my trial, because it was too painful, but she'd always believed what she had been told: that bloody fingerprints left at the scene of Brent's murder and other evidence proved they had the murderers who killed Brent. Over a series of visits with Rogers, Billie laid out the evidence that pointed to Herman's and my innocence—the bloody fingerprint that didn't match us and was never tested against the prisoners who lived on the walk, the bloody tennis shoes that were never given to the crime lab or brought up at our trials, all the contradictory testimony that pointed to lying "witnesses." In between Billie's visits, Rogers would later say, she did her own investigation, including talking to former Angola guards. She came to believe that a terrible miscarriage of justice had taken place. She wrote to Governor Bobby Jindal, asking him to find out who killed her husband.

In January 2008, our stories were taken to Washington, DC. King, Tory Pegram, Chuck Blitz, Gordon Roddick, and several other members of our advisory board, including Barry Scheck, the cofounder of the Innocence Project; Denny LeBoeuf, a Louisiana death penalty defense attorney who was directing the ACLU's efforts in Guantánamo at the time; Joan Claybrook, the founding executive director of Ralph Nader's Public Citizen; Ira Glasser, the former executive director of the ACLU's national office; Ira Arlook of Fenton Communications; Webb Hubbell, President Bill Clinton's associate attorney general and former chief justice of the Arkansas Supreme Court; the actor and anti–death penalty activist Mike Farrell; and Gordon's close friend and colleague

Ben Cohen from Ben & Jerry's, met with as many legislators and other potential national advocates as they could.

At one of these meetings Louisiana state representative Cedric Richmond (Orleans Parish), who was chair of the Louisiana House Judiciary Committee, Teenie Rogers, Billie Mizell, Tory, and King met with Rep. John Conyers, who was head of the federal House Judiciary Committee at the time and had assembled some of his colleagues. Our case was laid out. Then Billie introduced Teenie, who read aloud the letter she wrote to Governor Jindal.

> Brent and I both grew up on what everyone calls "The B-Line," which is a neighborhood behind the gate of the Louisiana State Penitentiary at Angola. As kids, we knew that Angola was a prison and a farm—but we just called it "home." Angola is where we lived, it is where we went to church, it is where we went fishing and hiking and played ball with our friends, and it is where Brent and I said our wedding vows. Not a day has passed in the last 36 years that I have not thought of Brent and the love we shared and the life we could have had. April 17, 1972 still feels like yesterday to me. I dropped Brent off that morning where he clocked in for duty and then I drove to beauty school in Baton Rouge. A few hours later, my sister showed up to tell me that Brent was dead. My brother, who was also a guard at Angola and on duty that day, had to see Brent's body—he never returned to work after that. My father also quit his job and we all left Angola. My husband, and my home, were taken from me by the men who stabbed Brent 32 times.
>
> For over three decades, I believed those men were Albert Woodfox and Herman Wallace. In 1972, I wanted both of them dead and would have killed them with my own hands if I could have. Even though I was too devastated to read the newspapers or attend the trials, I had no reason to doubt that the men who had been charged were the men who murdered my husband. Everyone on the B-Line had heard that a bloody fingerprint had been found at the crime scene, and when a fingerprint is discovered inside a prison, it does not take much effort to find out who left it there—the population is

captive and each inmate has a set of fingerprints already on file with the state. I assumed that a fingerprint left in my husband's blood provided the administration with an open and shut case against his killers. I had also heard that a bloody tennis shoe and a bloody knife had been found and that Woodfox and Wallace themselves had blood on their clothes so, for 33 years, I never doubted that the right men were behind bars. . . . What I found out was that there was a lot I did not know.

Since that day . . . I have learned that the bloody fingerprint found at the crime scene did not match Woodfox or Wallace. I was even more shocked to find out that no real attempt was made to find out who the fingerprint did belong to, which should have been a very simple thing to do. I have learned that the bloody tennis shoe never made it to the crime lab. I have learned that the knife could not be tied to Brent's death at all. I have learned that the clothes that the state claimed belonged to Albert Woodfox were missing from the crime lab for a week and only had a few tiny specks of what might have been blood. Since my husband was stabbed 32 times, that seems a bit unbelievable to me. I have learned that the entire case against Wallace and Woodfox came down to inmate testimony—because NO physical evidence could tie them to the crime—and yet more inmates testified on their behalf than testified against them. I have learned that the state's witnesses received rewards ranging from transfers to pardons to cigarettes and most of them have now admitted that they lied. I have learned that there was such a rush to judgement that a man named Robert King was also taken to solitary confinement and eventually told he was there under investigation for Brent's murder. He was left in solitary for 29 years, even though he could not possibly have committed the killing since he did not even arrive to Angola until days after Brent was murdered. I have recently met Mr. King, who is a gentle and kind man and is somehow not bitter about what was done to him.

I do not know what it is like to spend three decades in solitary for something I did not do, but I do know what it is like to lose a loved one to a senseless murder. Every time another newspaper article or

TV news story runs and every time a reporter calls me, I have to relive April 17, 1972 all over again. I do not know if you have ever lost someone you love to such a brutal crime, but I can tell you that it changes you—the grief overwhelms you, the "what ifs" haunt you. And now I have to live with another tragedy—the two innocent men, who have already spent 36 years in solitary confinement, who remain in prison for a crime that they did not commit. This is a tragedy that the state of Louisiana seems willing to live with. I am not. I hope you aren't either. . . . After over 36 years, there can be no excuse to deny justice for one more day. It is time for the state of Louisiana to finally compare the bloody prints found at the crime scene to every inmate who was incarcerated at Angola on the date of Brent's murder and find out who left his fingerprint on the wall of that prison dormitory before he walked out and left Brent there to die. I believe the recent promises to clean up the past corruption of Louisiana, so I am asking you to use the power of your office and your personal commitment to justice to put an end to this. Brent Miller was an employee of this state who was just doing his job. The state of Louisiana owes him justice.

After Rogers read her letter, nobody said anything. Some in the room were crying. While our group was still in his office, Congressman Conyers, who had described all black prisoners "political prisoners" at that New Orleans prison conference back in 1972, wrote to Attorney General Michael Mukasey, asking the Department of Justice to open an investigation into our cases. He wrote to FBI director Robert Mueller asking for any files on our case. And he wrote to Warden Burl Cain, asking to visit me and Herman at Angola, along with "other members of Congress and interested persons" he planned to bring with him.

That same month, January 2008, Herman, King, and I were deposed separately by the state's lawyers in preparation for our civil trial. Louisiana's attorneys asked me if I had sufficient clothing and I told them I did because I had family members and supporters who sent me money so I could buy clothes. Indigent prisoners, on the other hand, would put in a request for underwear and wait six months for a pair, I told them. They asked if we had fans in the summer. Yes, we did; but when it's over 100 degrees in the cell, fans don't help. They asked me if we were alleging anyone abused us in the lawsuit. "Not physical abuse," I said. "We're claiming the fact that we've been here in the cell so long constitutes cruel and unusual punishment." Our suit wasn't about the beatings, the dungeon, or the abuse by inmate guards or freemen that happened to us and all prisoners at Angola. It wasn't about yard time or blankets or medical care. Still, while deposing us, the state's lawyers repeatedly asked us questions trying to get us to say, one way or another, that being locked down 23 hours a day in CCR wasn't that bad. We had color TVs, we had ventilation, we had mattresses. Repeatedly we told them our complaint was not about having TVs. It was about how being locked down for 23 hours a day was cruel and unusual punishment and a violation of our constitutional rights. Our complaint was also that we were not given true meaningful equal treatment compared with other prisoners because, while dozens of other prisoners came and went in CCR, we weren't able to get out. We were denied our right to due process.

Louisiana's lawyers also examined our disciplinary reports trying to find legitimate reasons that could justify locking us up for decades. But, in all our time in Angola, we never got serious disciplinary write-ups. I was written up for declaring myself an emergency when I had the rash around my waist in the eighties. I was written up when I got sick on the Camp J work line and requested an ambulance. I was written up for having a "spear" in my cell. Brent Hicks was the lawyer for the state who questioned me about that incident.

Q. Mr. Woodfox, [in 1992] there was a telescopic pole concealed in a large envelope inside your locker box; is that correct?
A. Yes.
Q. And that was in fact inside your locker box?
A. Yes.
Q. What is that used for?
A. They call it a remote. We use that to change the TV with.

Q. What do you use the empty burned Coke can for? [Another disciplinary write-up.]

A. At the time we didn't have hot or cold water in our cells so we used it to warm water, to make coffee. They sold instant coffee in the canteen but we didn't have any hot water in the cell.

Q. Next I'm going to show you a Disciplinary Report dated February 5, 1992. According to this report, Mr. Woodfox, you had a homemade spear in your cell; is that correct?

A. Yes.

Q. That would extend eight feet long?

A. Yes.

Q. Is that a weapon?

A. Same thing, TV changer. We use them to turn the TV with. It's a routine practice at CCR at the time.

Q. I don't understand how it works, explain to me how it works.

A. All right, the TV is set up across the hall from the cell, [when] nobody is in the hall to change the TV [and] you want to change the TV to a certain station, you stick the stick out, press the button and change the TV.

Q. How would you make a spear from a roll of toilet paper?

A. You just roll it up. I mean, you shove it hard against the wall or something, it just collapses. Some officers didn't have a problem with it, some officers did.

Given that there was no serious misconduct to point to as justification for the extreme punishment of long-term lockdown, Louisiana tried to paint our personal and political associations as something threatening. They asked me about the Black Panther Party, as if my political beliefs could justify the extreme cruelty of being locked up in solitary confinement for 23 hours a day. Again I was questioned by Mr. Hicks.

Q. Did the Black Panther Party advocate violence?

A. No.

Q. This was all peaceful?

A. Well, by advocate violence, if you're saying to the point that they teach you to go out and attack people, no, I've never been taught by the Black Panther Party to attack any individual or organization.

Q. Were phrases such as "kill the pigs" affiliated with the Black Panther Party?

A. Affiliated with all organizations during that time. That was, I guess, for lack of a better word, it was a political rhetoric at the time.

Q. What did that phrase mean?

A. I guess it meant a lot of different things to different people. I know to the Black Panther Party it didn't mean literally to kill anyone, it was more or less defining the cause or to rally the cause to fight against police corruption, police racism, government racism, government corruption.

Q. Did you use the phrase?

A. Yes.

Q. In what context would you use the phrase?

A. As I said, it was a part of political culture, political rhetoric that was being used at that time.

Q. Was a raised clenched fist a symbol of the Black Panther Party?

A. It was a symbol of all organizations at that time. It was a symbol of unity. It has been misunderstood and misquoted over the years but the clenched fist meant you were in unity and there was strength.

Q. Unity of what?

A. Unity of the community, unity of the people of America against government corruption, unity of people, workers against unfair working conditions.

Q. Do you think the government was corrupt at that time?

A. Yes, I did.

Q. Why did you think that?

A. Because of the policies of the government.

Q. What policies?

A. The racism, blatant racism that was allowed to be practiced in a country against African-Americans and other minorities, oppression of the communities across America, unemployment, the wealth of the country, unequal distribution of the wealth of the country.

Q. Do you think the government was involved in racism?

A. Yes, I do.

Q. How so?

A. Because they allowed the racist practices of the country: African-Americans couldn't move into certain neighborhoods, they couldn't get certain jobs, other minorities, and the government failed to enforce constitutional rights to every citizen in this country, to live where they wanted, to work if they were qualified, to have access to education, opportunities that were not based upon the color of their skin.

Q. You felt that's what existed in the 1970s?

A. I knew it, I lived it, I saw it, I experienced it personally.

Q. Do you still believe that today?

A. I still think there is a lot of racism in this country.

Q. Do you still think the American government is corrupt?

A. Oh, yeah. . . . I think the government has a responsibility to all its citizens. I think they have a responsibility to protect them from events that take place in society they have no control over, such as unemployment—and I think the government has an obligation when unemployment, when this country goes through a recession that the federal government has an obligation to make sure that all its citizens have adequate homes, clothing, food, medical care, education and opportunities, and when the federal government or state government refuses to do this, I think that is a form of corruption.

Q. And you think this corruption was going on in the 1970s?

A. I think it's going on right now.

Q. What about unequal distribution, you talked about that a moment ago.

A. Yes.

Q. Explain what you mean by that.

A. Underpaid employees, benefits being thrown back, medical care being rolled back, working more hours for less pay.

Q. And when you talk about unequal distribution, are you talking about it being unequal based on race?

A. No, I mean being unequal period. Those who own the resources of this country, who own the means of production in this country, the industries, you know, when they pay a man for less than his work is worth, when they refuse to allow him the benefits from the wealth that they're making from his labor, when they cut back on medical care, when they cut back on benefits and trust funds or loss, I think that's a form of corruption.

Q. In the 1970s did you advocate violence in order to overthrow this corrupt government?

A. No. I advocated unity, organizing to petition the government, to protest.

Q. Did you advocate that a revolution had to take place?

A. Yes.

Q. Explain that to me.

A. Revolution meaning that things just need change, that the country had to change, that the government had to start protecting all of its citizens, that private enterprise had to stop being consumed, [it] was accumulating all of this obscene amount of wealth and not paying workers decent salaries, not giving them medical coverage or retirement benefits.

Q. So you advocated a peaceful revolution as opposed to a bloody revolution.

A. Yes.

Q. Do you think you've reformed these political views?

A. I'm not quite sure I understand what you mean, reform.

Q. Do you still have these same political views?

A. Yes, against corruption, abuse, racism. I think it's wrong, I think it's morally wrong for an individual to be this way or for the government to allow it to go on.

Q. So your political views haven't changed since the 1970s?

A. No.

Q. Do you still consider yourself to be a member of the Black Panther Party?

A. The Black Panther Party no longer exists but I still believe in the principles of the Black Panther Party.

Q. The principles we've been talking about this morning?

A. The ten point program, yes.

Q. What do you understand needs to happen in order for you to be released from CCR?

A. What do I understand? I understand that unless the courts intervene in this matter I will never be released from CCR.

Q. What is that based upon?

A. The last thirty something years when I go before the Review Board, the way I'm treated.

Q. Do you feel like you're being punished?

A. Yes.

Q. Why do you feel like you're being punished?

A. Because I've been held in a cell for thirty something years and no matter what self-improvements I've made, no matter what my conduct is, I've not been given an opportunity to work my way back into the main prison population.

Q. Do you feel like you're under constant pressure?

A. Yea, from being in a cell 23 hours a day.

Q. Do you recall meeting [Dr. D., a psychologist who interviewed me for the state]?

A. Yes.

Q. Have you read his report?

A. Briefly.

Q. Have you read it recently?

A. No.

Q. Would you agree with his conclusion that you've adapted to CCR reasonably well?

A. No.

Q. You don't think you've adapted reasonably well to CCR?

A. I've managed to survive without going insane, without having a nervous breakdown from being in a cell 23 hours a day.

On February 11, 2008, I experienced another painful loss: Michael Augustine, one of my best friends since we were little, my former running partner in the High Steppers, my brother-in-law, died from kidney disease. One of the last times he visited me was right after he'd had some surgery. We were playing dominoes and when he lost a game he insisted on dropping to the floor to do the requisite push-ups, smiling and laughing, even with stitches still in his side. Mike fell in love with my sister Violetta when we were children. They grew in separate ways, had marriages and relationships and their own kids. In their forties, single, they met again and got married. Michael's death was another loss I couldn't properly deal with from my prison cell. My will to stay sane wouldn't let me go into those emotions.

Warden Burl Cain didn't want Rep. John Conyers to visit Angola. Lawyers from both sides got involved and Conyers prevailed. On March 20, 2008, Conyers led a delegation that included Louisiana state representative Cedric Richmond, King, Barry Scheck, Joan Claybrook, and our attorneys Scott Fleming and Nick Trenticosta to Angola. Warden Cain met them and took them on a tour of the prison grounds, even bringing some of them to my tier. Representative Richmond and Congressman Conyers stood in front of my cell and introduced themselves. After that, Herman and I were taken to the visiting room. When we arrived I shook everyone's hand. Conyers hugged both me and Herman. He told us he had been shocked about our case. It was the first time I'd ever talked to Burl Cain. He had been on my tier numerous times and walked by my cell like I was the invisible man. He asked me and Herman how we were doing, putting a show on for the congressman and the others. I was impressed that a United States congressman and head of the House Judiciary Committee and a state legislator had taken an interest in the injustice by the state of Louisiana in our case. King brought some of his Freeline A3 candy and left a package with Warden Cain.

The next day Teenie Rogers, Congressman Conyers, and Representative Richmond met with Republican Louisiana governor Bobby Jindal as a follow-up to Rogers's letter and asked him to consider the evidence of our innocence and use his power over the Department of Corrections and the Board of Pardons and Parole to look into our case and help Rogers find Brent's real killers.

Within a week of those visits, in an attempt to undermine our lawsuit and take the pressure off the state, they let us out of our cells. We were not released into the main prison population but were put in a "CCR dorm" they had just created, called Eagle 1. On the surface, it might have looked like progress. It was pure PR. We would still be isolated from other prisoners. We would only be able to spend our days with CCR prisoners—in the yard, on the walk, and in the dining hall. We would still live under CCR rules, which prohibited us from participating in educational, vocational, or other programs or from doing any hobby crafts, like leatherwork, beading, or painting. (They removed the tables and chairs used for crafts from the day room in our dorm.) We had fewer contact visits than regular prisoners. We didn't have to wear restraints while we were walking to the dining hall, but whenever we went outside—as a group or individually—guards cleared the walk, shouting, "Eagle 1 on the walk!" Others on the walk had to go behind various locked gates. There was no penological reason for this. They did it to put psychological pressure on us. Even when we were on a call-out—to the clinic or for a lawyer's visit—and wearing full restraints, they cleared the walk when we were on it. It was a prison dorm in name only.

Twenty-five CCR prisoners were declared eligible to move into the dorm. Sixteen of us chose to be moved. Eagle 1 was at Camp D. Herman and I lived together for the first time in 36 years. It took no time to adjust. We trusted each other and knew one another well. Herman said being in the dorm lightened the burden and depression he felt in the cell. For me, it was wonderful to be able to see Herman and talk to him every day, but with all the security and the CCR rules I felt like I was still in the cell, only it was larger.

We were all given jobs, which I would have enjoyed if we were given the proper tools to do them. Herman and I were yard orderlies and our job was to cut the grass around the dorm. They wouldn't let us use the gas-powered lawnmowers that yard orderlies used at other dorms. We had to use old-fashioned push lawnmowers that had dull blades. There was no way for us to sharpen the blades. The grass was so thick the lawnmower handles broke while we pushed them. We asked several times why we weren't allowed to use the gas mowers that orderlies used at other dorms and never got a good answer.

Getting enough exercise on the yard was always a problem because we never got the amount of time we were told we could have. For months, there was no recreation allowed on the yard—no basketball hoop or weight pile. We had to make several requests to get a wheelchair for an inmate who weighed over 400 pounds and had difficulty walking. He couldn't make it to and from the dining hall in the allotted time. First, we asked if we could bring him a tray of food so he wouldn't miss his meals, and when authorities denied that we asked for a wheelchair. Eventually we got the wheelchair and took turns pushing him to the dining hall.

The highlight of my day was walking out of the dorm with no restraints to the dining hall to eat breakfast. For a while our dorm went to breakfast first, while it was still dark, and I was able to look up and see the stars. It had been many years since I could see stars above me. Inside the dining hall it was back to reality. The room would be empty except for CCR prisoners.

In April 2008, FBI director Robert Mueller got back to Congressman Conyers about our FBI files. He said they had recently been destroyed in a "routine" purge of departmental files. We were told no record was preserved of what was in those files. That same month Louisiana state representatives Cedric Richmond, Avon Honey (Baton Rouge), and Elbert Guillory (Opelousas) went with King to Governor Bobby Jindal's office to deliver a ColorofChange.org online petition signed by 25,000 people, calling for an investigation into our convictions and lockdown in solitary confinement. Governor Jindal refused to meet with them, but Representative Richmond left a message for him, publicly calling for the governor to reexamine our case and asking him to pardon me and Herman. "The state is too silent on this issue," Richmond told reporters, "so we need official government action. At some point, we're going to have to stand up as a state." He announced that the state legislature would hold hearings about the case. (In 2011, Richmond would join the U.S. House of Representatives. He would go on to serve alongside Congressman Conyers on the U.S. House Judiciary Committee and eventually be elected as chair of the Congressional Black Caucus. He would continue to speak out actively on our behalf until I walked out of prison, and he is still trying to get legislation passed that would limit the uses of solitary confinement.)

In May 2008, a panel of three judges in the First Circuit Court of Appeal ruled on Herman's claim. One of them, Judge Jewel "Duke" Welch, ruled that based on the evidence concerning Hezekiah Brown, Herman should get a new trial. Unfortunately, he was overruled by the other two judges, who denied Herman's petition. Herman would now appeal to the Louisiana Supreme Court. Meanwhile, I got hopeful news that month. Magistrate Judge Christine Noland reviewed my habeas petition and recommended that Judge James Brady return my case to state court for a third trial because I had not received effective legal counsel during my 1998 trial. Among other deficiencies, she specifically found that my defense counsel was constitutionally ineffective for failing to object to the reading of forensic expert testimony about blood spatters on the "lost" clothing alleged to have been worn by me and for failing to further investigate. Modern forensics, she noted, could have determined who wore the clothes and whose blood was on the clothing.

In June, the NBC *Nightly News* did a segment on us; our supporters had been trying since my trial in 1998 to get national network news to report on our story. "Let's understand something here," Herman's voice came over by phone in the report, "the SPCA would shut this prison down if they had dogs up in here like this. It's just cruel and unusual punishment." Teenie Rogers was interviewed for the NBC segment and also gave an interview to the *Los Angeles Times*.

As the months passed in the CCR dorm I was reminded of Herman's extraordinary resourcefulness. They say that necessity is the mother of invention, and that is nowhere more true than in prison, but Herman went beyond the norm. I once watched him fill his favorite pen with ink pulled from another pen. He attached the two pens somehow and spun them on a string until all the ink from one pen went into the other. He sewed pieces of thick white athletic socks onto his regular socks at the ankle to protect his skin from chafing when he walked in the leg irons.

He made gloves out of cut-off sweatshirt sleeves, tracing the fingers of his own hand on the sleeve and cutting it out with a razor blade, then sewing the finger seams together using thread from unraveling a sheet.

We were frustrated because we had no chance to talk to prisoners in the main prison. The only time we were in the same area with other prisoners outside CCR was when we were in the visiting room, and prisoners weren't allowed to talk to each other there. We discussed ways to reach them. "The only way to make change is to get among the 'gangsters' and 'gangbangers' and to arm them with new methods of thinking," Herman would say, quoting Mumia Abu-Jamal. "If our young brothers are lost," Mumia said, "then it is our duty to find them!"

While housed in the CCR dorm we had yard every day and Herman and I could be in the yard at the same time. We would never admit it or say it aloud, but the punishment of 23 hours a day in the cell had taken a toll on our health. We weren't as fast as we used to be. We were in our sixties now. My back stiffened on me some days and on those days I couldn't run at all. There were times when I suddenly felt fatigued and weak and I figured that was from the diabetes. I was on stronger medication for my high blood pressure now. Herman had his own aches and pains and was going deaf. He asked people to speak up, saying, "My ears are closing." After waiting for months he was finally sent to the hospital in Baton Rouge to have his hearing tested. The doctors told him he had severe hearing loss and prescribed two hearing aids. The prison gave him only one. He said it created an imbalance in his head.

On July 8, 2008, I got a message to call one of my attorneys, Nick Trenticosta. When your lawyer calls you in prison, part of you braces for bad news. There could be a death in the family. I called him back. Nick was joyful. He told me my conviction was overturned by Judge Brady, who had decided to follow Magistrate Judge Noland's recommendation of relief. Judge Brady overturned my conviction on the grounds of ineffective assistance of counsel and also found that prosecutors had unlawfully failed to turn over evidence they had that would have helped my defense. The state immediately asked Judge Brady to reconsider his decision.

On September 25, after denying the state's motion to reconsider his ruling, Judge Brady entered judgment, granting me habeas corpus relief. The state had 30 days to retry me or dismiss the charges against me. Nick gave me the news on the phone. He said, "Albert, it sounds like you're drunk." I said, "I am drunk. I'm drunk on justice." Nick made numerous attempts to meet with Attorney General Buddy Caldwell, but Caldwell wouldn't meet with him. "We call on the attorney general to do the right thing," Nick told reporters. "To act as a reasonable public servant in the pursuit of justice . . . to allow Mr. Woodfox to go home today." Caldwell talked to reporters, saying he would appeal Judge Brady's ruling all the way to the U.S. Supreme Court if necessary. "I oppose letting him out with every fiber of my being," he told the reporters, "because this is a very dangerous man." My lawyers filed a motion for my release on bail pending Caldwell's appeal, and a hearing for that motion was scheduled. At the bail hearing in October, my brother Michael's daughter, my niece Rheneisha Robertson (the director of a nonprofit health organization); and her husband, former professional football player Bernard Robertson, told the court I could live with their family in a gated community outside New Orleans. Michael testified about my character.

Nick told the judge how my already poor health, after more than 30 years of solitary confinement, would be jeopardized by my staying in prison and cited my outstanding conduct record. Assistant to the attorney general Dana Cummings argued against bail saying the state would be "irreparably injured" if I was released. She emphasized my criminal record and that I was "twice convicted of murder." Judge Brady reminded her that both of my murder convictions had been overturned. He asked her how the state would be "irreparably injured" if I was free on bail. Cummings replied, "If he goes out and kills one of our witnesses, we're irreparably injured." Burl Cain testified I was a danger to the community, "because he is not a rehabilitated prisoner. He will be a predator when the opportunity comes his way." Outside the courtroom, Buddy Caldwell painted me as a monster. He told the press I was a convicted rapist and a serial sex offender—all lies.

While the court considered the state's appeal of my victory, my niece was terrorized for agreeing to take me in. We heard that the attorney general's office contacted the homeowners' association where she lived and spread lies about me. Strangers somehow got into her gated community and repeatedly drove slowly by her house. Some neighbors received in their mailboxes flyers about me stating that I was a rapist. "Buddy Caldwell . . . embarked upon a public scare campaign reminiscent of the kind of inflammatory hysteria that once was used to provoke lynch mobs," wrote Ira Glasser, the former executive director of the ACLU. "He sent emails to neighbors calling Woodfox a convicted murderer and violent rapist; and neighbors were urged to sign petitions opposing his release."

One day Michael told me Rheneisha was home with her sick child when the doorbell rang. She opened the door to a mob of reporters, asking to talk to her. She didn't know what to do; she wanted to go to her child, who was in another room of the house, but didn't want to close the door on the reporters or say something that might come back to hurt me. Her neighbors stopped waving to her. I told my lawyers to tell the judge I was withdrawing her name as the person I would stay with on bail. I was concerned about my niece's family's safety and reputation. I didn't want to be the cause of friction between her and her neighbors. My attorneys informed Judge Brady and told him that they were looking for another place for me.

When I first heard about the false rape charges Buddy Caldwell was making against me I felt sick. I had risked my life protecting men from being raped in prison. Now I was being falsely accused of being a rapist. I called my closest supporters and lawyers and told them I wanted to speak out against the false accusations.

Nobody wanted me to talk publicly about the rape allegations made by Buddy Caldwell—not my lawyers, not my family, not my closest friends and advisers. Everybody had a different reason and begged me not to speak out. Some thought I shouldn't stoop to the level of Buddy Caldwell. Others thought it would make me look guilty to defend myself, or they feared that a "war of words" in the press would make Caldwell's charges look legitimate. Some thought that since the rape charges were bogus they would "die down." I knew the rape charges wouldn't die down. If you want to smear an African American man's reputation, all you have to do is say the word "rape." It is a bell that can't be unrung. I wanted to let our supporters know I was innocent of these accusations. For all of the people all over this country, all over this planet who had rallied to the cause of the Angola 3, who had fought for my freedom, I needed them to hear me say I never raped anyone. My support committee and attorneys asked me to let them deny it for me.

Buddy Caldwell based these false rape charges on old rap sheets created when the police emptied the books on me the night I was arrested for armed robbery in 1969. There has never been any real charge, arraignment, indictment, or prosecution of me for rape, ever. Caldwell was lying when he said there were witnesses and that there was evidence. There was no way he could prosecute me for rape. I was innocent. I knew I had comrades who would get my statement out to the public when I was ready, even if it was against their better judgment.

The attorney general's office filed more than 300 pages of exhibits and memoranda with the court to oppose my bail, documents that falsely stated that I was a "convicted sex offender" and misleadingly suggested that I had a number of "aggravated rape and armed robbery charges" from the late 1960s. Louisiana claimed I was never prosecuted for the rapes because I'd already been sentenced to 50 years for armed robbery. This was bullshit because the night I was arrested for the armed robbery was the same night the books were emptied on me charging me with rape. At that time rape in Louisiana carried the death penalty. If the state could have prosecuted me for rape, it would have. But Louisiana charged me with and prosecuted me for armed robbery, not rape, because there was no evidence of any kind, no eyewitness, no victim statement that supported the rape charges. And yet, Caldwell told the court, "No community should be so endangered by this admitted career criminal who still has outstanding, viable, unprosecuted aggravated rape charges."

Attorneys Chris Aberle and Nick Trenticosta responded with a memorandum of our own, pointing out the "numerous misrepresentations, mischaracterizations, and tenuous unsubstantiated accusations based on patently incredible hearsay" in the state's case. They pointed out that five of the six rape allegations in my arrest record were generated when the police arrested me on February 13, 1969, for armed robbery, when they emptied the books on me. My lawyers also made clear that I was never prosecuted for any of those charges except armed robbery.

The State first notes that Mr. Woodfox was arrested six times for aggravated rape in 1967 and 1969. Later in its memorandum, the State purports to list all of the crimes committed by Mr. Woodfox and includes six instances of aggravated rape so as to leave this Court with the false impression that Mr. Woodfox had been convicted of those offenses. What the State does not make clear is that the sole source of information regarding five of those six rape allegations is their appearance as unadorned charges in three arrest registers, each generated after the police arrested Mr. Woodfox on February 13, 1969, for the robbery with which he was ultimately charged and found guilty.

Mr. Woodfox avers, on information and belief, that during that period in history, New Orleans police routinely charged arrestees with unsolved crimes in the hope that the defendant could be connected to the crime. Such a practice would explain why those five capital offenses appear on the arrest registers, notwithstanding that the State never charged Mr. Woodfox with a single one of those aggravated rapes. One must assume that the State's decision not to prosecute Mr. Woodfox for any of those crimes arose from the lack of any evidence connecting Mr. Woodfox to any of those crimes.

The State also grossly misleads this Court regarding the sixth rape charge, alleged to have occurred in 1967. On page 15 of its memorandum, amid what purports to be a list of all of the crimes Mr. Woodfox has committed, the Attorney General avers that on 11/20/67, Mr. Woodfox committed the "aggravated rape of J.C." Following that entry, the State purports to allege another crime. Specifically, on 2/28/1968, Mr. Woodfox committed aggravated battery, a crime for which he pleaded guilty and received a 15-month sentence. According to the State, Mr. Woodfox admitted that "he and his girlfriend got into a fight." What the State conceals from this Court is that the battery offense described by the Attorney General is the same crime originally charged as the "aggravated rape of J.C." Although the Attorney General is in possession of an FBI document that makes this clear, he has chosen not to include it in the exhibits to his memorandum. If the State could not show that Mr. Woodfox committed aggravated rape 40 years ago, it surely cannot do so now. Hence, the Attorney General's repeated attempts to cast Mr. Woodfox as a serial rapist and a sex offender are baseless and grossly unfair. Such argument and allegation have no place in these proceedings.

Another shockingly false statement made by Louisiana that Nick and Chris addressed in our memorandum was that I was somehow linked to a plot to murder former warden C. Murray Henderson and "other Angola officials" so they couldn't testify at my 1998 trial. All I can say is we needed Henderson at my trial. We needed to put Henderson on the stand to ask him about how he paid Hezekiah Brown for his lies against us back in 1973—how he wrote letters to get Hezekiah Brown a pardon, how he had cartons of cigarettes delivered weekly to Brown, how he told inmate Leonard Turner he would lose his parole if he didn't give a statement against us. The "evidence" they had that I was allegedly connected to this plot to kill the former warden was an unauthenticated, unsigned memorandum based on triple hearsay, sourced by an unidentified confidential informant. In another false charge, Warden Burl Cain spouted a claim during a deposition that I also threatened the lives of Brent Miller's brother and prosecutor John Sinquefield, but he eventually had to admit this was not true, because he had no personal knowledge whatsoever to support the claims he made. There was, of course, no truth to what he said, therefore no evidence, no proof.

Caldwell continued to slander me in the press as my attorneys tried to get me bail. Herman was spared from Caldwell's lies—for the moment—because his case was still in state court. My conviction had just been overturned, so I was the target of Caldwell's campaign to destroy my reputation and justify keeping me in prison. Caldwell told National Public Radio that fall that I was "the most dangerous man in America," all while dodging questions about the weakness of Louisiana's case against me. In a three-part series on our case, NPR reporter

Laura Sullivan asked Caldwell about the bloody fingerprint that was left at the scene of Miller's killing and was never identified. Caldwell responded, "A fingerprint can come from anywhere. We're not going to be fooled by that."

On Saturday, November 1, 2008, I was reading on my bunk when Herman got word there was an article about me in that day's Baton Rouge *Advocate*. Since papers weren't delivered to the CCR dorm on weekends I called a friend and asked him to read it to me. It was a front-page article quoting Attorney General Caldwell as stating that if I was released he "would pursue six aggravated rape cases and six counts of armed robbery from 1967 to 1969" against me.

"If we let him out we will probably never see him again," Caldwell said in the article. "The guy's a serial rapist." Nick defended me in the article. "It's a flat out lie," he told the paper. "He has never been charged with six counts of rape. There is no case. It's offensive to the practice of law." Chris Aberle called it "a ridiculously absurd comment," adding, "If they have evidence . . . why didn't they supply it a long time ago?" To add insult to injury, at the end of the article Caldwell stated, "Albert's never been in isolation. He's had TV. He's had all the luxuries you can have in prison."

I sat on my bunk and wrote a four-page statement denying the attorney general's accusations. I called Noelle Hanrahan of Prison Radio and asked her to record me reading my statement and to broadcast it. I wanted my supporters to know how I was feeling and what I was thinking, in my own words. In part, I read,

The attorney general's office has decided to launch a smear campaign reminiscent of the federal government's counterintelligence program (COINTELPRO) to oppose my constitutional rights to be released on bail. . . . The techniques and tactics used by COINTELPRO were lies, deceptions, missing information, and character assassination. These techniques and tactics were used to cause chaos and disunity among members of any organization or group targeted by the government. . . . Shortly after my bail hearing on October 14, 2008, a smear campaign was started. First they spread lies about me in my niece's neighborhood. Someone contacted the homeowners' association that my niece belongs to and told them my niece was bringing a murderer and rapist into their community, which put her in the middle of a firestorm among her neighbors.

On the rape charges, I wrote,

> I welcome them [the attorney general's office] to put the evidence out there. Tell the public what you got. He says I'm a serial rapist. OK, show us what you got. Witnesses? DNA? Let's have it. Where's the proof. He's got nothing. There is no way he could bring these accusations through the courts . . . so he put his accusations before the media.

After I read the statement Noelle interviewed me. "My main concern now is the safety of my niece and her family," I told her. "I'm very distressed that the relationship she had with neighbors in her community may be destroyed because of this smear campaign by the attorney general's office, and the thing is, these people in positions of power and authority, they violate the Constitution, they break the laws and they have immunity from prosecution. Then they walk away and continue to live their lives, and all the people whose lives are destroyed by them, by their illegal actions, are left to fend for themselves." I continued, "The attorney general made the statement that two juries 'have spoken' and I have been convicted twice on this murder charge. What he failed to say is that, had the state of Louisiana followed the Constitution of the United States and the laws of the state of Louisiana to indict me and convict me, this case would not have been overturned twice. They were able to convict me because they used unconstitutional tactics—the discrimination against blacks in my grand juries, giving me incompetent lawyers, not turning over evidence that could have shed light on the real killers of Brent Miller. Everyone says my trials were overturned on a 'technicality,'" I said. "The Constitution is not a technicality." I put a copy of the statement I wrote in the mail to my friend and comrade Gail Shaw in Sacramento and asked her to post it online, which she did.

Someone in Buddy Caldwell's office must have decided it didn't look good for me to be living peacefully in a dormitory at Angola while Caldwell was going around telling everyone how dangerous I was. (Later we would learn prison officials started colluding with the attorney general's office to look for reasons to move me and Herman out of the dorm.) One day that fall a couple of guards showed up at the dorm and told me and Herman we'd violated disciplinary rule "30C." A 30C was a catchall charge standing for anything that was not specifically spelled out in the disciplinary rule book. They put us in the dungeon. George Kendall and his team went into action, filing for discovery on the reason we were put in the dungeon and seeking our release.

I was still in the dungeon on Tuesday, November 25, 2008, when Nick called me with surprising news. Judge James Brady had ruled I had the right to bail while awaiting the state's appeal, pending court approval of my housing plan. If I could find appropriate housing, I could go home. Judge Brady said he found no evidence that I was a danger to society, pointing to my age and my "exemplary record of conduct" in the last 20 years. He also pointed to my diminishing health, describing me as "frail and sickly." I hated that, but I had to admit it was true. Judge Brady called for my immediate release while we waited the appeals of my habeas relief.

The state filed an emergency appeal before the Fifth Circuit, asking that Judge Brady's ruling granting me appeal bail be put on hold until a hearing before a three-judge panel could be arranged. Assistant Attorney General Mary Hunley, citing my criminal convictions for "armed robbery, aggravated escape, aggravated battery, burglary and car theft," told the court: "It is evident that if he is released, this career criminal would be considered both dangerous and a flight risk." Notably, she said nothing about rape. A panel of judges on the Fifth Circuit blocked my release for another week and then denied appeal bail altogether.

I was in the dungeon for about a month when I was finally handed an investigatory report that told me why I had been moved there in the first place. I was removed from the dorm, placed in the dungeon, and then sent back to CCR based on charges that I had "abused phone privileges." I'd been on 10 three-way calls, which generally are prohibited in prison but are very commonplace. Six of those calls were with our lawyers, and we were allowed to have those. The other four were with Noelle Hanrahan of Prison Radio—the calls I made to her when I was giving her my statement refuting the rape charges. I was also charged with "deliberate misrepresentation of information on my call list," because I'd described Noelle as a "friend" and not as a journalist. Of course, this was no misrepresentation: I considered her a friend. Besides that, there was no place on the form that asked for or gave you space to write down the occupations of your friends. Finally, I was charged with releasing an "unauthorized press release" by speaking to her, and prison officials claimed I was making inflammatory statements that would provoke security issues in the prison. Herman was also charged with trumped-up disciplinary violations related to misuse of phone privileges.

Chris Aberle and Nick Trenticosta continued to defend me in the press. Nick told reporters that Attorney General Caldwell's charges were "scurrilous allegations, a litany of offenses that don't exist." But the truth didn't stop Buddy Caldwell, who continued to tell the *Advocate* that he would try me on rape if I was released. "Those charges are still viable," Caldwell told the paper. "We've got living witnesses out there. If we're going to err, let's err on the side of keeping him in prison." Recklessly, callously, he made these claims knowing that he could never support them.

In November 2008, I was deposed again for our civil trial. The state's attorney Richard Curry questioned me.

Q. Mr. Woodfox, what facts are you aware of that would support your allegation that you've been confined in lockdown for 28 to 36 years, and other adverse actions being taken against you, because of your perceived political beliefs and affiliations?

A. Well, the fact within itself that I've been held in CCR for approximately 35 years, with the exception of the three years I was in Amite City, Tangipahoa Parish Jail. I had the opportunity to see all the inmates with disciplinary records that were just horrible, released from CCR. Basically, that's all that we are evaluated on in CCR, conduct. I've seen guys come out of the dungeon or come from Camp J and a couple of months later they're released from CCR.

Q. Part of what you're contending, I believe, is that you've remained in CCR all this time because of your political beliefs?

A. Yes.

Q. What facts do you have to support that?

A. The fact that I'm still in CCR for approximately 35 years or more, the fact that I have an excellent conduct record, the fact that there's absolutely nothing that I can do to be released from CCR, while I've had the opportunity to observe other prisoners in CCR who have horrible conduct records and who have been released from CCR.

Q. And you're also contending that you've remained in CCR in part because of your perceived political viewpoints and opinions; is that correct?

A. Yes.

Q. And what facts do you have to back up that allegation?

A. Again, the fact that nothing that I can do will allow me to be released from CCR, as well as Warden Cain's own statements.

Q. And you're also claiming that you've remained in CCR because you've availed yourself of your fundamental right to court access. What fact do you have to back up that statement or that claim?

A. The fact that I've been held in CCR thirty-something years, the fact that I have an excellent conduct record, the fact that I've not been involved in any incidents that other prisoners have who have been released from CCR.

Q. You also allege that you've remained in CCR in part because of your race; is that correct?

A. Yes, the race part came in a statement Warden Cain made himself in the deposition he gave when he specifically singled out "Black Pantherism." All the members of the Black Panther Party were African-Americans, the Black Panther Party's philosophy was basically to help African-Americans.

Q. Are you contending Warden Cain is a racist?

A. I don't know enough about Warden Cain to say he's a racist.

Q. Are you contending that he's keeping you in lockdown because you're black?

A. Based upon his statements, yes.

In December, an art exhibit called *The House That Herman Built* opened at the Contemporary Arts Center in New Orleans. The artist Jackie Sumell had written to Herman years before, asking him what his dream house would look like. Over several letters, sketches, phone calls, and visits, he answered her. She created an art exhibit around his vision that included blueprints, architectural drawings, models, and a computerized virtual tour of the house Herman wanted to build. She incorporated his drawings, excerpts of his letters, and the paper flowers he used to make. She also built a walk-in wooden replica of a six-by-nine-foot prison cell. The installation would travel throughout the United States to cities including Philadelphia, San Francisco, and Augusta, Georgia, and around the world, to Poland, the United Kingdom, Germany, and France. It helped raise awareness about the horrors and abuses of solitary confinement among many who never would have been exposed to the issue. Visitors to art galleries and museums who walked into that wooden cell had a chance to imagine life in solitary confinement. A filmmaker, Angad Singh Bhalla, made a documentary about Herman's collaboration with Jackie, called *Herman's House*.

Herman had a garden filled with roses and delphiniums in the front yard of his dream house. He had a wraparound porch and a greenhouse on the grounds so that, as he explained to Jackie, he was "never far from growing things." There were six microwave ovens in his huge kitchen to accommodate all his guests. Portraits of John Brown, Harriet Tubman, and other abolitionists hung in the living room. The picture window was bulletproof. The swimming pool had a huge black panther painted across the bottom. Herman's bedroom had an escape hatch that led to a survivalist bunker. The house, he told Jackie, would be made of wood so in case of attack it could be burned to the ground.

Chapter 47

Never Apart

Back in our CCR cells, we were still a problem for Buddy Caldwell. Exposure about our case was growing. George Kendall told me and Herman to prepare to be separated for good. Apparently, Caldwell had approached Burl Cain and asked him to move me and Herman to separate prisons. We heard that Cain agreed because, in part, the publicity about the A3 was hurting the Angola brand. They moved Herman first, in March 2009, to the Elayn Hunt Correctional Center in St. Gabriel, about 12 miles southeast of Baton Rouge, creating a brand-new CCR there to house Herman (and adding other prisoners to fill it).

Herman and I were used to being apart. Except for the nine months total we'd spent together at Angola, in the dorm and in CCR, we had not lived together. We stayed close by sharing books, photos, music, and constant correspondence, passed back and forth over the years in the hands of orderlies, trustees, and sometimes even prison guards. We gave each other birthday bags filled with zuzus (snacks) and items from the prison store. When one of us was on the yard the other would call down from the window if he was out on his hour.

But the extraordinary, mysterious, and inexplicable success of our friendship was based on something else. In different cells, on different tiers, sometimes in different buildings, and now in different prisons, our keepers could never come between us. Herman had my back. I had his. If I needed him he was there. Not physically, but instantly. I'm not religious. I don't believe in God. But I believe in the human spirit and I believe human beings have a greater capacity than we understand. Behind the pain, the betrayals, the brutality, and the disappointments, Herman, King, and I existed somewhere, unhurt and together. After we were moved to different prisons, Hooks and I wrote to each other at least once a week, sometimes more. I adjusted. So did he. It's what we did best.

Later that year, on October 9, 2009, the Louisiana Supreme Court summarily denied Herman's application for review. He would have to seek relief in federal court. By now George Kendall and his team had taken over Herman's criminal case, as well as mine. George, Corrine Irish, Carine Williams, and Sam Spital were already working on Herman's first federal appeal, his petition for a writ of habeas corpus.

There were six claims in the writ, including that the state failed to correct false testimony it had presented against Herman, noting, for example, the statement from Howard Baker recanting his 1974 testimony, admitting that he lied when he said he saw blood on Herman and stating that it would have been impossible for Herman, or anyone, to burn clothes at the tag plant because there was no furnace there. The state also withheld impeachment evidence and exculpatory information from Herman's defense, failing to disclose, for example, an April 20, 1972, statement given by an inmate named Charles Evans. George said in the writ:

> According to the statement, Evans lived in the Pine 2 dormitory, next door to Pine 1. Evans stated that on April 17, 1972, he was awakened at 7:51 a.m. to see [a] "large group of people standing between Pine 1 and Pine 2. I heard somebody in [the] crowd say that it was a free man that was fighting. I saw an old man I know as 'Hezekiah' standing at the door of Pine 1." Evans further stated that he saw "a free man running toward Pine from Walnut dormitory." Unfortunately, prison officials failed to record any more details of Evans' recollections. What is clear, however, is that Charles Evans' recollection of events on the morning of April 17th, 1972 was inconsistent with the State's theory of the case and undermined the credibility of the State's witnesses. Certainly, Evans' testimony would have been valuable impeachment evidence for Mr. Wallace, inasmuch as it would have called into question the testimony of

all four inmate witnesses against him, each of whom—denying at times even the presence of each other—claimed that few people were present at the murder scene.

Moreover, if defense counsel had been provided Mr. Evans' statement, he could have investigated further, to interview Mr. Evans and to seek the names of other prisoners who were part of this "crowd" present at the time of the murder. One among the crowd may have had information as to who actually killed Brent Miller.

Another claim in Herman's writ was that he was "impermissibly convicted" because of the discriminatory selection of the grand jury that indicted him. His first grand jury indictment, in 1972, was quashed because the grand jury excluded blacks and women. When Herman was reindicted, in 1973, his second grand jury also excluded blacks and women. He filed a motion to quash that indictment as well. At a hearing on January 7, 1974, just before his trial, his judge denied Herman's motion. George's team went back and looked at the testimony at that 1974 hearing and at the law during that era and found that women were systematically excluded from grand juries at that time. According to Article 402 of the Louisiana Code of Criminal Procedure at the time, "A woman shall not be selected for jury service unless she has previously filed with the clerk of court of the parish in which she resides a written declaration of her desire to be subject to jury service." Ruth P. Daniels, a member of the West Feliciana Parish Jury Commission at that time, testified that registered voter lists compiled and sent to the jury commission only included male registered voters because "no [woman] had ever asked to serve."

"The trial court's refusal to quash the second indictment requires reversal of Mr. Wallace's conviction," George wrote, "because the systematic exclusion of female citizens from grand jury service violated the equal protection clause of the Fourteenth Amendment." On December 4, 2009, Herman's habeas writ was filed in U.S. District Court for the Middle District of Louisiana before Judge Brian A. Jackson.

In 2010, King and one of our longtime A3 supporters in England, Nina Kowalska, met with Tessa Murphy, who headed the U.S. research team for Amnesty International, about our case. Nina, I later learned, pretty much told those gathered for the Amnesty meeting that she wasn't leaving until they took us on. It didn't have to come to that. Amnesty wanted to look at the issue of solitary confinement in the United States and issued a press release, stating that our incarceration in solitary confinement was a violation of human rights and calling for our release from solitary.

That June brought a crushing blow. I lost the habeas relief that had been granted by the district court. A sharply divided three-judge panel of the U.S. Court of Appeals for the Fifth Circuit reversed Judge Brady's ruling, reinstating my conviction. The Fifth Circuit ruled Brady "erred" in concluding I had ineffective counsel in my second trial and maintained that while my trial "was not perfect," I couldn't prove there would have been a different outcome with different counsel. The court used President Bill Clinton's Anti-Terrorism and Death Penalty Act as the primary reason for reinstating my conviction. That statute requires that federal courts defer to rulings made by the state courts as long as those rulings are not "unreasonable" or "contrary to clearly established federal law."

I was depressed. I tried to sound upbeat with my brother Michael, my attorneys, and my friends. This news was just as hard on them as it was on me. So many people worked and fought so hard for me—my lawyers Chris Aberle and Nick Trenticosta, who had drafted my habeas petition and worked on the appeal; George Kendall and his team, who had joined my habeas case in 2008 while working on our civil lawsuit; all my friends and our supporters, who were raising awareness on the street and in Washington; my brother, keeping my spirits up in the prison visiting room. I couldn't believe the sacrifices they made for me, the commitment they made to me, I couldn't let them know the pain I was in. I fell back on self-discipline to fight depression. I kept up with my routine. I went on the yard when I was allowed, even though the thrill of being there was gone for me. I got no pleasure from that yard anymore. I only went outside to force myself to exercise. Herman wrote to me, asking how I was. I wrote back, "This one hurts but I'll be all right. It's just taking a li'l' longer to catch my breath on this one.

It's strange rearranging my hopes, dreams, plans, and expectations but I'll get it done."

There was one saving grace in the Fifth Circuit's ruling. The higher court sent my case back to Judge Brady for a determination concerning my final claim: that racial discrimination influenced the selection of my grand jury foreperson in 1993. This would be my last chance to get out of prison. The courts had already ruled on all of the other issues I was eligible for. A prisoner can only go to federal court on issues that were preserved in his original appeal. If the courts decided that this claim didn't warrant relief, then I would die in prison. I would get an evidentiary hearing on this issue.

I forced myself not to be discouraged, I forced myself not to give up hope, I somehow found the determination to fight on. But I wasn't unscarred by this back-and-forth, my hopes being raised and crushed over and over. Meanwhile, our civil suit claiming that our years in solitary confinement constituted cruel and unusual punishment progressed; we were told we might have a trial date soon. Psychologist Craig Haney came back to prison to interview me and Herman again. He noted "unmistakable, dramatic change in appearance and demeanor" in both of us. He wrote that I seemed "down, defeated and somber." Herman, he wrote, was "hesitant . . . voice cracking." Herman told Haney he was worried he'd reached "the end point" and was afraid he "can't stand up to it." "Herman began to tell me that he felt sad, but was trying to stay strong," Haney wrote. "And then he began to cry. After he regained his composure, he talked about the pain he could see in the men in the cells around him. He told me they 'act up terribly' but also that he understood it was not their fault."

On November 1, 2010, it was my turn to be moved out of Angola. I was taken to David Wade Correctional Center, a four-hour drive north, in Homer, Louisiana. I was now in the northernmost prison in the state; it is Louisiana's Siberia. Herman was in the southernmost. There was no CCR at Wade, so they created one, filling it with twelve prisoners from Angola who were moved with me. I never got the impression the other prisoners blamed me. They knew that I had no control over this move and had done nothing to cause it.

I'd heard about Wade. It was built as a "punishment prison" for the "worst of the worst" back in 1980. Angola officials told us our move wasn't a punishment. But it was impossible to view the move as anything but a punishment. I'd now be a six-hour drive from New Orleans, the base of my support. It would be impossible for someone to drive from New Orleans to visit me and return on the same day. I knew I'd be very isolated at Wade.

The day we arrived the guards were immediately in our faces, speaking harshly and being unnecessarily rude. "You have five minutes to get that gum out of your mouth," one of them yelled at a prisoner when we got out of the van. The man beside me looked at his hands, cuffed to his waist with a black box over them, obviously taking a second to figure out how to remove the gum from his mouth without his hands. The guard yelled at him again. Not all guards at Wade spoke in a rough and demeaning manner, but most corrections officers there had mastered the art of how to treat prisoners in the most degrading way possible. They did it because they could. Nobody was there to show them a different way. I also had the impression we were thrust on them without warning, that they were already overwhelmed and they aimed their anger and frustration at us.

It looked like they had emptied the cells of the new CCR tier the day before we got there. I could smell the disinfectant used to clean them. I had to tell the guards we were supposed to live under the same rules and have the same privileges that we had at CCR in Angola. The guards didn't know anything about CCR rules and privileges. They told me their rules: At Wade, there were no contact visits. There was no microwave for prisoners to use. No ice. We got yard only three times a week and didn't have the option to stay on the tier on yard days. That meant that if we didn't go to the yard we had to go straight back into our cells after we showered. At Angola, there were five TVs on the tier; each TV was shared by three prisoners and could be programmed separately based on what those three prisoners wanted to watch. At Wade the four TVs were programmed together, so all prisoners on the tier had to watch the same program. That would mean getting 12 men to agree on TV programming every hour of the day. There was less TV time, which was a great loss to guys who arranged their whole day around what would be on television. By the time I left Angola, the TVs had a chip in them so the volume came through radios in the cells. At Wade the TVs were blasting at full volume; the noise was deafening. By the time I left Angola we could have a phone in our cells when we made a call. To use the phone at Wade we had to stand at the end of the tier, in restraints, by the glass wall of the control booth.

The cell door shut behind me. It was steel mesh instead of bars, so prisoners couldn't pass anything through the doors or hold mirrors out to look down the tier. There was no space under the door to pass anything. The food slots had hinged flaps on them and could be locked from the outside. There were no slots in the cell doors to put restraints on our ankles or wrists, so every time we left the tier we'd have to hold our hands to the food slots to have handcuffs put on, then back away from the door as the guards opened it, face the back of our cells, and kneel on the floor so they could put leg irons on us. At 63, I had degenerative arthritis in my knees. I knew it would be painful for me to kneel on the concrete floor. I sat on my bunk. If I'd allowed myself to feel an emotional connection to my reality in that moment I would have gone insane. But I didn't feel the highs and lows that people in society feel anymore. I lived in the middle of every emotion.

The next day the warden and his assistant, a lieutenant colonel who was in charge of the South Side, where I was housed, called me out. I was put in restraints and taken to see them in a small room. They started questioning me about being in CCR and Angola and I felt they were dancing around whatever they wanted to talk to me about so I interrupted them. "Look," I said. "I assume you all called me out here trying to figure out my state of mind. Most rules don't apply to me because I don't participate in any prison games or bullshit. If your officers respect me, I'll respect them. If your officers disrespect me, I will disrespect them. If you put your hand on me you're going to have to kill me because I will fight you as hard as I can until I'm unconscious or dead. Other than that, you won't know I'm here." They looked at one another. The warden said, "We're glad to hear you aren't going to be a problem."

As I was being led back to my tier, I knew I was going to be a problem. Prisoners at Wade were treated like shit. We didn't have the CCR privileges that we were supposed to have under the state's own rules. As soon as my possessions were delivered I got out my writing materials and wrote to the warden, listing the privileges we had at CCR and asking when we could expect to have them, starting with contact visits.

The only privilege the warden turned over quickly was contact visits; we got those in a couple of weeks. For everything else, it took three to six months of pushing just to get an abbreviated version of what we had at Angola. The other prisoners worked with me. We all knew what they were doing was wrong. Acting by consensus I got petitions signed, wrote to the warden, filed ARPs. Throughout, guards routinely cursed at us and spoke to us disrespectfully, all of it unprovoked and uncalled for. Even on the walk from our cell to the shower we'd be harassed. Guards would call out to us, "Hurry up. Get in the shower, keep moving." If there was a sporting event on TV and prisoners on the tier cheered too loudly a guard would yell, "Get down on the fucking noise before I come down and put some of you motherfuckers in the dungeon."

Eventually we got ice. The day they put a microwave at the end of our tier it was such a novelty that security guards from all over the prison came to look at it. One of the guards said, "I never thought I'd live to see the day they'd have a microwave on a tier at David Wade." We couldn't use the microwave ourselves; we had to pass whatever we wanted heated into the guard center at the end of the tier and then get it passed back to us.

Some things the prison officials wouldn't change, no matter how much I protested and fought them. They refused to give us a shower curtain. The shower was directly across from the control center. We had to stand buck naked in the shower in full view of where the guards sat, including female guards. Wade was also not as clean as Angola. There were more insects and rodents at Wade; they sprayed insecticide only in the halls, not in the cells. They didn't pass out brooms or mops as often. When medical personnel needed to do lab work or other tests, they came to get us in the middle of the night—anytime from one to three in the morning. We had less access to legal material. This didn't affect me directly, because I was lucky enough to have lawyers who helped me. But it was a big loss for the other prisoners at CCR in Wade.

We finally got Wade to agree to let us stay on the tier if we wanted, instead of going out on the yard for our hour, but they put a line down the hall in yellow tape, one-third out from the wall, and told us we had to stay on that one-third side of the tier when we were out on our hour and not cross the line. That was a pain in the ass. It was hard to exercise or give things to people on the tier from the other side of the yellow line. If I was heating up a cup of coffee for someone in the cell or handing him a book I had to keep my toes behind the yellow line and lean over it. They used the yellow line as punishment for the whole tier because one of the prisoners programmed a porn channel on the DirecTV using the remote and security failed to catch it for a few hours. To punish everyone for the actions of a few, or even of just one prisoner, is the policy at every prison. We were always forced to live at the level of the lowest common denominator. That philosophy would eventually ruin our contact visits at Wade. When we first got contact visits we didn't have to wear restraints. Then a prisoner apparently threatened another prisoner, saying he was going to beat him and his family in the visiting room. After that we were all forced to wear shackles and handcuffs during our visits. That was Wade's solution to the problem.

Some months after I arrived the warden, Jerry Goodwin, called me out of the cell. I was taken to the room where the review board met. "I've got something I want to talk to you about," he said. "If you don't want to talk about it, it's OK with me. Either way, I'm telling you now, this conversation never happened. I will deny it ever took place." He paused. "Now, if you still want to hear it, tell me." "Well, yeah," I said, "What?" He said, "I talked with Buddy Caldwell at one of the budget meetings and he told me to tell you to be smart, and if you wanted to give testimony against Herman Wallace, you'd better make a deal now." I told him I'd think about it. As soon as I got back to my tier I called George Kendall to tell him to visit me so that I could tell him what

Warden Goodwin said. Nothing came of it. There was nothing we could do. Caldwell's offer came from a third party, which gave him deniability.

Soon after that I was reading when a crew of workers came onto the tier and started oiling and hammering the hinges on the rusty metal flaps that covered the food slots. I asked the guard on duty what they were doing and was told they were ordered to start locking the food slots in CCR after every meal. When they were done they locked all the flaps and left the tier. When a meal came the flaps were unlocked and the tray was passed to us. After we ate the trays were picked up and the flaps were locked again. We couldn't pass a book, a newspaper, or anything else when someone was out on his hour with the flaps locked. We couldn't open the flap to see the face of the person talking to us from the tier. There was no penological reason for it. It wasn't happening on any other cellblock. This was a punitive action created for CCR at David Wade Correctional Center. It added to our isolation. It made the cell seem more confining and it took time to adjust to that. I wrote to the warden to protest the action. When I told my lawyers about it they got involved. It took more than six months, but with my attorneys' help we got them to keep the food slots unlocked.

I was still getting claustrophobic attacks but that was nothing new. It always started the same way. I felt that the air around me was pressing down on me and the cell was getting smaller and smaller. If it was late at night or early in the morning and everyone was locked in his cell I would get naked. I couldn't stand the feel of clothes on me; my T-shirt and underwear felt five times too small. If the guard came down the tier for a count I would sit on the toilet until he passed, because I didn't want him to know. We were pushing this image, like Herman's poem, of men of steel. We hid weaknesses from security. Sometimes listening to opera helped. If I could find it on the radio I would sit on my bunk, close my eyes, and imagine the walls moving back to their normal distance from me. Most of the time there was no opera on the radio. Walking off the attacks usually worked better anyway. I paced the cell, back and forth. When it was summertime there would be a trail of sweat underneath me that formed a stripe down the middle of my cell floor, from one end to the other.

2011–2016

I feel my soul as vast as the world, truly a soul as deep as the deepest of rivers; my chest has the power to expand to infinity. I was made to give.

—Frantz Fanon

Chapter 48

Torture

In April 2011, the International Coalition to Free the Angola 3 and the ACLU National Prison Project held a congressional briefing on the abuses of solitary confinement, at the request of Congressmen John Conyers, Cedric Richmond, and Robert "Bobby" Scott. Tory Pegram co-organized the program and moderated the panel discussion with Robert King; Laura Rovner, an associate professor of law in the Civil Rights Clinic at the University of Denver College of Law; David Fathi, director of the National Prison Project; and Michael Randle, program manager for the Judge Nancy R. McDonnell Community Based Correctional Facility. There was a screening of a documentary about us called *In the Land of the Free*, directed by Vadim Jean and produced by the Mob Film Company, released the year before. (That film would be updated with new information and interviews and renamed *Cruel and Unusual* years later.) King and our attorney Carine Williams spoke after the film was shown.

That spring I got the news that my childhood friend Ernest Johnson had died from an illness. That was a shock because he was my age, 64. On June 2, 2011, former Panther Geronimo Ji-Jaga Pratt died of a heart attack. He was 63. There was no place in my cell to put these aching losses. I was still grieving for Althea Francois, a founding member of our support committee, who had died a year and a half before, after a long illness, on Christmas day. Althea, as a young member of the Black Panther Party in the 1970s, first visited me at Angola after I was accused of killing Brent Miller. In 1999, we reunited in the prison visiting room. A gentle but determined warrior, Althea was an activist in the black community her entire life. In the months after Hurricane Katrina devastated New Orleans, she worked to establish the city's Office of the Independent Police Monitor to uncover and expose the role of New Orleans police in post-Katrina killings. Herman and King were, of course, also devastated by Althea's death. When the *San Francisco Bay View* newspaper asked King for a few words about her, he spoke of Althea's giving nature, invoking a passage from the Bible, Matthew 25:35–36: "For I was hungry and you gave me something to eat, I was thirsty and you gave me something to drink . . . I was in prison and you came to visit me." I was used to being separated from people I loved, but separation by death was different. Althea Francois, Ernest Johnson, Geronimo Ji-Jaga Pratt, Anita Roddick, Michael Augustine, one of my very first supporters Opal Joyner, my sister Violetta Mable Augustine, my mom Ruby Mable. If I ever got out of prison, a part of me would always be looking for them.

I started getting swelling in my legs and ankles. As usual, I tried to run it off, but that didn't help. At one point my ankles were so swollen the guards couldn't put the leg irons on—they had to use two plastic restraints joined together for each of my ankles and attach the chain between my ankles to them. Eventually I saw a doctor and got a prescription for fluid pills and the swelling went down, but anytime my ankle restraints were too tight my ankles blew up like balloons.

I was still, after 39 years, being hassled about my books and mail. If I was sent anything that mentioned the Black Panther Party it was confiscated for "teaching racial hatred." "Give me a break," I wrote to Herman, describing the petty harassment. "I'm tired of this shit." One of my supporters sent me the book *The New Jim Crow* by Michelle Alexander, and, luckily, it got through. I shared it with the prisoners on my tier, telling them what a powerful book it was. There were issues in the book we used to discuss in the 1970s.

I stayed in close touch with Herman at Hunt and Zulu at Angola through letters, writing often. Although, as I wrote to Hooks, "It's hard to write to you and Zulu, what can I tell you about the beast's belly. Both of you are living my hell."

On October 18, 2011, the United Nations released a statement against solitary confinement:

> A United Nations expert on torture today called on all countries to ban the solitary confinement of prisoners except in very exceptional circumstances and for as short a time as possible, with an absolute prohibition in the case of juveniles and people with mental disabilities.
>
> "Segregation, isolation, separation, cellular, lockdown, Supermax, the hole, Secure Housing Unit (SHU) . . . whatever the name, solitary confinement should be banned by States as a punishment or extortion technique," UN Special Rapporteur on torture Juan E. Méndez told the General Assembly's third committee, which deals with social, humanitarian and cultural affairs, saying the practice could amount to torture.
>
> "Solitary confinement is a harsh measure which is contrary to rehabilitation, the aim of the penitentiary system," he stressed in presenting his first interim report on the practice, calling it global in nature and subject to widespread abuse.
>
> Indefinite and prolonged solitary confinement in excess of 15 days should also be subject to an absolute prohibition, he added, citing scientific studies that have established that some lasting mental damage is caused after a few days of social isolation.
>
> "Considering the severe mental pain or suffering solitary confinement may cause, it can amount to torture or cruel, inhuman or degrading treatment or punishment when used as a punishment, during pretrial detention, indefinitely or for a prolonged period, for persons with mental disabilities or juveniles."

Chapter 49

Forty Years

April 17, 2012, marked 40 years since Herman and I were first put in CCR. Our support committee and Amnesty International held our annual anniversary protest against solitary confinement; this year it was on the steps of the state capitol. Under a banner that read SOLITARY IS TORTURE, statements from me and Herman were read aloud, and several others spoke. "For me this day is bittersweet," King said, "Bitter with a deep sadness that we have to mark this day, but sweet, seeing our years of effort and struggle culminating in this day. The tide is changing and the time for change is now. We have the wind at our back and we need to keep on moving." "To be honest," I had written, "I am not sure what damage has been done to me, but I do know that the feeling of pain allows me to know that I am alive. If I dwelled on the pain I have endured and stopped to think about how 40 years locked in a cage 23 hours a day has affected me, it would give insanity the victory it has sought for 40 years."

Amnesty campaigners reached out to Governor Bobby Jindal to try to get a meeting. They wanted to hand him a petition demanding that Herman and I be released from solitary confinement; it had been signed by more than 67,000 people in 125 countries around the world. The governor refused to meet with Amnesty officials and King, referring them to the Louisiana Department of Public Safety and Corrections. Secretary James M. Le Blanc denied that conditions in lockdown 23 hours a day were inhumane and said Herman and I were kept in CCR because we were a danger to prison employees, other inmates, and visitors.

On May 13, 2012, the New Orleans *Times-Picayune* reported that Louisiana was the "prison capital of the world," incarcerating more of its people, per capita, than any other state. "First among Americans means first in the world," said staff writer Cindy Chang. "Louisiana's incarceration rate is nearly five times Iran's, 13 times China's and 20 times Germany's." Chang reported that, at the time of the article, 1 in 86 adults in Louisiana was incarcerated, nearly double the national average. Among black men from New Orleans, 1 in 14 was behind bars. She reported on Louisiana's harsh sentencing laws: "In Louisiana, a two-time car burglar can get 24 years without parole. A trio of drug convictions can be enough to land you at the Louisiana State Penitentiary at Angola for the rest of your life." The "hidden engine behind the state's well-oiled prison machine" she reported, "is cold, hard cash. A majority of Louisiana inmates are housed in for-profit facilities, which must be supplied with a constant influx of human beings or a $182 million industry will go bankrupt." Later that month, three days before I was to attend an evidentiary hearing in Baton Rouge regarding my habeas petition, Amnesty International started a new online petition, asking Secretary Le Blanc, who said I was a danger to myself and others, "Where is the evidence?" "On April 17, 2012, you issued a statement that Albert Woodfox and Herman Wallace are held separately from other prisoners to protect prison employees, other inmates and visitors," the petition read. "Where is the evidence to back up this statement? Records show that neither man has committed any serious disciplinary infraction for decades. Prison mental health records indicate that the men pose no threat to themselves or to others. . . . Where is the evidence?" Around 1,000 people who signed the petition also emailed Secretary Le Blanc directly, calling on him to produce evidence backing up his assertion that I was a danger to prison employees, other inmates, and visitors.

My evidentiary hearing took place at the Federal District Courthouse in downtown Baton Rouge. During the hearing I was held at the Elayn Hunt Correctional Center, where Herman was, but I wouldn't see him there. When I arrived I was immediately placed in the dungeon. I protested, pointing out I had no recent disciplinary reports in my record and that I never saw the reclass board or disciplinary court at Hunt. I was told the decision came from "higher up." They confiscated my socks and never gave me my toiletries or the clothes I brought from Wade. The other prisoners on the tier were loud, screaming, moaning, talking to themselves day and night—it was their way of dealing with the pressure. My lawyers tried to intervene, but prison officials would not move me from the dungeon. I didn't get any sleep. In the morning, I would be in court.

The stakes couldn't have been higher at this evidentiary hearing. My life was on the line. Because of the Anti-Terrorism and Effective Death Penalty Act, prisoners submitting habeas petitions are only allowed to raise issues that had been originally preserved in their postconviction relief application, and only those issues that had not previously been ruled on. I had two claims left by the time I got to Judge James Brady in federal court in 2006. Judge Brady had already ruled on one of my two claims: in 2008 he overturned my conviction on the grounds of ineffective assistance of counsel. The Fifth Circuit reversed that. Now I was before Judge Brady on my last claim: that my 1993 indictment by a West Feliciana Parish grand jury was tainted by discrimination because the judge, who handpicked the grand jury foreperson, almost exclusively selected white forepersons in a parish that was over 40 percent black. George Kendall, Sam Spital, Corrine Irish, and Carine Williams had done a mountain of research to prepare for this hearing, to prove the consistent underrepresentation of African Americans serving as grand jury forepersons in the parish and to debunk the state's case, which was that the judge's selections had been "race neutral."

The hearing lasted three days, May 29–31, 2012. Each day before leaving my cell I asked for my socks to wear under the restraints and my request was denied. Without socks my ankles were cut and bruised. In the courtroom, the state spared no expense in its attempt to defeat our claim, trying to prove the West Feliciana judge's selection of grand jury forepersons did not discriminate against blacks, presenting witness after witness who testified that objective factors, like education, supposedly made the appointments of the grand jury forepersons in West Feliciana Parish "neutral," even if they were handpicked by the judges. George's team refuted that, identifying African Americans on the panel of prospective grand jurors and showing that their employment and education were comparable to the qualifications of the white forepersons actually selected.

At the end of the hearing, the matter was in Judge Brady's hands. If he agreed with us, I would get a new trial. If he agreed with the state, I wouldn't. Judge Brady asked each side to submit a final brief three weeks after the transcript of the hearing was made available—which would take about another three weeks—and submit a final rebuttal to those briefs 20 days after that. In all it shouldn't have taken longer than eight weeks to get everything to the judge. The state dragged out the process, as usual, filing for extensions before submitting briefs. We wouldn't get a ruling for nine months.

When the hearing was over I expected to be transported back to Wade. Instead, I was kept in the dungeon at Hunt for nine more days. It was excruciating. I wasn't supposed to be in the dungeon, I hadn't broken any rules. Temperatures outside were in the 90s, and it was much hotter in the cell. There was one fan for the tier. I had no phone privileges, no canteen, no yard, no television, no ice, and no visits except with my lawyers. I wasn't allowed to call my brother. I was served food that was still frozen. I was only allowed out of my cell 15 minutes a day for a shower. I had to wear leg irons to the shower. I wasn't moved back to Wade until my lawyers threatened Hunt officials with contempt of court. (Later we sued Hunt officials for ignoring all transfer, classification, and disciplinary procedures required to justify putting me in the dungeon while I was there to attend my hearing. My friend New Orleans lawyer Emily Posner filed the suit, along with attorney Sam Dalton; it ended up being folded into our civil suit against cruel and unusual punishment.)

When I got back to Wade, hundreds of letters were waiting for me. Amnesty had launched a "Write for Rights" campaign for me and Herman, asking members to write to us. I sat on my bunk and opened the letters and cards from people all over the world, and I was deeply touched to read their words. Many had sent beautiful pictures of nature on the cards they picked out for me.

Preparing for the evidentiary hearing had taken George and his team months. Now that it was over, they could get back to focusing on our civil case and, we hoped, get us out of solitary confinement for good. The judge who'd been handling the case, Judge Ralph Tyson, had died in 2011, and our civil case was, coincidentally, passed to Judge James Brady, the same judge presiding over my habeas petition. Judge Tyson had been sitting on a number of pretrial motions regarding our civil case for more than two years; without rulings we couldn't move forward. Judge Brady ruled on them within a few weeks. One of those motions was related to an order issued back in February 2010 by Magistrate Judge Docia Dalby, granting my lawyers access to emails exchanged by Angola warden Burl Cain and Attorney General Buddy Caldwell's office that proved they colluded to manufacture a reason that would allow them to move me and Herman out of the CCR dorm and back into individual CCR cells in 2008.

In October, King received an honorary doctor of laws degree from Anglia Ruskin University in Cambridge, England. As always, he spoke of me and Herman in his remarks: "My evolution began in prison—in Angola State Penitentiary, in Louisiana—in an 18,000-acre former slave plantation," he said. "My experience in a six-by-nine-foot cell for 29 years in solitary confinement taught me the difference between legality and morality. It made me realize that despite the fact that the 13th Amendment allegedly abolished slavery, slavery was never abolished. I learned that a person could be actually innocent of a crime but convicted legally, and that this person would be designated a legal slave—as it was in 1864 where the Constitution decreed that if you were black being a slave was your lot. Modern-day slavery is alive and well in America but it has taken on a different form—from the plantation to the prison. . . . A case in point are my two comrades—Albert Woodfox and Herman Wallace who are now serving their 40th year in solitary confinement—and tens and thousands of others who have also been unjustly convicted but remain in prison in America in slavery."

Four months later, on February 26, 2013, U.S. District Court Judge James Brady overturned my conviction again, this time on the issue of racial discrimination in the selection of the grand jury foreperson. Judge

Brady saw through all the bullshit "science" state prosecutors spent a fortune creating in their attempt to prove there was no racial discrimination in the selection of the foreperson for my 1993 West Feliciana grand jury. I would get a new trial. I was ecstatic. Judge Brady ruled in his 34-page decision that the state had failed to show that "objective, race-neutral criteria"—such as education and employment—were used in the selection process. Brady agreed that the West Feliciana Parish judge who picked grand jury foremen favored the appointment of white people for that role. He also again granted a motion for my release on bail pending my appeal. The state immediately appealed to the Fifth Circuit, asking it to overturn Brady's ruling and for a stay of Judge Brady's order to release me on bail, because, the state claimed, I was "a danger to the public and a flight risk." The state argued that a stay would not substantially injure me, because "he has already been incarcerated for several decades."

Thirty thousand people signed an online Amnesty International petition calling for my immediate release after Judge Brady's ruling. In response, Attorney General Buddy Caldwell played his "rape card" again, replying to these petitioners with the same rape accusations he had made against me in 2008. He wrote that I was guilty of killing Brent Miller, saying, "There are no flaws in [the] evidence" that convicted me and Herman, and that we were never held in solitary confinement. "Contrary to popular lore," he wrote, "Woodfox and Wallace have never been held in solitary confinement while in the Louisiana penal system. . . . They have always been able to communicate freely with other inmates and prison staff as frequently as they want. They have televisions on the tiers, which they watch through their cell doors. In their cell, they can have radios and headsets, reading and writing materials, stamps, newspapers, magazines and books. . . . They can exercise in the hall, talk on the phone, shower and visit with the other 10 to 14 inmates on the tier. At least three times per week, they can go outside on the yard and exercise and enjoy the sun if they want."

In the following weeks retired Louisiana Supreme Court chief justice Pascal Calogero Jr., the NAACP Legal Defense and Educational Funds of New York and of New Orleans, and the nonprofit organization the Promise of Justice Initiative filed "friends of the court" briefs in support of a new trial. Former chief justice Calogero wrote about how grand jury forepersons can exert influence over other grand jurors. "Although the state has come a long way in eradicating racial discrimination throughout the grand jury foreperson selection process, we must not turn our back on those convictions that were tainted by the old system." I disagreed that the state had "come a long way in eradicating racial discrimination" in any part of the judicial system, and I still believe that racial discrimination and gender discrimination are very prevalent in today's judicial system in America, but I was extremely grateful for Calogero's support.

One afternoon in May I was getting ready to go on the yard at Wade when the guard who came to escort me said he had to strip-search me. I told him it was against Department of Corrections regulations to strip-search prisoners housed in maximum-security lockdown unless there was probable cause. I knew this by heart, because it was a ruling that came down when I sued the state on this issue back in 1978. "Going on the yard isn't probable cause," I said. He told me he was obeying orders from the colonel; it was a new rule at Wade. "I have to strip-search you," he repeated. I handed him my jumpsuit, my socks, and my tennis shoes. He went through them and handed everything back. He told me to drop my drawers. "Raise your arms, open your mouth, raise your tongue, raise your genitals, turn around, bend over, spread your cheeks."

I wrote to Warden Goodwin and told him the strip searches were unconstitutional, and about the 1978 19th Judicial District ruling on the lawsuit I filed, which stated prisoners could only be strip-searched under certain conditions. I asked him to stop the unlawful strip searches. I sent copies to my lawyers. I never heard back from him.

I talked to the men on my tier, telling them we didn't have to accept the strip searches, because the prison was breaking the law. I asked them to join me in fighting the strip searches; none of them wanted to get involved. Nobody stood with me. My lawyers pleaded with me not to physically resist the strip searches. "We'll take it to court," they said. Some sergeants and guards didn't do the strip searches; they didn't have the taste for it. Others acted as if it was their greatest pleasure to humiliate somebody. There were days when I was strip-searched as many six times, before and after I left my cell, even when I was only leaving my cell to walk to the guard booth—escorted and always within sight of at least one guard—to take a phone call from my lawyer. Having to bend over so a security officer can look at your anus gives you a terrible sense of being violated. It's one of the most humiliating things that can be done to you. Even the courts recognized this. As the ruling on my original suit stated, "Visual body cavity searches were a humiliating procedure" and "should only be used rarely." Some days I didn't leave my cell at all, to avoid being strip-searched.

That summer George Kendall asked me and Herman to meet with psychologist Craig Haney again so that Haney could finish his report on us, which would be used by our defense for our civil trial to show the impact of solitary confinement on us. I told him that at times I felt empty. I was losing interest in things. I said, "You don't know the horrors of fighting for your sanity." The pressure of being locked in the cell required all of my mental, emotional, and physical will to survive.

Chapter 50

Man of Steel

Maybe my soul is that of concrete
Maybe it is that of the wind
Maybe it is that of fire
Maybe it is the spirit of the people—the spirit of my ancestors,
Whatever my keepers wish my soul to be,
The man of steel is always free.

—Herman Wallace

Herman wasn't well. He'd been complaining of stomach pain and went to the prison hospital several times. He wrote to me that the doctors at Hunt told him he had thrush or a stomach fungus, and they were treating him for a fungal infection. I was relieved that he was finally getting some medical help. In June 2013, George Kendall and Carine Williams showed up at Wade for an unexpected visit. George told me they had asked our medical expert, Dr. Brie Williams, to update her report about our health status. In reviewing Herman's recent medical records, she grew very concerned and asked the prison health-care providers to further examine him and to allow her to examine him. The attorneys got permission to take Herman to a hospital in Baton Rouge. "Albert," George said, "Herman doesn't have thrush or a stomach fungus. He has advanced liver cancer. The doctors say he may have only three or four months to live." I started to say something but I wasn't able to speak. Herman's smile flashed in my mind. He was standing on the walk at Angola.

Dr. Williams didn't need a CT scan to examine Herman, George continued. She could see and feel the tumor on his liver as soon as she lifted his shirt; it was protruding in the shape and size of a toy football. After the diagnosis, Carine said, prison officials were planning to put Herman back in his cell. Even though he was dying, George and Carine had to fight to get officials at Hunt to keep Herman from being returned to lockdown. They won. When he was sent back to the prison from the hospital, Herman was put in an isolation room in the hospital unit.

George promised they'd do everything they could to get him out of isolation and into the hospital dorm. He told me they were filing for an expedited review of Herman's habeas petition (which had been sitting without any attention from the court for four years, since December 2009). They told me they were working to get prison officials to allow me, Herman, and King to meet with them together to discuss our civil suit, because the state was refusing to allow us to meet. "You will see Herman again," Carine promised me. After they left I called my brother. Michael took the news hard. He cried because he loved Herman. He cried because he knew what it would mean for me to lose Herman. We thought we were invincible.

George and Carine negotiated with the state to get Herman's classification reduced from maximum to medium security, threatening to go to the court if necessary. Because of their actions Herman was taken out of isolation and housed in a prison hospital dorm with a day room where he wouldn't have to wear leg irons. They were also able to persuade the court to order the prison to allow us to meet together with our lawyers. Because of this, Herman, King, and I would see one another again.

On July 10, Amnesty International launched a campaign directed at Louisiana governor Bobby Jindal, calling for Herman's immediate release on humanitarian grounds. "After decades of cruel conditions and a conviction that continues to be challenged by the courts, he should be released immediately to his family so that he can be cared for humanely during his last months," wrote Amnesty's Tessa Murphy. Once again

Governor Jindal hid, refusing to talk to Amnesty representatives and referring questions about Herman to the Louisiana Department of Public Safety and Corrections.

Dr. Brie Williams told George that between Herman's rapid weight loss, his medical history, the bloodwork, and the tumor protruding from his abdomen, there was no way any doctor could have missed Herman's liver cancer diagnosis. Yet Pam Laborde, spokeswoman for the Department of Corrections, insisted the prison "provides adequate health care to inmates." (In May 2015, a group of prisoners at Angola would file a class action lawsuit on behalf of thousands of men incarcerated there, claiming the prison's substandard medical care violated the 8th Amendment prohibition against cruel and unusual punishment. Their attorneys, who came together from four organizations—the Advocacy Center of Louisiana, the ACLU of Louisiana, the Promise of Justice Initiative, and Cohen Milstein Sellers & Toll PLLC—interviewed hundreds of men to build their case, documenting "one medical horror story after another," wrote journalists James Ridgeway and Katie Rose Quandt for *In These Times*. One prisoner repeatedly requested medical attention, starting in 2010, for extreme pain in his side. He was told he had gas. Over the next five years, Ridgeway and Quandt wrote, the prisoner "developed numbness in his feet, legs and fingertips, lost his appetite, and dropped nearly 100 pounds. When he finally received a CT scan in 2015, he was diagnosed with stage 4 cancer in his kidneys and lungs."

Angola routinely hired doctors with suspended licenses, a practice that is condemned by the National Commission on Correctional Health Care and the American College of Correctional Physicians. Between 2011 and 2016, when the article was published, Ridgeway and Quandt wrote, "14 physicians have been employed by Angola. Twelve came to Angola after receiving disciplinary sanctions from the state medical board for misconduct." The medical director at Angola in 2016, they wrote, "served a two-year prison sentence and had his license suspended from October 2009 to October 2014 for purchasing crystal meth with the intent to distribute in 2006 (he was hired at Angola in September 2010). The state medical board noted that [he] was diagnosed with amphetamine, cocaine and cannabis dependence, in addition to adjustment disorder and personality disorder with antisocial, narcissistic and avoidant features." Unsurprisingly, the death rate for prisoners at Angola, they wrote, dwarfed the nationwide average in state prisons.

On July 12, two days after Amnesty tried to meet with the governor, Rep. John Conyers wrote a letter about Herman's situation to the Civil Rights Division of the U.S. Justice Department, cosigned by ranking member of the U.S. House Judiciary Committee Congressman Rep. Jerrold Nadler (NY); ranking member of the Subcommittee on the Constitution and Civil Justice Rep. Bobby Scott (VA); and ranking member of the Subcommittee on Crime, Terrorism, Homeland Security, and Investigations Rep. Cedric Richmond (LA). The letter called for an investigation of the Louisiana Department of Public Safety and Corrections for its "abysmal history of protecting the rights of its prisoners," of which the "tragic story of the Angola 3 is a case in point."

About Herman, the congressmen wrote, "We have heard that he lost over 50 pounds within 6 months. Despite that dramatic weight loss, and at 72 years old, the prison did nothing to treat or diagnose him until he was sent to an emergency room on June 14. Given the late stage of his diagnosis, his treatment options are now limited. He is frail and ill, but is still being treated as if he is a threat to security, and we hear that he remains under lockdown conditions. This is unconscionable."

Our attorneys petitioned the court to get bail for Herman. His friend and A3 supporter Ashley Wennerstrom and her husband said they would take Herman into their home if he was released on bail, vowing to ensure Herman would comply with any restrictions placed on him by the court, whether it was electronic monitoring or curfew. They lived a block from his childhood home. Nick Trenticosta, Herman's friend and lawyer, who had known Herman for 17 years, also promised the court he would make himself available to personally monitor and ensure Herman complied with court orders if he was released on bail. Bail was denied.

My first meeting with Herman, King, and our lawyers took place on July 31. Wade transport officers drove me the five hours to Hunt and escorted me to the meeting room. Herman walked into the room swinging his arms, smiling, wearing his beret at a tilt on his head. He was very thin but relaxed, and animated. He told us not to worry about the cancer. With proper treatment now, he was going to beat it. I wanted to believe him. And I admit, looking into his eyes, I thought if anyone could beat cancer Herman could. We talked about his chemotherapy, which made him sick. He said he could handle the pain, but the air-conditioning in the prison hospital got to him. He was used to being in a steaming-hot cell in CCR. He was always cold in the hospital. We talked about legal strategy in our civil and criminal cases. We talked about world events, the latest news. When guards locked up my transport shackles to drive me back to Wade, I somehow felt hopeful. By the time I got to Wade reality had set in. Herman and I exchanged letters.

"I knew how you would face this," I wrote. "Like you said we have been friends/comrades for a lifetime. . . . I can't bring myself to talk to anyone about this now, the pain and fear is just too raw right now. Michael took the news very hard. . . . As for me I'm not gonna lie, I'm filled with so much pain and fear that I'm having trouble functioning day to day. Don't waste your time it is what it is. Stay strong comrade. Never apart."

At our next meeting, less than a month later, Herman was in a wheelchair. It was devastating to see. He'd lost even more weight. After we talked about our court cases, King and I forced ourselves to keep it like old times. We talked about Black Lives Matter, the civil rights movement that was just beginning to grow out of the injustice around the murder of Trayvon Martin, the black teenager who was shot and killed in broad daylight while walking home to his dad's house after buying candy at a store. Trayvon's killer, George Zimmerman, had just been acquitted of murder by a Florida jury. Herman spoke about how we had to protect Black Lives Matter. But he was also confused, talking about the past as if it was the present, talking about LSU games that happened years before. That's when I realized the seriousness of the cancer, because it was affecting his sense of time.

In August 2013, my attorneys Katherine Kimpel and Sheridan England, working with George Kendall and his team, filed a motion for a temporary restraining order on the strip searches at Wade, noting: "Defendants now strip search Plaintiff Woodfox and inspect his anus . . . even though he is shackled in wrist, ankle and waist chains when outside of his cell; is under constant observation or escort; and typically has no contact with individuals other than correctional personnel. Defendants continue this practice despite the fact that they are on notice that these strip searches are unlawful and previously agreed via consent agreement not to conduct such strip searches."

In early September, Herman released this statement:

On Saturday, August 31st, I was transferred to LSU Hospital for evaluation. I was informed that the chemo treatments had failed and were making matters worse and so all treatment came to an end. The oncologists advised that nothing can be done for me medically within the standard care that they are authorized to provide. They recommended that I be admitted to hospice care to make my remaining days as comfortable as possible. I have been given 2 months to live.

I want the world to know that I am an innocent man and that Albert Woodfox is innocent as well. We are just two of thousands of wrongfully convicted prisoners held captive in the American Gulag. We mourn for the family of Brent Miller and the many other victims of murder who will never be able to find closure for the loss of their loved ones due to the unjust criminal justice system in this country. We mourn for the loss of the families of those unjustly accused who suffer the loss of their loved ones as well.

Only a handful of prisoners globally have withstood the duration of years of harsh and solitary confinement that Albert and myself have. The State may have stolen my life, but my spirit will continue to struggle along with Albert and the many comrades that have joined us along the way here in the belly of the beast.

In 1970 I took an oath to dedicate my life as a servant of the people, and although I'm down on my back, I remain at your service. I want to thank all of you, my devoted supporters, for being with me to the end.

*   *   *

In September 2013, Herman was deposed again, this time on video-tape, so it could be shown to jurors when our civil suit against cruel and unusual punishment finally went to trial. Our lawyers wanted jurors to see for themselves who Herman was. The state was against it; in my opinion, the state's lawyers would have preferred to continue to slander him in the third person. There was no judge at the deposition. Any objections that were made by either side throughout the questioning were made for the record, for the purposes of future litigation. By then, Herman was in a great deal of pain even though he was on strong painkillers. He answered questions while lying on his side in his prison hospital bed. Speaking took a tremendous amount of effort and energy. He wanted to go through with it, in spite of his suffering and exhaustion. Our lawyer Carine Williams tried to make him as comfortable as possible, helping him take sips of water and covering him with blankets. She insisted a nurse sit with him during the deposition and alert them if she thought any part of the proceeding became too much of a strain. He threw up between some of the questions. Our lawyers repeatedly checked to see if he wanted to stop the deposition, and Louisiana's lawyers were definitely willing to end it. When they offered to pull back from questioning him, he insisted on doing it. "C'mon. C'mon," he said.

Attorneys Richard Curry and Ashley Bynum represented the state. Most of their questions centered on Herman's involvement with the Black Panther Party, conditions in CCR, and the fact that Herman at one time lived in the Pine 1 dorm and knew Brent Miller. They pressed him on whether or not he got along with Miller. (The state had always put forth a story that Herman and Brent Miller had been in an altercation in the Pine 1 dormitory when Herman lived there, before Herman was moved to Pine 3. Herman would have told me if that happened.)

On the second day of questioning, Curry asked, "Mr. Wallace, do you have any remorse today for killing Brent Miller?"

Herman didn't hesitate with his response: "I'm totally innocent of any killing of anybody, let alone that man," he said.

Attorney Sheridan England questioned Herman for our side.

Q. Mr. Curry asked you a number of questions yesterday and today about the murder of Brent Miller. Do you remember those questions?

A. Yes, I do.

Q. You're on your deathbed, isn't that right?

A. I beg your pardon?

Q. The doctors have told you that you don't have much longer to live; isn't that right?

A. Yes.

Q. And you're on your deathbed, is that your understanding?

A. Yes.

Curry: Objection.

Q. Do you believe that you will survive long enough to testify in open court in this trial in this case?

A. No.

Q. Are you able to say with a clean conscience, as you prepare to meet your maker, that you did not murder Brent Miller?

Curry: Objection.

A. Yes.

Q. I'm going to ask you, Mr. Wallace, because you know that you won't be around to say that directly to the jury, but I would like you to look straight into the camera and answer the question, with a clean conscience as you prepare to meet your maker, can you look into that camera and testify truthfully that you did not murder Brent Miller?

Curry: Objection.

A. Yes, I can.

Q. Are you able to look Mr. Curry in the eye and state truthfully that you did not murder Brent Miller?

A. Yes.

Curry: Objection.

Q. Are you able to look Ms. Bynum in the eye and tell her truthfully that you did not murder Brent Miller?

Curry: Objection.

A. Yes. Yes, I can with the slightest movement of my head.

Q. And if the jury were here today, would you be able to look each one of them in the eye and testify that you did not murder Brent Miller?

Curry: Objection. It's awfully repetitive for a dying man.

A. Yes.

Q. Mr. Curry asked you no less than 13 times whether or not you knew Brent Miller. Do you recall those 13 separate questions?

A. I recall.

Curry: Objection.

Q. And did I understand you correctly that you knew of Mr. Miller, but that you did not personally know Mr. Miller?

A. True.

Q. All right. And I believe Mr. Curry asked you some questions regarding burning down a prison. [This was referring to a prisoner protest Herman had participated in at Orleans Parish Prison before he was sent to Angola.] Do you remember those questions?

A. Yes.

Q. Can you describe to me what, if anything, you did in that incident?

A. We in that incident, we were making a statement basically because of the conditions that were a part of the prison. There were many people outside the prison and they wanted to know what was going on. And that was an opportunity for us to make a statement. It wasn't all that much of [what] you're talking about burning down the prison, . . . with all of us in it. It was an idea that culminated from that. . . . It was a victory in order to force the sheriff at that time to make changes. That's what we wanted.

Q. And were there any changes that were made?

A. We wanted—we really wanted changes in that prison. And the changes came about through the sheriff himself negotiating with us. So he began to—to agree that what was going on would stop.

Q. I would like to read you a portion of this article and I want to ask you if you wrote this statement. I'm reading from Page 133, quote, "I have always tried to help them," inmates, "overcome their destructive behavior by bringing them together and making them realize that being kind to one another is the best solution to making all of our lives more tolerable." Did you write that statement, Mr. Wallace?

Curry: Objection.

A. Yes. Yes.

Q. And do you still stand by the statement that you tried to help individuals overcome destructive behavior by bringing them together?

A. Yeah.

Q. And I believe Mr. Curry asked you a number of questions regarding Black Pantherism or your involvement with the Black Panthers. Do you remember those questions?

A. Uh-huh.

Q. Would it be fair to say that as part of your involvement, you were attempting to help inmates overcome their destructive behavior by bringing them together?

Curry: Objection.

A. Yes.

Q. At any time during your involvement with the Black Panthers, did you ever try to organize violent protests to kill anyone?

A. Never.

Curry: Objection.

Q. Are you aware whether any persons in the Black Panthers that you personally were involved with ever arranged to hurt or kill anyone?

A. Never.

Curry: Objection.

At the end of the deposition Sheridan England asked Herman:

Q. Yesterday you were asked a series of questions about what it was like for you in CCR. Do you remember those questions?

A. Yeah.

Q. I believe Mr. Curry asked you a number of questions regarding whether you had volunteered to go back to CCR and things of that nature. Do you remember those questions?

A. Yes.

Q. Can you please describe again how CCR affected you as you lived there?

A. CCR, you're asking me a question that when I think of CCR, it takes me into a cave. It takes me into a place where—where I don't want to be.

Q. Is it hard for you to talk about your time at CCR, Mr. Wallace?

Curry: Objection.

A. Oh, yeah. Yes, it do.

Q. And why is that?

A. As I just said. CCR, it's a place where—it's like a killing machine, mentally and physically. It's not a place where I can sit and isolate my thoughts, and there's nothing I can do about it.

Louisiana prison officials wanted to cancel my next meeting with Herman and King at Hunt. They said Herman was too sick to be moved from his prison hospital room to a visitation room and expressed some made-up security concerns. George Kendall and Carine Williams refused. Not wanting to go to court, Wade's warden finally said that if I agreed to wear the black box over my restraints the whole time, they would allow the joint attorney-client visit to proceed in Herman's prison hospital room. The black box is usually used only during transport. It is worn with a waist chain, leg chain, and leg irons and covers the keyhole to these restraints so that the lock cannot be picked. A chain runs through it that is used to tighten a prisoner's wrists against his stomach. Because the black box cuts off circulation in the hands, wearing it for just one or two hours can be extremely painful. Keeping one on during the entire attorney-client visit meant I'd be wearing the black box for 15 or more hours: on the five-hour drive to Hunt and back, as well as during the meeting. Prison officials obviously didn't think I'd accept their terms. What they didn't know was that nothing short of death would have prevented me from seeing Herman again. I didn't care if my hands fell off. On October 1, 2013, I was put in the black box and driven down to Hunt prison to see Herman.

While I was in the van, Carine Williams was driving King and attorney Katherine Kimpel up to the prison for our meeting from New Orleans when George called her on her cell phone with news: U.S. Middle District chief judge Brian A. Jackson had issued his decision that morning as to Herman's pending petition for habeas review. George read the decision over the phone, skipping over much of the legal analysis to get to the ruling: Judge Jackson's decision granted

Herman full habeas relief because in violation of the 14th Amendment, women had been wrongfully excluded from the West Feliciana Parish grand jury that indicted him in 1973. Judge Jackson had taken the unusual step of not only granting habeas relief but also ordering Herman's immediate release.

We gathered around Herman in his hospital bed before telling him. He was curled up in a ball and extremely weak. He had stopped taking food and fluids days before. I sat on one side of his hospital bed and could just reach him with my hands in the box. I put my hands on his arm. King sat opposite me on the other side of him. At first, when Carine told him that habeas relief had been granted, Herman thought she said I was the one who had won. He smiled and pointed to me, nodding his head. When we clarified that *his* conviction had been overturned, it took a moment for him to process. "Herman, this is your case," Carine said. He looked at her and said, "My conviction?" It was extremely difficult for Herman to speak. Struggling, he said, "If he only knew," pausing. "If Judge Jackson only knew what it was like in that cell," he said.

Carine got up to call George back so they could discuss next steps. As she opened the door to leave the room, someone told her George was on the line to speak with her. They needed to act quickly, before Louisiana filed an appeal of the judge's ruling. To put pressure on the prison to comply with Judge Jackson's order, George arranged for a private ambulance to pick Herman up. After hanging up with George, Carine went straight to Warden Howard Prince's office to tell him an ambulance was on the way and to ask him to process Herman's release. The warden had heard the order from the state's lawyers but refused to see Carine. His assistant told her that, since he didn't have a copy of the order, he couldn't know if what he was being told (by the state's own lawyers) about the decision was actually true. The warden wouldn't release Herman, Carine was told, before he saw a copy of the decision ordering release.

Carine got in her car and drove until she found a local library that let her access the court's electronic database. She printed out copies of Judge Jackson's decision. When she got back, the ambulance was parked at the curb, some distance away from the prison security gates. The warden was also outside, parked in his pickup truck at the security gates, with his windows up and engine running. Carine went up to him to tell him she had a copy of the order for him. The warden wouldn't roll down his window to talk to her. She placed the document facedown on his windshield so he could see it and spoke to him through the glass, telling him the judge had ordered Herman's immediate release and that he would be in contempt of a federal court order if he failed to comply. She then went back into the prison and left a copy of the order with the warden's secretary and brought another copy of it back into the room with us. She held it up to show Herman. "Herman, here's the order," she said. "You're free." Herman made like he was looking around the room and said, "Girl, I still know where I am. I'm not free."

I didn't say much. My communication with Herman was mostly silent. I didn't know how much time he had left. I silently told him how much I loved him, and that when we didn't have his back anymore, the ancestors would. My heart was breaking. I think of these hours I had with Herman and King together in the same room. It was a surreal coincidence that the three of us were all together on the day that Herman would get this momentous news. That we could share in this victory with him. That he would go home. My memories of that day are always a reminder to me of how our lawyers went above and beyond to help us, how they never failed us. The same way our supporters came through for us, above and beyond. I didn't know how we could be so lucky. Herman asked if we could pray. We all held hands. Carine said a prayer, then Katherine said a prayer. I looked at King. Tears were steadily falling down his face.

In Herman's ruling, Judge Jackson wrote, "The record in this case makes clear that Mr. Wallace's grand jury was improperly chosen in violation of the Fourteenth Amendment's guarantee of 'the equal protection of the laws,' . . . and that the Louisiana courts, when presented with the opportunity to correct this error, failed to do so. . . . Our Constitution requires this result even where, as here, it means overturning Mr. Wallace's conviction nearly forty years after it was entered."

Our visit ended as scheduled, around three p.m. King left the building. Carine and Katherine stayed with Herman. The transport officers who were taking me back to Wade led me to a room on the hospital tier for a while, as a favor, so I could be in the prison when Herman left. A lot of the guys in the hospital were rooting for Herman. One of them asked me, "If Mr. Herman is going home now, how do you feel?" I said, "Well, I'm at peace. Whatever happens from now on, I'm at peace." After about an hour the lieutenant escorting me told me we had to get on the road. No one was moving to prepare Herman to leave. I figured they were delaying his release, stalling to give Buddy Caldwell time to file a motion to stay Judge Jackson's ruling. That turned out to be true—Louisiana filed a motion for a stay of the decision. When we pulled away from the prison grounds, I saw the ambulance at the curb, waiting for Herman. Later I learned the warden had left the prison; the rumor was he went to dinner, thinking if he left prison grounds he wouldn't have to release Herman.

George and Carine thought Judge Jackson and his law clerks might soon leave chambers for the day and called to see whether the judge might stay late so that they could file a response to the stay motion. They didn't get an answer, but very shortly after that Judge Jackson issued another order. This decision denied Louisiana's request for a stay and ordered the prison to release Herman immediately or be held in contempt. Warden Prince returned to the prison. He knew if he didn't he could be in front of the judge's bench the next day himself, possibly in handcuffs.

Herman had a dream once about leaving Angola. He described it in the film *Herman's House*. "I get to the front gate," he says, "and there's a whole lot of people out there and, you ain't going to believe this but"—Herman laughed—"I was dancing my way out. I was doing the jitterbug. And I was doing all kinds of crazy stupid-ass shit, you know. And people were just laughing and clapping until I walked out that gate. And . . . I look and there are all the brothers in the window waving and throwing a fist sign, you know."

Carine told me the sun was setting when Herman was brought out of prison on a stretcher and put in the ambulance. He was conscious but very weak. After he was put inside the ambulance he asked, "Is everybody smiling?" Many of his friends had gathered outside the prison and called out to him, shouting words of support. Herman's fiancée, Maria Hinds, and friend Ashley Wennerstrom were in the ambulance with him. Carine and Katherine drove behind the ambulance, following it to a New Orleans hospital emergency room. After they arrived, Carine walked up to Herman as he lay in a hospital bed. He looked at her and smiled. "Now I'm free," he said.

That night, George released a statement: "Tonight, Herman Wallace has left the walls of Louisiana prisons and will be able to receive the medical care that his advanced liver cancer requires. It took the order of a federal judge to address the clear constitutional violations present in Mr. Wallace's 1974 trial and grant him relief. The state of Louisiana has had many opportunities to address this injustice and has repeatedly and utterly failed to do so."

On the drive back to Wade, my hands were numb and in pain from the black box. I was numb and in pain too. I was elated that Herman was getting out, but the miracle I ached for now was his life. The next day Herman was taken from the hospital to the home of Ashley Wennerstrom and her husband for hospice care. I called the house and spoke to several old friends and comrades who had gathered. They told me Herman was resting and in and out of consciousness, but he knew where he was. He knew he was in Ashley's house. He knew his family, supporters, lawyers, and friends were around him, coming and going. They played music for him, took turns reading to him and holding him. Ashley brought him flowers to smell.

On the next day, October 3, District Attorney Samuel D'Aquilla had Herman reindicted by a West Feliciana Parish grand jury for the murder of Brent Miller. East Baton Rouge Parish district attorney Hillar C. Moore III asked the Fifth Circuit Court of Appeals to return Herman to prison. The vengeance by the state of Louisiana against us had long been incomprehensible to me, but this move pushed at the boundary of sanity. Herman was dying. Nobody ever told him he was reindicted.

If he'd known there is no doubt in my mind he would have begun to mentally prepare the way he did for every battle, without hesitation.

On October 4, I woke up around four a.m. with a very strong urge to call Ashley. When I got through to her she told me Herman had died in the night. He went to sleep and never woke up. He was 71. I sat on my bunk and wrote a statement for our supporters.

> The old man has decided to leave us. I am sure it was a very hard choice for him, Who will I serve? The ancestors who have called me home, or humanity who I love so much?
>
> "Old man" was my term of endearment for him—it had to do with the age of everything—his heart and his soul. Herman "Hooks" Wallace was not a perfect human being, and like all men, he had faults and weaknesses, but he also had character. He could make me so mad that I wanted to rip his head off. Then he would melt my heart with a word, or an act of kindness to another human being.
>
> On October 1 sitting in a hospital room, with the other part of my heart, Robert King, I tried to will a miracle and a miracle was granted, not the miracle of life that I wanted for Herman, but the miracle of freedom. After 42 years of tireless struggle against evil, he was a free man.
>
> I had a chance to say good-bye to my comrade in the struggle, my mentor in life, my fellow Panther, and most of all, my friend. Herman taught me a man can stumble, even fall, as long as he gets up. That it's OK to be afraid, but hold on to your courage. To lose a battle is not the loss of a war.
>
> Herman Wallace's greatest pride was joining the Black Panther Party for Self-Defense. He believed in duty, honor, and dedication. He never broke the faith of the party, his comrades, or the people. As I bent to kiss his forehead, my heart said good-bye—I love you forever. My soul said—separated but never apart; never touching but always connected. He was the best of us. As long as we remember him, he lives on.

In Washington DC that day, Rep. John Conyers read a tribute to Herman on the floor that would go into the Congressional record.

Mr. Speaker, we rise to commemorate and celebrate the life and contributions of Herman Wallace, one of the bravest champions for justice and human rights whom we have ever met. Nicknamed "The Muhammad Ali of Justice," Mr. Wallace was a member of Louisiana's "Angola 3" who spent 41 years in solitary confinement. Mr. [Cedric] Richmond and I had the opportunity to visit Mr. Wallace at the Louisiana State Penitentiary in Angola, justifiably called "the Alcatraz of the South" several years ago. I was impressed by his courage, determination, and dignity. We received word that Mr. Wallace passed away earlier this morning, only three days after he was freed pursuant to a federal judge's ruling that he had not received a fair trial in 1974. . . .

Mr. Speaker, it was with great sadness that we learned of Mr. Wallace's passing earlier this morning, nine days shy of his 72nd birthday. Mr. Wallace's personal fight against injustice and the inhuman plight that is long term solitary confinement has ended for him. The larger fight against that injustice must go on, however, and his legacy will endure through a civil lawsuit that he filed jointly with his fellow Angola 3 members, Albert Woodfox and Robert King. That lawsuit seeks to define and abolish long term solitary confinement as cruel and unusual punishment.

Mr. Speaker, we ask my colleagues to join me in honoring Mr. Wallace for his many-decades-long fight for the humane treatment of prisoners. We, and all of us, owe Mr. Wallace a debt of gratitude.

Three days later, the United Nations special rapporteur on torture, Juan E. Méndez, called on the United States to immediately end the indefinite solitary confinement imposed on me. "This is a sad case and it is not over," he said. "The co-accused, Mr. Woodfox, remains in solitary confinement pending an appeal to the federal court and has been kept in isolation. . . . Keeping Albert Woodfox in solitary confinement for more than four decades clearly amounts to torture and it should be lifted immediately."

Herman was buried on October 12. Friends and loved ones visited me and told me about Herman's memorial service and funeral, held in a community center in the Treme, a block from where I grew up. People sent me photographs. Somebody had made a light blue tapestry with a large black panther across it that was draped over Herman's coffin. Six former Panthers were pallbearers, including King and Malik Rahim, all wearing blue shirts and black ties—Panther colors—and black berets. There were drawings and paintings of Herman, me, and King on the walls. Herman's sister sang. Many friends and family members spoke, remembering Herman's spirit, his commitment, his humor, his courage, his heart. How he never gave up. Carine held up her phone and played a recording of one of Herman's favorite songs, Etta James singing "At Last."

I looked at the photos from Herman's funeral and memorial service several times in the following weeks. I told myself, and everyone, "Don't think of what we lost, remember what we had." The day Herman died I felt a great pain and sense of loss that is still with me, and I will carry it to my grave.

Two weeks after Herman died, Amnesty International tried to deliver yet another petition to Governor Bobby Jindal. This one requested that the state drop its appeal to keep me in prison. Fifty thousand people signed it. The governor was not in his office so it was left with his staff.

It was strange: this time instead of demanding our freedom, Amnesty was demanding my freedom. I had never felt more alone. Before they delivered the petition, our supporters held a press conference on the state capitol steps. They had spread calendar pages on the steps to represent the time I had spent in solitary confinement and held signs that said REMEMBER HERMAN WALLACE and FREE ALBERT WOODFOX. Malik spoke, demanding that state legislators get involved in ending my confinement in solitary, calling it a human rights issue. King spoke, saying we would never stop pushing for justice. Billie Mizell read a statement for Teenie Rogers: "Each time I look at the evidence in this case, I remember there is no proof that the men charged with Brent's death are the ones who actually killed him. It's easy to get caught up in vengeance and anger, but when I look at the facts, they just do not add up." Rogers said she hadn't been planning to sign Amnesty's petition, but after Herman was reindicted on his deathbed she changed her mind. "That's not anything I want to be a part of, and I don't think it's something Brent would have done," Rogers said. "If the state had a strong case, I might feel differently. But I have not seen anything yet that proves to me these men murdered Brent."

My brother Michael read the statement I gave him, "On good days I am allowed, at most, an hour of exercise in a cage outside. I do not have the words to convey the years of mental, emotional, and physical torture I have endured. I ask that for a moment you imagine yourself standing at the edge of nothingness, looking at emptiness. The pain and suffering this isolation causes go beyond mere description."

The next month I was in federal court, testifying about the strip searches and visual cavity searches that were still going on at Wade. My attorney, Sheridan England, asked me how having multiple strip searches a day made me feel. I told him the visual anal cavity inspections were humiliating and stressful. They made me feel hopeless and helpless.

Richard Curry, representing Louisiana prison officials, argued that strip searches were necessary in maximum-security prisons to prevent prisoners from having contraband, like drugs or razor blades. "Weren't you once found guilty of having a handcuff key in your possession?" Curry asked me. "No," I said. Curry showed me a disciplinary order that was issued 36 years earlier at Angola, in 1977, stating that a handcuff key had been found in my cell. I told him if I had a handcuff key in my cell in 1977, it was planted in my cell. Especially back in those years many guards hated me. "You were never found innocent of this charge," Curry countered. No contraband had been found on me or in my cell since I'd been at Wade, I pointed out. The warden at Wade confirmed that.

Back in my cell, I was feeling out of balance. It was December. Most years run into the next when you are locked down 23 hours a day. A few years stand out for being worse than others. The year my mom died. The year I lost my sister. That year, 2013, was one of those years. Herman was gone. The degrading strip searches continued. I was being slandered in the press by the attorney general's office—again. The state of Louisiana, which had already spent millions of dollars to defend my wrongful conviction and to keep me in prison, was now expending considerable resources to fight to restore my conviction—again. I was reminded of a valuable lesson I'd learned, and relearned, many times before. Whenever you don't think you can take another step, the human spirit keeps going, even when you don't want to.

Chapter 51

The Ends of Justice

Would the loss of Herman finally tip the scales of sanity against me? Would this be the year of justice and freedom or another year of the same? My habeas case was before a three-judge panel of the most conservative judges on the Fifth Circuit. Two of them were appointed by President Ronald Reagan. The third was appointed by President George W. Bush. I didn't have a lot of hope for justice and freedom. But I was feeling the support of the people. I was receiving thousands of letters from people through Amnesty International. And that gave me strength. I wanted to write back to each and every person who wrote to me, but it wasn't physically possible. In January 2014, I released a statement, which Amnesty distributed. "To the many people around the world who have taken us into your lives and your hearts, who have told us 'I know you, and what you have given to this world,' who have taken the time to write to me and to Louisiana State officials, you have no idea what a source of strength and courage you have been in my darkest moments. It is impossible for me to personally respond to the 1000s of letters and cards that encourage me to stay strong, don't give up, don't lose hope and to fight on. Thank you. The message is heard. I ask that this letter feels as if I am reaching out to you personally and saying, in solidarity and struggle, All Power to the People!"

On January 31, 2014, eight months after the strip searches at Wade began, my attorney Katherine Kimpel called me to say Judge James Brady had issued a preliminary injunction against them. In his ruling Judge Brady wrote that routine searches were not shown to be necessary or justified for security "as is required constitutionally of such policies. Therefore," he wrote, "Woodfox's human dignity [as] protected by his fourth Amendment rights" outweighs the "legitimate penological interest. In this circumstance."

The state appealed immediately, not on the grounds that the strip searches were legitimate, but on the grounds that Judge Brady, a federal judge, didn't have the jurisdiction to enforce a state-issued consent decree. Louisiana argued that my case could only be heard in the 19th Judicial District Court in Baton Rouge. During the appeal process I was protected from strip searches, but every other CCR prisoner at Wade was still being strip-searched. Some officials in the administration tried to play it to the other prisoners as if I was getting special treatment, as if I'd orchestrated the whole thing. Most of the guys saw through it. I reminded all of them that I had asked them to join me to fight the strip searches but they didn't want to get involved.

Next, the Fifth Circuit reversed Judge Brady's injunction, not because the court agreed with the strip searches, but on the grounds that the matter had to be adjudicated in a state court. Officially, Wade corrections officers could start strip-searching me again, but most of them didn't. My attorneys immediately filed for an injunction in the 19th Judicial District.

Over the winter and spring of 2014, King was on yet another A3 tour. He spoke on solitary confinement at California state legislative hearings in Sacramento; on the impact of solitary confinement at a scientific meeting in Chicago; at the Toronto Black Film Festival; at the Rutland Institute for Ethics Presidential Colloquium at Clemson University in South Carolina; and at Central Connecticut State University. At each stop he spoke about the horrors of solitary confinement and about our cases. I was worried about him—he had given his life up for me, and for Herman. He answered every collect call we ever made, spent part of each week on conference calls with our lawyers, with Marina Drummer, with Tory Pegram, with individual supporters and members of our advisory board; he took every call from every reporter who ever contacted him and sat down for interviews with anyone who could give us publicity for our case. I knew the travel was exhausting, that he sometimes got stopped by airport security. He never complained.

In May 2014, Rep. Cedric Richmond introduced HR 4618, called the Solitary Confinement Study and Reform Act of 2014, to study and reform the use of solitary confinement in the U.S. prisons, jails, and juvenile detention facilities. In July, it was referred to the Subcommittee on Crime, Terrorism, Homeland Security, and Investigations. That was the last action taken on that bill. (In early May 2018, Rep. Richmond introduced HR 5710, the Solitary Confinement Study and Reform Act of 2018. Later that month it was referred to the Subcommittee on Crime, Terrorism, Homeland Security, and Investigations.)

In July 2014, Amnesty International released a 54-page report on solitary confinement in U.S. federal prisons that began, "The USA stands virtually alone in the world in incarcerating thousands of prisoners in long-term or indefinite solitary confinement, defined by the UN Special Rapporteur on Torture and Other Cruel, Inhuman or Degrading Treatment or Punishment as 'the physical and social isolation of individuals who are confined to their cells for 22 to 24 hours a day.' More than 40 US states are believed to operate 'super-maximum security' units or prisons, collectively housing at least 25,000 prisoners. This number does not include the many thousands of other prisoners serving shorter periods in punishment or administrative segregation cells—estimated to be approximately 80,000 on any given day."

That fall, I got unbelievable news. In November, the conservative Fifth Circuit panel reviewing my claim that racial bias tainted the selection of the grand jury foreperson who presided in my case had ruled in my favor. It was a unanimous decision. All three of the Fifth Circuit judges agreed with Judge Brady's ruling. Judge Patrick Higginbotham wrote a powerful decision for the panel (which included fellow circuit judges E. Grady Jolly and Leslie Southwick).

We begin with an important observation. Woodfox's claim is not just about the selection of the grand jury *foreperson*. Rather, it is also about the selection of the grand jury itself. The grand jury system used for Woodfox's re-indictment was the same as the

one challenged in *Campbell v. Louisiana*. As the Supreme Court
explained, the Louisiana system of grand jury foreperson selection,
at that time, was unlike most other systems. Under most systems,
"the title 'foreperson' is bestowed on one of the existing grand jurors
without any change in the grand jury's composition." But under the
Louisiana system at issue, "the judge select[ed] the foreperson from
the grand jury venire before the remaining [eleven] members of the
grand jury [were] chosen by lot." The foreperson had the same voting
power as all the other grand jurors. Thus, in effect, the judge chose
one grand juror. This case then is one that alleges discrimination in
the selection of the grand jurors, an important constitutional challenge. For well over a century, the Supreme Court has held that a
criminal conviction of an African-American cannot stand under the
Equal Protection Clause of the Fourteenth Amendment if it is based
on an indictment of a grand jury from which African-Americans
were excluded on the basis of race.

The state appealed the decision, asking for what's called an "en
banc" review so it could present its case before every judge in the Fifth
Circuit, the full court, and if a majority of the active judges on the Fifth
Circuit agreed to rehear the case, the three-judge panel's decision would
be vacated, and the full court would deliberate and decide my fate. Not
one judge called for a rehearing. The state lost that round. Undeterred,
Louisiana appealed to the U.S. Supreme Court, and lost again. Judge
Brady's ruling would stand. I would get a new trial.

On February 11, 2015—seven years after my conviction was overturned by Judge Brady the first time and two years after it was overturned the second time—the Fifth Circuit issued a mandate to Judge
Brady to issue the final writ of habeas corpus. The next day, the state
once again brought my case before a West Feliciana grand jury. I was
reindicted for the murder of Brent Miller.

Later I would read the affidavit for my arrest warrant, written by an
investigator from the attorney general's office, which rehashed Buddy
Caldwell's false claims of rape and robbery as if they were fact. Everything in boldface type in this arrest affidavit is a lie:

Between January 4 and February 13, 1969, Woodfox engaged in a very violent crime spree committing 7 armed robberies and 5 aggravated rapes. [Not true.] As prosecutors worked their way through these cases [Prosecutors were never assigned to these cases.] the first case they brought to trial [The only case brought to trial.] ended with Woodfox being convicted for armed robbery (of Tony's Green Room) on July 31 1969. . . . Woodfox was remanded to Orleans Parish Prison to await further court appearances [Not true. I was taken to Orleans Parish Prison to await sentencing on the armed robbery conviction.] on the other pending armed robberies and rape cases. [There were no other pending armed robbery or rape cases.] Woodfox was possibly facing five death penalty sentences on the aggravated rape charges that were pending at the time. [Not true. There were no pending charges. The judge dropped all charges except for the armed robbery. I was not facing any charges for rape.]

The affidavit, which I can only assume was read to the grand jury that indicted me, went on to say:

Prosecutors believed that Woodfox had nothing to lose in committing this heinous murder [Obviously not true.] as he believed he was already facing the possibility of 5 separate death penalty sentences [Not true.] for the aggravated rapes he had committed just three years earlier. [All lies. Slander.]

And:

[A] United States Supreme Court opinion was released on June 29, 1972, making the death penalty unconstitutional, effectively making it impossible for prosecutors to try Albert Woodfox for the death penalty [What made it impossible for prosecutors to try me was that there were no charges against me, no indictments, no arraignments.] for the murder of Miller or for the five aggravated rapes he committed [Because I did not commit these crimes.] during the New Orleans crime spree during January and February, 1969.

[There had been no crime spree and Judge Brady saw through the lies. After looking at these charges and finding nothing that substantiated them, he granted me appeal bail. Which, on state appeal, was blocked by the Fifth Circuit.]

The arrest affidavit went on to attribute to Chester Jackson a whole new story about the events leading up to Miller's murder—different from Jackson's testimony at Herman's trial and different from what Jackson had said in his original statement taken in 1972. The affidavit claimed that I showed Jackson "a letter" the night before the murder (the same letter Warden Henderson would describe the day after Miller's murder, a letter that the deputy warden had no knowledge of and that was never produced at either my or Herman's trials).

"Upon information and belief" the affidavit accused me of writing the letter taking credit for burning the guard in the booth, which was signed by "The Vanguard Army." "The Black Panther Party," the affidavit erroneously stated, was "also known as the Vanguard Army." The affidavit also claimed that Leonard "Specs" Turner "without hesitation" broke the case for investigators, telling prison officials I murdered Brent Miller with Herman and Chester Jackson; "armed with Turner's statement" (a "truth" the man who took the statement couldn't remember at my trial), investigators then "reinterviewed" Hezekiah Brown. "Upon hearing the details, Brown confirmed the information Turner had provided was true." Leonard Turner was never called to testify at my first trial, and at my second trial he denied making the unsigned, undated statement presented to him as his. The former captain who allegedly took the statement from Turner testified he couldn't remember taking it and he didn't remember what the statement said, which would be highly unlikely if the statement had been real, because it would have cracked the case for investigators.

At the time, I wasn't aware of these new false accusations against me. All I knew was that I was reindicted for the murder of Brent Miller. I was transferred from David Wade Correctional Center to a jail in West Feliciana Parish. It happened so quickly I didn't have a chance to give my things away to other prisoners on the tier at Wade.

*   *   *

The West Feliciana Parish jail is small. There were four solitary cells on my floor. The first was a holding cell for drunks, where people were put to sober up. I was in the second cell. The two cells on the other side of me were used to hold prisoners for short durations, a few weeks at most. The cells had solid steel doors. The only way I could talk to someone was if I bent over and spoke through the food slot. There was a small TV in the cell and a window that didn't open that looked out on the yard. Any relief the window might have provided me was counteracted by the steel door. I still got claustrophobic attacks. When I started getting mail at my new address I received dozens of birthday cards. I had turned 68.

Since I was no longer in state custody, my strip search lawsuit had become moot. George Kendall wanted to continue litigating it for the CCR prisoners at Wade and tried to find another prisoner who would take over for me as plaintiff, but nobody wanted to do it. Meanwhile, George was also looking ahead in my criminal case. We were still hoping Judge Brady's unconditional release order would hold up in the Fifth Circuit. In case we lost, though, George brought in two new lawyers to join my legal team to focus on my defense at trial, Billy Sothern and Robert McDuff. They started reinvestigating the murder of Brent Miller and moved quickly to defend me in court, filing to have the latest indictment thrown out and to get me out on appeal bail. Meanwhile, Buddy Caldwell continued his unethical, inflammatory campaign of lies, publicly accusing me of being a rapist (still never pressing charges). "The facts of the case remain solid," Caldwell told reporters. "Despite Woodfox's last-ditch efforts to obtain a 'get out of jail free' pass on grand jury selection issues, the proof of his guilt in committing the murder is undeniable."

As the weeks passed I felt drained of energy. I stopped taking my hour out of the cell. The guard would come and ask me if I wanted yard and I'd say, "Nah, not today." In my cell, I watched CNN. I'd been watching the news about police shootings of unarmed black people and following the Black Lives Matter movement. It hurt me to see organizers of Black Lives Matter painted as being racists. It hurt me to see black people needing to state the obvious: that we mattered. I thought of the black sanitation workers who went on strike in Memphis in 1968; black workers wore placards that read I AM A MAN. Fifty years later, and the humanity of a black person is still in dispute?

It didn't make sense to me. The top 1 percent of Americans own more wealth than the bottom 90 percent of all Americans of all races, combined. And yet Americans believe that people of other races, religions, sexual preferences, and cultures are the problem. An unjust economic system can only be perpetuated if we, the majority of the population, are at odds with one another. Black Lives Matter was formed to campaign *against* violence and systemic racism toward black people. How was that being racist? When you see organizations like Black Lives Matter under attack for being "racist," you are seeing the agenda of an unjust economic system at play—a system that seeks to separate groups of people within the majority to benefit the top 1 percent. If we can't allow diversity, if we can't accept our differences, if we can't see one another as equal, if every race can't begin to function on an equal footing with every other race in this world, we will never be able to unite, which means we will never be able to demand economic justice for all. We won't be able to advance as a species. Capitalism can't be "fixed" or made to be fair or just; it must be destroyed. The very nature of a capitalistic economy prevents unity and fosters class struggle. Under capitalism there is division in labor and division among the workers themselves because they are taught to look out for the individual and not for their fellow workers. There is no equal distribution of the wealth of the nation under a capitalist system. We have to come together and look out for one another. In 1968, Martin Luther King spoke before a mixed-race crowd who had gathered to support the striking black sanitation workers, honoring the unity of the group. "You are demonstrating that we can stick together." King said, "You are demonstrating that we are all tied in a single garment of destiny, and that if one black person suffers, if one black person is down, we are all down."

I had no energy at the parish jail, but I would always leave my cell to meet a visitor who came to see me, even though it required a lot of effort to be positive throughout the visit. The visits were keeping me connected to the world, and I loved the people who came. The room where we met was antiquated. I had to sit in a booth and look through a window to see my visitor. I put my head down to the mesh screen beneath the window to speak and to hear what was being said. Most of the time they kept handcuffs on me, but sometimes they didn't. It depended on the personnel working. My most regular visitors were old friends: Maria Hinds, Professor Rebecca Hensley, and Jackie Sumell. Michael came every month. He begged me to go out on the yard. I told him I would, but I didn't feel like it. George and my other lawyers got on my case too, pressing me to get out of the cell for my hour and exercise. When I did go out on the yard I didn't feel like running. Sometimes I walked. Sometimes there was a deputy working who was up on current events and we talked about politics or whatever was in the news. Almost all of the guards at the jail used to work at Angola. Sometimes we talked about Angola.

George set up an attorney-client visit with me and King at the West Feliciana jail to talk about our civil case. I was looking forward to it. King was a stabilizing force for me. When he arrived for the visit, they told him he couldn't enter the prison visiting room unless they strip-searched him. He allowed the strip search. He didn't tell us about it until the end of our meeting. He wanted to brush it off because he knew if he didn't submit to a search, this would be our last visit. I wanted to see King. I needed to see him. But not at the expense of his dignity. "I don't want you to be strip-searched anymore," I told him. George said that we would fight it in court. I told King, "If we can't stop the strip searches, don't come back."

I met my daughter in person for the second time since she was a baby at the West Feliciana jail. She came to visit with my grandson and three of my great-grandchildren. It was strange looking at my great-grandchildren knowing they were a third generation removed from me, that no matter what the system did to me my legacy was still moving on. I appreciated the visit so much; it was another step in building a bond with my family and it supported my ongoing effort to preserve my humanity.

*　*　*

In June, Judge James Brady issued my habeas corpus writ. To ensure justice for me, and my freedom, he went beyond my wildest expectations, issuing what's called an "exceptional writ," an extremely rare, unconditional writ that orders the state to release a habeas petitioner from prison and bars the state from retrying him.

"The Supreme Court has long instructed that habeas corpus relief must be applied with an eye toward 'the ends of justice,'" Judge Brady wrote. "The Fifth Circuit has identified two categories of rare and extraordinary cases where 'law and justice' require the permanent discharge of a petitioner: either the circumstances of the case involve a 'constitutional violation [that] cannot be remedied by another trial' or 'other exceptional circumstances [must] exist such that the holding of a new trial would be unjust.'" Judge Brady listed five "exceptional" circumstances that justified his decision: "Mr. Woodfox's age and poor health, his limited ability to present a defense at a third trial in light of the unavailability of witnesses, this Court's lack of confidence in the State to provide a fair third trial, the prejudice done unto Mr. Woodfox by spending over forty-years in solitary confinement, and finally the very fact that Mr. Woodfox has already been tried twice and would otherwise face his third trial for a crime that occurred over forty years ago."

Brady agreed with my claim that the state's conduct demonstrated extreme prejudice against me. "Additionally, Mr. Woodfox has served over forty years in solitary confinement," he wrote. "The Court agrees with Mr. Woodfox that the time involved here results in extreme prejudice. The State understates the extent of the prejudice done to Mr. Woodfox.... A habeas court must consider all of the circumstances involved when defining relief. The prejudice of an unconstitutionally obtained indictment is only one of the relevant circumstances."

Brady also cited the evidence of my innocence in favor of an "extraordinary" remedy and noted the Fifth Circuit had said before that it failed to see the "overwhelming evidence" the state claimed to have against me. "There was an abundance of physical evidence available at the crime scene in 1972," Brady wrote, "but not one piece of physical evidence incriminated Mr. Woodfox." He cited the following indications of my innocence that were raised in my writ: "(1) a statement from State's key witness Leonard Turner admitting Mr. Woodfox was not involved in Miller's murder; (2) statements from two women with whom Chester Jackson ... spoke about Woodfox's actual innocence upon his release; (3) a reliable scientific review of the bloody print at the scene, exculpating Woodfox; (4) evidence that severely undermines the credibility of State's three prisoner witnesses; and (5) a polygraph examination indicating that Woodfox truthfully denied involvement in the crime."

He noted the hardship of my continued solitary confinement even after I'd "demonstrated an ability to live peacefully with others," writing, "Mr. Woodfox has remained in the extraordinary conditions of solitary confinement for approximately forty years now, and yet today there is no valid conviction holding him in prison, let alone solitary confinement. Last year a unanimous panel of the Fifth Circuit observed: '[C]onsidering the duration of the solitary confinement, the severity of the restrictions, and their effectively indefinite nature, it is clear that Woodfox's continued detention in CCR constitutes an "atypical and significant hardship on the inmate in relation to the ordinary incidents of prison life" according to any possible baseline we consider.'" In conclusion, Brady wrote, "The only just remedy is an unconditional writ of habeas corpus barring retrial ... and releasing Mr. Woodfox from custody immediately."

The state immediately appealed Judge Brady's decision to the Fifth Circuit. A three-judge panel from that court issued a temporary stay that would keep me in prison until a more permanent ruling would come down, within the next four days. Representative Cedric Richmond (of the U.S. House) released a statement calling for my release. Of Buddy Caldwell, he said, "This is an obviously personal vendetta and has been a waste of tax payer dollars for decades. The state is making major cuts in education and healthcare but he has spent millions of dollars on this frivolous endeavor and the price tag is increasing by the day."

Four days later, on June 12, Carine Williams came for a lawyer's visit to keep me company while we waited to hear if I'd be released from prison that day or not. We were in a ground-floor room that had a window looking out on the parking lot. There were some reporters and a film crew outside. The visit started around ten a.m. and the court had said it would rule before one p.m. We sat together at a table, talking. We both watched the clock on the wall. The later it got, the more hopeful we became. If they were going to rule against me, why would they wait until the last minute?

In my cell that morning, I'd made a list of what I'd do when I got out of prison. I'd never done that before. "Visit Mama's grave. Spend time with my daughter. Learn how to live in society." As the hour hand moved closer to the deadline I saw outside the window, over Carine's shoulder, that one of the reporters who had been standing with the others was leaving. He got in his car and drove away. I knew then that the Fifth Circuit would not grant my release. I didn't have the heart to tell Carine. I thought of all the hard work she had done, along with my other attorneys, and felt a wave of sadness come over me. Some of the most difficult times for me in prison were moments like these, when it wasn't only a loss for me, but for everybody who worked so hard on my behalf and who cared about me. The guards brought her a cordless phone, which rang shortly afterward. George was on the line. He gave her the news: the Fifth Circuit decided to leave the stay in place and to keep me in jail pending the state's appeal of Judge Brady's exceptional writ. Carine and I put a brave face on for each other. We said our good-byes. Carine walked out of the jail to give a statement to the reporters. I was taken back to my cell.

In his exceptional writ Judge Brady wrote that I would not be able to get a fair trial anywhere in the state of Louisiana. My arrest affidavit alone was proof of that. That summer we got further corroboration. The foreperson on the grand jury that indicted me in February came forward with concerns about the grand jury hearing; she had misgivings about the process. A white, Christian, lifelong conservative Republican, Deidre Howard, a dental hygienist for 41 years, didn't know anything about me before the prosecutors made their case against me. She trusted Assistant Attorney General Kurt Wall, Special Assistant Attorney General Tony Clayton, and West Feliciana Parish district attorney Samuel D'Aquilla, who she knew personally. The prosecutors told the grand jurors my conviction was overturned on a "technicality" and made the case for my indictment. The grand jury indicted me. Deidre signed the indictment and gave it to the judge and was dismissed. She believed I was guilty. But something felt wrong. One day she was working as a dental hygienist and the next day she was deciding the fate of a man's life. She felt unprepared to do what she had just done.

She talked to her twin sister, Donna, stating she didn't want to be in that situation ever again. She had taken an oath not to reveal details of what happened in the grand jury room but when my indictment was reported in the newspaper the next day Donna knew that was Deidre's case. In the following weeks Deidre had trouble sleeping. Out of concern for her sister, Donna and her husband typed my name into a search engine online and found out I could be innocent and that I'd been kept in solitary confinement for 40 years. On Deidre's next visit to Donna, her sister told her, "The whole world has been trying to get him out." Deidre Howard's knees gave out and she fell to the floor. She felt betrayed and used because she had trusted the attorney general's office to be honest and now she knew she didn't get the whole story. She felt the weight of the world was on her now. Her first reaction was to try to undo the indictment, which, she learned later, could never be undone.

Deidre hired a lawyer because she wasn't sure how to proceed with a complaint about the grand jury and still comply with the grand jury secrecy she swore to at the time. She wrote a personal letter to Judge William Carmichael of the 20th Judicial District Court, who oversaw the grand jury hearing and would be the judge on my third trial. Her attorney mailed her letter to Judge Carmichael and Judge Brady, with a letter of his own, stating that his client "has had serious misgivings about that process from the date of the jury's decision." Judge Carmichael informed my attorneys about it and put the letter under seal. When Deidre didn't hear back she wrote to the special assistant attorney general, Tony Clayton; and to the West Feliciana Parish district attorney, Samuel D'Aquilla. "In my opinion, after reading everything I can get my hands on, articles, books, trial transcripts, visual and audio interviews," she wrote, "I believe Mr. Woodfox is innocent of the murder." When she didn't receive any response, she wrote to the assistant attorney general

Kurt Wall. When no response came, she wrote to Attorney General Buddy Caldwell and then, after hearing nothing back, Deidre wrote to Governor Bobby Jindal. "I wish that I could go back and redo that morning but sadly I cannot," she wrote. "I decided that I could cry and hurt, or take action, because as his plight goes so does mine. . . . Please, can you do anything? When the dust settles one day on this case, it is going to be one of the darkest chapters in our state's history." Later she would say she kept thinking to herself, "How did Louisiana hold a man in a cell for over 40 years on the word of an eyewitness who was given free cigarettes for years? Didn't anybody wonder why?"

With nobody responding to Deidre, her sister Donna wrote a heartfelt letter of her own, describing Deidre's experience and "begging for help," to every member of the Louisiana legislature, members of the media, and others in influential positions who she thought could help. Before it was over, she had sent more than 500 letters.

In June 2015, I once again applied for pretrial bail. As usual, the state fought back, starting with delaying tactics. First, prosecutors claimed that my case was a capital case and therefore my right to bail was limited. My lawyers Robert McDuff and Billy Sothern actually had to cite case law that made it clear beyond question that my case wasn't a capital case and that I was, therefore, eligible for bail. In the end, though, I wouldn't get bail.

The first time I heard about Deidre Howard was in July. At that point, because her correspondence had been placed under seal, I didn't know her name. But Billy told me he was going to file a motion to be allowed to read a sealed letter written by a woman who was the foreperson at my grand jury. He told me the woman had raised issues about the actions of the grand jury. In September, my attorneys were able to view the letter and filed a new motion to quash my indictment on the grounds of prosecutorial misconduct. That motion was eventually denied. Still, the integrity and courage that Deidre Howard displayed in coming forward to speak out about her experience, even early on, before she knew if I was innocent or guilty, were so noble and rare. I am grateful to this day. Later, Deidre would say it took months for her to process everything that happened. "As a citizen, I was taught to respect those in authority," she said. "I was not prepared to second-guess them. A citizen coming from [her] own job doesn't walk into the courthouse with the mind-set that the prosecutors are not going to be honest, or that they would knowingly leave out facts that would change the whole story. I felt completely disillusioned, because the rules that I, and most citizens, try to live by were not the ones that I found the officials lived by."

Chapter 52

Theories

That summer my criminal defense attorneys Billy Sothern and Rob McDuff filed a motion to dismiss my case, as key prosecution witnesses had died since my 1998 trial. With so few still alive, it would be impossible for me to exercise my constitutional right to confront witnesses and cross-examine them about information we had uncovered since 1998. (Many of those who led the investigation had also died, meaning we couldn't question them on why they didn't pursue other leads revealed in the deputy's notes or the bloody tennis shoe that was found near the scene of the crime.) That motion was denied.

Billy and Rob filed 33 pretrial motions that would be ruled on in coming months, most of them seeking fairness, such as asking for a change of venue so I wouldn't be tried in St. Francisville, in West Feliciana Parish, where I'd had two or possibly three unconstitutional grand juries; asking the court to compel the state to allow modern DNA testing on all remaining physical evidence and to compare the fingerprints from the crime scene against Angola's fingerprint archives from the 1970s as well as the FBI's recently expanded Integrated Automated Fingerprint Identification System (IAFIS) database; asking for blood testing; and asking for a unanimous jury. They filed to exclude the impeached, discredited testimony of state's witnesses Joseph Richey, Hezekiah Brown, and Paul Fobb, all deceased.

Billy and Rob also reinvestigated Brent Miller's murder. In part, they looked at several statements former prisoners had given our investigators over the years—statements about who killed Brent Miller. Their investigation got yet another statement—sparking a new theory.

This first account we got of Brent Miller's murder, though, came years before, from Billy Sinclair, who had been a longtime editor of the prison magazine *The Angolite*. In 2001, one of our lawyers had reached out to Sinclair to ask him if he'd heard anything about the murder; as an editor at the magazine he had a lot of freedom at Angola and knew a lot of prisoners. Sinclair, who was still incarcerated at the time, responded right away, writing to my lawyer that he believed Herman and I were innocent because a prisoner named Irvin "Life" Breaux told him so back in 1973; that he killed Miller, and told him that Herman and I were innocent. Sinclair had nothing to gain by coming forward. I had never met him. He and Herman were on the same CCR tier for six months back in 1974. He said that he wanted to set the record straight, writing, "I do not know Woodfox but I did get to know Hooks. I met him in 1974 when I spent about six months in CCR. I had a tremendous amount of respect for him. He is one of a half-dozen inmates who, over the last three decades, left a lasting impression on me for his courage, character and commitment."

Billy Sinclair gave this sworn statement to my attorneys:

In March or April 1973, I met and became close personal friends with an African-American inmate named Irvin "Life" Breaux. I met Breaux through the Prisoner Grievance Committee, a 36-inmate grievance committee created at the Louisiana State Penitentiary by former Corrections Director Elayn Hunt. I was on the "Executive Committee" of the Prisoner Grievance Committee and a representative from the Big Yard. Breaux was a member of the general committee, a representative of the Main Prison's maximum-security cellblocks.

A recognized inmate leader, Breaux had been placed in maximum-security lockdown status for alleged "black militant activities" following the April 1972 killing of an Angola prison guard named Brent Miller. Breaux and I were part of a seven-member inmate team given quasi-official approval to educate and encourage the general inmate population of the Main Prison Complex regarding both the need and inevitability of the racial integration of the Louisiana State Penitentiary.

In the spring and summer of 1973, Angola was experiencing a horrific wave of prisoner violence and homosexual rapes. Breaux was instrumental in creating an organization called the Brotherhood, a group of African-American inmates committed to saving young inmates from homosexual rape and slavery. It was through the integration/Brotherhood efforts that Breaux and I cultivated and maintained a very close personal relationship—a relationship fueled by our mutual personal and political beliefs that the lawless, corrupt, and evil conditions prevalent at Angola had to be changed.

Breaux was possessed by a militant ideology that subscribed to the belief that violence was an acceptable and, under specific circumstances, a preferable means to bring about changes at the state penitentiary. I was a budding "jailhouse lawyer" who believed that concentrated legal action offered the best opportunity to produce the changes we both desired.

Breaux and I frequently discussed and debated our common objectives but different methods of accomplishing those objectives. A strong bond of mutual trust developed between us; we became "comrades in the struggle."

It was during these discussions and debates that the subject of the killing of Brent Miller surfaced, especially since Breaux had been one of the scores of African-American inmates who had been placed in lockdown for "militant activities" in the wake of the Miller killing. In these conversations, Breaux initially alluded to involvement in the Miller killing, stating that prison officials either knew or believed that he was involved in that crime.

It was common knowledge throughout the prison system that four inmates known as "the Angola Four" had been locked up and were placed in CCR as the ones responsible for the killing of Brent Miller. Breaux repeatedly insisted to me that those inmates were "innocent"; that they had been "framed" by Custody Warden Hayden J. Dees. He was contemptuous of the notion that two of the Angola Four inmates, Chester "Noxzema" Jackson and Gilbert Montegut, could even be called "black militants" (a term that Breaux took particular pride in)

He became especially incensed when talking about how the other two Angola Four inmates, Albert Woodfox and Herman Wallace, had been "framed" by Warden Dees.

I placed significant credence in what Breaux told me. Hayden J. Dees "ruled" Angola in that era; Angola belonged to him. He operated with an official fanaticism against "black militants" and communism. Following one of the first disciplinary hearings at Angola at which I was allowed to participate as an "inmate counsel," Dees approached me, livid and irrational, and accused me of being a "communist."

So it was natural for Breaux and I—the "black militant" and the "white communist"—to discuss Dees and his role in the "Angola Four" case. One day Breaux told me—and it was the first of several times that he told me—that he and others had actually killed Brent Miller. He stated that in April 1972, he and others were committed to a plot to kill twelve known black "snitches." The plot called for all the snitches to be killed simultaneously in different parts of the prison on the day Miller ended up being killed.

Breaux told me that Brent Miller walked into the Pine dormitory as he and other inmates were separating for distribution the weapons that would be used in the attacks on the snitches. He described a confused scene in which the inmates initially tried to subdue Miller but that Miller was either stabbed or cut. Breaux said a collective and instantaneous decision was made by the inmates to kill Miller because he had recognized them, and then to "get rid" of the weapons.

I never once asked or probed Breaux about this incident. The information was far too sensitive even to know and, frankly, it was not a subject matter that I wanted to talk about. But there was certainly more than one conversation during which he told me that he had killed Miller . . . ; that Dees and other prison officials knew he was involved; that they could not charge him with the crime because it would expose the fact that the "Angola Four" had been framed; and that he would eventually "be killed" because of his role in, and knowledge about, the Brent Miller killing. Irvin "Life"

Breaux was stabbed to death at the Louisiana State Penitentiary on August 11, 1973, by two inmates named Gilbert Dixon and Willie Carney.

In another statement, the one that Rob and Billy got with an investigator, a prisoner who was a teenager in 1972 swore he was in Pine 1 the morning Brent Miller was killed. He said that two "sissies"—gal-boys—and their prisoner-pimp, who "owned" them, were arguing with a fourth prisoner, Leonard "Specs" Turner, when Miller walked in. "They had knives and Miller saw it" the witness said. He said the snitches and their pimp jumped Miller and started stabbing him. "Albert Woodfox was not there," he stated. "Neither was Herman Wallace or Gilbert Montegut. Chester Jackson was not involved with the stabbing. I left the dorm, past Miller on the ground, and went over by the laundry. That's when they locked everything down."

Another prisoner told one of our investigators that a prisoner paid by the pimp to protect the snitches in Pine 1 attacked Miller. He was a very powerful prisoner who ran gambling operations and drugs on the walk, known as a "shot caller", and was supposedly very close with some security officers because he made money for them, selling dorm assignments and jobs to prisoners. Also, in this version, Chester Jackson allegedly helped the shot caller, who he was supposedly good friends with, kill Miller. In this version, Irvin Breaux and a few other prisoners who didn't live in Pine 1 were also there. (Had they come to the dorm that morning to kill the snitches but instead got involved with killing the guard? We don't know.) The shot caller who allegedly killed Miller in this version supposedly confessed to his girlfriend close to his death. He said he felt sorry Herman and I took the fall for Brent Miller's murder, but he didn't want to go back to prison. Another purported witness who was interviewed said he saw prisoners who didn't live in Pine 1 walk toward the dorm that morning "suited up," meaning armed, and "dressed in raincoats with hoods up and tied in front of their faces," but he didn't see what happened next.

*   *   *

I don't know what to make of these theories. Most of them came to us through investigators from statements that were not signed. Every prisoner who claimed to have seen Brent Miller's murder and who talked to an investigator—or to anyone—about the killing had his own interests in play, either protecting himself or his reputation, or protecting someone he liked, or possibly hurting someone he didn't like. We also got a statement from Chester Jackson's younger brother, Noel Murphy, who had been a prisoner at that time of Miller's killing. He swore Jackson told him he (Jackson) killed Miller, and that Herman and I were innocent, but Jackson lied about me and Herman to protect Murphy, who was 20 at the time, as well as to protect his stepson (who was also at Angola then). Murphy said Chester Jackson was told by authorities that he, Murphy, would be tortured along with Jackson's stepson if Jackson didn't lie about us. He said Jackson had promised his mom he would take care of him in prison. Did Chester Jackson kill Brent Miller? I saw him in the dining hall that morning at breakfast. Everett Jackson, who was with me during the time Miller was killed, also testified he saw him at breakfast. A different prisoner claimed in another statement to have seen Irvin Breaux at breakfast that morning. Did the murder happen earlier than the coroner said? Did it happen later? There is no way to know. The only value these statements have to me is the one consistent thread that runs through them: that Herman and I weren't there.

Billy Sinclair was the first person who had any knowledge of Herman's and my innocence to come forward. As a journalist and editor of *The Angolite*, he had a deep knowledge of Angola and its administration and history. He was known outside the prison for work he did in the community while he was still a prisoner. In his first letter to my lawyer, Sinclair wrote of an encounter he had with Hezekiah Brown: "In the early 1980s *The Angolite* did a feature on Angola's infamous 'Dog Pen.'... Brown was assigned to the Dog Pen after his testimony against Wallace/Woodfox. The prison took care of him back there. I spoke to him briefly at the Dog Pen—'a niggah got to do what a niggah got to do to get by—white folks run this prison,' he said to me. In convict parlance, that was his way of saying ... that he had lied for the State in exchange for the lifetime position at the Dog Pen."

Chapter 53

The Struggle Continues

In the summer of 2015, while Buddy Caldwell was running for office for the third time, 18 members of the Louisiana House of Representatives introduced a resolution (HR 208, 2015) asking the attorney general to withdraw his appeal of Judge Brady's ruling to release me, barring further prosecution of me. The resolution didn't pass, but I believe press coverage of the legislators' bill may have helped expose Caldwell's unreasonable actions against us, including how he used taxpayer money to indict Herman Wallace on his deathbed. In November, Buddy Caldwell was voted out of office. In the eight years he was in office, this self-serving demagogue acted as if he was obsessed with finding justice for Brent Miller, and yet he refused to test the bloody fingerprint left at the scene of Brent Miller's killing against the fingerprints of all the prisoners on the walk that morning. He brought no integrity to the office of attorney general or to the state of Louisiana. Instead of prosecuting cases based upon the merits of the evidence, he was more interested in publicity. He abused his authority as attorney general and he made our case a personal vendetta. I was happy the majority of the people of Louisiana saw through him and voted him out of office. Unlike a court ruling, it couldn't be undone.

On November 9, 2015, in response to the state's appeal of Judge Brady's exceptional writ, a randomly selected three-judge panel in the Fifth Circuit—different from the one that had ruled on my case previously—agreed with the state and ruled that Judge Brady overstepped his authority when he denied the state the right to retry me.

It was a split decision. Judge Carolyn Dineen King wrote that my case did not "present a constitutional defect that cannot be cured at retrial" and that Judge Brady was wrong to assume the state courts would not provide me with a fair retrial. Judge Priscilla Owen agreed. The court vacated Judge Brady's order to release me without a retrial. I would go to trial. In a powerful dissent, Judge James L. Dennis wrote, "If ever a case justifiably could be considered to present 'exceptional circumstances' barring reprosecution, this is that case.

"The writ of habeas corpus is the fundamental instrument for safeguarding individual freedom against arbitrary and lawless state action," Judge Dennis wrote. "Today, as in prior centuries, the writ is a bulwark against convictions that violate 'fundamental fairness.'" He wrote that he shared Judge Brady's lack of confidence in the state to provide a fair third trial. He wrote, "Clearly, the wrongful harm done to Woodfox, not only as a litigant but also as a human being by his two unconstitutional convictions and his egregious four decades of solitary confinement, cannot be rectified by the usual remedy of reversal and reprosecution."

Judge Dennis also pointed to the recent allegations made by grand jury foreperson Deidre Howard that proceedings at my third grand jury were improper. "Recently surfaced allegations that the State made inflammatory statements to the third grand jury in order to obtain a third indictment create even greater uncertainty as to Woodfox's ability to obtain a fair trial in the State's third prosecution," he wrote, quoting a supplement citing the state's "'inequitable conduct' during the [grand jury] proceedings as one factor weighing in favor of barring reprosecution." Judge Dennis went on to say that "these myriad prejudices" might be "easier to swallow if there were strong evidence of his guilt, but the evidence against him is, at the very best, extremely equivocal. Although there was an abundance of physical evidence available at the crime scene, none of this evidence incriminated Woodfox, and other evidence has emerged since the first trial that casts even further doubt on the State's case against him."

The court returned the case to Judge Brady, with instructions that he would have to issue an ordinary conditional writ that would require the state to release me only if it failed to retry me within a reasonable period of time.

In November, I got the news that one of our most dedicated supporters, Leonard "Mwalimu" Johnson, a longtime prisoner activist and mentor to hundreds of prisoners, had died after a long illness. He was 78. Mwalimu came up in poverty. "The choice was either sit around and starve or step beyond the law," he would later write. He was imprisoned for robbery in the sixties. In prison he almost died of pneumonia in a strip cell—where prisoners were placed naked, with nothing except a hole in the floor. "I had to lie there completely naked," he wrote, "my cell flooded with water, drawing upon my spiritual, mental and physical faculties in order to survive." He was sent to Angola in 1977 and spent the next 15 years there. He documented 62 cases of abuse by personnel while he was there, some of which resulted in prisoners dying. After he was released he spent many years working at the Capital Post-Conviction Project of Louisiana. I never met Mwalimu personally, but he was beloved in our support committee, an unwavering light at every protest and event, always committed to peace and justice. "Initially I was unable to entertain any thought of forgiveness," he wrote in 2010, "but slowly I came to realize that bitterness only creates bitterness. Negative experiences are a kind of cancer, and my choice as a human being is either to encourage the spread of that cancer or to arrest it and apply a solution. I opt to be part of the solution, part of the healing."

Thanksgiving was approaching. Normally holidays meant nothing to me. The only thing different about a holiday in prison was sometimes there would be a different item of food on your tray. At Angola, they once handed out oranges to prisoners in CCR on Christmas Day. This Thanksgiving would be different. The warden at the West Feliciana jail told prisoners that we could each get two plates of food from our families at Thanksgiving: one plate for dinner, the other for dessert. It would be my first home-cooked meal in over 40 years. My good friend Professor Angela Bell and my brother Michael cooked my favorite dishes: stuffed crab, hot sausage, turkey, seafood stuffing, and creamed corn. Angie added slices of homemade pies, cake, and cookies, packaging two layers of food on two of the largest dishes she could find that could still be considered plates. She drove to the West Feliciana jail on Thanksgiving Day to drop off the plates. The lengths to which she and Michael went to cook for me and deliver the food on Thanksgiving touched me a lot. The prisoners around me were grateful too. I shared both plates with them.

In December, George Kendall petitioned the U.S. Supreme Court, asking it to restore Judge Brady's exceptional writ. This would be one of 10,000 petitions the Court receives each year, about 80 of which are heard. George believed the country's highest court might be persuaded to hear my case—which he felt fueled a national debate about solitary confinement—because six months earlier, Justice Anthony Kennedy seemed to invite a constitutional challenge to the use of solitary confinement. The case, *Davis v. Ayala*, centered on an unrelated issue—the exclusion of a defense attorney from part of a hearing on jury selection. The defendant in the case, though, had been kept in solitary confinement for the better part of 20 years. That seemed to touch a chord with Justice Kennedy, who wrote a concurrence on the issue, laying out the history and brutality of solitary and citing the case of Kalief Browder, a teenager who spent more than two years in solitary confinement (and three years total) on Rikers Island while being held, without a conviction, for allegedly stealing a backpack. After his release Browder committed suicide.

In closing Kennedy wrote: "In a case that presented the issue [of solitary confinement], the judiciary may be required, within its proper jurisdiction and authority, to determine whether workable alternative systems for long-term confinement exist, and, if so, whether a correctional system should be required to adopt them." In light of my settlement, we voluntarily withdrew our petition for review by the Supreme Court.

Chapter 54

A Plea for Freedom, Not Justice

In January 2016, I was waiting for two trials to be scheduled by the courts, one for our civil suit challenging the use of solitary confinement, and another for a murder I didn't commit. I was looking forward to both. I believed we could prove our decades in solitary confinement constituted cruel and unusual punishment and I wanted to be exonerated of the murder of Brent Miller. I had the best lawyers in the world.

By early 2016, though, we had lost many important pretrial motions for my criminal defense. Judge William Carmichael would not grant us a change in venue. My third trial would be in St. Francisville, in West Feliciana Parish. Billy Sothern and Rob McDuff appealed the judge's decision to a higher court, but we lost on appeal too.

The judge sided with the prosecution and ruled that the testimony from certain dead witnesses, Joseph Richey, Hezekiah Brown, and Paul Fobb, could be read to jurors, meaning this critical testimony would be delivered by actors reading a script. In another blow to fairness, the courts found that I would have a nonunanimous jury, meaning that only 10 jurors had to agree on a verdict instead of 12. Louisiana and Oregon are the only two states in America where defendants can be convicted by fewer than 12 jurors, a system created to marginalize the votes of black jurors when courts were first required by law to allow blacks on juries. Since it is easier to get a conviction with a nonunanimous jury, the system was also established in Louisiana to help fill its prisons when it relied on convict labor to replace slave labor during Reconstruction.

For some incomprehensible reason, Judge Carmichael would not allow us to test the bloody fingerprint left at Brent Miller's murder scene against the FBI's Integrated Automated Fingerprint Identification System (IAFIS) database. He ruled we would only be able to test the bloody fingerprint against Angola files—whatever was left of them—from 1972. We didn't know what condition those 1972 files were in. The judge did grant our motion to DNA-test various pieces of physical evidence, but the state prosecutors claimed to have lost the clothing they said I wore, so I wouldn't be able to prove the clothes they said I was wearing weren't mine. The state also lost the bloody tennis shoes investigators found and hid from my defense, so we couldn't test them either.

On January 11, former member of the U.S. House of Representatives Jeff Landry, a Republican and Tea Party member, was sworn into the office of Louisiana attorney general.

Deidre Howard wrote to the new attorney general, twice. "Please hear me out," she wrote. "I am exhausted from my attempts to be heard. . . . My friends at work who see me exhausted and stressed tell me that I have done all that I can do. I just look at them and say that it will never be over for me." My lawyers went to meet with Landry, hoping that he could look at my case without the biases of Caldwell's office.

George Kendall and Carine Williams came to see me. They got to the point. Given a new attorney general to work with now, they asked me if I would consider taking a deal for time served instead of going forward with the retrial. They weren't asking me to plead guilty. They knew I wouldn't consider that. I had never once thought, even in my loneliest moments in more than 40 years of solitary confinement, that I would do "whatever it takes" to get out of CCR, or prison. I was offered a chance to get out of CCR if I gave up my political beliefs, and I refused. I was offered a chance to lie about Herman to benefit myself, and I refused. Before Attorney General Landry took office, I had been offered a chance to plead guilty for the murder of Brent Miller, and I refused. They asked me to think about a plea of "nolo contendere," which means "no contest." They didn't know if they could get it, but with a nolo contendere plea I could maintain my innocence but my conviction would stand. If I took the plea I would not be admitting guilt, but I would be implicitly acknowledging that the state had enough evidence to convict me again at trial. I knew the state had no evidence that I killed Brent Miller, but I also knew I could still be reconvicted for his murder.

With a nolo contendere plea deal, George said, the outcome would be certain: freedom. A trial in St. Francisville, George said, "is like a trip to Vegas. We don't know the outcome." George and Carine didn't press me. They knew it would be a difficult decision. I told them I would think about it. Before she left that day Carine told me she believed I'd be more useful to people in the free world than locked up in prison. When I talked to Michael he urged me to take a plea. He reminded me I could begin a relationship with my daughter. I hardly knew her. He knew that weighed on me. "You can get to know your great-grandchildren," Michael said. "You can be in their lives."

Billy and Rob, who were appealing a number of Judge Carmichael's rulings to the Louisiana Supreme Court—including the judge's denial of my unanimous jury—also visited me. "We will fight for you in court," Billy told me. "We will do everything we can to convince the jury to find you not guilty." But he asked me to weigh the outcomes. "What if you are convicted?" he asked me. We both knew that meant life in prison. "If you take a plea," he said, "you will be free immediately." He reminded me my trial hadn't even been scheduled yet. There was no guarantee I would get a trial in 2016. "You deserve to be happy, Albert," Billy told me. "You deserve to have a life outside Angola prison."

I thought of the next to last time I saw Herman. We were temporarily alone in the visitation room of the prison hospital, after our lawyers left. He was sitting in a wheelchair, covered in blankets. He started talking about being free, about freeing me, about my freedom. At first, I thought he was drifting off onto a tangent because he was tired. Then he said, "Albert, we both know I'm dying, you're not." He paused. "What if I say . . . ?" I stopped him, "Hooks, don't go there." He said, "They've already offered me a deal. You can go free." Our eyes met. I wanted to knock him out. I knew he was coming from a place of love—revolutionary love, brotherly love, soul to soul. We were family.

"I will never forgive you if you do anything like that," I told him. He nodded and closed his eyes. He knew I could never live with myself knowing that he had lied for me. Now, I was asking myself, could I live with myself for lying to take a plea?

If I made a deal I'd have freedom. But I'd never get justice. My lawyers reminded me if I lost at trial I wouldn't get justice *or* freedom. I was almost 69 years old. It had taken 18 years in court to get to this point, a new trial. In his ruling, even Judge Brady asked if I had another 18 years in me if I was convicted at trial again. I kept thinking of Michael. He had never asked me for anything, but now he was asking me to take the plea deal. I thought of my mom, who had wanted so badly to see me walk out of prison. I thought of my daughter, who I wanted to know. I had spent my life teaching men to take a stand for what's right. Would I be letting them down? I had lived my life as an example to everyone around me. I paced and slept and read that week. I'd always prided myself on facing difficult decisions head-on. I made a decision. I called my lawyers and told them I would make a deal for freedom.

By pleading nolo contendere I wouldn't be innocent in the eyes of the law. But I knew I was innocent. The struggle inside me didn't go away. There isn't a day that goes by that I don't think about breaking my word to take that plea.

I sat in my cell and waited for a week. George, Billy , and Rob had to coordinate several parties to get agreement on the details of the deal: the judge, the DA's office, the attorney general, the lawyers. It was my understanding the Miller family had to be involved; how they felt had to be considered.

Ultimately, the deal was for me to plead to manslaughter, and Louisiana tacked on a burglary charge in order to compute the punishment to match the exact amount of time I had been held in prison. As part of the deal, King and I settled our civil suit with the state. (Herman's family had already settled years before, after he died.) A date was set. By pure coincidence, it was my birthday, February 19, 2016. That morning they put restraints on me and took me to the 20th Judicial District Court in St. Francisville. I stood before Judge William Carmichael. When he asked me for my plea on manslaughter and burglary, I replied, "Nolo contendere."

After the court appearance, I was taken back to my cell and my restraints were removed. The door was closed and locked behind me. I'd already laid out the street clothes George had brought me but I didn't change right away. I sat down on my bunk.

Brent Miller's family was in the courtroom that morning. His brother Stan had stood before Judge Carmichael, speaking on behalf of the Miller family. Describing the pain of losing his brother he said, "A piece of our hearts has been jerked out of our bodies." I understood how the Miller family felt double-crossed. I felt genuine sympathy for him in that moment, and then a flash of bitterness. I was being forced to take a plea for something I didn't do. The Miller family pushed for us to stay in prison, even though they knew that no physical evidence linked us to the murder, not even the bloody fingerprint left at the scene. Even after it was revealed that there were bloody tennis shoes and inmates wearing bloody clothes and scratches on a prisoner that were never investigated, and that the inmate testimony against us was paid for, and even though none of the "witness" testimony matched up. Now I was being forced to choose freedom over the integrity of my word, which was everything to me. My word was my mother's gift to me. For 44 years I survived by my word. My word kept me alive in the darkest darkness; it kept me safe, it kept me sane, it kept me human. Now I was breaking my word. I was innocent. Herman was innocent. Part of my heart had been ripped from me too.

I put on the clothes George brought me: black jeans and a black sweatshirt. I folded my jumpsuit and laid it on the bed. I was supposed to enter my plea, come back and get my things, and go. But there was a paperwork foul-up somehow, so my release was delayed. I stood at the window of my cell, looked outside, and waited. There were two news vans parked at the curb with satellite dishes on top. From now on, everything was unknown.

The door to my cell opened and a guard asked me if I was ready. He wasn't carrying restraints. I picked up the plastic bags that contained my possessions and followed him down the hall to an office. The sheriff allowed my brother Michael to come inside while George and I waited for the paperwork to come through by fax from the DOC. We sat at a small table and talked. Michael was only 8 years old when he started visiting me in prison with my mom. When he was 18, he came alone and vowed he'd stay with me until the end. "Until I perish or you perish," he promised. I looked at him now. He was smiling. My rock. Barring disaster my brother was in the visiting room every month. We had our brotherly clashes over the years. If I thought he was being irresponsible on the street or making bad decisions I told him. He never let it come between us. There was a light in his eyes today.

I turned to George and asked, "What time is it?" We'd been waiting more than an hour. George got up again to press the prison officials. Then, the paperwork came through.

Michael and I walked out the door of the jail together. I squinted in the sun. My knees buckled. He tightened his hold on me so I wouldn't fall. Many of my friends had been waiting there to celebrate my release. Marina was there. Scott was there. So many of my local, New Orleans friends and supporters had come. Tory had traveled from across the country to be there, and held her phone up so Gordon Roddick, on a video call, could watch me walk out of prison. I heard their cheers and I smiled and raised my clenched fist. Their faces were a blur. I got in my brother's car. Michael, fighting tears, fastened my seat belt. He drove me directly to the graveyard in New Orleans where our mom is buried. It was closed. I wanted to climb over the wall but Michael wouldn't let me. That evening he took me to an event in our old neighborhood hosted by my childhood friend, the activist Parnell Herbert. It was the same place, the Carver Theater, that I used to sneak into as a child. The event had been scheduled weeks earlier, before anyone knew I was to be released that day.

My one fear upon getting out of prison was that I wouldn't be accepted in my community, in the African American community, in the Treme neighborhood, where I had grown up and did so much damage and harm. Parnell called me to the stage. Michael walked with me. As we made our way out of our seats and up to the stage people started clapping, then standing and cheering. King was called to the stage, along with Malik Rahim and others. There was a feeling of togetherness in the room I hadn't felt in so long, a feeling of unity, a feeling of relief and victory for all of us, a feeling that we all shared. I was being welcomed back into my community. I was speechless, moved to tears. I raised my fist.

The next day Michael and I went to Walmart and bought almost every flower there. Longtime supporters and friends came with us. We took flowers to my mom's grave. I felt the loss of her as if her death was fresh, as if she had just died. It was more painful than anything I experienced in prison. I told her that I was free now and I loved her. I went to my sister Violetta's grave, in a different cemetery, and to the grave of her husband Michael Augustine, my oldest childhood friend. I went to Herman's grave.

That night I couldn't sleep. I didn't go to bed. I sat up in a chair and dozed on and off. It was my second night out of prison. I looked at the watch on my wrist. Michael had given it to me back in the prison office. When George got up to talk to prison officials about the delay, I turned to Michael and asked, "What time is it?" He took his watch off and put it on my wrist, saying, "Yours now."

Epilogue

My fear was not of death itself, but a death without meaning.

—Huey Newton

My brother Michael took me home and I lived with him and his wife and son in their house for almost a year. I got medical care that I needed. In my mind, heart, soul, and spirit I always felt free, so my attitudes and thoughts didn't change much after I was released. But to be in my physical body in the physical world again was like being newly born. I had to learn to use my hands in new ways—for seat belts, for cell phones, to close doors behind me, to push buttons in an elevator, to drive. I had to relearn how to walk down stairs, how to walk without leg irons, how to sit without being shackled. It took about a year for my body to relax from the positions I had gotten used to holding while being restrained. I allowed myself to eat when I was hungry. Gradually, over two years, I let go of the grip I held against feeling pleasure, and of the unconscious fear that I would lose everything I loved.

Michael told me I needed to make new memories, and I did. I'd always dreamed of going to Yosemite National Park after seeing a National Geographic special about it years before in CCR. At the invitation of old friends and former Panthers Gail Shaw and BJ, I flew to Sacramento. Scott Fleming came up from Oakland to meet us and we drove to Yosemite together. We hiked to the falls I wanted to see, and we stayed in the park overnight.

I've been privileged to speak to law students around the country and to speak out in Europe, in Canada, and here in America against the abuses of solitary confinement. I was honored to meet Teenie Rogers,

Brent Miller's widow, who had the courage and character to speak out against our convictions. I met Deidre Howard, the foreperson who came forward with her misgivings about her grand jury experience, proving that Judge Brady was correct in his assessment that I would never get a fair trial in the state of Louisiana. Deidre and her sister Donna are taking steps to get Louisiana to create a guidebook for grand jurors, explaining their rights.

A great joy has been getting to know my daughter and her children. My great-grandchildren are my hope. The innocence, intelligence, and happiness in their eyes give me strength. I want to keep going for them, keep speaking out, keep fighting. I hope to leave them a better world than the one I had. I hope they can find the spirit of my mom, their great-great-grandmother, when they need her, as I did.

I bought a house. I'm still a news junkie and usually have news on the TV. I can still only sleep a few hours at a time. I am often wide awake around three a.m., when I used to get some "quiet time" in prison. Many people ask me if I ever wake up and think I'm still in prison. I always know where I am when I wake up. But sometimes I walk into a room in my house and I don't know why, and then I walk into all the rooms for I don't know what reason. I still get claustrophobic attacks. Now I have more space to walk them off. For peace of mind, I mop the floors in my home.

People ask me how America has changed in 44 years. I see changes, but in policing and the judicial system most of them are superficial. In 2016, the year I was released from prison, a black man named Alton Sterling was fatally shot by police while he was pinned to the ground by officers in Louisiana; a black man named Philando Castile was shot and killed at a traffic stop by police while he was reaching for his wallet in Minnesota, while his girlfriend screamed, "You told him to get his ID, sir"; a black behavioral therapist named Charles Kinsey, caring for an autistic man, was shot in the leg by police in Florida as he lay in the street with his hands up (later the chief of police stated the cop was aiming for the autistic man who was holding a toy truck that the cop thought was a gun); an unarmed black man named Terence Crutcher was shot and killed as he was walking in the middle of a street outside his vehicle in Oklahoma, obviously drunk or drug-impaired. That was just 2016. As I write these words, in March 2018, a 22-year-old unarmed black man named Stephon Clark was fired at 20 times—with 8 shots hitting him, mostly in the back—and killed by police officers in his grandmother's backyard in Sacramento.

The officer who killed Terence Crutcher was acquitted and her record was expunged. The officer who killed Philando Castile was acquitted. Black people make up 13.4 percent of the U.S. population, but the year I was released, according to the *Washington Post*, 34 percent of the unarmed people killed by police were black males.

In 2016, according to the NAACP, African Americans were incarcerated at more than five times the rate of whites. The imprisonment rate for African American women was twice that of white women. Also according to the NAACP, nationwide, African American children represented 32 percent of all children who were arrested, 42 percent of all children who were detained, and 52 percent of all children who ended up in criminal court. Though African Americans and Latinos combined make up approximately 32 percent of the U.S. population, they make up 52 percent of all incarcerated people.

Racism today isn't as blatant as it was 44 years ago, but it is still here, underground, coded. We have to make changes that are deeper, as a society. Without roots, nothing can grow. The systemic hatred of a human being based on his or her skin color or hair texture or cultural heritage or gender or sexual preference is pointless. These are trivial things; we are more alike than we are unlike. We will never advance as a species if we see each other as enemies based on race. Frantz Fanon wrote, "Superiority? Inferiority? Why not simply try to touch the other, feel the other, discover each other?" Can we shift the focus of our insecurities, fears, and anger from other races and work together to deal with the unfair distribution of wealth on this planet? Back in the seventies Huey Newton wrote, "Youths are passed through schools that don't teach, then forced to search for jobs that don't exist and finally left stranded in the street to stare at the glamorous lives advertised around them." This is happening right now in this country, in 2018, for all children of all races.

I have hope for humankind. It is my hope that a new human being will evolve so that needless pain and suffering, poverty, exploitation, racism, and injustice will be things of the past. I am thrilled to see young people obeying the call of their own humanity, even though it so often seems to come at a terrible price. The year of my release, quarterback Colin Kaepernick "took a knee" during the national anthem before National Football League games to protest and bring awareness of the deaths of black people at the hands of police and other social injustices. As his protest spread throughout the NFL, critics subverted the message of the players, ignoring the reason for the protest—to call attention to the very real problem of police violence against black people—and severely criticizing Kaepernick and the other players who took a knee during the national anthem for "not respecting the military" and "not respecting the flag." Kaepernick was slandered by presidential candidate Donald Trump. He was abandoned by the NFL, exiled from the game he loved. Although he was considered one of the most gifted quarterbacks in the league, no team would hire him the next year. He put his career on the line to use his platform to speak for those who aren't being heard. His efforts weren't in vain. Because of his actions, taking a knee has come to mean something different now.

Another bright spot for me was to see how Black Lives Matter had spread: to meet youth in London and Paris who told me they are part of the Black Lives Matter movement in their countries, and to learn that the movement had spread to Brazil, South Africa, and Australia, among other places around the world. I can't tell you how proud I was to meet Alicia Garza, one of the founders of Black Lives Matter, at a panel discussion.

I was heartened to hear that, as a result of the civil lawsuit that Herman, King, and I filed, there is now an oversight board that reevaluates decisions made by the reclassification board at Angola. Prisoners call it the "Woodfox board." In early 2017, the Louisiana Department of Public Safety and Corrections partnered with the Vera Institute of Justice for a two-year study of Louisiana's prisons, with the objective of reducing the use of solitary confinement. The Vera Institute program, called the Safe Alternatives to Segregation Initiative, had already been rolled out in Nebraska, Oregon, North Carolina, New York City, and New Jersey. I am encouraged by other actions. In 2018 the New Orleans activist group VOTE (Voice of the Experienced), formed by former prisoners, launched a "Stop Solitary" campaign in conjunction with the ACLU and others to end solitary confinement in Louisiana. The ACLU offers online tools and contacts for activists in every state to participate in Stop Solitary campaigns. In May 2018, after more than 40 years as a punitive place of torture at Angola prison, Camp J was closed. At its peak, Camp J held 400 prisoners in solitary cells for longer than 23 hours a day. Prison officials cited the deterioration of the building's infrastructure as the reason for the closure rather than admit that Camp J was a form of solitary confinement and brutal treatment. The infrastructure at Camp J had been deteriorating for decades.

Herman wanted our suffering to be for something, not in vain. He hoped knowing about his life, my life, and King's life could somehow help change the way prisoners are treated; the way security officers are trained; the way biased police departments, DA offices, and courtrooms operate. When King and I are in public, Herman is with us as we speak out against solitary confinement. He's with us as we educate people about political prisoners in America. One of our biggest concerns is that people do not realize that there are political prisoners in the United States, men who were set up by COINTELPRO and similar illicit actions decades ago and are still in prison: Mumia Abu-Jamal, Sundiata Acoli, Mutulu Shakur, Jamil Abdullah Al-Amin, Leonard Peltier, and many others, all repeatedly denied parole, denied release, denied justice.

Herman is with us as we call for people to come together and speak as one voice to demand congressional hearings on the clause in the 13th Amendment that legalizes slavery within prison walls. He's with us when we ask people to understand that there are wrongful convictions in this country. We were the tip of the iceberg. Bias, prejudice, racism, laziness, and an aggressive "need to win" mentality on the part of district attorneys' offices and others haunt our "halls of justice." One hundred and thirty-nine wrongfully convicted people were exonerated and released from prison in 2017, according to the National Registry of Exonerations (NRE). On average, each was incarcerated for a little over ten and a half years. Government officials—defined as police, prosecutors or other government agents—abused their authority in more than half of the cases.

Herman is with us when we speak out about criminal justice issues that have an impact on the poor. In just one example, bail for poor people today is as much of a problem as it was when I was in the Tombs back in 1970. Excessive bail for petty crimes keeps people locked in public and private prisons. It's a business. The overwhelming majority of people held in city and county jails have not been convicted of a crime; many of them simply can't afford bail. Too often the families of people in jail have to choose between paying bail or buying groceries. The cost to these human beings who can't make bail cannot be calculated: people lose their jobs; their children are taken by social services. That's just one example.

Herman is with us when we talk about abolishing solitary confinement. People have to see solitary for what it is, morally reprehensible. Solitary confinement is immoral. There are still more than 80,000 men, women, and children in solitary confinement in prisons across the United States, according to the Bureau of Justice Statistics. That figure doesn't include county jails, juvenile facilities, or immigrant detention centers. "We have abused the practice of solitary confinement to the point where it has become modern-day torture," Rep. Cedric Richmond said in 2015. "Too many prisoners, including the seriously mentally ill and juveniles, are locked away for 23 hours a day often with little to no due process and at steep cost to the taxpayer.... Instead of being reserved for the worst of the worst, solitary confinement is too often being overused for 'administrative' reasons to avoid providing treatment for the mentally ill and rehabilitation for those who will return to society."

In May 2018, King and I spoke at the University of California, Santa Cruz at a conference on the psychological and physical effects of solitary confinement. Craig Haney, the psychologist who had met with us several times in preparation for our civil trial, brought together the world's experts in the field to develop principles that would limit the use of solitary confinement based on the scientific evidence that shows the devastating physical and mental effects of isolation and loneliness. There was strong support at the conference for the United Nations' "Nelson Mandela Rules," which would prohibit solitary confinement for juveniles, pregnant women, the mentally ill, the elderly, and the physically infirm and limit solitary confinement to no more than 15 continuous days for anyone else. King and I asked those assembled to go one step further, calling for an absolute ban on solitary confinement, for everyone.

We need to admit to, confront, and change the racism in the American justice system that decides who is stopped by police, who is arrested, who is searched, who is charged, who is prosecuted, and who isn't, as well as look at who receives longer sentences and why and demand a fair and equal system. Racism in police departments and in courtrooms is not a secret. It's been proved. Racism occurs at every level of the judicial process, from people of color being disproportionately stopped by police (racial profiling) to their being sentenced.

The U.S. Sentencing Commission found that between 2012 and 2016 (the length of the study), black men got sentences 19.1 percent longer than white men for the same federal crimes. A 2014 study published by the University of Michigan Law School found that, all else held equal, black arrestees were 75 percent more likely to face a charge by prosecutors with a mandatory minimum sentence than white arrestees, for the same crime.

In 2018, black people in Manhattan were 15 times more likely to be arrested for low-level marijuana charges than whites, according to a *New York Times* investigation. In Missouri that same year, the state attorney general's office reported that black drivers in Missouri were 85 percent more likely than whites to be stopped by police—a 10 percent increase over 2017. Also in 2018, two professors at Harvard Law School found by examining the sentencing practices of 1,400 federal trial judges over more than 15 years that judges appointed by Republican presidents gave longer sentences to black defendants. The study also showed that white men were more likely to get their sentences reduced under the judge's discretion than black men and that white men got larger reductions than the ones black men got.

*   *   *

We need to confront the realities of the prison-industrial complex. America has the largest prison population, per capita, in the world. Money is made off prisoners' backs. Prisoners are forced to shop in prison stores. They (or their families) are forced to pay astronomical fees to outside companies to make phone calls, and in some cases, forced to visit through video services, which also cost the prisoner money. In some prisons, inmates are forced to work full-time making products for multinational corporations for almost no pay. The legal definition of "slavery" is "the state of one person being forced to work under the control of another." The U.S. prisons are contracted by a range of government entities and private corporations to make their products. In most prisons, wages are well below poverty level. In some states prisoners aren't paid. These working prisoners aren't allowed to get benefits, they aren't allowed to form unions, they aren't allowed to negotiate the terms of their work conditions. It's legal slavery to exploit prisoners in this way. Under the 13th Amendment prisoners are slaves of the state and are treated as such.

Private prisons—prisons run by corporations in order to make a profit, are dangerous. When the goal of a prison is to make a profit, human beings suffer. Corners are cut; rules are devised to keep people in prison longer; there is no incentive to rehabilitate prisoners. A 2016 Justice Department report issued by the Obama administration found that there is more violence at privately run prisons and less medical care than at government-run facilities. In 2016 President Obama directed the Justice Department to reduce the use of private prisons. The following year, under President Donald Trump, Attorney General Jeff Sessions rescinded Obama's order within three weeks of being sworn in. The private prison industry is booming.

If there is something you can do, even one thing, to ensure humanity exists behind bars, do it. If you don't know where to start, follow Solitary Watch and Prison Legal News on social media to find out what's going on. There are organizations that are trying to change prisons as we know them, such as Critical Resistance and the Malcolm X Grassroots Movement. As human beings, we need to insist on the humane treatment of prisoners and the rehabilitation and education of prisoners. Prisoners who are mentally ill need treatment, not paralyzing drugs and 23 hours a day in a cell. Prisoners who are uneducated need education. The RAND Corporation has published study after study showing that educating prisoners who lack basic academic and vocational skills reduces future criminal behavior. RAND research has shown that every dollar invested in correctional education creates a return of four to five dollars in the reduction of future criminal justice costs. Don't turn away from what happens in American prisons.

On October 3, 2016, I was invited to speak at the Southern University Law Center. Afterward I was approached by the Honorable Judge James Brady. I'd never met him before. He graciously introduced me to his wife. I was so humbled that he took time out of his day to be there. I thanked him for saving my life. "Judge Brady, I'm honored to shake your hand," I told him. "I want to thank you for the integrity you showed during my case and with the rulings you made." He said, "Well, you had the law on your side, and I was just doing my duty as a judge, following the law." Just over a year later, on December 9, 2017, Judge Brady died after a brief illness. "He believed in justice for all," his obituary read, "regardless of wealth, power or position. He believed that whether prince or pauper, in his court you were equal in the eyes of the law. He was, as friends and family called him, 'Atticus Finch in the flesh.'"

If there's a moral to my story it's that salvation comes with the will to be a better human being. I have been asked many times what I would change about my life. My answer is always the same: "Not one thing." All I went through made me the man I am today. I had to be a better person, a wiser person, a more disciplined person to survive. I paid a heavy price. Herman and King did too. In his autobiography, *From the Bottom of the Heap*, King wrote, "My soul still cries from all that I witnessed and endured. It mourns continuously." The agony and pain from all we saw and experienced will never leave us, it will always be part of us.

To those of you who are just entering the world of social struggle, welcome. To those of you who have spent years struggling for human rights and social justice: Don't give up. Look at me and see how the strength and determination of the human spirit defy all evil. For 44 years I defied the state of Louisiana and the Department of Corrections. Their main objective was to break my spirit. They did not break me. I have witnessed the horrors of man's cruelty to man. I did not lose my humanity. I bear the scars of beatings, loneliness, isolation, and persecution. I am also marked by every kindness.

Acknowledgments

With eternal gratitude and love to Herman Wallace and Robert King, to my brother Michael Mable, and to the brave and inspiring members of the Black Panther Party, who accepted me as I was and taught me the principles and values that saved my life.

I give thanks to all who came together on behalf of the A3.

To our tireless and dedicated lawyers who stood with us and never gave up, going above and beyond to help us in our darkest hours: Scott Fleming, Nick Trenticosta, Chris Aberle, George Kendall, Sam Spital, Harmony Loube, Carine Williams, Corrine Irish, Katherine Kimpel, Sheridan England, Billy Sothern, and Robert McDuff. (And to Scott, George, Carine, Corrine, and Billy, for your help with this book.)

To the International Coalition to Free the Angola 3—our support committee and advisory board—I think of you always, for your unending faith, hope, trust, and strength, and the many actions you took and sacrifices you made on our behalf.

To Anita Roddick, I miss you; your passion still inspires.

To Gordon Roddick, Samantha Roddick, and the Roddick family for your vision and love, and for the support of the Roddick Foundation.

To Marina Drummer for taking care of us and keeping us on the rails.

To my comrade, mentor, and brother, former Black Panther Malik Rahim, for all you have given in more than 50 years of social struggle and continue to give.

To Tory Pegram for your passion, commitment, and friendship; for helping me gather materials for this book (and to your children, my godchildren, love always),

To Maria Hinds, for your heart.

To my comrades Gail Shaw and BJ, for your friendship, activism, and for keeping the flame for the Black Panther Party at itsabouttimebpp.com.

To artist Rigo 23 for your A3 murals, for making art that inspires change, and for your strong support.

To Jackie Sumell for your friendship, and devotion to Herman's vision, and for the art exhibit *Herman's House*.

To Angad Singh Bhalla for making the film *Herman's House*.

To Rebecca Hensley, for your friendship and wisdom during many visits.

To Anne Pruden, my Brooklyn connection.

To Nina Kowalska, Ambassador of Truth.

To Amnesty International and the staff involved in the A3 campaign: Tessa Murphy (USA), Angela Wright (USA), Jasmine Heiss (USA), Everette Thompson (USA), Kate Allen (UK), Kim Manning-Cooper (UK), Nicolas Krameyer (France), and all the members and supporters of Amnesty International, for your thoughtful letters, your commitment to justice, and for broadening awareness of and the discussion about the abuses of solitary confinement in the United States of America.

To filmmaker Vadim Jean, producer Ian Sharples, and the Mob Film Company for the documentaries *In the Land of the Free* and *Cruel and Unusual*.

To our investigator and friend Billie Mizell and all of our investigators over the years.

To Shana Griffin, Brice White, Anita Yesho, Brackin Kemp, Luis Talamantez, Ashaki Pratt, and everyone else who attended my trial in 1998: you blew my mind.

To Parnell Herbert for your friendship and social activism, and for writing the A3 play.

To Bruce Allen, for your many years of dedicated friendship and support.

To Noelle Hanrahan for Prison Radio and for giving voice to the voiceless.

To Mumia Abu-Jamal for your courage and dignity and for being a role model—thank you for speaking out about us.

To Black Panther Party alumnus Emory Douglas, valued comrade, for your support and your creative art on behalf of the Angola 3 and all political prisoners.

To all alumnae of the Black Panther Party who spoke out for us, fought for us, and welcomed me and Herman and King home.

To my good friend Professor Angela Bell, for being a lighthouse, and for keeping us all connected to the news we need to know.

To Emily Posner and Jen Vitry, for being fierce supporters and valued friends.

To Yuri Kochiyama and Kiilu Nyasha, for your friendship and support all these years.

To Kenny Whitmore (Zulu), comrade, friend, brother,—your time is coming.

To Rep. Cedric Richmond, to former representative John Conyers, and to the members of Congress and the Louisiana state legislators who fought for us and are trying to make laws against the abuses of solitary confinement.

To Teenie Rogers, for seeing through hate to find truth and for having the courage to speak that truth.

To "The Twins," Deidre and Donna, for your principles, honesty, and bravery.

To James Ridgeway, Amy Goodman, Brooke Shelby Biggs, and all the journalists who kept our stories alive over many years.

To Richard Becker for spreading the word about us from the beginning, and for calling the WBAI–Pacifica Radio newsroom in New York City to report on my 1998 trial.

To the Prison Activist Resource Center, for all the work you do on behalf of prisoners and to change prisons, and for working with Scott Fleming to set up our first website in 1999.

To Colonel Nyati Bolt, for being a true comrade.

To Mwalimu Johnson, your steadfast wisdom is greatly missed.

To every person who visited us in prison: your friendship is priceless.

To every individual who wrote to us, signed a petition, wore a button, appeared at a hearing, held a banner, and made art, music, or theater telling our stories: your actions touched my heart.

To my family, for your embrace.

To my agent, Gail Ross of Ross Yoon Agency, who believed in my story.

To Jody Hotchkiss, for your dedication to getting the Angola 3 before a wider audience.

To Leslie George for having the courage, above all, to put up with me while helping me write this book. You might think that this is her strongest point, but how far from the truth that is. Les is a woman of infinite wisdom and heart, not to mention patience. Good or bad, right or wrong, she is always honest. Make no mistake, without her support and love, this book could not be.

To Grove Atlantic, for taking me in.

To the entire team at Grove Atlantic behind this book, including Julia Berner-Tobin, Justina Batchelor, Deb Seager and Michael O'Connor.

To George Gibson, my editor, for your deep humanity.

I am humbled, inspired, and awed by all of you; by your loyalty, your hope, your spirit, your belief in justice, and your love. Thank you for being there for me, Herman, and King. You have proved to me that "Power to the People" is an achievable goal, as long as we never give up our commitment to serve and protect one another.

And to my mom, Ruby Edwards Mable, most of all: I want to thank you for giving me life and the lessons that have carried me through for 72 years. You are truly my hero.

—Albert "Shaka Cinque" Woodfox

Index